Writing Reminders

Tools, Tips, and Techniques

JIM BURKE

D1463443

HEINEMANN
Portsmouth, NH

Heinemann
A division of Reed Elsevier Inc.
361 Hanover Street
Portsmouth, NH 03801–3912
www.heinemann.com

Offices and agents throughout the world

The author and publisher wish to thank those who have generously given permission to reprint borrowed material:

"Big6™ Overview for Research Projects" is reprinted with permission of Big6 Associates. Copyright © 1987 by Michael B. Eisenberg and Robert E. Berkowitz. For more information visit www.big6.com.

"6+1 Traits" by the Northwest Regional Educational Laboratory, Portland, Oregon. Copyright © 1997 by Northwest Regional Educational Laboratory. Reprinted by permission.

Library of Congress Cataloging-in-Publication Data
Burke, Jim, 1961–
    Writing reminders : tools, tips, and techniques / Jim Burke.
        p. cm.
    Includes bibliographical references and index.
    ISBN 0-86709-521-0
    1. English language—Composition and exercises—Study and teaching (Secondary).   2. Language arts (Secondary).
    I.   Title.
    LB1631.B774 2003
    808'.042'0712—dc21

                                                            2003010236

Editor: Lois Bridges
Production: Abigail M. Heim
Typesetter: Kim Arney Mulcahy
Cover coordinator: Renée Le Verrier
Cover design: Judy Arisman
Cover photography: Steve Bernier
Manufacturing: Steve Bernier

Printed in the United States of America on acid-free paper

07   06   05   04   03   RRD   1   2   3   4   5

To my wife,
Susan,
Who made me
a writer years
ago by giving me
a reason to write

One of the best examples of good teaching I have ever encountered was with a golf professional. On my first lesson, he said, "Here is a bucket of balls . . . hit 'em." A few minutes later, he wandered back and said, "Keep hitting them, only this time, keep your head down, eye on the ball." By the next bucket of balls, he had introduced one more skill for the day . . . no more. Before a few weeks were out, he had quietly attended to my feet, grip, shoulder level, and follow through. A few years later, I realized with a start that every single one of my problems was visible on the first lesson. If he had attended to all of them that first day, I would probably have missed the ball entirely and resigned in disgust from ever playing golf again.

—*Donald Graves, from* **Writing: Teachers and Children at Work**

Contents

. . . .

Teach and Support Students 53

WHAT STUDENTS MUST BE ABLE TO DO

Appendices

Acknowledgments

. . . .

When I entered the teacher education program at San Francisco State University in 1987, I arrived with a degree in developmental psychology. Needless to say, I felt unprepared for the course I had charted for myself: to become an English teacher. At some point in my program, I enrolled in a course with Rosemary Patton. I had written much, even fancied myself a writer, though I had published nothing. After studying the sentence—for an entire semester!?—with Rosemary Patton, I sought out a course on the paragraph with Catherine Lucas. This unexpected detour into the realm of writing and instruction culminated in a seminar with the program's creator, Bill Robinson. I have always felt the deepest possible gratitude to Rosemary Patton, Catherine Lucas, and Bill Robinson for all they taught me, for their teaching included not just how to write but how to teach, how we learn, why we write, and how language works. It has been some fifteen years since I sat in their classes at San Francisco State, and not a day goes by that I do not use what they taught me or feel inspired to teach my students as well as these three professors taught me.

In the years since then, others have mentored me, through friendships, collaborations, or books. My colleague Diane McClain, whose exemplary teaching appears throughout this book, teaches me more during our twenty-minute lunches each day than most graduate programs can cram into a year. For her example, her friendship, and all that she teaches me, I am grateful. My other colleagues, especially Elaine Caret, Marilyn Nelson, and John Harris, constantly teach me about what is possible as we discuss what they do and how they do it; they are also great friends and colleagues. My colleagues Sandy Briggs and Rebecca Shirley help me better understand what English learners and students with learning differences need. For their guidance and friendship I remain grateful.

Don Graves has become one of my teachers. Through his books, his e-mails, and our conversations, he has taught me more than my two hands can hold. I am particularly grateful to him for his passionate commitment to and reminders about the importance of writing and all that it can accomplish.

The people at Heinemann continue to provide me with everything a writer needs: support, ideas, and resources. In particular, I would like to thank Renée Le Verrier, Maura Sullivan, Eric Chalek, Kären Clausen, Alan Huisman, Susie Stroud, Leigh Peake, Roberta Lew, Pat Carls, Deb Burns, Steve Bernier, Peggy Wishart, and Marla Berry, and my copy editor, Beth Tripp. Two people, however, merit special mention. Abby Heim, my production editor, has overseen the publication of every one of my books. I am grateful for her guidance and friendship. The second person is Lois Bridges, my editor. Every book I write is the result of our conversations, her encouragement, and her wisdom about what teachers need.

As always, it is my students who teach me the most. They teach me what works and what doesn't. At the heart of each book is my genuine desire to better meet the needs of the kids I work with every day at Burlingame High School.

Special thanks to Nichole Snider for all her help preparing this manuscript and organizing all the logistical details such as permissions.

Finally, I must acknowledge the contribution my family made to this book. My sons are moving into the upper-elementary and middle school grades now, which gives me the chance to learn more about the early development of writers. As they write more and more for school, they teach me what writers need. For example, Evan, my oldest son, has taught me to ask him *how* I should read the paper he wants to show me, instead of automatically whipping out my pen and turning on the lasers. My wife, Susan, made this book possible through her support and our conversations. In a much deeper way, she made it possible by helping me learn to write. Years ago, while in the Peace Corps, I wrote her a letter, expecting no response. We had known each other in high school and I had heard she was traveling the world. When her letter arrived weeks later, I began what would amount to a crash course in writing while living in Tunisia, trying to translate the sights, smells, and experiences of my travels to her through the little Brother typewriter I had brought with me. By the time we met up two years later and moved to San Francisco, I had become a writer; soon after, we became teachers at the same school. She has been my most important teacher ever since.

Introduction
The Challenge of Teaching Writing

. . . .

Instead of *Writing Reminders*, I might have titled the book *Remember Writing?* Many leading figures in education—Don Graves, George Hillocks, Alfie Kohn—have voiced their concerns about the effect our nation's obsession with testing is having on learning in general and writing instruction in particular. The obsession and its associated problems are real, but they by no means represent all the challenges teachers face when it comes to writing instruction these days. A short list of such challenges might include:

- Finding the time to write

- Handling the paper load for the number of students you teach

- Choosing an effective instructional approach

- Creating the conditions needed for effective writing instruction

- Maintaining academic freedom in an era of high-stakes testing

- Providing students with diverse and serious instructional needs

- Ensuring that the work students submit is, in fact, *their* work in this era of online papers; in other words, ethical dilemmas—for teachers *and* students—are present in the classroom in ways they have not always been

Given the size of these different challenges—and the others I chose not to include—it's a rather daunting list. No wonder committed teachers struggle: they are trying to accomplish so much. And the stakes are high: few skills contribute more to students' success than their ability to write clear, effective prose. Writing also gives students a greater sense of achievement and engagement in classes, according to Richard Light's *Making the Most of College* (2001). Through his study of college students, Light found that they themselves place great importance on good writing. Light goes on to say that "[students] reveal that including extensive writing in classes does much to enhance student engagement. . . . They believe they learn most effectively *when writing instruction is organized*

So mom, tell me the truth. Just how important *is* this alphabet thing the teachers are saying we have to learn?

STEPHEN PETERSON, KINDERGARTNER

xi

around a substantive discipline" (59). Of course, Light is talking about college; yet his findings hold true for high school also: writing is work and kids know it. Courses that demand that students write, that use writing to engage students with ideas, that teach students how to write what the course demands—these classes challenge students and give them a feeling of accomplishment. They soon learn that they must think in this class and the teacher will help them do it. Such classes create a culture of intellectual discipline that takes students' ideas seriously even as it pushes them to study subjects they do not yet understand and, by learning about them, develop ideas about the subjects over time.

Having spelled out the obstacles, I ask you to give yourself permission to believe that it is possible to teach students—*all* students, so long as they make a genuine effort—to write clear, cohesive prose. Vicki Spandel, in *Creating Writers: Through 6-Trait Writing Assessment and Instruction* (2001), argues that "the key is language. *Writers'* language. . . . Writers must know about leads, correctness, brevity, clarity, development, detail, fluency, conventional correctness, conclusions and so much more—and must use these terms with ease in discussing their own and others' work" (2). Spandel's list, along with the Six Traits writing model (which I discuss throughout this book), makes visible what writers do and thus makes instruction possible. Knowing what they must do, and what they must learn, teacher and student can get to work. These are teachable skills; they are abilities and capacities that students can study, experiment with, and adopt as they begin to create a working draft of themselves as writers.

Thus, writing is always personal, even when it is academic. When we help students learn to write the different types of texts the world uses, we help them develop not only a skill but a voice, one that has something to say and a way to say it. Reflecting on the process by which students develop this persona, this voice, Tom Newkirk (1997) writes, "All forms of 'self-expression,' all our ways of 'being personal' are forms of performance, in Erving Goffman's terms, 'a presentation of self'" (3). Newkirk's observations make sense to me, for my road to my current selves was a long and winding one. Since I barely managed to graduate from high school, I had to learn the different performances and selves that school and the adult world demand.

This book offers you resources and reminders that will build on what you know and help you learn to be a better writing teacher. I want this book to help us each address the needs of the student I was but also provide us with ways to challenge the teacher we strive to be, though not by drowning ourselves in papers so that we cannot be the partner or parent we need to be when we come home each day. We can always do more, be better; this book is designed to help you work smarter and more effectively as you teach students to write the poems, journals, and other types of text they want while also preparing them to write the essays and research papers the colleges and state exams expect. Thus, this book strikes a balance between what the teacher and the student need to learn and do, between what the student and the state want, between academic and personal writing.

Reading Reminders (Burke 2000) grew out of my classroom, where I still teach full time. That book began a conversation about what works and why; *Writing Reminders* continues that conversation. The connection between reading and writing has always been apparent to me; after all, I began as a writing teacher and have much more formal education about writing than reading. For that reason, this book feels like a return to my roots as a teacher and a student. Carol Booth Olson provides a succinct description of what she calls "the reading/writing connection":

> . . . researchers have increasingly noted the connection between reading and writing, identifying them as essentially the similar processes of meaning construction. Experienced readers and writers share a surprising number of common characteristics. Both readers and writers:
>
> - are actively engaged in constructing meaning from and with texts;
> - go back to go forward in a recursive process;
> - interact and negotiate with each other (i.e., the reader keeps the writer in mind and the writer keeps the reader in mind);
> - access a common tool kit of cognitive strategies, including planning and setting goals, tapping prior knowledge, asking questions and making connections, constructing the gist, monitoring, revising meaning, reflecting and relating, and evaluating;
> - use skills automatically; and
> - are motivated and self-confident.
>
> (2003, 17)

When it comes to writing, however, I believe, as poet William Carlos Williams once wrote, that "the virtue is in the effort." In other words, I know the obstacles are out there, but still I persevere, guided by my faith in the importance of writing and the difference it has made in the lives of my students these many years. I persevere for another, more personal reason: during the years when I was not doing school, when I was not writing the papers my teachers assigned, I wrote when no one was looking. Inside me, a voice, a self, grew. Only one person knew about it: my English teacher. I often failed to do his assignments; but still I wrote, and he made room for me in his classroom. In fact, he *gave* me—and those who wanted to write—a room adjacent to his classroom in which to write. He frequently invited speakers to come to his class and share their views of the world with us. When they left, we could write letters to these people reflecting on what we learned and thanking them for coming. We received extra credit if we wrote these letters, and even more if we typed them. Somehow these speakers engaged me, as did the opportunity to sit in the back room at a typewriter. There, in that back room, I began trying on the self it would take me years to accept. The speakers, my teacher, perhaps even the sound of the typewriter—these started a fire in me, inspired in me ideas, gave birth to a voice I am committed to helping each of my students find in themselves through the daily writing and more ambitious projects we do. Let this book remind us daily how important that challenge is. Let it remind us of all that we know. Let it and the many voices within it provide you the light and company you need as you journey through each revision of the teacher you are becoming.

Jim Burke

Teaching Composition:
A Position Statement
From the Commission on Composition, National Council of Teachers of English

. . . .

The NCTE Commission on Composition has prepared this position paper to state essential principles in the teaching of writing. We hope that this statement will guide teachers, parents, and administrators in understanding the power of writing and in teaching it effectively.

THE ACT OF WRITING

Writing is a powerful instrument of thought. In the act of composing, writers learn about themselves and their world and communicate their insights to others. Writing confers the power to grow personally and to effect change in the world.

The act of writing is accomplished through a process in which the writer imagines the audience, sets goals, develops ideas, produces notes, drafts, and a revised text, and edits to meet the audience's expectations. As the process unfolds, the writer may turn to any one of these activities at any time. We can teach students to write more effectively by encouraging them to make full use of the many activities that comprise the act of writing, not by focusing only on the final written product and its strengths and weaknesses.

THE PURPOSES FOR WRITING

In composing, the writer uses language to help an audience understand something the writer knows about the world. The specific purposes for writing vary widely, from discovering the writer's own feelings, to persuading others to a course of action, recreating experience imaginatively, reporting the results of observation, and more.

Writing assignments should reflect this range of purposes. Student writers should have the opportunity to define and pursue writing aims that are important to them. Student writers should also have the opportunity to use writing as an instrument of thought and learning across the curriculum and in the world beyond school.

THE SCENES FOR WRITING

In the classroom where writing is especially valued, students should be guided through the writing process; encouraged to write for themselves and for other students, as well as for the teacher; and urged to make use of writing as a mode of learning, as well as a means of reporting on what has been learned. The classroom where writing is especially valued should be a place where students will develop the full range of their composing powers. This classroom can also be the scene for learning in many academic areas, not only English.

Because frequent writing assignments and frequent individual attention from the teacher are essential to the writing classroom, writing classes should not be larger than twenty students.

Teachers in all academic areas who have not been trained to teach writing may need help in transforming their classrooms into scenes for writing. The writing teacher should provide leadership in explaining the importance of this transformation and in supplying resources to help bring it about.

THE TEACHERS OF WRITING

Writing teachers should themselves be writers. Through experiencing the struggles and joys of writing, teachers learn that their students will need guidance and support throughout the writing process, not merely comments on the written product. Furthermore, writing teachers who write know that effective comments do not focus on pointing out errors, but go on to the more productive task of encouraging revision, which will help student writers to develop their ideas and to achieve greater clarity and honesty.

Writing teachers should be familiar with the current state of our knowledge about composition. They should know about the nature of the composing process; the relationship between reading and writing; the functions of writing in the world of work; the value of the classical rhetorical tradition; and more. Writing teachers should use this knowledge in their teaching, contribute to it in their scholarly activities, and participate in the professional organizations that are important sources of this knowledge.

The knowledgeable writing teacher can more persuasively lead colleagues in other academic areas to increased attention to writing in their classes. The knowledgeable teacher can also work more effectively with parents and administrators to promote good writing instruction.

THE MEANS OF WRITING INSTRUCTION

Students learn to write by writing. Guidance in the writing process and discussion of the students' own work should be the central means of writing instruction. Students should be encouraged to comment on each other's writing, as well as receiving frequent, prompt, individualized attention from the teacher. Reading what others have written, speaking about one's responses to their writing, and listening to the responses of others are important activities in the writing classroom. Textbooks and other instructional resources should be of secondary importance.

The evaluation of students' progress in writing should begin with the students' own written work. Writing ability cannot be adequately assessed by tests and other formal evaluation alone. Students should be given the opportunity to demonstrate their writing ability in work aimed at various purposes. Students should also be encouraged to develop the critical ability to evaluate their own work, so they can become effective, independent writers in the world beyond school.

How to Use This Book

. . . .

I designed this book, as I did its predecessor, *Reading Reminders* (2001), to support classroom teachers who are trying to help their students write better and professors who are preparing future teachers. I designed this book to give you useful ideas after only a two-minute read—between periods, while planning, even while teaching. I also tried to write a book that would help teachers of any subject improve their writing instruction.

This book is divided up into the following parts:

• *Reminder.* Each reminder is summed up in its title, which itself is phrased as a reminder. To this end, I hope that you can look at the table of contents and get an idea that will help you in thirty seconds. If you then want more information, you can go to the actual reminder and read it for more detailed instructions or view examples of student work or actual activities.

• *Rationale.* Each of the sixty-plus reminders begins with a brief explanation of what the reminder means and why you should remember to do the specified activity. These rationales are always based on both my own experiences in the classroom and current research. (In the section titled "Write in Many Genres," this is replaced with "Description.")

• *What to Do.* This section is the main course of each reminder. Here you will find examples of student work, questions to ask, activities to try, or strategies to use. On occasion, I include actual sample assignments. (In the section titled "Write in Many Genres," this is replaced with "Prompts for Practice.")

• *Classroom Connection.* Whenever possible, I include sample assignments from my own classroom or, in a few cases, other teachers'. Also, in addition to the actual assignments, I try to include representative student samples to show the kind of work the assignment yields. In some cases I include different examples to show you a range of possible responses or approaches.

• *At a Glance.* In the section titled "Write in Many Genres," I include a short list of what each type of writing should typically include and what it should accomplish.

Writing is one third imagination, one third experience, and one third observation.

WILLIAM FAULKNER

• *Recommended Resources.* At the end of each reminder you will find information on books, Web sites, and other sources that offer additional guidance in that area. Some books, such as Donald Murray's *A Writer Teaches Writing, Writer's Inc.*, and Nancie Atwell's *In the Middle* (to name a few), appear more than once. These books and authors should be considered essential reading and sound investments for the teacher looking to continue working on their writing.

My goal was to create a book that you could use in your own way to meet your own needs, regardless of what grade level, ability level, or subject you teach. Between the headers, table of contents, and subheaders, I have tried to structure this book so you can get the information you seek as easily and quickly as possible.

This book has one final, more ambitious objective: Schools need to develop and remember to use a common set of strategies, habits, and terms to help students become better writers in all subject areas. I wrote this book, as I have all my books, while teaching full time at Burlingame High School. Every suggestion herein grew from my own daily effort to solve the problems I face in my own classroom, with kids I care about, whose needs challenge me as much as your own students no doubt challenge you. This book should be treated as a companion to *Reading Reminders*; throughout this book, I have tried to reinforce the essential connection between reading and writing. As you read *this* book, I hope it will help you teach your students to write as well as they must to succeed in your class and the world for which you daily endeavor to prepare them.

Create a Community
of Writers

Draw your chair up
close to the edge of
the precipice, and I'll
tell you a story.

—F. SCOTT FITZGERALD

In *A Community of Writers: Teaching Writing in the Junior and Senior High School* (1988), Daniels and Zemelman assert that "writing, real writing, requires that teachers create a special kind of group climate in their classrooms . . . " (47). The authors go on to emphasize the connection between reading and writing, which I discussed briefly in the introduction: "Both educators and the general public have suffered for too long under the delusion that reading and writing are essentially solitary skills that develop best through isolated, individualistic practice" (47). Thus, traits of a community of writers might describe a classroom that is:

• *Participatory.* It is interactive, dynamic; students can speak up and share their writing in the class or with partners.

• *Supportive.* Kids can take risks, share their ideas or even what Annie Lamott (1994) calls their "shitty first drafts" without fear of humiliation. They know they will get the help they need to do the assigned work and thus meet their teacher's expectations.

• *Inclusive.* What students read, write, and discuss is always respectful and mindful of all students in the class. No one is left out of the conversation or the assignment. While the teacher differentiates instruction (Tomlinson 1999), *every* student feels included and supported, challenged and capable of succeeding.

• *Responsive.* Students' writing topics and the content of the course respond to the students' academic and personal needs as they arise.

• *Committed.* Everything the teacher and students say or do reflects the values of the class and reinforces the sense that this is a class that takes ideas and writing seriously.

• *Authentic.* Students feel that the work they do is real and meaningful; while such a class prepares them to succeed on state requirements, instruction is kept in check so as not to intrude on the larger, more compelling reasons that students write.

Don Graves (1994), reflecting on what writers need, identified seven "conditions for effective writing" (103):

• *Time*. Students should write *daily*, working through their ideas and developing their abilities by working as writers. Graves says if you can only "teach writing" one day a week, then "don't teach it at all."

• *Choice*. Choosing their subject and what to say about it engages writers; it helps them commit to their writing because they feel a sense of ownership.

• *Response*. Responding to students' writing throughout the composing process signals that people—students, teachers, other readers—take them and their ideas seriously. Graves describes different ways and times to respond but emphasizes that "students need to hear the responses of others to their writing, to discover what they do or do not understand" (108).

• *Demonstration*. The teacher is "the most important factor in creating a learning environment in the classroom. . . . When you actually take your own text and put it on the chalkboard, an overhead projector, or chart paper, and show your students how you read it, they will receive the clearest demonstration of what writing is all about" (109). We demonstrate many things, Graves points out: passion, curiosity, problem solving, craft. Through these demonstrations, you demystify the process of writing by allowing students to "see you struggle to match your intentions with the words that reach the page" (110).

• *Expectation*. Most compelling to me is Graves' remark that "to have high expectations is a sign of caring." The classroom must be a place where students and teacher continually revise and raise their expectations of each other and themselves. Graves' favorite question, one that conveys these high expectations, is, What are you working at in order to be a better writer?

• *Room structure*. Graves stresses the importance of structure as a defense against the fragility of the writing process. Students need to know what to expect so they know how to—and that they *can*—work on their piece of writing. He describes this as making the room "predictable" for productive work.

• *Evaluation*. Graves expands this concept to include evaluation of not only the piece of writing at hand but the bigger picture of the student's progress as a writer over the course of the year. His expectation that students "be prepared to tell [him] about their work and how it is going" reinforces the value of self-evaluation, a process by which students learn "to know how to decide if their choices [about topics] are good ones."

Maxine Greene (1995) sums up the feeling one finds in a classroom where a community exists: "In thinking of community, we need to emphasize the process words: making, creating, weaving, saying, and the like" (39). Greene's words apply equally to students *and* teachers. A community is not a team, or a family, or a crew; it is an evolving, organic notion that describes how people relate to and work with each other. People play different roles, and the community itself meets needs common to all students. In classes where students feel their needs—academic and personal, intellectual and emotional—are met, they feel a great sense of belonging; they also feel challenged. Consider the following needs and ask whether your classroom and the work students do in there meet these different needs: comfort, safety, control, tradition, friendship, nurturance, recognition, success, independence, variety, curiosity, and enjoyment (Osborn and Osborn 1997, 104).

Creating communities is hard but essential work. We need them as much within the classroom as we do within the school at large. Writing, after all, is the business of the whole school, not just the English teachers. Judith Langer (2002) found that all "beat the odds schools" had one thing in common: "they provided an environment that fostered teacher professionalism" (41). Langer elaborated on this finding, saying these schools established and maintained a climate that:

- Coordinated efforts to improve student achievement

- Fostered teacher participation in a variety of professional activities

- Created instructional improvement activities in ways that offered teachers a strong sense of agency

- Valued commitment to the profession of teaching

- Engendered caring toward students and colleagues

- Fostered respect for learning as a normal part of life (47)

Langer's findings emphasize the importance of creating such a community within the class as well as throughout the school. Writing and reading—literacy in general—cannot be something valued in one department and dismissed in another; all departments must accept responsibility for students' literacy. Schoenbach et al. (2000), whose work through the Strategic Literacy Initiative stresses the importance of a schoolwide approach to "academic literacy," focuses on four "dimensions of classroom life" that support what they call the "reading apprentice":

- Social

- Personal

- Cognitive

- Knowledge building

Students in such a supportive classroom receive a complete, well-rounded education that honors their need for social interaction and inquiry while simultaneously developing the skills and knowledge they need to succeed in other domains outside of that class. At year's end, I ask students in my ACCESS (Academic Success) program to write letters to the incoming students explaining what the program is all about. The following excerpt from Brian Blanton's letter captures what the different researchers say about effective classes:

> After being in ACCESS for two years I feel like I'm part of a family. Every year I succeed more than I can say. Taking this class is paying off. This class brings us together and helps us prepare for our future. This class taught me to work, work until you know inside yourself you are happy. Real world people come in and show you what they do. It's a real eye-opener!

Such work is not possible if the class lacks a sense of shared mission and togetherness. Of course, it's not like that every day! But the values that underlie the community of our class, values we must reaffirm constantly if we are to live by them, keep us all coming back the next day to try to do it better. These values and the commitment to each other give us a feeling that the class will only be as good, as effective, as our individual contributions.

What then do I, the teacher, contribute to this community? The truth is we teachers do not provide just one thing; rather, we fulfill many needs, play many roles over the course of the year. Sometimes we must be leaders, governing and even pushing the students to rise to the occasion. On other occasions we are masters of our craft, modeling to our apprentices how to do what we ask or they must learn. Certain qualities are constant and essential to a dynamic community: honesty, passion, commitment. We act out these qualities by being advocates and activists, coaches and generals, parents and partners in the process. Joseph Tsujimoto (2001) emphasizes two essential traits all effective writing teachers have and that we must strive to keep alive in our own teaching: persona and passion. Tsujimoto explains:

> The teacher's persona is a professional façade. It is the character the teacher presents to the classroom. It is the teacher's genuine personality shorn of the characteristics that detract from or are irrelevant to effective teaching and learning. The persona is

made notable through the distillation and emphasis of the characteristics that help the teacher communicate with unquestioned confidence and memorable intensity. (185)

Passion is who you are, what you teach, and the way you teach it that—at different moments, to different degrees—dissolves into a single, luminous sound, tumultuous or tremulous, that signals like a pulsating light at the roof of your students' skulls. At its most intense, the signal reads, "Here is something important, here is something powerful and fine, here is something that I ought to look into more closely." Students are infected, suddenly or gradually, by a teacher's dementia—for all the right reasons that the teacher shows. (189)

Tsujimoto captures what we all know, as teachers *and* students, about effective classrooms: there must be a sense that something is going on, that something is always about to happen, that each day is an occasion to which every member of that class community must rise, for the work is important, the time is short, and the stakes are high.

1 Write with Your Students

RATIONALE

Students can't be the only learners in a classroom. Teachers have to learn, too.

NANCIE ATWELL, *IN THE END*

Writing is a performance, an invitation, and a challenge; writing with our students keeps us honest, reminding us that it is not always so easy to "just jot down your ideas for a few minutes." Writing with students also creates a community of writers. It seems almost too simple, but students often comment on the fact that I get down there with them and write. It conveys the idea that I would not ask them to do something that I would not do myself; it also allows me to provide a model and think aloud about my process. This last benefit, being able to describe how I approached the writing topic, is useful when students are struggling to begin. When I gave a class of struggling readers the following quote to write about, I was not prepared for their difficulty in getting *something* down. So I sat down with them so that we could write about it together.

Begin somewhere; you cannot build a reputation on what you *intend* to do. (Henry Ford)

I wrote:

You cannot learn to swim by standing on the side of the pool. There comes a time when you must jump in, even if it means looking silly or making an error. When I lived in Tunisia, for example, I had to learn Arabic. Only the people who blundered their way into saying things learned to speak it well. The only problem was that each mistake I made seemed to somehow be very embarrassing to both the person and myself. One night I asked a man where his butt was when I thought I was asking for the park. But I learned, and built a reputation for myself as someone who was willing to do whatever was necessary to get the job done.

When I finished, I read it aloud to my class. I talked about the questions I asked myself to gather and elaborate on my ideas. I keep a standard composition book in my desk in the class for such writing.

WHAT TO DO

• While reading aloud from a class read-aloud book (*Tuesdays with Morrie*, Albom 1997, for example), keep a sheet of paper out to stop and model how to find and develop topics. Create a Cornell Notes page format (see Burke 2002c). As you read, stop and note possible topics to write about. Tell the students to write them down. Tell them why you are writing them down, what you might come back to and discuss. Then, say, "Okay, now I will read for a few more pages, but you have to listen for and generate your own topics." At the end of the reading, ask them what they have. This informal assessment tells you who still struggles to generate ideas and who is on their way. Meanwhile, they are free to pick whichever topic they wish, circle it, and then write about it. This technique addresses their needs as writers and readers, listeners, and thinkers.

• Share what you wrote when it will help, but not when it will confuse or intimidate. Use your writing when necessary to show *how*—not to show *off*.

• Write with your students—on an overhead transparency or computer monitor so you can model for them.

• If appropriate, think out loud about your own writing so they can see how you arrived at the result. You might also talk about what you found difficult and how you solved that problem while writing.

• You can also write *to* your students. I often write notes, sometimes even letters, to students. I do not dumb them down, but instead assume that students will challenge themselves to read my letters since they are personal mail.

• Writing with students is especially helpful when you are introducing a new technique or type of writing. My students write in their journal after they complete their silent reading; responding to this reading was a new idea, however, for many kids. So I did my own reading and then did the daily SSR reflection myself, which I then used as a model to help them see what they could do on this assignment:

> I jumped right into my book because I was very eager to find out what happened to David's father. Would he actually begin a criminal investigation of his own brother? But after five minutes I began getting distracted. Michael, then Guiselle, and then Shane, came in late, each one making more noise than the last. Then someone kept popping their gum and I couldn't concentrate because I wanted to know who it was. Finally, I got myself to concentrate again by just staring at the page and focusing

myself to read. This helped me regain my concentration, especially when I found out what his brother, a respected physician in the small town, had done.

Go to Reminder 45 to see Tommy Chong's journal excerpt for further clarification of this strategy.

RECOMMENDED RESOURCE

Atwell, Nancie. 1998. *In the Middle: New Understandings About Writing, Reading, and Learning*. Portsmouth, NH: Heinemann.

Confer with Your Student Writers

2

RATIONALE

Conferencing calls to mind the image of the master at the apprentice's shoulder, guiding, helping the apprentice master their craft. It also helps create a community within the class, a place where students know they will get the guidance they need to improve. Large class sizes often preclude the kind of conferencing we wish we could provide, but still there are ways to meet. Those classes that use a writing workshop model can also build in room for writing partners or groups to meet and conference with each other, sometimes for a specific purpose such as generating ideas for the paper, which teachers can monitor and guide as they move around the classroom. Conferencing allows you to individualize instruction, a key element of effective writing instruction, given the range of needs in any given class. English learners, for instance, may have specific needs that a quick small-group conference can address. Advanced writers, more concerned about style and voice, can get what they need and not feel eclipsed by the other students' more basic needs.

Being edited is like falling face down into a threshing machine.

MARGARET ATWOOD

WHAT TO DO

Meet with individuals at their desks, at your desk, in the hall, on the steps—whatever space will allow for a productive, focused, and supportive discussion of their writing. Remember that writing is personal, and so you must always ask whether talking to a student about their writing in the presence of others will embarrass or distract the student and thus prevent them from learning from you.

Meet with groups who have a common need or are writing about the same topic. This is especially helpful in larger classes, where it is almost impossible to conference effectively with thirty-five students individually. This configuration also allows you to provide targeted instruction or support for struggling students or English learners who might, for example, need extra help getting started or even understanding the writing assignment itself.

9

Meet at students' desks as they work, to confer about such issues as their subject or topic sentence. These curbside conferences allow you to move through the whole room and either approve of what they have or quickly guide them as needed. This type of conference sustains the supportive atmosphere in the class and allows you to gather helpful information about what people need. For example, after moving through the entire class to check their topics, I might have noticed that many made very obvious statements. So we might do a quick write, using such questions as So what? to get beyond the obvious topics and into the real source of heat hidden within their ideas.

Have students meet with each other in writing groups to provide support, feedback, and community as they move through the writing process of a paper. Students are not able to provide all forms of help that developing writers need, but they can, through talking about and reading each other's papers, be very helpful if taught which questions to ask and how to talk about writing. Remember, however, that writing is personal and not all papers are for everyone's eyes, so check with students first before demanding they share their writing.

Meet with them in the hall later that day. Sometimes at lunch I will see a kid whose writing I read that morning. I might have realized something later on, a possible addition or change the student might consider. Or perhaps I remembered something I could not when we met that morning. I will walk up to her and say, "I was thinking about your paper some more, and I thought you might find it helpful to try. . . ." Such efforts outside the classroom pay off by creating a rich community of writers inside the classroom.

Confer with the whole class using the overhead and a student example. This is really just a variation on the minilesson, but it's still a form of group conferencing about a common issue. Take an exemplar from a past student or from another period (removing the name) and copy it to a transparency. Use it to discuss a problem or a trait of good writing that you realize everyone needs to address in the current assignment.

Help students via e-mail if you can and are inclined. Remember that there are equity issues involved: are you providing extra instruction to students who can afford computers? Since students can reach me through our classroom Web site, I have experimented with this form of conferencing and found it productive for several reasons. First, students have to formulate the question or identify what they need help doing. This evaluative step gets them much more focused than the student who plops his paper on your desk and asks, "Can you check my paper?" On-line conferencing also allows me to respond in writing, which I can do quickly and much more legibly on the computer.

Before students meet with you, have them identify their greatest need so you can use the time well. As soon as you sit down, ask them, "What is the one thing you want to discuss about your paper?" Or put them through the paces of a targeted activity such as identifying all their verbs or transitions; then, if you are teaching them to use transitions or more active verbs, meet with them to just look at what they circled. Begin such discussions by asking, "What do you notice about your use of transitions?"

When reading through students' papers, instead of correcting them, jot down one or two main issues in the paper at the top. Examples: focus, verbs, supporting details. Then, instead of grading them, return them to students and ask them to meet with you. As you sit down, you have already determined what this student needs to improve on this paper and you can direct all your remarks accordingly.

When meeting with students, especially those from other cultures, ask them to explain their ideas so you can better understand what they think they are saying. Peitzman and Gadda (1994) suggest using the following questions when meeting with English learners:

- Why did you begin and end this paper this way?
- How do you think this kind of writing should sound?
- What do you think your reader already knows about what you say?
- What do you think you have to tell them?
- How do you expect your reader to follow you from Part 1 to Part 2?
- What do you expect your readers to understand by this?
- How do you expect this piece of writing to affect your readers? (56)

It must be clear to students that you are genuinely interested in their writing and ideas. They are entrusting their stories, their selves, to you as you try to improve their writing. The questions you ask, the comments you make, the tone of your voice—these all matter when you meet with students to discuss their writing.

Instead of writing all over a student's paper, consider using Post-its. I have a clipboard with a pad of Post-its taped to it; I write on that and then stick the note on the student's paper in the proper place when we meet. Another alternative is to use a conference sheet that contains helpful questions you can ask or the traits of good writing. See the example shown in Figure 2.1 and adapt it to meet your own needs. When done

11

Writing Conference Notes

Student: _____

Date: _____   Assignment: _____

1. This is the _____ draft.
2. The *subject* of this paper is:
3. The *main idea* of this paper is:
4. Which of the following traits are we talking about?

   ☐ Idea development
   ☐ Organization
   ☐ Voice
   ☐ Word choice
   ☐ Sentence fluency
   ☐ Conventions

5. Title: It should intrigue and inform the reader.
6. Discuss ONE aspect of the paper per conference.

   ☐ What does this story say *in one sentence*?
   ☐ Why will the lead capture the reader?
   ☐ What are the reader's five questions about this paper?

   1.
   2.
   3.
   4.
   5.

7. Are these questions answered by the paper's end?
8. What proof or support does the writer offer?
9. What is the question this paper is trying to answer?
10. Other useful questions to consider:

    ☐ What works?
    ☐ What doesn't work?
    ☐ What is the writer trying to accomplish?
    ☐ To what extent does the writer succeed?
    ☐ What surprised you most in this paper?
    ☐ How is this draft different from the previous one?

11. What does the writer need to do for the next conference?

Conference Notes

FIGURE 2.1   Conference Notes template

May be copied for classroom use. Writing Reminders *by Jim Burke (Heinemann, Portsmouth, NH); © 2003.*

with the conference, give the sheet to the student and ask them to attach it to their final paper.

RECOMMENDED RESOURCE

Kaufman, Douglas. 2000. *Conferences and Conversations: Listening to the Literate Classroom*. Portsmouth, NH: Heinemann.

3

Use Writing to Assess, Synthesize, and Extend

RATIONALE

To write is to think. Thus, a classroom that works as a community writes for many different purposes. For teachers, writing is a tool, a means of seeing what students know and how well they understand it; it is also a means of extending what students know. It is a performance that makes visible what kids think, what they learn. You cannot connect or produce coherent writing about things you do not understand. Writing is a means of discovering and making meaning. However, none of this is possible if students do not work within a classroom that supports writing as reflection or meaning making.

WHAT TO DO

Assess understanding of ideas or texts students read by having them write about them. Options include essays, retellings, summaries, reports, and notes. The example in the following bullet shows a student demonstrating his understanding of ideas and texts through notes, annotations, and his essay. This allows me to assess his ability to take notes, to understand what he read, and to incorporate ideas from the reading into his essay. The example in Figure 3.1 comes from a freshman in my ACCESS (Academic Success) class at year's end and shows me all that he has learned to do.

Have students synthesize different texts and ideas using writing. Whether students use Synthesis or Summary Notes (see Figure 16.1 and Burke 2002c), or just a page of informal writing to tie it all together, writing helps them make sense of what they read and learn about. Tommy Chong, a student in my sophomore ACCESS class, here explains the Henry Ford quotation (*see* Reminder 1); he also reflects on how he writes and what he finds difficult.

> I think that this quote means if you want to do something you won't say you are going to do something, and then expect it to happen for you. Like in doing your homework. You can't say, "I'm going to do all my homework the whole year, and I am going to

get As," and then when you go home you just sit there and watch TV. Then when you go turn in your homework, you have to make up some excuse. Then when your report card comes and you have all Ds and you can't understand why. I know how that goes because I use to do this all the time. Then when I started trying my hardest and I would still have a bad grade in the class. So that's why this year I made a pact with my friends, and I have followed through, I have already finished all my homework for the week and so now I feel that I can do good this whole year.

[I then asked students to draw a line under their last sentence and explain how they came up with ideas and what happened while they wrote.]

Writing is pretty hard for me so I need people to help me start. But it doesn't end there. I need someone to help me spell, and help when my mind goes blank. I draw a lot of blanks so I need someone to feed ideas to me. Like last year I would only do my essays in Mrs. Shirley's class because she would help me when I was stuck. So I did okay on the essays. But when I started doing them at home, I noticed that they wouldn't get done because I would go into a blank and get frustrated and just stop.

Synthesize a period's discussion by taking the last five or ten minutes to have them explain what they read and discussed. They could write notes, a journal entry (in which, for example, they retell and respond to what they studied), or a letter to the teacher. All of these methods would help them better understand the information and also allow you to assess and monitor their understanding.

Have them synthesize and extend their thinking after they finish creating graphic representations of events, ideas, or stories. Using any of the tools in *Tools for Thought* (Burke 2002c) is useful, as are such techniques as character mandalas, but using such graphic tools as prewriting improves their capacity as writers. Thus, after they finish any art project or graphic organizer, have students explain it. Many of these graphic tools further improve students' writing by teaching them to organize their ideas based on the clusters of the different tools. Tony's Conversational Roundtable (Figure 3.1), for example, organizes his ideas into clusters that could become paragraphs in his essay. It is also a good idea to take data from interviews and research and write a summary of those findings to synthesize the ideas and extend them into a deeper form of a report or essay that draws its examples from the interview or research data.

Extend the text by having students recast it into new forms or new possibilities. For a fun example of this, visit the Web site Fair E-Tales

15

<www.three.org>, which carries classic and contemporary fairy tales re-written from multiple points of view. Such extensions of the original text also demonstrate one's understanding of the original text, since one cannot adapt or extend what they do not initially understand. Such extensions offer other important opportunities for students to connect learning with their own ideas and cultures as they recast stories into new cultural contexts to better understand them. Finally, such extensions, as demonstrated by the examples you can find at Fair E-Tales, teach students about style and voice and the conventions of genre as they work within each genre's conventions to create their own pieces.

CLASSROOM CONNECTION

The following assignment—Self-Evaluation: Progress Report Time—incorporates all three goals of assessment, synthesis, and extension. The sample included is one I wrote so students in my reading classes had a concrete exemplar to help them.

Self-Evaluation: Progress Report Time

Overview   The following assignment asks you to reflect on your progress this semester. You need to think about your progress (or lack of it) in several different areas; also, you must show evidence of your progress in these areas. If you do a very good job, you will explain why you made such good progress and what type of progress you made. Use this work-sheet to prepare you for the paragraph assignment at the end.

Prepare to Write

1. Identify the areas (e.g., skills, behaviors, habits, performance in classes) in which you feel you have shown improvement this semester.
2. Identify those areas, if there are any, in which you have had trouble or not done well. Explain the causes of these troubles as best you can.
3. The most appropriate grade for me this semester is . . .
4. This grade is fair and accurate for several reasons.
5. So far this semester, my most important accomplishment is . . .
6. Using the answers to these prompts as notes, and your returned work as examples, write a paragraph that begins as follows:

   There are several reasons that I should have a _____ in this class.

There are several reasons why I should have a ___B___ in this class. First, I have improved in several areas since last semester. For my SSR books, for example, I am just finishing my third book. *This shows that* I am reading not only better but more than I did last semester. *I have also improved* my attendance. I realize this is not important to some people, but my attendance last semester was terrible. So being here every day on time this semester is one more way I have improved. *My participation in the class has improved* more than anything, and I am very proud of this. *Last semester I hardly talked at all, but this semester* I contribute almost daily to discussions. I have taken my participation a step further by going to Washington Elementary School, where I read to a kindergartner every Thursday. *This work proves* how much my confidence has grown, since I never would have done something like this at the beginning of the year. *Finally,* though I have improved in many ways, I still have areas in which I need to improve. I still need to work on my behavior in class. Most days I am no trouble at all, but at least once a week I seem to disrupt the class. I have also not reached my personal goal of finishing four books by the end of the grading period. I will continue to work on this, but for now a B seems like the grade that best describes my work so far.

Here is another synthesizing assignment:

ACCESS Final Exam

Overview   The purpose of this final exam is to show what you know and can do at the end of your freshman year. You have the entire period. At the end of the period, you will have read three selections from the anthology *Multicultural Voices,* all of which are about America. The question you are reading to answer is, What does it mean to be American now? The story, essay, and poem, combined with your own experiences, will prepare you to write a final paper near the end of the period. Finally, you will also show me your ability to take notes and discuss several different pieces of writing in one paper. Good luck!

STEP ONE: BEFORE READING

• Write down your initial response to the question, What does it mean to be American now? Do whichever helps you most: list, cluster/brainstorm, or write your ideas. Just get your mind thinking about the topic.

- After doing the previous step, write down a statement that answers the question, What does it mean to be American? You can revise it later if your thinking changes.

- Read each of the following, in this order:

  ▸ "The Struggle to Be an All-American Girl," by Elizabeth Wong (page 215)

  ▸ "Only Approved Indians Can Play: Made in USA," by Jack Forbes (page 107)

  ▸ "Becoming American," by Vern Rutsala (page 220), OR "West Side," by Naomi Shihab Nye (page 37)

- *Remember to skim the text, including the study questions and other notes, before you read.*

STEP TWO: DURING READING

- Take notes as you read. Jot your notes down in the boxes of the Conversational Roundtable. You should write down only the examples, quotes, or ideas that help you answer the question, What does it mean to be American? You will use these when you write your paper.

- Read actively: ask questions, make connections, take notes.

STEP THREE: AFTER READING

- Use your notes to write your final answer to the question, What does it mean to be American? Your paper should:

- Include examples or quotations *from each reading selection*

- Organize your ideas into paragraphs, each with one main idea

Figure 3.1 shows Tony's Conversational Roundtable for this assignment. Following are the first two paragraphs from the in-class essay that Tony then wrote; note how the organizer prepared him to write:

AMERICAN OR NOT

To be American is a very special honor for many people. But sometimes many people get adapted with other cultures, and leave their own behind. To be American is to be yourself, to never forget where you come from. To be American is special, but to forget your own ethnic group is wrong. To be an American is very hard. You always have to make important decisions.

Elizabeth Wong says, "I preferred tacos to egg rolls; I enjoyed Cinco de Mayo more than Chinese New Year." In her

Conversational Roundtable

Name Tony Arteaga	Date 6/13
Topic Essay	Period 2°

Suggestions for Use: Ask yourself what is the focus of your paper, discussion, inquiry. Is it a character, a theme, an idea, a country, a trend, or a place? Then examine it from four different perspectives, or identify four different aspects of the topic. Once you have identified the four areas, find and list any appropriate quotations, examples, evidence, or details.

What You Think

- Never forget your own culture
- She should never have given up her culture.
- people have been discriminated against for not being of American descent.

What Elizabeth Wong says:

- To be American she changed her way of life.
- Instead of liking her culture she prefered others.
- She never liked going to Chinese school, and her brother always made fun of her mother.
- She preferred tacos to egg rolls.

What does it mean to be American?

What Jack Forbes says:

- Since the Tuscon team was not enrolled they could not play.
- This meant they were discriminated against.
- An Indian was excluded because his tribe was unknown.
- No one listened to him.

What the poet says:

- people easily change their culture or they adopt a new language, or new culture.
- In his poem he writes that many people want to learn new languages. They want to know their stubborn tongues are kept tame.

FIGURE 3.1   Conversational Roundtable: This tool has many uses, but in this case, freshman Tony Arteaga uses it to prepare for his final exam essay.

world this is what being an American really means. To be an American is to be American. In her way being American changed her way of life. Her mother wanted them to go to Chinese school, but they hated it. Her brother always made fun of how their mother spoke.

RECOMMENDED RESOURCE

Wiggins, Grant. 1998. *Educative Assessment: Designing Assessments to Inform and Improve Student Performance.* San Francisco, CA: Jossey-Bass.

Use Writing Across the Curriculum

4

RATIONALE

Every field demands that people know how to communicate effectively. Whether writing reports or taking notes, writing brochures or creating Web sites, successful adults need to be able to write a variety of texts with clarity. We do not just write to communicate, however; in school we often use writing to learn, to think, and to assess. The following examples of writing in different subject areas illustrate what Howard Gardner means when he says in *The Disciplined Mind: What All Students Should Understand* (1999) that students "must spend several years mastering the elements of these literate systems and learning how to use them fluently and flexibly" (29). Writing is not something students use in the English class alone; all scientists and historians write constantly, using the same set of mental habits and organizational and rhetorical devices that writers in all disciplines use.

> Three hours a day will produce as much as a man ought to write.
>
> ANTHONY TROLLOPE

WHAT TO DO

Let's begin with what is common to most if not all writing across the disciplines. Student writers working in all disciplines need to be able to:

- Make statements or claims about events, ideas, or processes

- Support these statements using details and evidence from other texts or research

- Write with clarity, organizing information in the way that best meets their and their audience's needs

- Determine the purpose for this piece of writing: to persuade, inform, explain, entertain, learn; these are common to all subject areas at one time or another

21

Social Studies

Have students write:

- A letter to an official (e.g., in response to recent legislation or proposing some change).

- An op-ed article on a current or historical event; students could write from their own point of view, or write from several different points of view to better understand the event. Writing an op-ed piece (from the perspective of a politician, someone in support of, and someone in opposition to the decision) in response to Roosevelt's decision to intern the Japanese Americans, for example, would help students understand the different implications and sentiments of such a decision.

- Their own version of some primary source document they study. For example, students learning about the Constitution could write their own personal constitution or bill of rights. Such activities help students understand the ideas in the documents and teach about such elements as style, rhetorical devices, and organization of information.

- An advertisement for a politician or idea that they are studying, or a speech that leaders might give to convince the public that, for example, going to war is in the best interests of the country.

- An essay or essay exam.

- A short story based on historical events, which helps them enter into history and better understand the reality behind the facts. Or they could write a journal or letter from the perspective of a historical figure they are studying. A student who writes their own slave narrative or keeps a journal of their days in a concentration camp will be able to better understand the history they are reading.

- An investigative report on the history of an idea, person, place, or object.

- A response to Steve Mills' French Revolution Digital Storybook assignment (see Reminder 47).

- A formal paper on an important historical topic for publication in *The Concord Review*, whose Web site offers the following information:

  The National Writing Board will read and rate serious academic papers by high school students of history in July against an international standard. Reports will be sent to authors, who can then decide which college admissions officers should receive them to add to the information they now have with which to evaluate prospective applicants.

These papers will be evaluated externally against an independent academic expository writing standard developed by **The Concord Review**, since 1987 the only quarterly journal in the world for the academic work of high school students writing in English. *<www.tcr.org>*

Science

Have students write:

- Lab reports that follow the standard guidelines for such reports

- Speech or multimedia presentations of findings from a recent lab or scientific investigation

- Research papers on a subject of scientific importance (e.g., cloning, the genetic code, robotics)

- Brochures for a proposed or fictional product (e.g., a new drug treatment)

- Directions for a scientific procedure

Math

Have students write:

- An explanation of the process they used to arrive at their solution

- An investigative report on a subject related to math (e.g., "No Mathematics, No MP3: How Mathematics Creates the Music You Love")

- Their own word problems in order to better understand how they work and the conventions that govern such problems

Health

Have students write:

- An informational brochure about a specific topic (e.g., teen pregnancy); extend the assignment to include document design ideas, and publish the brochures for the school

- A public service announcement. Visit *<www.adcouncil.org>* for actual examples of such ads in different media forms, all of which require writing (for script, proposal, text of print ads)

- An investigative report

- An interview or survey that they then conduct; follow up the survey by having students analyze their data and examine it in a paper, brochure, or newspaper article

- A grant proposal for a health-related program (e.g., in-school day care program for teen mothers, teen center, presentation by a special speaker for school or your class)

- A letter of advice to someone with a certain problem about which they must make a decision

- An analysis of the consequences of a decision, using a Decision Tree (see Figure 16.1) to map out the possible outcomes of different decisions and explaining the benefits and disadvantages of each choice

CLASSROOM CONNECTION

Math Reports

Due Dates: Friday, November 15th
                 Thursday, December 5th

Goal   The goal of this Math Report is for you to see math from different perspectives, to see how math has come to be developed and gain a better understanding in how you may use math in everyday life and practical application.

Content   The report is to be a one-page summary of something you have read or researched that you can relate to math. This may be about a person, theorems/formulas, the subject of math, real-use applications, and so on.

Some examples are as follows:

- *People:* Descartes, Einstein, Fibonacci

- *Theorems and Formulas:* Pythagorean theorems, Siope formula, quadratic formula

- *Subjects:* When was algebra first used? When was the concept of zero first used? What culture used zero first?

- *Applications:* How do you convert Celsius to Fahrenheit? How are kelvins used? What kind of math does a doctor use? An architect?

Format

- Minimum one page, maximum two pages, TYPED.

- Reports will be graded on content, grammar, and spelling.

- You must have at least one source of information, and you must CITE this source in your report.

- You may use a bibliography or a footnote to cite your source of information.

- You may use conventional books, the Internet, magazines, newspapers, documentaries, or even interviews for your source of information.

If you have any questions regarding the Math Report, do not wait until the night before to ask. If you need ideas or help getting started, make sure to see me as soon as possible.

The following sample comes from Lourdes, a student in my sophomore ACCESS class:

I know a person that has to use math no matter what. He has to do it for his job. That person has to be my dad because he has to use it whether he likes to or not because his job is installing carpet. Working with the carpet always has to do with length and width. The formula for this measuring carpet is P = 2L + 2W. He uses another formula to calculate the cost per yard and the number of yards there are in the whole house.

All of this information comes from my dad himself. He uses a lot of math because by the end of each week he has to add his checks all up. In that kind of job you always have to double-check everything because that amount is what is going to be his salary and has to be divided between three different people. Installing carpet is a job that requires that you make many decisions because my dad has two other workers in addition to himself.

What have I learned? I learned that wherever you go there is no way you would be able to do a job that does not involve algebra. I understand my father's job and what it involves now that I took a better look.

RECOMMENDED RESOURCE

Maxwell, Rhoda. 1995. *Writing Across the Curriculum in Middle and High Schools*. New York: Pearson.

5 Be Patient, Consistent, Courageous, and Confident

Try again. Fail again.
Fail better.

SAMUEL BECKETT

RATIONALE

Writing is a craft and thus takes time to master. Sure, some show apparent talent early on, but most need to be coached into having a conscience about their craft. Others have real challenges that only time and direct instruction can overcome. Because it is a performance, writing makes errors public. Students who don't understand what they read can just hide in the back of the class and not answer questions; writing will not let you hide out like that. Writing errors light up a paper like an airport runway.

Creating a supportive community within your class makes it okay to learn, which is to say, make errors. But such a commitment to the process of growth demands patience from both teacher and student. Both need to know that what they do will make a difference, will result in improved writing. There is a difference between being patient and being tolerant, however. As the Chinese proverb says, "Be not afraid of growing slowly, but of standing still."

Writing progress comes in many forms because kids struggle with different aspects of the process. For some, beginning a piece of writing feels impossible. They must know that they can improve in this aspect of their performance and that you can help them do this. Others are haunted by spelling or grammatical errors that seem to have taken up residence in their sentences and never given notice. Still others have stamina problems, which make the mere act of sitting and writing very difficult for them.

Writing requires patience, but it also requires consistent practice and instruction. To continue on in the face of what for some teachers seem insurmountable difficulties requires courage, a confident belief by both teacher and student that improvement will come, though at a different pace for some than others. Such faith in teachers and students, and in a process, reinforces the values of the classroom and makes it a hopeful community.

WHAT TO DO

• Look for any sign of progress that is genuine. Celebrate it with comments or, if possible, by using it as an example for the class.

- Be sure the students know what progress looks or feels like so they know what to watch for. Students with stamina difficulties, for example, need to know that sitting and writing for the entire period as they did today shows great improvement.

- Create some means of measuring their progress—amount written, length of time, number of pieces, number of *to be* verbs—so both of you can see and celebrate it.

- Put up a continuum of performance on your classroom wall like the one in Figure 5.1 and refer to it regularly to remind students that they are working at progressively more difficult writing assignments that demand more from them. This awareness of the growing difficulty can help allay anxieties that they are not making progress, which can undermine their confidence in their ability and perceived improvement.

- Be consistent in your expectations; every student needs a reachable but meaningful goal and a teacher like you to help them reach those goals.

- Provide examples whenever possible to help them see what an improved performance looks like.

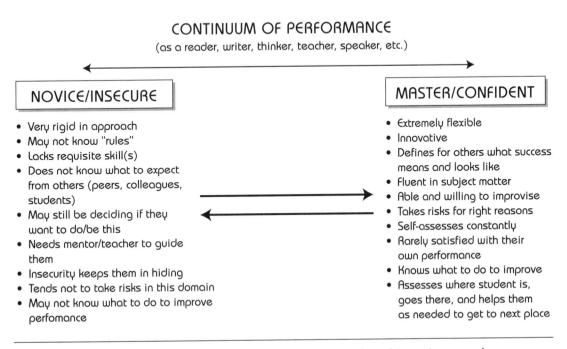

CONTINUUM OF PERFORMANCE
(as a reader, writer, thinker, teacher, speaker, etc.)

NOVICE/INSECURE

- Very rigid in approach
- May not know "rules"
- Lacks requisite skill(s)
- Does not know what to expect from others (peers, colleagues, students)
- May still be deciding if they want to do/be this
- Needs mentor/teacher to guide them
- Insecurity keeps them in hiding
- Tends not to take risks in this domain
- May not know what to do to improve perfomance

MASTER/CONFIDENT

- Extremely flexible
- Innovative
- Defines for others what success means and looks like
- Fluent in subject matter
- Able and willing to improvise
- Takes risks for right reasons
- Self-assesses constantly
- Rarely satisfied with their own performance
- Knows what to do to improve
- Assesses where student is, goes there, and helps them as needed to get to next place

FIGURE 5.1 Continuum of Performance: Writers continually move along this continuum as they learn new ways of writing or write about different subjects.

• Be consistent in your instructional methods so students are not distracted by what seem to them like random approaches or tricks to help them.

• Be consistent and fair in your grading so that emerging writers do not feel grades are a matter of popularity or privilege.

• Provide opportunities for revision so students know they can keep working to improve both their writing and their grade in your class.

• Use earlier drafts of a paper to show them the difference their efforts made in improving their paper.

• Speak of errors as invitations and opportunities to learn, especially if these errors appear in patterns that can be identified and addressed in a systematic way (e.g., you use only *to be* verbs in the entire paper; you use the same sentence pattern; you always use *your* when you mean *you're*).

• Praise improvement in one domain—for example, ideas—even if they do not show the same progress in other areas, such as grammar. The excerpt in Figure 5.2, for example, comes from a special education student who at the beginning of the year could write little more than a couple of basic sentences. Figure 5.2 shows his response to the final exam (see page 16 for the assignment).

CLASSROOM CONNECTION

Fallon's reflection (see Figure 5.3) shows how her writing has progressed but also reveals her awareness of what is involved in writing. Along with this progress, her confidence in her ability to do this challenging work has improved.

Zack, a freshman with learning differences, found writing a real torture when he arrived in September. He would muddle through a couple of sentences in the time it took others to write a page. His essay from the first-semester final exam (this was not all they had to do; see page 17 for the final exam guidelines) shows his progress (see Figure 5.2). Patience was crucial for both of us; we both needed to know that the efforts we made would result in improvement. Looking beyond the interference of his language difficulties, you see here a thoughtful piece of writing about what it means to be an American.

RECOMMENDED RESOURCE

Shaugnessy, Mina P. 1977. *Errors and Expectations: A Guide for the Teacher of Basic Writing*. New York: Oxford University Press.

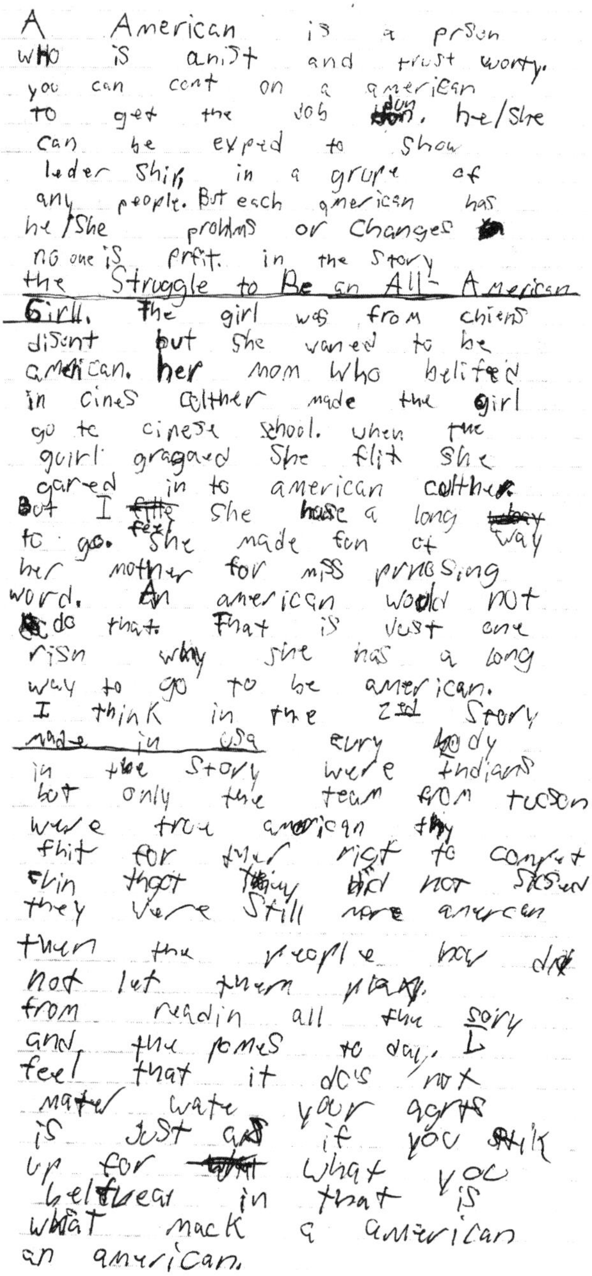

A American is a prson who is anist and trust worty. you can cont on a american to get the job don. he/she can be exped to show leder ship in a grupe of any people. But each american has he/she problms or changes no one is prfit. in the story the Struggle to Be an All-American Girll. The girl was from chiens disent but she vaned to be american. her mom who belifed in cines colther made the girl go to cinese school. when the guirl gragaed she flit she gared in to american colther. But I flit she have a long way to go. she made fun of her mother for miss prnosing word. An american would not do that. That is just one rison why she has a long way to go to be american. I think in the 2nd story made in usa eury body in the story were indians but only the team from tucson were trou american they fhit for ther rigt to conpet then thaot they did not sksen they were still more amercen then the people hoy did not let them play. from readin all the soiry and the pomes to day, I feel that it dos not mater wate your agrts is just as if you stik up for what you belfear in that is what mack a american an american.

FIGURE 5.2

Strengths	Improving	Need to improve
• generate ideas	• using good words	• word choice - how I use i-
• ideas are focused	• voice of the writing	• incomplete sentences.
• ask questions before I write	°	• sent. don't connect each other
		• spelling errors
		• pun, tuation
		°

```
|————————⊕———⊕———————————|
° novive          • developing      • accomplished
° ineffective     • improving       • distinguished
• unsuccessful    • average         • expert
```

    When I get my Seamus Heaney poems back I always seem to do good, but when I do major essays like, "memorable person" or "Jasmine", I seem to freak out. I would be average for my writing skills. I wouldn't say I'm terrible or I'm an expert, but I seem to work hard and develop ideas. Picturing myself as a writer, is hard. I'm not a writer who stay's on one topic and only that topic. If I'm writing about dogs, I'll end up writing about cats. It's really hard for me to stay on one topic. As for word usuage, I really don't know what half my words mean. I just use them, so it could make my essay look great. After I got my Memorable Person essay back, I look at my essay, and saw words that didn't seem to belong.

FIGURE 5.3   Reflection on progress: Here Fallon Parekh considers her improvement and those areas she needs to continue to address.

Provide Students Options When Appropriate and Possible

6

RATIONALE

Students do not always get to choose their topic. State tests and other exams such as the AP or Regents provide topics and expect students to be able to write about them. So students need to be able to write well about a topic they just met. But they will always write better—because they will care—if the topic is one that matters to them, one they can make their own. Options come in many forms. Is it okay to write a piece of fiction or batch of poems about this topic even though it is a history class? Can they write a series of letters? Can they write from someone else's point of view so they can get a feeling for what it was actually like, for example, to be an Irish farmer during the Potato Famine?

Choice within the topic is another way to provide options. You might say the students need to write about a theme, but do you have to define which one of the many themes in the book they must write about? You can ask them to write about an important character or to compare two books, but must you determine which ones? Making room for students in the writing assignment makes room for them in the classroom; they will see it as a place they come to think about those things that matter to them and see you as someone who will help them learn to write well about these topics.

Options are important for another reason. What sometimes seem like great topics that could not possibly offend or trouble some students are emotional bombs to others. You think you are providing them a nice topic about "how their family came to this community or country," but some might feel you are asking them to relive the horrors or despair they fled to come here. This was made too clear to me when I assigned such a topic one year, only to find a wonderful girl sobbing after class, saying only, "I can't write about that. It's too painful, Mr. Burke." It turned out that her family immigrated to the United States after most of them had been killed by death squads in Nicaragua. Telling her she could write about something else made her feel safe again in the classroom and allowed us to work together to find a topic she could write about.

I write for myself and strangers. This is the only way that I can do it.

GERTRUDE STEIN

One more related choice is whether to share what they write: just as students need to be able to choose what they write about, they need to be able to choose, when possible, whether or not to share what they write.

WHAT TO DO

• Decide what you want them to learn or demonstrate on this writing assignment. Ask yourself what evidence of their understanding you are willing to accept. Such a question might help you realize, for example, that a poem is as appropriate as an essay, or a journal is as valid as a formal report.

• Provide a list of possible topics to choose from; make one of the options "Develop your own topic," but require them to check with you before they write about it.

• Encourage them to connect what they write about in one class to what they are learning in others. Students who read *Catcher in the Rye* and have a health or psychology class might, for example, appreciate the option to examine Holden's behavior in light of recent discussions about mental health.

• Allow students from other cultures to connect what they study in your class to their own experiences in their culture. This will allow them to feel more welcome in your class and more successful in their work.

• Using Leila Christenbury's Dense Question Strategy (see Figure 7.1), students can create their own topics; shaping these topics becomes part of the writing process that prepares them to write.

CLASSROOM CONNECTION

Sophomore English Final Exam

Overview　So we come to the end: your final assignment in which you show me all you can do as readers, writers, and thinkers. The following essay will be evaluated based on how well you:

• Read not only *All Quiet on the Western Front* but also your outside book(s) and *Macbeth,* as demonstrated by your insights and comprehension.

• Write about a complicated idea or topic, incorporating into your essay examples from those books you read and discussions we've had.

- Think, as shown by the connections you make to your own life and between the different books we've read.

- Organize your ideas into paragraphs and coherent sentences.

OPTION ONE:

Using the notes and Conversational Roundtable graphic organizer from the poetry packet (the one with all the Yusef Komunyakaa poems in it; the one with "masks," "memories," "losses," and "what matters" in the center area), write the best essay you can about one of those four topics. You should show me how well you can develop a topic (hint: ask yourself, What questions should I ask myself to help me write about _____?). You must include examples—mostly from *All Quiet* but also from your outside books and, to be eligible for an A, *Macbeth*, too—and explain your ideas.

OPTION TWO:

Use the notes and graphic organizer we created last week for the Human Needs assignment. You can approach this option two different ways: (1) you can write about the different types of needs we have and how they apply to the novel, your outside books, yourself, and (to be eligible for an A) *Macbeth*; (2) you can take one need (e.g., the need to feel secure) and write your whole essay around that, again discussing how it applies to the novel, your outside books, yourself, and (to be eligible for an A) *Macbeth*.

In an effort to diversify the types of texts my students read, I created *The Weekly Reader*, a digital textbook that includes a range of texts in different media (see Figure 6.1). The assignment for this is included in Reminder 7.

RECOMMENDED RESOURCE

Graves, Donald. 1994. *A Fresh Look at Writing*. Portsmouth, NH: Heinemann.

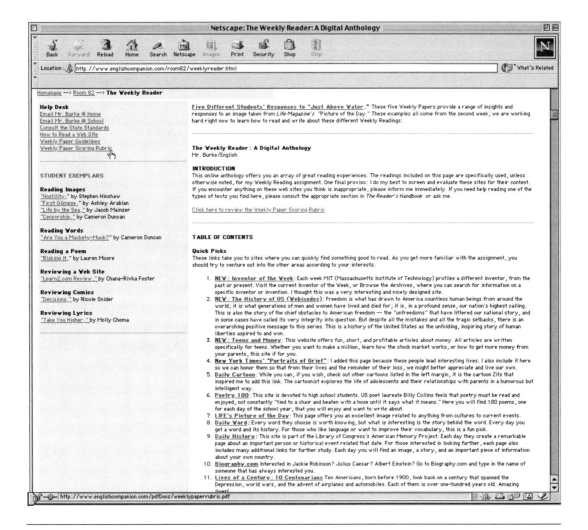

FIGURE 6.1   *Weekly Reader* homepage. Visit <*www.englishcompanion.com*> to see it; while there, check out the *ACCESS Digital Text Book* also.

Have Students Write About Subjects of Personal and Social Importance

7

. . . .

RATIONALE

Through writing we make meaning. Thus, if kids do not write about worthy subjects, their writing will mean little to them. When our subjects challenge us, when we care about them, we write better. We must be able to make a subject our own in some sense so that we may, through our writing, enter into it and say something intelligent about it. Writing about personal importance is not to say students should always write about themselves; rather, they should write about subjects that challenge them to expand what matters to them, to connect who they are to what the world is becoming. Finally, asking students to write about ideas and subjects they recognize as important fosters a culture of serious inquiry in the class. They see it as a place where they are taken seriously and can thus give themselves permission to do the serious thinking that leads to improved writing.

In their book *The Freedom Writers Diary* (1999), students and their teacher, Erin Gruwell, embody the concept of community and illustrate the benefits of writing about important subjects. Living in a community troubled by serious gang problems (Long Beach, California), the students decided to write Zlata Filipovic, author of *Zlata's Diary*, and tell her how their lives were similar. Erin Gruwell, who was a first-year teacher, wrote in her own journal:

> I just got off the phone with Zlata and I told her that she's the inspiration for our latest writing project. Using her as our muse, the students will begin compiling the diaries they've been keeping into a collaborative book. She still keeps a journal and feels honored to be passing the baton. . . . Zlata said writing was her salvation during the war and it kept her sane. She suggested that writing might be one of the best vehicles for some of my students to escape their horrific environments and personal demons. . . . For some of my students, my classroom is one of the only places where they feel safe. Room 203 is a place where they can seek refuge from all the mayhem. (139)

All of us, ages four to ninety-four, want our reading and writing to be meaningful, to make sense and to be good for something.

NANCIE ATWELL, FROM *SIDE BY SIDE*

35

WHAT TO DO

- Let students choose or develop their own topics (see Reminder 6)

- Use the Dense Question Strategy (see Figure 7.1)

- Teach students to identify what is important—to them, a work of literature, a subject they are studying

- Ask students to keep a topic journal

- Allow them to adapt topics or otherwise make connections to their own experience, culture, or ideas

- Begin each day by reading them a passage, quotation, or proverb to which they can respond in their journal. Such daily practice improves their ability to respond to texts if they are trained to ask the right questions

- Create a digital textbook similar to *The Weekly Reader* (see Figure 6.1)

CLASSROOM CONNECTION

The Weekly Paper

Overview   The following guidelines apply to the Weekly Paper, which is due each Monday. It is based on whatever you read from *The Weekly Reader*. This assignment, both the reading and the writing, has several important goals. It asks you to:

- Read a variety of types of text (images, essays, films, articles, poems, stories, and multimedia productions)

- Improve your familiarity with how to use the Web and its resources

- Reinforce and extend your knowledge of how to write paragraphs that are focused, organized, and developed, using examples and details

- Write about a subject of interest to you and your audience that demonstrates your ability to read a variety of texts with insight

- Write with an emphasis on clarity and correctness

STEP ONE

Decide what you will read. Go to:

<www.englishcompanion.com/room82/weeklyreader.html>

If you don't have much time, try one of the Quick Picks. If you have more time or the inclination, take time to investigate one of the other sites listed in *The Weekly Reader*.

Overview

Good readers build meaningful links between what they read, what they think, and the world in which they live. This assignment asks you to generate a basic question that the text can answer, then add to this some component that links what you are reading to your own experiences, thoughts, beliefs, and opinions. Eventually, you should create one single question called a "dense question," about which you can write an essay. In this essay you would write about the intersection between your reading this semester, your life, and the world. Easy stuff! I have provided example questions related to *Catcher in the Rye*, but you should be able to translate these into helpful samples for whatever book you are reading.

Type of Question	Description	Example
TEXT	Info found in text	Who is the narrator of the story?
READER	Reader's experience, values, ideas	Have you ever felt fed up with everything and just wanted to take off, get away on your own?
WORLD or OTHER LIT.	Knowledge of history, other cultures, other literature	What other character—in a book or a movie—would you compare the main character to?
SHADED: TEXT/READER	Combines knowledge of text with reader's own experiences, values, ideas	What characteristics do you share with the main character?
TEXT/WORLD	Combines knowledge of text with knowledge of history and cultures	In what ways is Holden similar to teenagers today? In what ways are today's teenagers different?
TEXT/OTHER LITERATURE	Combines knowledge of text with knowledge of other pieces of literature	How does Holden's relationship with his sister compare with Esperanza's?
READER/WORLD	Combines knowledge of reader's own experiences with knowledge of other cultures, people	In what ways are teenagers in other countries similar to American teens? In what ways are they different?
READER/OTHER LITERATURE	Combines knowledge of reader's own experiences with other pieces of literature	In what ways are you similar and/or different from Holden and Esperanza?
DENSE QUESTION TEXT/READER/WORLD or TEXT/READER/OTHER LIT.	Combines knowledge of all three areas into one DENSE question	Why does Holden feel alienated and how is that related to what many of today's teens feel? Include in your answer a discussion of the extent to which you do or don't share these same feelings and why.

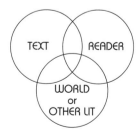

FIGURE 7.1 The Dense Question Strategy, developed by Leila Christenbury. Used by permission.

STEP TWO

Read the text you chose. I say "text" because you might choose an image, a Web-based documentary, a painting, a poem, or a video essay. *Before you begin,* jot down some questions about the text you chose, questions that will help you read it better. If you are not sure how to take your reading to the next step, go to the appropriate section of the *Reader's Handbook* (Burke 2002a).

STEP THREE

Write a one-page paper that:

- Is double-spaced and typed; uses 12-point serif font and 1.25-inch margins

- Establishes a clear thesis in your opening paragraph

- Organizes itself into paragraphs, each with a main idea that relates to and builds on your thesis

- Includes examples and details from the text you read; these examples should maintain the focus, organization, and development of each paragraph

- Carries a title that helps clarify or even extend the idea of your paper. It should *not* be anything like "The Weekly Paper"

- Shows you know how to properly format titles:

  ▸ *Quotation marks:* poems, articles, stories, essays, songs
  ▸ *Italics:* books, CDs, movies, magazines, newspapers

- Is revised

- Is proofread

(Figure 18.1 shows the scoring rubric we used for the Weekly Papers. We created it as a class and revised it to meet our evolving needs.)

RECOMMENDED RESOURCE

Gruwell, Erin, and The Freedom Writers. 1999. *The Freedom Writers Diary: How a Teacher and 150 Teens Used Writing to Change Themselves and the World Around Them.* New York: Main Street Books.

Provide Opportunities to Write for Real Audiences

8

RATIONALE

Everyone works harder, tries to do their best, if it counts, if it's "for real." A real audience, whether live or virtual, adds a sense of importance to what we are doing. Thus, one reason we want to provide students with actual audiences is because it motivates them to do better work. If students do well, their success before a real audience amounts to a real achievement. When students in my freshman English class interviewed centenarians (people one hundred years or older) and wrote a book containing their centenarians' biographies that was then published by the sponsoring hospital, they achieved real success. Students who created, designed, and published a resource directory, complete with a short history, of Burlingame felt a sense of genuine accomplishment. This satisfaction was deepened when, during the process, Maria Fererra wrote a grant proposal to the district superintendent asking him to buy us the desktop publishing software we needed. Her proposal, written as a letter, required that she get the message and its mechanics just right. She got them right, and we got the money, as well as the superintendent's future support for our program.

Whether they are writing for a contest or a Web site, the superintendent or an unknown recipient in a small town in Alaska, students care more and thus take the time to write well. This is significant, for we all have students who we know have the ability to write well but who submit inferior work because they do not care about the topic or the assignment does not challenge them.

Whether an audience likes *it is less important than whether they* understand *it.*

STEPHEN SONDHEIM

WHAT TO DO

• First, remember that your class can be a "real" audience if it becomes a community of peers whose opinions matter. With this in mind, consider having students:

> ▶ Read aloud a text—whether dramatic or expository, poetic or fictional—they wrote

- ◗ Publish their annotations and written response to the class by reading them aloud or putting them on the overhead (e.g., have them write their annotations on a transparency)
- ◗ Share their writing with their writing group during writing workshop

• Have them publish their poetry to an online "zine" for teen poetry, such as <*www.itvs.org/poeticlicense/*>.

• Ask them to write letters (or e-mail) to:

- ◗ Students around the country, inviting them to tell your students what, for example, counts as American literature in their area. Diane McClain's juniors do this every year. One of my favorite letters and its original invitation, written by Nefertiti Altan, appears in "Classroom Connection."
- ◗ People from the countries you are studying. Students in my freshman honors English class, which is integrated with their modern world history class, posted letters to a South African newsgroup one year. We brainstormed the kind of questions they should ask, what made a question good. Students received remarkable responses.
- ◗ Officials within the school, school district, or local or state government. When they changed the state requirements for a driver's license, my sophomores downloaded the bill and read it, then wrote formal letters arguing their case to their state senator.
- ◗ Speakers or other guests who visit your class, thanking them for coming and reflecting on what the students learned from their presentation.

• Have them write formal proposals for:

- ◗ Programs the school should have or continue to support
- ◗ Speakers to come to your class or school
- ◗ Changes in the students' schedule or new classes they want to see offered
- ◗ Books or other items to contribute to a local program. My juniors one year, after reading to little kids all year long, wanted to get books for all the kids at the school. They wrote a one-page proposal for books or contributions; $2,500 later, they had enough new books to give one to every kindergartner *and* first grader at the school. When the local Ben and Jerry's agreed to come to the Gift of Words book giveaway at the elementary school, it was that much sweeter. Thank-you letters to the superintendent, Ben and Jerry's, and the contributors provided that many more opportunities for authentic writing.

- Use the opportunity of writing for these different audiences to discuss:
  - Word choice
  - Voice
  - Purpose
  - Organization
  - Correctness
- Consider these other venues for publishing student writing:
  - Newspapers (school and local)
  - Web sites
  - Bulletin boards
  - Performances
  - Newsletters

CLASSROOM CONNECTION

Here is the letter exchange between Jory Barnhill and Nefertiti Altan, a student in Diane McClain's American literature class:

Nefertiti Altan
English Dept.
Burlingame High School
Burlingame, CA

June 5

Juneau-Douglas High School
Juneau, AK

Dear fellow student(s),

What is it like being you? How different are we? Well, my name is Nefertiti Altan. I'm 16 and I am a student at Burlingame High School in California. My teacher thought it would be interesting to write to other high school students to see, or well more to just recognize that there are other people my age living totally different lives. (I think it can become a neat experience as well.) I chose your school out of a fat book of high schools and why I chose it I'm not sure, it just sounded appealing so I became curious, especially at the number of students in your school. I've also been fascinated with the natural beauty of Alaska and its mysterious presence. Or maybe there is nothing that great about it. I don't know. I was hoping you could help me out with learning more not just about Alaska but your community.

Before I describe where I live, I'm curious of knowing what assumptions, or if you have any, you have about California? Well it's big and diverse geographically. I live about 15 minutes south of San Francisco and go there and around surrounding towns that are connected through massive freeways on weekends. I'll sometimes go to the beach if I can in a town called Half Moon Bay and just listen to water, to crashes, to wind. What is a problem though is that my community and the ones that surround me are heavily dependent on automobile transportation. It's more fun I think walking, riding the train, or riding on the back of trucks (kidding). I can't do much about it because everyone "needs!" a car, so I've become very passive about it.

My school has roughly about 1300 diverse bodies running around the school thinking about doing homework for next period, going to the office, buying lunch, flirting with silly boys, material for the next test, and humming songs in their heads. When it's passing period it seems like all of us are just herds of cattle mooing our way through hallways in large groups making a lot of commotion and noise. It's pretty funny and helps me out when I get tired of being at school or having a stressful day.

So what are you guys reading in class? What do you like learning about? My junior year this year in English has to do with the American Dream (I don't know if I like that term) and different kinds of American literature. Right now we are reading *Beloved* by Toni Morrison which is one of the most powerful and beautiful pieces of art I've ever experienced. It is about slavery, humanity, strength, being African American, and so many more aspects of life I never thought about or felt existed. We haven't really read contemporary novels or novels by very many different authors that are not Caucasian. Does it mean to be American if you are white? I don't know but outside of class I try to read different authors from different backgrounds to get a sense of how other people live, or lived. What I'd really like to do is have two books to choose from each time we begin a new one, then we just select what books we want to read from that list during the year. What and how do you guys read in class? Earlier in the year we examined different Native People's storytelling and literature, different American speeches, and now we are writing short stories. I like the short story because it is a much more active way of learning which I feel is more motivating to people, you feel me on that one?

I'm going to head on out and do the other 3 hours of homework I need to do. I would greatly appreciate any response concerning what you're learning, life, whatever. Can't wait to hear back.

Sincerely,
Nefertiti Altan

Here is the letter she received in response:

May 7

Nefertiti Altan
c/o Burlingame High School
Burlingame, CA

Dear Nefertiti,

Ah, to be us! Well, we are all different, so to be me is very different than to be you. I can tell you that in a way, we are very alike. We go to high school, see the same movies, drive, and even maybe eat the same foods. Yet, in these simple activities, we might be extremely unique. Have you ever eaten Moose Nose soup? I can tell you that it isn't my favorite, but it is a common food up "here." Can you tell me that you have ever ridden a snow machine to school or a four-wheeler? I have, and it is very thrilling.

My name is Jory Barnhill. I am just recently seventeen, and I am a want-to-be senior in the small school named Galena City High School. In my class, there are roughly sixteen kids, eleven boys (not including myself) and five girls. I've never taken the time to count the kids in our school, just because none of them take the time to show up every day. I'm guessing around seventy kids. Most of the kids in my school have some native heritage in them. It was very interesting when I first moved to Galena, having to learn how to live amongst a town where I was the minority. Fortunately, once I settled in and announced my intentions as an "ok dude," life grew less hard and the harassment and jokes primarily ceased to exist.

I do have some inquiries about where you live. I have a game that is called Flight Unlimited Two. It is a game where you fly a plane around the skies of the San Francisco Bay Area. I occasionally, in my game, take off from Oakland tower and land at Half Moon Bay International. The reason I state this in my letter is because I couldn't help thinking of such a coincidence. In your letter I felt that I knew exactly what you were talking about when you described the water crashing on the shore of Half Moon Bay.

In my English class, we each have a goal of what we want to learn by the end of the school year. How many books, what kind of books, and so on and so forth. I read a few books this year. I read *Of Human Bondage*, *The Fountain Head*, and *All Creatures Great and Small*. All three of those books were very good, and I enjoyed all of them. You mentioned homework in your letter. Well, fortunately I haven't done more than three hours of homework for the entire year. Or as my English teacher would say, homefun!

So Galena isn't that different from Burlingame. I've had people from the states ask me if I lived in an igloo before. I usually laugh and let them think what they want.

They'll only change their minds if they come up and see Galena with their own eyes. One gallon of gas here is three dollars and ten cents, compared to one sixty down there. A gallon of milk is five bucks. I'm not sure, but I think that Galena was rated as one of the most expensive places to live in the US. There are no roads, so everything has to fly in or come by boat, you feel me on that one?

Well, I've hoped you've enjoyed listening to me talk about Galena life. I can't wait to graduate.

Sincerely,
Jory Barnhill

Newsletters and pamphlets offer students a chance to write for public audiences. Here are the guidelines for a class newsletter:

Monthly Class Newsletter

Overview   At the end of each month, a group of students will submit a desktop-published newsletter that covers what this class has been doing, reading, thinking; it may also address other issues the newsletter's staff wants to tackle. The objective is to improve your computer skills, enhance your ability to work in a group, and keep the public (i.e., your parents) informed about all the excellent, interesting work you are doing in here. (Pressure's on: we'd better do interesting things worth reporting about!) Finally, each newsletter will be published to the class' Web site for all the world to see. You may not turn it in until it is perfect.

Standards   Writing, technology, speaking, collaborating

When   The first newsletter is due with absolutely no exceptions or excuses Wednesday, the 19th (the day of Back to School Night). It will be published and distributed to all parents *that night,* so make it look great. Otherwise, the newsletter will be due on the last day of each month.

Who   We can do this one of two ways: a group of three to four volunteers can show us all how it is done—set the standard by which all others will be judged!—OR I can just take the first four names and say YOU will do it. Unless I get volunteers, it is Option Two.

How   You get together ASAP and just map out a few ideas, maybe talk to me, then make some notes about anything interesting that happens along the way. When it comes to computer work, you have the computer in our classroom, the computer lab over by the English office, or your computer (if you have one) at home. It is up to you to work out the logistics of this part of the project. I have a digital camera, scanner, and laser printer available as well as Macs and PCs. *Note*: There is an early example on the Web site that I hope to replace with *your* better example!

Ideas   Consider including in your newsletter some of the following:

- *Quotes:* humorous, brilliant, interesting

- *Excerpts:* from something we read or a student wrote

- *Summary of what was discussed:* an index of themes, ideas, issues, books, stories, poems, cultures

- *Connections:* how does what we do in this class relate to Mr. Firpo's class and the cultures you study in there?

- *Editorials:* take a stand on some issue we are studying

- *Art:* comics, art related to what we are studying

- *Book list:* parents need reading ideas: keep a list of what people are reading outside of class and come up with your own monthly top books

- *Reviews:* of books you/others read; movies based on books you read (compare them in the review); Web sites that students, parents, or teachers might find helpful

Option   You could, if you wanted to, do the newsletter as a Web page. Look at Web sites like Time.com for possible examples and ideas. I would love to see someone try this.

Assessment   Your newsletter will be graded based on its thoroughness, the quality of its writing, its aesthetic appearance, your ability to work as a group, your originality, and your demonstration of the use of technology. Everyone must be able to provide evidence of their contribution.

Endnote   Your newsletter may NOT exceed one piece of paper!

Writing contests also provide fun and sometimes exciting opportunities to publish students' work.

RECOMMENDED RESOURCE

Visit *<www.publishingstudents.com>* for resources and links to help publish students' writing.

9 Establish and Reinforce the Value of Good Writing

RATIONALE

Good writing matters. It represents clear thinking and, to most people, intellectual ability. Writing is, after all, a public performance, one people often use to judge others' qualifications. In the town where I teach, one opening for a position in the fire department drew five thousand applicants. A paper screening reduced the applicant pool down; they then gave the remaining applicants a writing test. I like this example and use it often with my kids because it shows them that the world expects people to be able to write well.

WHAT TO DO

• Whenever possible, refer to the way people in the adult world use writing. In my academic literacy program, speakers come each Friday; we always ask them what they have to read and write.

• Consistently mention and include on any assignments a rubric or other guidelines that reinforce the values of good writing. The homework rubric (see Reminder 18) shows the criteria for homework; I create this and other rubrics to establish my expectations and a culture of seriousness when it comes to the essential domains of effective writing.

• Put up posters and other visible reminders that relate to writing on your classroom walls. Some teachers make enlarged photocopies or brightly colored posters of strategies, rubrics, or examples to help support student writers and reinforce the culture they are trying to create in their class. A teacher focusing on sentence fluency, for example, might post sample sentences from both students and professional writers to which the class can easily refer. The presence of such examples reinforces the value of writing by keeping it constantly before the students' eyes.

• Reinforce the important role academic language and good writing play in college acceptance and success.

• Use student examples of good writing. You can put these on an overhead and explain why they are so effective. You can also copy them for students who are just learning to write a certain way or a certain type of text.

• Don't say things like, "Spelling doesn't count," or "Grammar doesn't matter." Instead, say, "We will focus on spelling (or grammar) later on, but for now we are concentrating on getting our ideas down." You want to always convey that content counts, as does correctness and clarity, though you can also emphasize that they can tend to these aspects later in the process. It is worth pointing out, however, that state writing exams do not allow such time; thus, being able to generate, organize, and write well about ideas without time for revision is important.

RECOMMENDED RESOURCE

Daniels, Harvey, and Steven Zemelman. 1988. *A Community of Writers: Teaching Writing in the Junior and Senior High School.* Portsmouth, NH: Heinemann.

10 Establish and Foster a Culture of Revision in the Classroom

RATIONALE

Writers need room to grow, which means freedom to make mistakes and the opportunity to learn from those errors. To this end, they need a classroom where the teacher and their peers encourage them take risks and improve on their initial efforts. Revision comes in different forms: concept, content, coherence, and correctness. Students who are still learning English, for example, need time to get their ideas down; they also need time to revise this initial work for clarity and, eventually, for correctness. If they get the message—from their teacher, from the state, from the school—that correctness is all that counts, they will not develop their ability as writers of substantial content. Revision also means experimenting with different forms, voices, and perspectives. Thus, a writer in a class with a culture of revision can try a poem to see if that is the proper genre for an idea—and then, if it is not, try an essay. It is important to add, however, that students cannot always revise; tests such as the SAT and state tests put students' abilities to the test on the spot, and they must know how to deliver.

Revision offers both teacher and student much more than a means by which to improve their writing. It is a metaphor for a larger process, one that suggests improvement—of a person, a paper, a product, an idea—is always possible. In my own classes, for example, I refer periodically to my own past errors as a teacher or a student (I barely graduated from high school) and how grateful I am for the chance to revise myself, my teaching, my relationships.

WHAT TO DO

Georgia Heard (2002) identifies three ways to foster a culture of revision:

1. Conduct weekly "process shares," where students share their processes of writing rather than their finished writing
2. Share examples, quotes, and reflections from professional writers about their writing and revision processes
3. Encourage students to reflect on and write about their writing and revision processes in their writers' notebooks (3)

Here is a sample sequence that describes a process for one essay my students wrote:

1. Give students the assignment and the rubric by which their paper will be scored.

2. Have students generate ideas on their own (using Think in Threes tool from *Tools for Thought*; see Reminder 17).

3. Have students share and compare what they came up with; they should use this session to come up with new connections or ideas, which they can then add to their notes.

4. Have students organize these ideas into categories and identify those which are most viable.

5. Students then write a quick draft in class. This means writing as if they are beginning the essay but writing recklessly for only about fifteen minutes to get ideas out by a different means than the organizers.

6. Next, students get into small groups or pairs and read aloud what they did. Encourage or even require students to interrupt with questions or suggestions to help the writer better understand their topic. The writer jots down notes during this phase.

7. Writers take feedback and write their next draft. This might be considered the first actual draft, as the quick draft was really a second round of idea generating.

8. Have them do a read-around in their writing response groups. Each person reads the draft and poses questions in the margins (or on Post-it notes) to the writer to help them get more clear about or go deeper into their topic.

9. Students take their draft and revise it, asking the question, So what? after every sentence. This will help them go deeper by adding the necessary details to answer that question.

10. Have them repeat Step 8 despite their groans and sighs and general rebellion.

11. You can, at this point, collect their drafts and identify a couple of issues you want to discuss with them in a conference. Write these at the top of the page so when they come, you can get right down to business.

12. Have students type what they think is the final draft and bring it, along with all notes and drafts, to class.

13. Depending on your goals for their writing at the time, you can ask students to do any of the following at this point:

    ▶ Identify all verbs and revise for stronger verbs (or more precise, concrete nouns)

> ▸ Code their paragraphs (e.g., "MI" = main idea, D = detail; E = example; C = commentary) to check that their paper is focused, organized, and developed
> ▸ Identify all transitions (or places where they should be added)
> ▸ Cut one hundred words from the paper and then revise

14. When they bring in their final draft and all other accompanying notes and drafts, have students write a note on the back describing the process and the difference it made in their writing.

15. Using the rubric you gave them, have them evaluate their own essay.

16. Finally, they turn in the completed paper with all drafts. After you evaluate them, offer students with a grade lower than a B the chance to revise and resubmit. Make yourself available to those students who need additional coaching or more guided instruction.

Decide what your policy will be about revision of papers early on. Then stick to it and apply it equally to all students.

Remember that English learners need time to improve and benefit from the opportunity to write multiple drafts. This allows them to concentrate on different aspects of writing instead of feeling pressured to do it all at once. As Gadda and Peitzman (1994) write, "We need to look beyond surface errors to recognize the strong points a speaker or writer is making" (20).

Develop students' awareness of certain changes by having them explain what they did and why they did it. For example, if they deleted a word or paragraph, have them explain why they did this and how it improved their paper. This not only improves their knowledge about their writing process but develops their ability to discuss their writing. If this way of thinking about writing is new to them, model such revision for them so they not only see how to do it but understand the difference revision makes (see Figure 10.1).

CLASSROOM CONNECTION

Here are two students' post-responses about the essay they wrote using the sequence I described earlier:

> I learned that even though you may think your essay is done, it's not and there are many things you can do to create a final draft ten times better than the first. Each revision along the way taught me something new to look for when I edit my papers. The last change was the one that helped me the most. Having to identify the reason each sentence was there helped me stay focused in my essay.

Word Choice/Sentence Fluency

Burke/Fall

Read through the two versions. The one on the left, written by a student, is a good piece of work: it shows careful reading, intelligent insights, and effective organization. Read the version on the right and note the omissions and additions. Discuss the effect these have on the writing. Be specific; provide examples when explaining the difference. Take your notes at the bottom of the page and/or in the margins. The **boldfaced words indicate additions.**

Heaney's "The Schoolbag" *makes* comparisons between life and a bag *used* for school. In the first stanza, Heaney *talks* about how his teacher, John Hewitt, *was* "nel mezzo del cammin," in the middle of his life, when he *was* a schoolboy. In the second verse Heaney *makes* reference to the Italian *used* in the first *by saying* "in the middle of the road to school" *were* daisies and dandelions. The comparisons with life and the mind *are* most evident in the third verse of the poem. It *says* that the school was "unemptiable." This *could be saying* it *was* unemptiable because there *was* nothing in it, or that knowledge *can never be* lost. It then *says* to take the bag for a "word hoard" (to *put* papers in, or to *keep* knowledge and memories in your mind) and a hansel, which *is* a good luck token. The last two lines *tell* the reader to take the schoolbag as you *leave* your parents.	In "The Schoolbag" **Seamus Heaney compares** his schoolbag to life. In the first stanza, Heaney **remembers** his teacher, John Hewitt, **who** was "nel mezzo del cammin," (in the middle of his life), when **Heaney** was a schoolboy. In the second **stanza** Heaney **alludes to the earlier Dante quotation,** saying "in the middle of the road to school" **he found** daisies and dandelions. The comparisons with life and the mind **grow more poignant** in the third **stanza** of the poem **where Heaney describes** the school **as** "unemptiable." **Here Heaney implies that his young mind contained** nothing, **and what it gained from teachers such as Hewitt** could never be lost. **Finally Heaney urges the reader (and Hewitt?) to** take the bag for a "word hoard" (to **store** papers, **to** keep knowledge and memories in your mind) and a hansel, **or** good luck token. **In** the last two lines **Heaney suggests that the schoolbag holds all he will need—if we have learned our lessons well—as we** leave **our** parents to **walk our own "cammin."**

FIGURE 10.1   Word Choice/Sentence Fluency activity: Formatting texts this way allows you to maximize the features of computers to help students better see what is happening in a writing sample.

The time that we spent taking time to self-evaluate and reread our essays proved to help me the most. Since I corrected my own paper, I saw where my OWN strengths and weaknesses are. From my mistakes, I realized my faults and now am aware of these minor glitches. Next time I write, I will not have as many glitches as I had before.

Early in the year, to help create such a culture of revision, I ask students to jot down some ideas about revision. Their responses tell me what they think and give me some guidance as to how I should introduce it. Here are Mimi Franco's comments to the questions I asked:

What is revision?

It is going back and changing something to make it better. When you revise you check for mistakes (and correct them). You re-do something you already have making slight or drastic changes to make a newer, better, improved product. You relate your ideas and make it flow.

Why do it?

We (I) revise so that my final product can be the best that I can possibly make. I want the best because I want the world to know what I am capable of which is why I revise, so each time there will be a better reflection of myself.

How do you do it?

I revise my work by re-reading it many times, looking for and correcting mistakes, thinking about how I can better state or relate my ideas, and by just re-writing it several times each time generating a better, more thoughtful product.

How do you feel about revision?

When I was younger I used to hate revising, but now I realize that although sometimes rough drafts have good ideas there are usually better ways they can be stated and portrayed. Now I like revisions because they help me express myself in the most interesting and flowing way I can.

RECOMMENDED RESOURCES

Heard, Georgia. 2002. *The Revision Toolbox.* Portsmouth, NH: Heinemann.

Lane, Barry. 1999. *The Reviser's Toolbox.* Shoreham, VT: Discover Writing Press.

Teach and

Support Students

Most of us can run
pretty well all day
long on one
compliment.

—MARK TWAIN

Everyone wants to succeed; not everyone knows how to. Our students come in needing to learn many aspects of writing, yet sometimes we treat them as if they are supposed to know everything already and are in our class simply to show us that they know. Allison Zmuda and Mary Tomaino (2001) dared to ask their students what was wrong with their class. "A common theme emerged—[students] were angry with us not because we expected a lot of them, but because they did not understand how to be successful. Frank explained . . . 'Do you really expect us to work hard in here if we know that we are not going to do well?' . . . Our students were telling us that they wanted to know exactly what we expected of them sooner. They did not appreciate or appear to benefit from the drama of training for a goal without knowing what the goal was" (xiv).

The era of computers and other sophisticated tech tools has taught us to value support, to realize how difficult it can be to move along the continuum of competence. We forget too often that students enter our classes to learn what they do not already know; thus, they rely on us for support, depend on our ability and commitment to guide them from the novice end of the spectrum toward the experienced end. *Support* is the perfect word, for it acknowledges the emotional and intellectual, even the physical aspects of learning: they need to know that we will help them cope with and resolve the problems they encounter along the way; that we will assign work that will develop their capacity and resilience to keep at it until the work is as good as they can get it for this round; that we will choose texts and design work that will get progressively more difficult, even as we support their intellectual development.

These different forms of support have one common goal: independence. At some point, students must take state tests or AP exams, write college term papers, or create work-related reports on their own. The reminders outlined in this section discuss various aspects of instruction that must eventually fall away so the students can launch themselves. Graphic organizers, for example, develop students' ability to generate and organize ideas, but these tools must become internalized, must become transparent cognitive habits that they decide to use on their own when appropriate; in other words, they must learn to choose the right tool for the job and know when and how to use it in a particular instance. Other reminders, such as "Prepare students to write," can achieve their maximum effect only if students learn to prepare themselves. They must discover and learn to use those questions and other strategies that help them not just complete but succeed on all writing assignments in the class and the testing hall.

Of course, not all students are the same, which means each student must learn how he or she best learns, most effectively generates ideas, or prepares to write about a text. What prepares one distracts or confuses—or simply does not work for—another. When we design our lessons, we must then consider the different needs and styles of our students. Students with learning differences may benefit from opportunities to first talk about or visually represent their ideas (in clusters, outlines, or other visual formations). It is not enough for us to provide such opportunities, however; as with so many other aspects of writing and learning, students must study their own minds, learn what works for them, so that they can become independent, fluent writers with the confidence to use the cognitive tools and tricks of the trade they know work for them.

As you read this section, keep in mind the ways in which your students differ but also are similar. All benefit from learning a writing process, but one person's process is another's problem. Tools such as computers are helpful to all students, but not appropriate to all assignments; kids do not, for example, get to use computers for the state writing tests or AP exams and so must continue to know how to write by hand, something I myself find increasingly difficult as I rely more and more on computers. Throughout this section the message is, I hope, clear: we must teach our students, giving them the tools and techniques they need to work independently, then support them as they begin and continue to do that work at progressively more difficult levels.

Use Models to Support Instruction

RATIONALE

Everyone needs to know what good writing looks like, how a writer achieves a successful result. When you were first learning to teach, you watched other teachers to learn what to do—and what *not* to do. Thus, models serve different purposes and allow teachers to achieve different ends. Models help both teacher and student by showing them what they must know and be able to do when, for example, writing a persuasive essay. Models are essential when we are trying to teach something new; they guide us in our teaching and allow us to support our students by showing them examples of what to do as well as how to do it.

Some people argue for and others against the use of professional models (e.g., essays written by professional writers); the opponents say that it is unfair to kids. Let's choose our models not according to who writes them but how much they can support our students' learning.

Perhaps the most important aspect of modeling is the teachers themselves. We shape students' attitudes toward reading and writing by the way we talk about them. Do you write with your students and for your own purposes? Do you talk about what—and how—you write with your students? Do you convey your passion for writing and language to your students, or do you say, "You need to be able to write (e.g., a biographical sketch) because it's on the high school exit exam"? In the end, modeling that writing matters is vital to a good writing instruction program.

> Read, read, read. Read everything—trash, classics, good and bad, and see how they do it. Read! You'll absorb it. Then write. If it is good, you'll find out. If it's not, throw it out the window.
>
> WILLIAM FAULKNER

WHAT TO DO

I provide models in different media and formats, depending on what I am trying to accomplish:

- *Photocopies.* If I want them to be able to have a copy at hand to consult when writing, or if I want them to be able to mark it up.

- *Overhead transparencies.* If I want to be able to directly model how to approach a writing task, or if I want to think aloud about a model (e.g., a sample of a good opening paragraph written by a student) I am using to improve their performance.

• *Computer monitor/projector.* If I want to be able to emphasize different aspects of a piece of writing by using the mouse or using color to direct their attention to certain elements (e.g., verbs, introductory phrases, organizational structure) of a text. Working on a computer like this also allows you to manipulate writing or, when using PowerPoint, create slide shows depicting the effect of different changes to a sentence.

• *Video.* If I want to help a student better understand their process in a way words can't accomplish. This is particularly helpful in small classes of struggling writers. I just hit the record button and then, with them sitting by my side, play an appropriate segment of the video back on my classroom computer as we discuss what the student was doing and why.

• *Whiteboard.* To help them see what we might be talking about, I will always try to put the language on the board. Different-colored markers allow for extra attention to details, a technique that helps students with different learning needs or styles.

The following sequence provides my students with the maximum support while also developing their independence. It also, in some cases, helps reduce my paper load for some phases of the writing process.

1. Introduce the writing task, providing a rationale for why they need to be able to do this. When teaching my students to write about their reading, for example, I include several examples of different quality. (See "Sample Responses and How to Respond to Reading.")

2. Have students read through and rank the different examples from best to worst. Have them identify the criteria by which they evaluated the examples and support their ranking with specific examples.

3. Have a quick anchoring session in which individual students or groups report their rankings. Develop a rubric on the board for the qualities of, for example, a good response to literature, based on everyone's comments.

4. Have them reevaluate the model text(s) according to the rubric.

5. Provide them, when appropriate, prompts or other models of the language they should use when writing this type of text. For example, if teaching them to compare, include in their handout samples of comparative language to integrate language study into the writing instruction.

6. Have them try their hand at the assignment. When introducing a new technique or type of writing, break it into smaller pieces if time allows. For example, have students choose what they think is the most important aspect of a chapter and write one response to that when they finish reading a chapter.

7. Collect their work and read it through that night. Instead of responding to each individual student, look for common areas of need and choose examples that you can use to address those needs. Prepare them according to how you want to present or work with the samples. To demonstrate certain features, you might put the samples on the computer to provide a before-and-after model. Or you might want to format the examples a certain way (e.g., exemplary language in bold font for emphasis and easy reference), in which case you should type them up on the computer monitor using PowerPoint. Or you might want to be able to write on them; in such cases, use transparencies and give students a copy on paper if possible. (See Figures 30.1 and 30.2 for examples of this process.)

8. The next day, present the model to the class. Return all their papers to them so they can have their own work to consider alongside the examples. Consider giving them all a completion grade (e.g., a check or five points) to expedite this part of the process. Think aloud about what the writer did well that can help others improve. Walk through and point out, for example, the questions the writer must have asked or strategies they used to arrive at this result. You might, depending on the assignment, have them go through their papers and identify the places where they used the kind of language or prompts you required.

9. Have them trade papers with a partner. After modeling how to do the following, have them read each other's papers and write down any questions the writer needs to answer to improve their paper. When modeling this step, I will create my own representative example on the overhead, then read through it with them and have them brainstorm questions I should have asked when writing it. Here is a sample sentence from my version: "In this chapter, the character makes a very important decision that changes his relationship with his friends." The kids know what questions to ask: "What was the decision?" one asks, while another asks, "Why was it important?" Others ask, "What is an example of the change in their relationship?"

10. After they read each other's papers, jotting down questions in the margin or asking them aloud—while I move around guiding, prompting, encouraging—they give the papers back to the owners, who must then use these questions to revise their writing.

11. Having moved toward the next rung of improved performance, they go home to try it with the next draft (or paragraph, or whatever comes next).

12. As long as it is appropriate, I keep using this model-based feedback cycle to improve performance until we reach the standard we are striving to achieve.

Make available examples of assignments for those who want to see what your favorite big project looks like when it's all finished. Such a use of models can significantly improve student performance by giving them a standard to reach—or surpass. Some years I have students write children's books based on folktales and myths (which we then share with the local elementary schools so their work has an authentic audience). I always copy a few of the best and use those the next year as models. Inevitably, a few do even better work that year. In this way, the kids of one year challenge and help the students in the following year to do better work.

When preparing students for writing tests—the AP exam or state writing exams—seek all available models to support your instruction and their learning. State departments of education usually provide not only samples but rubrics on their Web sites. Using these and the process outlined earlier will improve students' performance while developing their ability.

One last use of models merits discussion. When reading or teaching students to write specific genres such as the ode or a persuasive essay, it is essential to provide models they can imitate or even adapt until they achieve Pablo Neruda's "Ode to My Socks" and Gary Soto's "Ode to Weight Lifting" or "Ode to La Tortilla"; that way, they can have fun but also steal what they need to learn what they can.

CLASSROOM CONNECTION

When possible, I provide students support through examples from past students. Here are some samples I use to prepare students to write about Homer's *Odyssey*. The three examples represent different levels of performance. Students rank them according to how effective they are, then defend and discuss their ranking.

Sample Responses and How to Respond to Reading:

HELPFUL BEGINNINGS

- This means that . . . because . . . (Why do you think that?)
- This is important because . . . (Why do you think that?)
- This shows . . . because . . . (Why do you think that?)
- This anticipates/suggests/implies . . . because . . .
- The consequence of this is . . . (So what?)
- Because of this . . . (So what?)
- As a result of this . . . (So what?)

1. Odysseus is usually a man of wisdom, but he did not know his own homeland or who Athena was when she was disguised. When he found that he was home he kissed the ground to show how thrilled he was. He was heroic in these scenarios because he had the strength to walk up to his son and meet him again after twenty years.

2. Odysseus had to do this if he wanted him and his men to escape, to live. He shows his intelligence by tricking the Cyclops with wine. He is heroic in this situation because he saves his troops from certain death and allows them to continue their journey home. Also he triumphs by brains not brawn here, a form of heroism that further distinguishes Odysseus.

3. This [opening the bag of wind] was not heroic but an act of stupidity and greed that cost them dearly. Their lack of trust for Odysseus cost them the respect of Aeolus and his people and the progress they had made towards home. It also cost the crew what little morale or strength they had left since this put them back to square one just when they thought they were about to get home. Such actions, however, further reinforce the idea that Odysseus' reckless actions cost him credibility in the eyes of his crew who no longer trusted him as they should and as they need to if they were to survive.

Sample Observational Writing Assignment

Overview   The ability to make careful observations—of processes, behaviors, people, events—is essential. We use this capacity as parents, consumers, employees, and citizens all the time. Throughout *All Quiet on the Western Front*, the narrator, Paul, makes observations about what he sees happening on the battlefield, with the soldiers, and in his and others' minds. Here is an example:

> Kat has lost all his fun since we have been here, which is bad, for Kat is an old front-hog, and can smell what is coming. Only Tjaden seems pleased with the good rations and the rum; he thinks we might even go back to rest without anything happening at all.
>
> It almost looks like it. Day after day passes. At night I squat in the listening-post. Above me the rockets and parachute-lights shoot up and float down again. I am cautious and tense, my heart thumps. My eyes turn again and again to the luminous dial of my watch; the hands will not budge. Sleep hangs on my eyelids, I work my toes in my boots in order to keep awake. Nothing happens till I am relieved;—only the everlasting rolling over there. Gradually we grow calmer and play skat and poker continually. Perhaps we will be lucky.

59

All day the sky is hung with observation balloons. There is a rumor that the enemy are going to put tanks over and use low-flying planes for the attack. But that interests us less than what we hear from the new flame-throwers.

We wake up in the middle of the night. The earth booms. Heavy fire is falling on us. (Remarque 1995, 105)

Assignment   This assignment asks you to write one to two pages about some portion of your day or life, specifically paying attention to the following:

• *The voice and style of your writing* (note how Remarque's disaffected, re-moved voice reflects what the war has done to Paul). *What* and *how* you write (your writer's voice) should compliment what you write about. Think of voice this way: movies choose lighting and music to match the scene and action they are shooting; thus, if it is a scary scene, they must use lights and music (e.g., nervous violins) to heighten that feeling. That's how you should use voice.

• *The moments, ideas, or people you comment on.* Look at the previous excerpt and ask yourself what events, moments, or people you could write about if you were writing about school instead of a war, as Paul is.

• *Use of detail.* Remarque makes excellent use of crucial details that help us see and feel what the characters are experiencing. You might write, for example, a little vignette about what you see on the desk you occupy in a particular class (e.g., graffiti, scars, etc.). Try to use precise verbs and specific, descriptive nouns so we, too, can see what you see.

Due   The following are due this Friday:

• Notes (from your observations) of ideas, observations, details. You might consider creating a three-column organizer of nouns, verbs, and adjectives to use.

• Observations (one to two pages) as described above.

• Paragraph in which you describe Remarque's writing style and include examples to illustrate your observations about his writing. Consider focusing on the following: style, voice, structure, genre, language, images.

RECOMMENDED RESOURCE

Spandel, Vicki. 2001. *Creating Writers: Through 6-Trait Writing Assessment and Instruction.* 3rd ed. New York: Longman.

Develop Writers' Independence

12

RATIONALE

All teaching techniques and tools are useless if they do not help the writer become independent. Students must learn to generate and organize ideas on their own; the tools and techniques discussed in this book, combined with the teacher's own professional experience, should develop in each student a voice, a set of mental habits they can use on their own long after they leave your class. As the Continuum of Performance (Figure 5.1) illustrates, students are always moving along a continuum. Just as students become more independent, they face more complex tasks or topics that return them to the novice phase. Over time, students learn which questions and strategies help them the most; thus, they become more independent. Of course, *independence* is a misleading term, implying that the student learns to work alone, in isolation; the truth is that effective writers turn to others for help and feedback all the time. This is not a measure of their dependence, but instead a mark of their independence, for testing their ideas on a real audience has become a strategy they use to clarify their thoughts.

> You just sit down and write every day for three or four hours. You do it like piano scales until you have a story to tell.
>
> ANNIE LAMOTT

WHAT TO DO

• Whenever you introduce a new technique, model it for students (see Reminder 11); if possible, provide them with exemplars so they can see what you expect and what good work looks like. As they begin to use the tool or technique, however, provide fewer models and more guided feedback so they can make the individual progress they must if they are to achieve independence. A subsequent strategy might be to provide a list of possible sample essays by different authors, but only the list of titles; seeking out examples and guidance must become the students' responsibility.

• Develop their awareness of the different choices writers face before, during, and after they write a text. Teach them to ask (and use) these questions to help them, for example, generate their own ideas for a topic or create their own topic. Such independence also includes making informed choices about style, format, genre, voice, and content.

• Teach students to determine how they arrived at a solution so they can become more cognizant of their processes. If you have them brainstorm a bunch of ideas, for example, have them go back through and ask, What question did I ask to arrive at this fine idea? This trains them to ask questions and improves their sense of which questions to use at different stages of the writing process.

• Develop each student's identity of themselves as a writer (i.e., one who is able to write). This is crucial, as it influences their confidence. Independence is predicated on the notion that they could sit down and write about anything with reasonable success if asked to. To foster identity and confidence, teachers can:

> ▸ Refer to students as writers
> ▸ Talk to students as if they are apprentice writers whose ideas and words matter (e.g., "Nazreen, what questions did you ask yourself as a writer when you wrote this paper [or this section]?")
> ▸ Constantly point out and celebrate those moments when the student is really writing or working well. Such efforts, while small, help the student recognize and, if we are lucky, reexperience that feeling of engagement with the world of ideas

• Strike a balance between useful praise and honest criticism. Independence is not real if it is built on a foundation of false praise and inflated grades. College professors routinely complain about the quality of student writing, even at the upper-division level, where the students consider themselves quite independent despite evidence to the contrary. As one professor said, "independence comes from instruction not promotion and encouragement (Fearn 2001)."

• Make them independent in many kinds of writing. Writing letters and other, more formal business documents requires different strategies than writing fiction. Thus, a crucial part of helping students achieve independence involves training them to use the conventions and language of a given format. The obvious example would be academic writing.

• Provide students with generic tools—bookmarks, prompts—to help them when they get stuck. Here is a short list of heuristics that students sometimes find helpful:

HEURISTICS, OR HOW TO WRITE DESPITE YOUR BEST
INTENTIONS NOT TO

The Quick Write

Sit down, put pen to paper and, without stopping, empty your mind onto the page. If you have a topic but don't know where to go with it, see where this technique takes you. If you don't know what to write about, use it as a way to explore your mind. Whatever you do, do not stop writing; if you cannot think of what to say, write, "I cannot think of what to say about . . ." until your brain tires of that thought and coughs up new ideas. You won't have to wait long. Try this for about ten to fifteen minutes, or, as novelist Jack Kerouac said, "until your hand cramps up."

So What?

This works best with either your rough draft or right after you do a quick write. Take a breather, then read what you have. Next, ask yourself, *after each sentence*, So what? or What's the big deal? Your mind should retaliate with a new crop of ideas that will try to answer the question So what? You can use this technique several times with drafts or quick writes, each time feeling yourself getting deeper into the paper.

Ask: Who/What/Where/Why/When/Which/So?

Try asking yourself these questions either while you are writing or when you are revising your paper and find your ideas a bit vague. Chances are, by answering these questions to yourself, you will be able to write or revise the paper to better inform your reader. If you don't ask these questions, your reader will—then what will you do?!

Write a Letter

Having a hard time getting into the groove to start the paper? Not sure what you want to say about it? Sit down and pound out a letter to someone—even yourself!—telling them about this paper or the subject about which you must write. What happens is your brain is on the lookout for that paper, ready to keep procrastinating, and never suspects this letter—which your brain figures you are doing to avoid your paper—is actually a rough draft or quick write.

Shopping List

Simply jot down everything that comes to your mind about your topic like a shopping list. I mean *everything*!

Topic Log

This is either an actual journal or just a scrap of paper you carry around with you throughout the day. You know you have to write a paper about X. You find yourself sitting in your math class, spacing out, when suddenly, BLAM! you come up with the greatest example of X, or the most original idea about X pops into your head. Jot it down and come back to it later.

Beat the Clock

Try setting deadlines for yourself. Some people really thrive under pressure. Set a goal to have your introduction finished or drafted by dinnertime or by the time baseball practice begins.

Bedtime for Bonzo, but Not for You

I know people who try this as a last resort: try writing when you are sleepy or very tired. Your brain is so sleepy, it often ignores the fact that you are taking great ideas out of it. The problem with this technique is that it is not good for your health, so do not rely on this method.

Freshman Molly Choma gave me a good sense of how these and other methods helped her when she wrote in June:

> If you were to contrast the work that I did in the first few months and the last few months of the school year, you would see a major gap between my capabilities then and now. With all the organizational tools we used, I learned to keep my focus on a certain topic throughout the entire paper and not just a sentence. My grammar and sentence structure improved dramatically. I learned to become a long distance writer. I started to include details in my work and slowly but surely my papers became longer without having to increase the font size on the computer. As an added bonus, a page of work would take me only about twenty minutes to do.

It is such sheets as that shown in Figure 12.1 that helped Molly learn to determine what matters most, or as she put it, "keep [her] focus." Other tools, such as the Conversational Roundtable used by Alex Montalvo (Figure 12.2) show how early structure can develop the confidence to write about difficult topics.

RECOMMENDED RESOURCE

Elbow, Peter. 1973. *Writing Without Teachers*. New York: Oxford University.

What Matters Most: How to Tell What's Important

Name _____   Date _____

Subject _____   Period _____

Suggestions for Use: Fill in the blanks with words like *Author, Teacher, Teenagers, Parents, Society,* a character's name, or some other person or agency appropriate to your inquiry. Think also about *when* it is important: always, the past, the present, or the future.

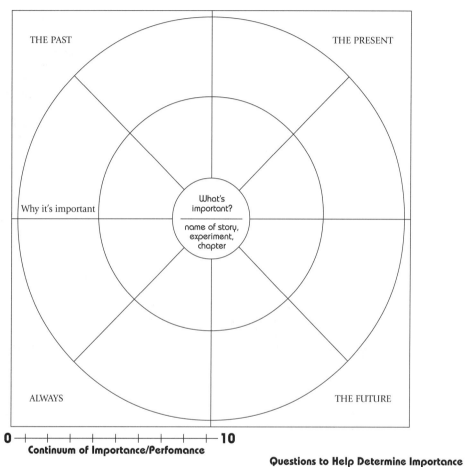

THE PAST

THE PRESENT

Why it's important

What's important?

name of story, experiment, chapter

ALWAYS

THE FUTURE

0 —+—+—+—+—+—+—+—+—+—+— 10

Continuum of Importance/Perfomance

Questions to Help Determine Importance

Vocabulary of Importance

1. important	7. urgent	13. necessary
2. significant	8. imperative	14. prominent
3. critical	9. main	15. remarkable
4. essential	10. substantial	16. key
5. crucial	11. eminent	17. major
6. vital	12. invaluable	18. primary

1.

2.

3.

FIGURE 12.1   What Matters Most Target: Graphic tools like this target or a continuum help students find and focus on what is most important.

Odysseus	Penelope
• He is a great and famous soldier. • He is a religious man, always sacrificing to the gods for their appreciation. • He is very smart. He was the mastermind behind the Trojan Horse. • The gods have sent him on a collision course, preventing him from coming home.	• She is just as accomplished as Odysseus, the only one worthy to be married to him. • She is very beautiful. She has suitors constantly calling on her. • She is very brilliant; just like Odysseus. • She has chosen not to remarry until it has been proven that he is dead and buried. • She has remained strong for many years, besides the tempts of the suitors.
Telemachus	**The Suitors**
• He is rumored to be the son of Odysseus. • When his father left he was a little boy. He has grown to be a young man without his father's guidance. • He is still searching for a way to follow in his father's footsteps. • He is trying to find the courage to break from his beliefs and continue his own life.	• They are slobs who are trying to call on Penelope. • They are slobs and invade the house for food. • Telemachus is trying to find it in him to send them away without his father's help.

By the end of Book I in Homer's *Odyssey*, we know several important details. Regarding Odysseus, we know that he is a brilliant and well-respected man. He is known for his devotion to the gods, always sacrificing and praying. He is also a great warrior. He was the hero of the Trojan War, creating the Trojan horse, which got his army into the gates. But know the gods have forbidden him from returning home, to see his family. But he will return, since his devotion to the gods was strong. But for now, he is stuck at sea, going on journeys, until the gods let him return home.

As for Penelope, his wife, she is beautiful and the nearest equivalent to Odysseus. She constantly has men calling on her, but she is remaining close to Odysseus, even though his health is a mystery. Because of this, she refuses to remarry. So she has put up with the disgusting suitors for years on end, hoping for Odysseus' return.

Now we come to Telemachus, the misguided son of Odysseus. He has a lot to do in order to live up to his family's name. When his father left, he was a young boy. Now he has matured into a young man and is still without a father. He must now gain the courage to go his own path and make a name for himself, even without his father's guidance.

The last major piece of the puzzle is the suitors. They are a group of men who have invaded Odysseus' house, hoping to win the affection of Penelope. Since Telemachus has not found the courage to make him leave, they must feed every man, day in and day out. The men are sloppy and show no appreciation for their home. Until Telemachus finds his inner self, their torment will continue.

FIGURE 12.2   Conversational Roundtable for *Odyssey*

Use Groups
to Improve Writing

13

RATIONALE

Groups make public the private, silent conversations in our heads. Groups remind us that learning and communicating are social in their very nature. While groups are not appropriate to all instructional situations, they offer important support during different phases of the reading and writing process. Taking time to discuss what they will read or write about, for instance, prepares students; it gets them thinking and helps them understand their subject and their purpose better. Groups also bring kids together, allowing them to learn about each other through the discussion of their writing. Another benefit of groups is that they provide a useful step toward independence, as students move away from the teacher's guiding hand and learn to represent their own writing and ideas to others. Finally, if used effectively, groups support those students still learning English; these students can turn to each other for guidance or allow their teacher to address their group's specific challenges on the given assignment.

> It helps if you have someone to talk to, it really helps. I don't think you can write a book completely alone.
>
> JUDITH KRANTZ

WHAT TO DO

Before you begin, ask yourself the following questions:

- What are you trying to accomplish during this period?
- What are you trying to accomplish through this assignment?
- What is the problem for which groups are the solution?
- What is the proper configuration for these groups, given your instructional goal? For example, do you need mixed groups (e.g., both genders, all levels of ability, etc.)?
- What is the appropriate group size—pairs or trios (i.e., small groups) or larger groups?
- Should students stay in the same groups throughout this assignment, unit, or semester? Why?
- How will you evaluate their work as a group and as individuals?

Depending on your objective, try the following ways of using groups:

- *Read-around.* Have kids huddle up, then read and respond to each other's papers, writing questions, comments, or suggestions on the papers, a sticky note, or a separate sheet of paper.

- *Responsive listeners.* Have students read their text (essay, poem, speech) to a partner. The partner can *only* ask questions that the writing should but does not answer. As the writer reads, for example, the partner might ask, "What is an example of that?" or "How does that relate to your main idea?" The writer must then stop and note down the question.

- *Discussion groups.* These can come before, during, or after students write. When students meet and what they discuss depend entirely on the teacher's instructional goal or students' needs as writers. Discussing their ideas before they write or read prepares students. Discussing their current ideas or initial drafts during the writing process allows for cross-fertilization and new connections. Discussing their work and process after they are finished improves their awareness of the techniques they used when they wrote.

- *Peer response.* Whether for editing or revising, brainstorming or planning, peers have much to offer at different steps throughout the writing process. There are also times, however, when they are the equivalent of the blind leading the blind; if students do not genuinely have ideas to contribute or intelligence to guide them, groups are not an effective instructional approach. Students can, however, be trained to be effective participants in the peer response group.

A few other procedural issues are worth mentioning briefly:

- *Emotional and intellectual integrity.* Kids must be able to trust that others in their group will take them and their ideas seriously and will not insult them.

- *Privacy.* Students must be able to pass if they are not comfortable sharing their writing assignment with others in their group; nor should they have to convince the teacher to allow them to do so. If students do not feel free and safe to write about what matters most to them, in their own way, from their own perspective, they will either not do the assignment or write about an issue that is safe.

- *Participation.* Group tasks must be structured so that all students can and do participate. This can be addressed sometimes by assigning specific roles, which should be appropriate to the task.

- *Grading.* If you grade students' work within the group, be clear and fair about the standards and the process. Tell them up front what successful group work looks like and how you will grade it. If you will be using a rubric, give them a copy to help them better meet your expectations.

- *Grouping criteria.* Do you put all the English learners in one group so you can speak to their specific needs, or do you assign them to different groups of native speakers? My answer is that it depends, but you should have a sound rationale for whatever you do; part of that rationale should ensure that the grouping improves learning by meeting students' individual needs.

- *Teacher's role.* While they work away in groups, what is the teacher doing? Different things, but mostly moving from group to group to advise, clarify, push, provide direct instruction, model, or affirm. In certain circumstances, the teacher may need to confer one-on-one to discuss a student's writing or how that student can better contribute to the group.

- *Purpose.* The group's purpose must be made explicit and members must provide concrete evidence of their work and, I hope, progress.

Here is a short passage from *Wall of Fame* (Freedman 2000, 117), a book that describes the Advancement via Individual Determination (AVID) program for academic success. In this passage, students are asked to describe how they help each other with their writing:

"The papers I'm getting from AVID students are better than AVID students could possibly write by themselves. I think that tutors are writing the papers for them."

Nina and James bristled and Judy wanted to answer this charge, but Mrs. Swanson held up her hand. "How would you answer that?" she asked the students.

"It's not true," they said. "Nobody writes it for us."

"Then what *does* happen?"

"When we get an assignment, we put it on the board," the student explained, pointing to the tutoring schedule. "Then everybody from different class sections, you know, who's got that same paper, gets together to brainstorm."

"Brainstorm?" asked an American literature specialist, frowning.

"Yeah, we get together and talk off the top of our heads . . . or dig it out of our notes . . . or look in the textbook . . .

brainstorming ideas!" the students cried, voices blending like a jazz band.

"Hold on, brainstorming is just the beginning," Judy interjected. "To write a good essay, we have to narrow the focus. Each student must come up with an original thesis. Then they have to defend that thesis to the group."

"Can you demonstrate this for us?" asked the history teacher.

Judy nodded, leading the students in an unrehearsed discussion.

"Okay," said the tall black girl with braided hair, "my thesis is: The cause of World War II was that Hitler invaded Poland."

"But what caused Hitler?" piped up a shorter boy with freckles.

"Depression in Germany," answered the girl.

"What does depression mean?" James probed.

"People were sad because they lost World War I," she answered.

"Why else?" asked Nina.

"Too poor to buy bread," answered the Vietnamese student, who knew hunger.

"And why were they poor?"

"Inflation . . . their paper money became worthless, so they blamed the United Nations for everything."

"You mean the League of Nations," James said.

"Hold on, those are pieces of a puzzle," Mrs. Swanson interjected. "What was the underlying force driving Hitler?"

"Power," said a voice from the back. (117)

RECOMMENDED RESOURCE

Visit the Center for English Learning and Achievement at <*http://cela. albany.edu*>, where you will find a wealth of reports, many of which deal with working with groups.

Provide Good Directions

14

RATIONALE

In order to write successfully, students must understand what the assignment is asking them to do. Directions—written, spoken, explained, or created—are complicated or helpful to the degree that they consider the student's needs. A single word in a sentence—*compare* instead of *contrast*—can make a crucial difference in one's performance on the task. The directions for writing assessments, if well crafted, include specific wording that signals the criteria on which the essay will be assessed. When directions say, for example, that the student should "identify three main causes," that student's paper better include the *three main causes* (not two, not minor causes!) the teacher or evaluator will be looking to find. Also, what might seem like obvious words—*essay*, for example—might not be familiar to students from other cultures; thus, you should take time to introduce all levels of academic vocabulary students need to complete their assignments.

Other words and issues arise when it comes to directions. Some students will interpret certain words differently unless told what they mean on this assignment. The word *story*, for instance, has different implications, as do the words *paragraph* and *essay*. When asking students to write about what they think is important, teachers need to take time to clarify or establish the criteria for importance; otherwise, the student's work may well be off-topic or otherwise incorrect. With regard to importance, for example, students often interpret that to mean what is important to *them* as opposed to what is important to the author, the characters, or the world in general.

> They didn't want it good, they wanted it Wednesday.
>
> ROBERT HEINLEIN

WHAT TO DO

• Here is a sample sequence for helping students read the directions well:

  ▶ Step One: Read the directions aloud while students follow along on the same sheet.

  ▶ Step Two: Have them underline any important words (those such as *define* that indicate specifically what they are supposed to do) so they can revisit and refocus throughout the reading.

> Step Three: Model for them what the assigned task looks like, narrating your decisions and actions as you go.

> Step Four: Provide a student example if appropriate and possible so they see what a student should be able to achieve.

> Step Five: Have them try it on their own, stopping to check their initial effort against the criteria for success that you have already established.

• Teach them to use any of the following strategies when reading directions:

> Annotate the directions—underline key words, jot down questions, note down ideas—focusing on useful information or questions they want to ask the teacher.

> Turn the directions themselves into a checklist of what students should do.

> Look first for the verb (e.g., *categorize*); then ask what they should, for example, categorize (e.g., different elements in a cell); and finally, ask the extent to which, in this instance, they should categorize the information.

> Establish the sequence in which the activities should be done or in which they occur.

> Paraphrase the directions in their own words to better understand them.

• Think in threes: they should hear or see it, read it, and try it before getting under way.

• Be sure to establish the following in your directions:

> Purpose (why they are writing this)

> Method (how they should write this)

> Specifics (how much they should write, by when)

> What this assignment is asking students to do that they have not done before

• Good directions should be:

> Written in short, coherent sentences

> Organized sequentially (using numbers or bullets to emphasize each step)

> Illustrated through examples

- Grammatically, syntactically, and semantically correct and clear: Instead of writing "The definition of *looming* is . . . ," write, "Define *looming.*" Not only is this more efficient, it's also more clear by virtue of the verb and sentence structure

- Designed with the writer in mind not the task or the teacher

- Consistent in usage, for example, don't use words like *summarize* and *explain* interchangeably

- Written with appropriate, standards-aligned terms such as *tone, plot,* and *argument*

- Make any constraints or warnings (e.g., "Do not write on the form") clear by using typography and layout for emphasis.

- Remind them—and in the early stages of the learning process, stop them—to return to the directions throughout the task so they can check what they are doing against what they are supposed to be doing.

- While it is essential to go over directions with them in the early stages, teachers must simultaneously show students how to read directions on their own so they can be independent readers when the time comes. Having students read and then annotate and/or paraphrase the directions provides a useful opportunity for the teacher to ask what they underlined, why they thought something was important, or what they thought the directions asked them to do.

CLASSROOM CONNECTION

The "screens" in Figure 14.1 would normally appear on my class computer monitor, where I can use color to emphasize certain features—in this case, the key words in each set of directions.

RECOMMENDED RESOURCE

Sebranek, Patrick, Dave Kemper, and Verne Meyer. 2001. *Writer's Inc.: A Student Handbook for Writing and Learning.* Wilmington, MA: Great Source.

73

#1

Sometimes an important character makes a mistake that has significant consequences for himself and others. Write an essay in which you identify the character, describe the mistake, and explain the consequences. Include the title and author.

#2

Sometimes an important character makes a mistake that has significant consequences for himself and others. Write an essay in which you identify the character, describe the mistake, and explain the consequences. Include the title and author.

#3

- important character
- makes a mistake
- significant consequences
- write an essay
- identify the character
- describe the mistake
- explain the consequences
- include the title and author

FIGURE 14.1   Use computers to help introduce direction or support students during assignments. Such features as color and size, as well as a series of screens, allow for powerful instruction.

Use a Variety of Instructional Techniques

15

RATIONALE

In *Side by Side* (1991), Nancie Atwell writes, "Bottom line, what they need is a Teacher. Today I'm striving for the fluid, subtle, *exhilarating* balance that allows me to function in my classroom as a listener *and* a teller, an observer *and* an actor, a collaborator *and* a critic *and* a cheerleader" (21). Her point is important to our work: not only must we use a variety of techniques, but we must use a variety of personae, an array of teachers who are always on call. Howard Gardner (1999) emphasizes the importance of "multiple points of entry" when teaching a concept students might struggle to understand. Some techniques are more appropriate to use before students write, while others are best used during or after; some, such as asking questions, serve the writer well at any point in the writing process. Just as the reader and writer must have a tool belt of different strategies to use for different tasks, teachers must maintain their own tool belt of teaching strategies from which they can draw as the situation demands. See "Teach by Design" (Reminder 35) for further discussion.

I never write exercises, but sometimes I write poems which fail and call them exercises.

ROBERT FROST

WHAT TO DO

• Begin by asking yourself what you are trying to accomplish and which technique(s) can best achieve that end. Here is a short list of questions to consider:

  ▶ Should I use groups?

  ▶ What techniques will help them visualize this idea or relationship?

  ▶ What do they need to do *before* they write to prepare them?

  ▶ What models would best help them understand what to do?

  ▶ Do I have a scoring rubric so they know what they must do and the standards by which they will be evaluated?

  ▶ What role should discussion play?

• Use discussion to generate or refine their ideas before and during the writing process.

• Use graphic strategies to help them generate, refine, and organize ideas and details for their writing assignment.

• Use note-taking strategies to help them gather and organize material throughout the composing process.

• Use direct instruction when teaching them something new so as to guide them through the experience. Teaching students to use such modifiers as appositives and adjective clauses, for example, usually requires a guiding hand that moves them through scripted, imitative practice toward independent use.

• Use manipulative techniques to help them see the relationships between ideas or elements within a text. When teaching them paragraph organization, for example, you can cut a paragraph into its individual sentences. Students must then arrange the strips into the original (i.e., correct) organization, providing a rationale for their arrangement.

• Use the right technique for the right students. Sometimes not everyone needs a particular strategy. English learners, for example, might have a hard time seeing the different categories into which information should be organized when they write. You might take them aside and use a target organizer to help them identify and generate details about the main characters in the story you are reading, for example.

CLASSROOM CONNECTION

The examples in Figures 15.1 and 15.2 show two assignments I used to help students read and write about Anne Sexton's poem "Pain for a Daughter." These notes, along with small-group discussion of the notes, prepared Amanda to write the following response to the poem:

> The people in this poem all feel the same emotion: Love. I have noticed that the style and word choice is kind of harsh. The author wants you to feel the pain that these people are feeling. The author repeats the word "blind" many times. Blind with love, blind with loss, blind with pain, blind with fear. Every stanza started with one of these; blind with _____. The girl feels not as loved, maybe. She gets hurt when the horse steps on her. But when he steps on her, she's not thinking about pain. When she died, I think, she died with her heartache, not in reality. She felt heartbroken that her horse that she loved so much would hurt her. She would do anything for this horse. She does all the dirty work, but still does it all for love. This poem compares with the relationships between Winnie and Pearl [in Amy Tan's *Kitchen God's Wife*, which we were reading at the time].

Project Pain for a Daughter

Idea

Page

First Scene
She does a lot for a horse. I think that this girl really is given herself to the horse. She's scared of things, but not of horses. Nothing about them makes her sad. This is important b/c she feels that the horse is hers

Second scene
She loves the horse so much, that she even will do the most outrageous things for horses. She poured out the boil and its very important b/c she will do very much for horses

scene three
The father is helping the girl fix her wounds. This is important because it shows that the girl is still into horses b/c she didn't die a: in reality, but in her heart

It also shows a father/ daughter relationship.

FIGURE 15.1

Directions Sensory Notes is a tool and technique designed to help you pay closer attention to details while you read. Effective readers use all their senses while they read. Use this sheet to take notes on what you see, hear, smell, feel---and think---as you read. Be specific and, if possible, write down the page numbers for future reference.

	Most Important Image
I SEE... the excitable muscles and the ripe - her pony blossom with distemper neck - rain like milk on the barn floor - the flaming horses - the thoroughbred resting like building.	the flaming horses
I HEAR... - her daughter crying nightly for horses - gritting of teeth. - her tugging at the horses	**Most Important Sound** the daughter crying nightly for horses
I FEEL... - Gritting her teeth with love - Squeamish to pull a thorn from the dog's paw. - Blind with loss all winter - Blind with pain. - Blind with love.	**Most Important Sensation** Blind with love.
I SMELL... - the boil with hydrogen peroxide. - of the horse burning like a - smell of burning wood furnace.	**Most Important Scent** the smell of the farmhouse burning.
I THINK... - the daughter truely loves the horses. - the daughter feels pain, but mostly for her love of the horses	**Most Important Thought** She feels that the horses & her belong together

FIGURE 15.2

Pearl is trying to grow apart from her mother, and so is the girl in this poem. The poet is trying to explain how many different feelings people go through. The weird thing is that everything is connected to love. When the horse steps on her, she feels betrayed, but I still think she loves her horse.

RECOMMENDED RESOURCE

Gardner, Howard. 1999. *The Disciplined Mind: What All Students Should Understand.* New York: Simon and Schuster.

16 Use Graphic Organizers

RATIONALE

Graphic organizers are essential tools for both teachers and writers. They come in many forms and have proven valuable for writers at all levels because they:

- Support all learners, but especially those with special needs

- Provide structure and guidance as writers move toward greater independence

- Offer a visual means of explaining and organizing information and ideas

- Ask students to evaluate and actively manipulate information, which helps them see the connections and relationships between the ideas

- Teach students to think categorically

- Provide useful tools to prepare for and facilitate writing, thinking, and discussing

- Help students remember and make greater cognitive associations between information and ideas

- Force students to evaluate information in order to determine what is important

- Prepare students for the world of work, where such tools are used with increasing frequency

- Improve writers' understanding of the text

- Help develop students' knowledge of textual structures and their general textual intelligence

WHAT TO DO

- Try out the graphic organizer(s) you want to use before assigning them to students. Sometimes it turns out that they do not work as we imagined or we find better ways to adapt them to the unit. Either way, using them ourselves provides a model to show our students, it helps us think better about the text, and it tests the appropriateness of the tool for this assignment.

• Before writing: use organizers such as Target Notes (see Burke 2002c) to generate and organize initial ideas. Such tools get students thinking about possible connections as well as the organizational structure of the information.

• While some graphic organizers are prescriptive and very structured, I prefer those that are more open-ended or adaptable (see Figure16.1). Such tools challenge students to think outside the box by envisioning new ways to use them that I had not imagined. I think of these organizers as somehow archetypal—that is, they tie in with the ways we are naturally inclined to think. The Target Notes tool, for example, makes immediate sense to most people yet can be used in many different ways. The Conversational Roundtable also allows for many alternative uses.

• Avoid the reflexive use of graphic organizers. If their use becomes predictable, you lose the element of surprise that makes them a source of energy.

• Use different organizers to help students:

  ▶ Classify ideas, words, characters prior to writing about or discussing a text

  ▶ Organize a sequence in a process they are reading about

  ▶ Take parallel notes, for example, comparing what they read with the experiment or lecture that followed

  ▶ Identify what is important in a text

  ▶ Examine and understand the organizational pattern of the information or story

• Use graphic strategies to develop their skills, but as you use them, discuss why you chose the ones you did. Gradually allow students to choose the method that works best for them so they can become more independent. Be sure to ask students why they made the choices they did so they can be more aware of their thought processes when making such decisions as which tool or technique to use when reading or writing a particular type of text.

CLASSROOM CONNECTION

The Toolbox (see Figure 16.1) shows a set of graphic organizers I developed for use in all of my classes.

RECOMMENDED RESOURCE

Burke, Jim. 2002. *Tools for Thought: Graphic Organizers for Your Classroom.* Portsmouth, NH: Heinemann.

Toolbox

Character Directory	Conversational Roundtable	Decision Tree	Episodic Notes (3-Square)	Episodic Notes (6-Square)	Idea Cards
Interactive Notes	Linear Array	Outline Notes	Plot Notes	Pyramid Notes	Q Notes
Reporter's Notes	Spreadsheet Notes (3-column)	Spreadsheet Notes (Multicolumn)	Story Notes	Summary Notes	Summary Sheet
T Notes	Target Notes	Think in Threes	Time Line Notes	Venn Diagram	Vocabulary Squares

FIGURE 16.1   *Tools for Thought* collection of graphic strategies and tools. *Tools for Thought,* by Jim Burke (Heinemann, Portsmouth, NH); © 2002.

Scaffold Your Writing Instruction

RATIONALE

Students become good at writing—and everything else—the same way we do: step-by-step. Some have a measure of talent, but all learn through a steady progression that, if followed carefully, culminates in excellence. One skill or habit builds on others until eventually the student learns to write, to read, to speak, or to think. Such teaching and learning require that we think more about the learning process than we often do, to acknowledge that some things must be done before, during, and after any lesson. While beneficial to all students, scaffolded instruction is crucial for second language students, as they are still building the foundations of their learning. As Langer and Close (2001) write, "Learners often need support when facing new or difficult tasks. When appropriate support (or scaffolding) is not provided, they may go off task, lose interest, or give up completely. . . . Teachers need to be careful listeners and observers so they can determine when and what kind of support students require at any given time. As students internalize the process, scaffolding can be decreased and finally eliminated." Langer and Close go on to discuss two kinds of instructional scaffolding: ways to discuss and ways to think.

Time is a great teacher.

CARL SANDBURG

WHAT TO DO

• *Structural or prescriptive methods.* Teachers such as Jane Schaffer have created extensive curricula that walk students (and teachers) step-by-step through a guided sequence when writing, for example, a persuasive essay. While some bristle at these highly structured approaches, seeing them as intrusive, many have great success with them. Schaffer herself developed her materials in her own classrooms, where struggling students came year after year without any idea of how to write an essay. You can argue with the method but not her results.

• *Generative strategies.* Prepare them to write and teach them to generate ideas for writing by using discussion, note taking, and graphic organizers.

• *Sequential instruction.* Though not sequential by nature, scaffolded instruction helps students more if it is sequential because it keeps them organized and oriented. English learners and those with learning differences will benefit the most, but all students will appreciate the help.

Here is a sample sequence that illustrates scaffolding for any lesson:

1. Introduce the skill or task
2. Provide a rationale
3. Demonstrate the skill or technique
4. Have students try it in class
5. Check for understanding and level of mastery
6. Revise or adjust criteria and instruction as needed
7. Allow time for independent practice
8. Evaluate performance
9. Have students rehearse and practice
10. Assess understanding and progress toward objective
11. Extend
12. Reinforce and revisit over time

CLASSROOM CONNECTION

Here is my plan for an *Othello* assignment:

1. Give them the assignment, which I know will be difficult because it is about an abstract idea.
2. Have them brainstorm anything that comes to mind when thinking about the subject of power. Have them take time to reflect on how they arrived at their ideas so they become more aware of their process.
3. Have them use the Think in Threes tool to both organize and generate ideas about the theme of power.
4. Ask them to choose those items from the organizer that have the most interest and potential and organize them into columns around the theme. This is the beginning of their paper's organization.
5. To get them going, have them write a practice introduction using their notes. This helps them process their ideas and gets them to think about new ones as they begin producing language that will lead to their essay.

The following sequence describes Omar's process for this assignment. Each step prepares Omar for the next. In the first step (Figure 17.1), he brainstorms possible topics and aspects of the topic of power, making some initial connections to *Othello*, which we were reading at that time. Figure 17.2 shows Omar moving deeper into his subject and establishing some initial organization for his early ideas. Such graphic strategies (see Reminder 16) help to generate ideas even as the student begins to organize them. Figure 17.3 shows how Omar moves toward the essay he is preparing

*mental
* active
* controlling
* military
* sports
* education
* people
* leadership
* evilness
* goodness
* political
* phsycological

- I got what I have by listing all the different kinds of power I experience, see on T.V. and hear about

- Iago has power over all mentally wise. Othello has power over all physically.

- The duke has power politically overall.

FIGURE 17.1

Area	Othello	S. Africa	Your World
Power: kinds	-Iago: Mental -Othello: Physical -Desdemona: Beauty	-social -racial -military -government	-Political -Peer Pressure -Satisfaction -law
Who:	-Iago -Othello -Desdemona	-British -Zulus -Africaners	-George Bush -Friends|peers - teachers - parents - authority
Why:	-actions and people affected -by power	-People, especially blacks, effected by these powers	- everyone is affected because power is just like that.
Examples:	-Iago makes everyone go after eachother. -Othello is a military general -Othello fights for Desdemona for her love and beauty	-Zulus had great military power -British have military, social and political power - Afrikaners have racial and social power.	- Friends have power over eachother. - Parents have power over kids. - Teachers have power over students - Police have power over people's future & safety.

FIGURE 17.2

Think in Threes

Name Omar Khayat   Date 5-06

Project Othello Paper   Page English

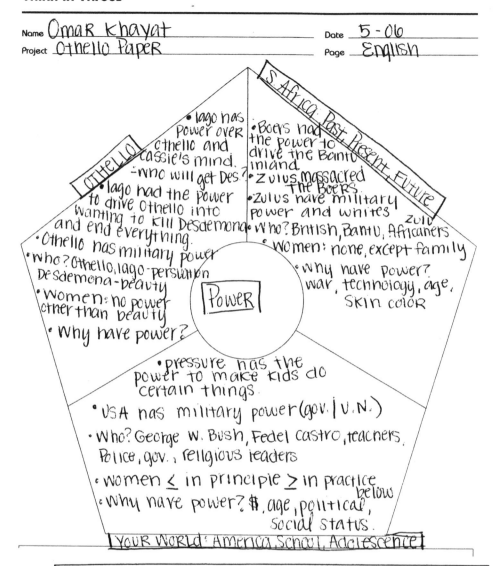

OTHELLO

- Iago has power over Othello and Cassie's mind.
  -who will get Des.?
- Iago had the power to drive Othello into wanting to kill Desdemona and end everything.
- Othello has military power
- who? Othello, Iago-persuasion Desdemona-beauty
- Women: no power other than beauty
- Why have power?

S. Africa: Past, Present, Future

- Boers had the power to drive the Bantu inland.
- Zulus massacred the Boers.
- Zulus have military power and whites Zulu
- Who? British, Bantu, Africaners
- Women: none, except family
- Why have power? war, technology, age, skin color

Power

- pressure has the power to make kids do certain things.
- USA has military power (gov./U.N.)
- Who? George W. Bush, Fedel Castro, teachers, Police, gov., religious leaders
- women ≤ in principle ≥ in practice below
- Why have power? $, age, political, social status.

YOUR WORLD: America, School, Adolescence

Directions: There are many different types of power. Obvious forms of power include physical power or military power; others—political or psychological power—are more subtle. Your final paper on *Othello* requires you to identify different types of power and the sources of that power. You must also examine the consequences of that power---on individuals, groups, institutions, or societies. Finally, you must include in your paper a careful examination of this theme as it relates to not only *Othello*, but your studies of South Africa, and your observations about your own life, institutions, and society as adolescents. This paper is due next Monday, along with the completed version of this thinking-in-threes tool. Any notes, outlines, drafts, or other evidence of your thinking will only improve your work and thus your final grade.

FIGURE 17.3

to write; in Figure 17.3 you see him organizing his ideas around the theme of power and generating specific examples he can use in the essay he will soon write.

Here is the opening to the essay he then wrote:

How does one's power affect others, the world, the universe, or even themselves? Power generates in infinite ways, it depends on the person to generate in the way his personality is. In *Othello*, power was apparent mainly in three different ways. The first way was generated by Desdemona. Her unique power was her beauty. The second power was generated by Othello. His power was his physical strength. The last and most important power was Iago's cunning and sly intelligence. All of these powers gave the play its fame and uniqueness. Iago, Othello, and Desdemona's power affected everyone in the play. South Africa has the most unique and odd power of all other countries. Their power is centered on Apartheid and conquering. South Africa generates its power in the social, racial, military, and governmental areas. These four powers led South Africa to what it is today. In my world I recognize power coming from the government, teachers, parents, and most of the peers. All these powers are the most significant in my world. My future is in the hands of all these kinds of people. Whether power comes from Othello, or South Africa or even the world, it is generated everywhere in a significant manner.

RECOMMENDED RESOURCE

www.janeschaffer.com

18 Provide Scoring Rubrics Before Students Begin to Write

RATIONALE

Assessment should improve performance. Grades are irrelevant if students do not learn to write better. For standard assignments, generic rubrics can provide quick and useful feedback; for other assignments, people require more specific guidelines. This really is the purpose for rubrics: they point the way, telling writers not only what they must include but how they will be scored. Such information gives students what they need to perform well and to improve; they know, for example, what questions to ask when they get stuck or must begin to write. These scoring guides provide valuable support for second language students, many of whom are still learning how to write an essay. Finally, in addition to helping students, rubrics provide teachers with a helpful guide and a viable means of providing writers good and quick feedback, thereby diminishing their workload.

WHAT TO DO

• Provide examples that illustrate the different levels of performance. If, for example, you are teaching students to write college application essays, put three or four different samples on the overhead or pass them out. Have students generate their own descriptors of the different performances, then apply these criteria to additional examples and their own essays. In short, you want them to know what a 4 or a 2 looks like.

• Have students turn the rubric into a checklist of the things they must include or accomplish in their essays.

• Create department- or even schoolwide rubrics that can be posted to the class or school Web site. Such schoolwide rubrics invite meaningful dialogue between other teachers and departments, all of which can improve the academic climate of the school by providing a common set of expectations in all classes when it comes to writing.

• Obtain copies of any rubrics with which your students will be evaluated for state, local, or national assessments. This includes the AP exam and such state exams as the high school exit exam. You can usually find these rubrics on the state's department of education Web site.

• Copy six or seven samples of student writing for the same assignment. Put kids in groups and ask them to score the set of writing samples. Then have them list the traits of the best to the worst, organizing them into three columns. Finally, have students develop the criteria for a 1, a 3, and a 5 on a rubric; be sure they include the rationale for their criteria. Though the final outcome is inevitably predictable, the process of creating it develops their awareness of the traits of good (and ineffective) writing.

Figures 18.1 through 18.6 illustrate a variety of rubrics and scoring guides.

RECOMMENDED RESOURCES

www.relearning.org

Also, consult your state's department of education Web site for sample rubrics used to score state tests such as exit exams.

Weekly Paper Rubric

Student Name _____

Be sure your paper includes the following when you turn it in:

☐ A copy of the text/image or the URL
☐ Proper citation format (see sample Weekly Paper or *Writer's Inc.*)
☐ Any notes or drafts you may have

FOCUS	1	3	5
Idea	☐ Text lacks clear ideas, purpose, and details.	☐ Text's ideas are focused but general, obvious.	☐ Text is clear and focused; captures reader's attention.
Organization	☐ Order is missing or random; no identifiable structure.	☐ Order moves reader through with confusion.	☐ Order compels, enhances, and moves ideas.
Sentence Fluency	☐ Writing lacks flow; it is difficult to read.	☐ Writing moves along but feels more businesslike.	☐ Writing flows with rhythm and cadence. Elegant.
Word Choice	☐ Words are simple or vague; limited in scope.	☐ Words are common and obvious; they lack energy.	☐ Words are precise, interesting, engaging, powerful.
Voice	☐ Writer is indifferent, distanced from topic/audience.	☐ Writing seems sincere but not engaged; it's plain.	☐ Writing is compelling, engaging; aware of audience.
Conventions	☐ Errors distract the reader and make reading difficult.	☐ Reasonable control of conventions; distracting errors.	☐ Observes and uses standard conventions; few errors.
Formatting (Presentation)	☐ Does not follow requirements.	☐ Follows *most* requirements.	☐ Satisfies *all* requirements.

COMMENTS:

FIGURE 18.1   Weekly Paper scoring rubric

Homework Evaluation

❏ **1**   **Completion:** Your work satisfies all the assignment's requirements.

❏ **2**   **Understanding:** Your work demonstrates an adequate understanding of the ideas or skills this assignment is designed to develop or improve.

❏ **3**   **Writing Quality:** Your writing is:

     ❏ Coherent
     ❏ Grammatically correct
     ❏ Free of spelling errors

❏ **4**   **Idea Development:** When appropriate, you include:

     ❏ Examples from your experience, class discussion, or the text you read
     ❏ Details to help your reader see and understand what you mean
     ❏ Specifics to make your writing more precise

❏ **5**   **Handwriting:** Your handwriting is acceptable.

FIGURE 18.2   Homework scoring guide

Newsletter/Publication Evaluation

Student Name: _____

Period: _____

1.	1	2	3	4	5	**Collaboration**: Everyone worked, contributed, helped equally, consistently, and to the best of their ability.
2.	1	2	3	4	5	**Layout/design**: Your final production follows the principles described. The product has: ☐ Columns ☐ Header/subheaders ☐ Bylines ☐ Different-sized but appropriately formatted fonts ☐ Captions for illustrations, photographs, or infographics
3.	1	2	3	4	5	**Mechanical fluency**: There must be no errors: this is publishing writing for a public audience. This section includes the mechanics of writing—grammar, spelling, punctuation, and paragraph organization/focus/development.
4.	1	2	3	4	5	**Aesthetics**: In writing assignments, this refers to neatness and legibility; in art/visual projects, this refers to the presentation's look, the quality of its appearance.
5.	1	2	3	4	5	**Technology**: The product was created using a program like MS Works, MS Word, Adobe PageMaker, or AppleWorks. You may not use programs like Creative Writer. In addition, your publication must include the following in order to demonstrate mastery of certain standard skills: ☐ Digital image(s) (from digital camera, scanner, or Web) ☐ Infographic (table, graph, chart, or something similar) ☐ Newsletter format as described in the accompanying page of exemplars
6.	1	2	3	4	5	**Content**: The publication must contain engaging, appropriate content that supports the issue's theme(s). Every article or other piece of information should be able to answer the question, Why would the reader want/need to know about this?
7.	1	2	3	4	5	**Writing**: This is not related to the mechanical fluency; it refers to the quality of the writing itself. The language is appropriate, lively, well written. It has voice, style.
GRADE						**COMMENTS**

FIGURE 18.3   Sample newsletter or classroom publication rubric

Journal Evaluation

Student Name: _____

Period: _____

1.	1	2	3	4	**Use:** Degree to which each entry shows you use the journal as a tool to explore your ideas and develop them through writing and, on occasion (if you are so inclined), through images. Entries whose main purpose appears to be filling up the page during the allotted time do not constitute good use no matter how much you write. An example of such use would be when every day's entry sounds the same and talks about the same things.
2.	1	2	3	4	**Completeness:** Extent to which your entries satisfy the requisite number of entries in the journal; this means daily writing of varying lengths, depending on the amount of time given to write in class and homework assigned to be done in the journals.
3.	1	2	3	4	**Organization:** Refers to the degree to which your entries are clearly and appropriately marked (e.g., with the date and/or type of entry).
4.	1	2	3	4	**Insight:** Degree to which your writing demonstrates your ability to go beyond the obvious when considering a subject or idea. It has to do with the quality of your thinking and the extent to which you effectively communicate your insights into these subjects.
5.	1	2	3	4	**Homework:** Quality of work done in the journal as assigned for homework. For example, how well do you respond to reading in the journal, if that is the assignment? An important part of the journal grade.
6.	1	2	3	4	**Daily Work:** Quality of your daily responses; reflects the extent to which you use the allotted time well and do quality work.
7.	1	2	3	4	**Benchmark:** Overall quality of your work here compared with both past work and ever-increasing expectations of better work.
GRADE					**COMMENTS**

FIGURE 18.4   Sample journal evaluation rubric

Project Rubric

Distinguished	Competent	Unsatisfactory	Incomplete/Undone	COMMENTS

NAME: **PERIOD:**

Formal Proposal: Write a formal proposal to me in which you outline the following in some detail: what you will investigate; why you want to do this; how you will do it; what you expect to find; what obstacles you foresee and how you might solve them.

Oral History/Interview: Interview someone or some people in depth about your particular subject. You can satisfy this requirement in person, over the phone, or via the Internet so long as the content of the interview is substantial. Remember that you will need evidence (e.g., notes, printed e-mail, etc.) of this.

Movie or Documentary/Movie Review: After watching a film, write a review of the film/documentary in which you discuss what they tried to show about the subject and how well you felt they succeeded. Good work here will explain why you thought it was a good or bad film.

Write Your Paper/Web Site: This paper must be at least five typed pages and written on the computer. It must also be: double-spaced; 12-point font; no more than 1.25-inch margins on any side. It should have a cover page with your name, title, and so on; and a bibliography at the end.

Presentation: Each student will give a ten-minute presentation of his/her work during the final two weeks of class. It must include a visual component such as charts, images, family tree, art, video. The presentation can be in any of the following forms: dramatic performance, multimedia presentation, video documentary, formal presentation—or some other form you might invent.

Bibliography: All outside reading, films watched, and sources quoted must be documented and included in a properly formatted bibliography (please use the provided style and usage guide).

❑ Read five outside sources (only one of which can be an encyclopedia)
❑ Use the Internet
❑ Find a poem about your subject
❑ Include all notes, drafts, outlines

OVERALL GRADE

FIGURE 18.5   Sample project scoring rubric

     May be copied for classroom use. Writing Reminders *by Jim Burke (Heinemann, Portsmouth, NH); © 2003.*

Essay Scoring Rubric

Student Name: _____   **Date:** _____

Period: _____   **Topic:** _____

1.	1	2	3	4	5	**Requirements:** Contains all notes, drafts, and final draft.
2.	1	2	3	4	5	**Focus:** Your essay establishes its central idea clearly and effectively in the opening paragraph and maintains this focus throughout the essay. Each paragraph is logically linked to the main idea and all sentences within the paragraphs serve to further develop and maintain this focus.
3.	1	2	3	4	5	**Conventions:** Your essay's prose is written in grammatically correct English; it has no spelling or grammatical errors; it shows a sound understanding of the structure of a good sentence and paragraph.
4.	1	2	3	4	5	**Organization:** Your ideas follow and relate to each other in a logical and effective way. Information is organized within the sentence and paragraph, as well as the paper itself, for maximum rhetorical effectiveness. Also means ideas and topics within the essay are balanced.
5.	1	2	3	4	5	**Insight:** The degree to which you show insight into your theme. Your essay explores your subject in all its complexity and reveals and examines the nature of that complexity. Such insights should not be implied but revealed and developed through good examples from the texts.
6.	1	2	3	4	5	**Development:** Your essay uses specific, concrete examples from the text to illustrate the ideas your essay develops. The examples are clearly cited (e.g., "In *Jasmine*, Bharati Mukherjee says that America has changed . . .").
7.	1	2	3	4	5	**Process:** Refers to evidence of revision, planning (e.g., brainstorms or clusters, outlines or notes), and careful work (e.g., does it look like it was written or created at the last minute?). Also relates to your ability to work in writing response groups throughout the different stages of the writing process.
8.	1	2	3	4	5	**Benchmark:** Quality of this work in relation to what I expect you to be able to do in this class at this time on such an assignment.
GRADE						**COMMENTS**

FIGURE 18.6   Sample essay scoring rubric: While this is a more generic version, teachers might consider aligning it with their state standards.

19 Teach Students to Ask Useful Questions

RATIONALE

Tear off the curtain of doubt by questions.

EGYPTIAN PROVERB

Questions are the engine of all good reading, writing, and thinking. The answers we get are only as clear and useful as the questions we asked in the first place. Just asking questions is not enough, however; we must also know which questions to ask and when to ask them. There are, in short, three periods during which we must ask questions: before, during, and after. The word *question* itself comes from the Latin word *quaerere* (to ask, to seek). Just as ancient heroes went on a quest for gold, writers launch out on a quest to find, to persuade, to inform, to learn. Questions make them active participants in that process. Good writers, as do good readers, ask questions to help them clarify, develop, organize, and so on. Students, therefore, must learn to ask—and *use*—questions that will help them write with clarity and purpose.

A brief note of caution about questions: They can threaten, offend, and confuse some students. Students must always feel safe from questions they perceive as too personal. Moreover, students from other cultures are often taught *not* to question authorities such as authors, teachers, and adults in general. Thus, we must be sensitive to the difficulties some students face when learning to ask questions.

WHAT TO DO

Teach writers (and readers) to think in sets of questions:

- *Before* writing, they should ask:
    - What is the question this poem/essay/article is trying to answer?
    - Who is my audience?
    - What is my purpose?
    - What is the most appropriate genre for this text?
    - What is the most appropriate voice, style, and design for this text?
    - What do I need to know or be able to do to write this text?

- *During* writing, they should ask:
  - ▶ What is the main idea in this paragraph?
  - ▶ How does that relate to the main idea of the paper?
  - ▶ What is an example of that?
  - ▶ How does that example relate to the main idea of the paragraph?

- *After* they finish a piece, they should ask:
  - ▶ What were the questions I asked to get this sentence?
  - ▶ What questions come up that I did not answer but need to?
  - ▶ What did I leave out?
  - ▶ How effective was I in communicating my ideas?
  - ▶ Does this paper satisfy the requirements outlined in the assignment, directions, or rubric?

  Here is one example of how questions can help improve writing:

1. Students pair up to share a draft of their written text.
2. Student A reads his paper aloud to Student B. Student B's job is to interrupt as often as possible to ask questions about the writing. The trick is that the questions must result in improved writing. So, for example, Student B should only ask questions like, "What did that look like?" or "Why did the character do that?" or "What is an example of that?" Student A must write down the answers to all these questions as they come up; or, if time is short, he must write down the questions and answer them later in a revision.
3. Student B then reads her paper to Student A, repeating the same process.
4. Students then take their draft, complete with comments and questions, and revise it for the next round of work.

Introduce the various types of questions:

- **Opinion questions.** The answers to these questions can be found in your head or your heart since they ask you what you think.

  Example: Are kids today as well educated as their parents were?

- **Factual questions.** The answers to these questions can be verified, proven, observed.

  Example: How did the candidate vote on education legislation?

- *Analytical questions.* The answers to these questions will usually be found between the lines because readers must make inferences to answer them.

    Example: How will the new education legislation affect schools?

- *Reflective questions.* These are questions that do not have answers but are, instead, invitations to think.

    Example: What is the purpose of school?

- *Reporter's questions.* The questions reporters ask—and answer—when they write. Students who learn to ask these questions will be prepared to write (and read) effectively:

    - What?
    - Who?
    - When?
    - Where?
    - Why?
    - How?
    - So?

RECOMMENDED RESOURCE

Elbow, Peter. 1981. *Writing with Power: Techniques for Mastering the Writing Process.* New York: Oxford University Press.

Teach Students How to Talk About Writing

20

RATIONALE

We process ideas and information in different ways, each one offering us new perspectives that can lead to greater depth and clarity when writing. We also talk much more than we will ever read or write; thus, knowing how to talk, whether about writing or a scientific concept, is important for students. Talk is also generative; there is a reason we say two heads are better than one. Talk must also be purposeful, however, and result in improved performance. To this end, we must sometimes make an extra effort to help students see that talking is a writing strategy as well as an instructional technique that you are using to achieve a specific outcome. Otherwise, some kids might think they are "just talking about stuff" until the real work comes along—or the bell rings.

Growing up with five brothers taught me that it's good to be the guy telling the story after the lamp gets broken.

JON SCIESZKA

WHAT TO DO

• Scaffold instruction so students develop the ability to discuss their writing (see Reminder 17 for more ideas on this). You can do this by:

  ◗ Modeling

  ◗ Providing prompts that will help them develop the academic language necessary to speak about their writing or ideas (see examples on pp. 100–102)

  ◗ Structuring discussions to ensure success until they learn to facilitate such discussions independently

  ◗ Providing the questions (or types of questions) you want them to discuss

  ◗ Assessing the effectiveness of the discussion by having students share what helped and what did not

• Teach them *what* to talk about:

  ◗ Direct their attention to specific aspects of the writing (e.g., "Please go through and find all the nouns in both your papers; then have a discussion about which ones could be more specific." "In your groups, discuss the different types of faith in Anaya's novel *Bless Me, Ultima*.")

> ▸ Provide prompts that direct their attention to specific aspects of the writing (e.g., *The author's purpose in this essay is . . .*)

> ▸ Give them a topic, for example, women in the *Odyssey*, and tell them to find the main women and describe them using adjectives. Then, through their discussion, they should generate traits and examples of these traits throughout the book

• Teach them *how* to talk about writing:

> ▸ Give them prompts to help them learn the academic language needed to discuss writing. Examples might include:

>> • One thing I noticed when reading your paper was . . .

>> • I got lost at this point when . . .

>> • Your paragraph's main idea is . . . but all the examples seem to be about . . .

CLASSROOM CONNECTION

I include here two different ways I use discussion in class: "Conversations" (Figure 20.1) and "Discussion Roles." Talk in these contexts helps prepare students to write by helping them better understand what they read or learned prior to writing.

Discussion Roles

While the following roles are more for a literary discussion, it is such discussions, if run effectively, that prepare students to write successfully.

Asker

Your role: You ask questions about the topic. They should not be yes/no questions, questions whose answers are obvious or facts. You are the fire starter. You are extending an invitation to people to *think*. Here are some examples:

• Does _____ have a right to . . . ?

• Is democracy the best form of government?

• Why did _____ behave as she did?

Wild Card

Your role: You can choose any role you wish. If, as you listen to the discussion you see a connection, act as a Connector (see following description). If someone makes an interesting comment, act as a Validator and

Conversations

Overview   Follow these steps to prepare for and contribute to a conversation about an idea, event, or person. Conversations involve talking not only to yourself but to others both past and present, people similar to and different than yourself.

Objectives   The goal of this assignment is to improve your ability to:

- Generate ideas
- Use strategies (e.g., questions, tools, etc.) to help you think
- Write for various purposes: to understand, to think, to inform
- Participate in and contribute to a thoughtful discussion of an idea or text
- Listen to others' ideas in order to understand what they are saying and why they think as they do
- Think about and better understand yourself and the world in which you live

Directions   Complete each of the following steps:

1. *Brainstorm ideas* about, responses to, or examples of the subject (try listing, clustering, or a Main Idea Organizer). These examples can come from your own observations, personal experiences, or subjects you have studied at school.

Subject

Main Idea
What are you *saying* about the subject?

Development
- Stories
- Details
- Examples

2. *Read the text* I gave you. This might be a page of quotations, a poem, or a longer piece of prose. Unless I say otherwise, *please* mark it up: underline ideas or quotations you think are interesting or important.
3. *Write a paragraph* about your subject, using your ideas from the reading and your text to guide you. Get as much down as you can in the time provided.
4. *Write down two or three questions* about your subject. These should be questions about things you did not understand or about which you simply wondered.
5. *Gather in small groups* (unless I tell you otherwise) and share your ideas, questions, and quotations. *Make sure everyone shares their ideas.*
6. *Discuss the subject as a class*, sharing ideas from your writing or discussion. This is also a perfect time to ask questions you think will help us have a great conversation.
7. *Write a final reflection* on the day's conversation. You might focus on any of the following:

    ✔ Did your thoughts about this subject change after all this work?
    ✔ What surprised you the most today?
    ✔ What did you learn about this subject that you did not know before?
    ✔ How does today's subject connect to your own life?

FIGURE 20.1   Conversations introductory handout

compliment them. Here is an example: "I'm using my Wild Card role to be a Connector. Miguel's idea just reminded me of something . . ."

Clarifier

Your role: You make comments and ask questions to help the group members better understand their ideas—and the question they are trying to answer. Your responses should extend and support the discussion. Here are some examples:

- Interesting, but is that answering the question . . . ?
- I'm not sure I understand; can you explain that . . . ?
- Does that mean . . . ?

Connector

Your role: You connect the current discussion with other topics you've studied or books you've read. Your role is to extend the conversation into new areas that the others might not have considered. Here are some examples:

- When you said . . . you reminded me of . . .
- _____ is a lot like _____ because . . .
- What is another way to look at that?

Validator

Your role: Your job is to listen and recognize good ideas or successful participation. Here are some examples:

- That's a really interesting idea, _____. I hadn't thought of it that way before.
- Oh, that's a good connection. How did you come up with that?
- I like what you said, even though I'm not sure I agree.

RECOMMENDED RESOURCE

The Center for English Learning and Achievement offers a variety of excellent, research-based reports on the role of talking in writing. Visit <*http://cela.albany.edu*>.

Use Minilessons to Provide
Specific Instruction

21

RATIONALE

Writers' needs change as the demands of each assignment unfold. One assignment asks them to persuade the reader of something. Another assignment requires that the writer describe a process. Still another asks them to organize the ideas in a paragraph a certain way in order to achieve some rhetorical or stylistic effect. These and other needs, such as using a variety of sentence patterns, require specific, targeted instruction within the context of the current assignment. Other contexts for minilessons arise, however, that may or may not involve everyone in the class. Those learning English, for instance, might have a set of common needs that can best be addressed through a minilesson designed just for them. Another group of students might be making the same errors or showing the same weaknesses in their writing; a minilesson at the teacher's desk or huddled around those students' desks can help the teacher better meet their needs. The point is that minilessons allow teachers to respond to the needs of all or some writers in their class by teaching within the context of what they are already doing. They are not, however, the only way or even the best approach. Minilessons are, like most ideas in this book, a tool available to the experienced teacher who decides that such a technique is right for the current situation.

> Cross out every sentence until you come to one you cannot do without. That is your beginning.
>
> GARY PROVOST

WHAT TO DO

Nancie Atwell (1998) tucks index cards into her lesson plan book so she can jot down minilesson ideas for later on or the next day. I keep index cards in my pocket and sticky notes in my *Teacher's Daybook* (Burke 2002b) to write down ideas for the lessons we need next. If, for example, I am working with kids in class and find one after another struggling to get started or to get a hold of a good topic, I might pick the one or two kids in class that have made good progress and make their success the focus of our lesson. "How did you come up with this?" I will ask them, "What questions did you ask to arrive at your topic?" "What makes it a good topic?" We will then expand the lesson to include the other topics students have. We will put one up on the board or overhead and workshop it, putting all our heads together to ask the questions that will help the writer find the *real* topic. In this way, we teach others to write a good opening, collaborating as we learn. If we need to, we will leave the criteria for a good topic on the board so we can refer to them as we work.

Teachers of subjects other than English sometimes wonder how to help kids write for their subject area. A short minilesson on, for example, how to write about an abstract idea, or how to properly cite references for a science paper, develops students' capacity to do the work we ask.

An effective minilesson is:

- Specific

- Timely

- Brief but adequate (ten to twenty-five minutes)

- Not isolated: that is, you reinforce the idea as time goes on in order to strengthen the skill and extend their ability

- Prepared ahead of time, or spontaneous if context allows and you are able to come up with one on the spot

- Structured

- Scaffolded

- Focused on students' writing whenever possible (this might mean, for part of the lesson, using examples from the past)

- Interactive

- Responsive to local, individual needs

- Modeled

- Integrated with assessment; the assessment is used to inform teaching and improve performance

Nancie Atwell (1998, 158) identifies four categories of minilessons:

- *Procedural.* The rules and routines of the workshop

- *Literary craft.* What authors consider when they create literature

- *Written conventions.* What writers and readers need to know about writing and language

- *Strategies.* What readers and writers do to successfully communicate

Here's a short list of sample minilessons:

- Writing effective introductions (or conclusions)
- Paragraph organization
- Sentence patterns
- Concrete nouns
- Active verbs
- Writing about a fictional character
- Grammar
- Punctuation
- Using details
- Opinion versus fact
- Tone
- Voice

Books like *Writer's Inc.* (Sebranek, Kemper, and Meyer 2001) or *Write Source 2000* (1999) provide a year's worth of minilessons and the re-sources to support such instruction. Better yet, learn from the master in Nancie Atwell's *Lessons That Change Writers* (2002).

CLASSROOM CONNECTION

The following example comes from a minilesson on how to begin a pa-per about a place. Students in a sophomore English class had a hard time knowing how to begin in an interesting way. I wrote three openings in PowerPoint (see Figure 21.1) and put them up on the computer mon-itor so we could evaluate each one. I asked them to identify what works and what does not in each one. We then used these elements to brain-storm the traits of an effective opening for this essay, generating possible ideas for them to include in their openings. This minilesson on begin-nings then led to a good discussion about voice and the tone a piece about a place should have.

RECOMMENDED RESOURCE

Portalupi, JoAnn, and Ralph Fletcher. 2001. *Nonfiction Craft Lessons: Teaching Information Writing K–8*. Portland, ME: Stenhouse. (See also: *Fiction Craft Lessons*)

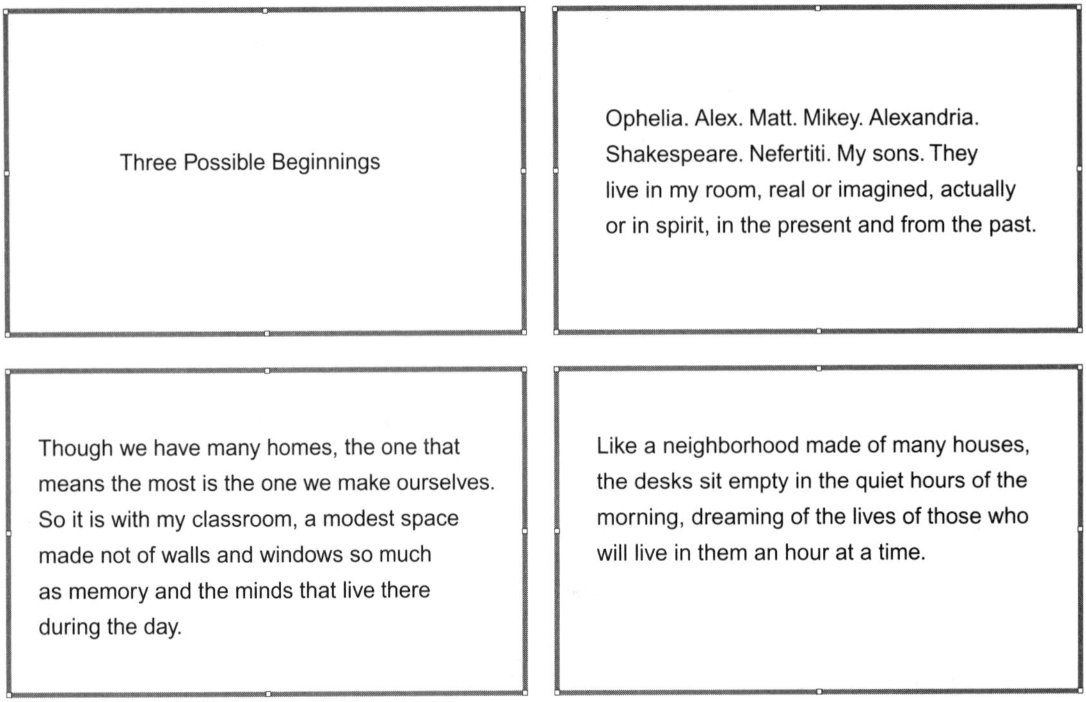

Three Possible Beginnings

Ophelia. Alex. Matt. Mikey. Alexandria. Shakespeare. Nefertiti. My sons. They live in my room, real or imagined, actually or in spirit, in the present and from the past.

Though we have many homes, the one that means the most is the one we make ourselves. So it is with my classroom, a modest space made not of walls and windows so much as memory and the minds that live there during the day.

Like a neighborhood made of many houses, the desks sit empty in the quiet hours of the morning, dreaming of the lives of those who will live in them an hour at a time.

FIGURE 21.1   Sample PowerPoint screens from a minilesson

Use a
Writing Process

22

RATIONALE

Good writing is built, not born; it requires time, but not talent. Of course, talent helps, but using a process approach to writing enables everyone to write effectively. Some writers' processes might be more efficient or have fewer steps than others, but all can communicate successfully through writing if they follow their own process. Like many great ideas, process-based writing suffers in the hands of those who would prescribe certain steps, as if it were a recipe that could be followed step-by-step to arrive at a uniform but excellent result.

A process approach is valuable for both students and teachers for several reasons. Teachers struggling to provide effective writing instruction better understand where they fit in and what they can offer when students use a process. Teachers know, for example, that they can teach students different strategies for developing their topic. The process lends itself to a series of targeted, contextualized minilessons (see Reminder 21) that support the writer through the process. The student, on the other hand, benefits from such an approach for the same reasons any writer does: good writing is an act of discovery that takes time. A process approach gives all writers, both the talented and the struggling, room to learn, to think, to improve as they work on their paper (see Figure 22.1). Students with learning difficulties and English language learners benefit from such an approach since they often need a guiding hand and time to concentrate on one aspect of their writing at a time. All benefit from this approach, however, since most kids find it difficult, for example, to begin. Using a process gives students permission to write what Annie Lamott calls "shitty first drafts" that get them on the road; Don Murray (1985) calls them "down drafts," by which he means getting something down on paper so you can work with it.

Remember that not all writing allows students to use such an extended process. Time constraints or the nature of the task (e.g., a timed or in-class writing test) does not always provide the time needed; thus, you must also equip students with a range of processes for different situations. When using a writing process approach, we are constantly reminded of that eternal teacher problem: time, and the difference between what we should do and what we can.

I have forced myself to begin writing when I've been utterly exhausted, when I've felt my soul as thin as a playing card . . . and somehow the activity of writing changes everything.

JOYCE CAROL OATES

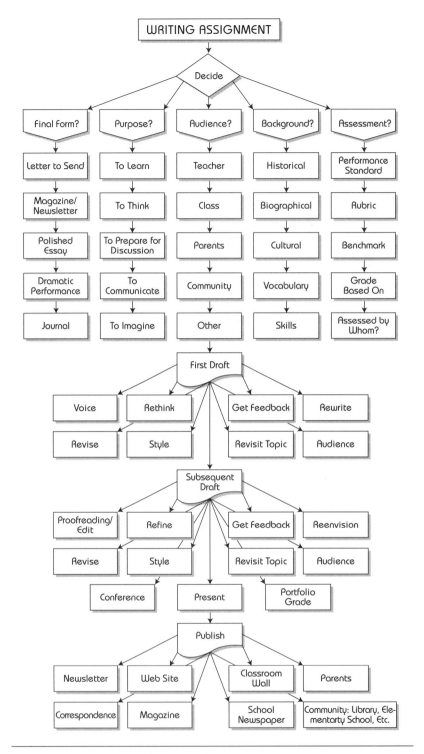

FIGURE 22.1   One schema for a writer's process

WHAT TO DO

A process is as much a set of mental habits as it is a technique. The goal here, as with so many aspects of teaching writing, is to achieve independence. A process is not linear or fixed; a good process will adapt to the needs of both the writer and the teacher so they can learn as well as write successfully. Depending on your objective, for example, you might interrupt their process to have them rewrite whole sections of their paper in a different voice or style to better understand how such changes affect their paper. Or you might have them revise, as I occasionally do, their entire paper, using the question So what? to guide them. They read a sentence and ask, So what? in hopes this will yield new insights as to the importance of their argument or details to support their claim.

The following list describes what students could do before, during, and after they write a piece.

BEFORE

- Generate ideas using any or all of the following techniques:
  - ▶ Talking
  - ▶ Brainstorming
  - ▶ Reading to get ideas
  - ▶ Completing graphic organizers
  - ▶ Outlining
  - ▶ Taking notes
- Determine your purpose
- Identify your audience and their concerns
- Choose the appropriate voice and style
- Select the genre and medium most appropriate to your message

DURING

- Select and refine your topic
- Gather and organize your supporting details and examples
- Draft your ideas into a working form
- Discuss your ideas and draft with other writers and the teacher
- Read for more ideas; look at exemplars to better understand what you should accomplish on this assignment

• Do read-arounds to get other students' feedback on specific aspects in your paper

• Revisit the rubric or directions—if possible—to be sure you are heading in the right direction. Turning rubric or directions into a checklist can help you focus on what you must accomplish

• Confer with other writers at this point if possible and appropriate

DURING (TEACHERS)

• Provide students with a range of examples—professional or student-created—to inspire new ideas and clarify their purpose

• Watch for struggles and offer minilessons or individual instruction on those subjects

• Evaluate the effectiveness of their topic and the examples they have included so far

AFTER

• Revise for clarity

• Revise for style

• Revise for content if you find that your examples, for instance, do not adequately support your ideas

• Edit for correctness

• Edit for content

• Finalize format according to appropriate style and usage guidelines

• Confer with helpful and willing readers

• Publish to the appropriate venue and audience

A few related reminders:

• If kids are using a computer, which typically supports a process model, have them print and keep a record of each revision. Too often, kids toss their drafts as they revise on the screen and then turn in the "process paper" without any evidence of having revised.

• Have them label (e.g., date, version) the different drafts and related exercises so they can keep track of the steps they went through.

• Have students reflect on their own process—what helped, what did not—so they begin to know how to run themselves through it as needed without you having to require it.

CLASSROOM CONNECTION

Here is a sample process paper I assigned each September for the last few years:

Summer Reading Wrap-Up/Process Paper

Overview   The different components of this assignment are designed to evaluate your ability to:

- Write

- Read

- Think

- Collaborate

The assignment also provides a useful opportunity for people to get to know each other through conversations about important ideas expressed through these different stories.

STEP ONE: THINKING

Using the graphic organizers provided, make connections between the books you read over the summer vacation. You might, for example, write down a word in the middle like *relationships* or *different worlds* and see what you come up with. Take a minute to develop some useful questions to generate interesting connections: for example, Are there different types of relationships? What examples of these different types can we find in the different books (*Mockingbird, Ultima,* and the third book you chose)?

STEP TWO: TALKING

After you have generated a big mess of rich or potentially wonderful ideas, discuss in groups what you would like to write about. Agree on a topic or develop a question. This should be a question you all find interesting and which your notes and discussions have prepared you to write. You should spend the rest of your time developing ideas, finding examples, and making connections for your individual essays (since after this step you are on your own!).

STEP THREE: WRITING

Using the notes and the question or topic you developed with your group, write an essay in which you show me everything you can do. Remember,

111

the primary purpose at this point of the semester is to establish what you can do (this is called a baseline, if you want to be more precise) at the beginning. Your essay should be as long as you decide it should be. I will not answer the question, "Mr. Burke, how long should this be?" I will give you a look, and that look will mean, "You're the writer: it should be as long as you think it should be."

STEP FOUR: PRESENTING

Return to class with your completed essay—do *not* throw out any graphic organizers, notes, or drafts (even if you did them on the computer)—and get back into your groups and do a read-around as directed. Pay close attention to how the other writers solved the problems you faced as a writer. How are their papers similar to and different from yours? Do these differences make their papers stronger or weaker than yours? Why do you think that?

STEP FIVE: DISCUSSING

After presenting your papers within the groups (during which time I will be circulating around, listening, making notes, and evaluating), we will have our first class roundtable discussion in which we will use the papers to have a culminating discussion about the books you read. This will conclude our work on this unit.

RECOMMENDED RESOURCE

Murray, Donald. 2002. *Write to Learn*. Canada: Heinle.

Develop Writers' Capacity

23

RATIONALE

Developing students' ability to write is not enough; they must have the capacity to use and improve upon the skills they learn. *Capacity* refers to not only the stamina and fluency needed to write but the will to persist in the face of confusion or even failure. Writing demands that students commit to the process of beginning, improving, and finishing a piece of writing. It demands more, though: writing requires deep and sustained attention as the student moves toward a clarity of understanding that will culminate in clear writing. Finally, writing demands that students be "generative thinkers" (Langer 2002), thinkers who can come up with compelling topics, useful questions, and powerful details or examples that support the point they are trying to make. The key capacities we strive to develop in all students are to:

- Generate ideas for writing

- Evaluate and choose the best topic (i.e., the one most appropriate to the assignment and the one about which they can write the best)

- Identify the main categories into which the topic can be organized

- Use those categories to generate ideas and examples to support what they want to say about those ideas

- Express themselves

- Develop their ideas using details and examples from various sources

- Write in different styles according to the demands of the situation

- Read as writers (i.e., study the writer's craft)

- Detect errors and flaws in language, arguments, and content

Once student writers know they *can* write well in different styles about various subjects, they will choose to write, because they will know they can say what they mean. Thus, the final, and in some respects most crucial, capacity is to develop in students the sense that they have something to say, something worth putting down on paper, something so

> People who can't afford to get writer's block don't get it. That tells you everything you need to know about writer's block.
>
> MARSHALL J. COOK

113

important, so true that they will write it well, no matter how many times they must revise it.

WHAT TO DO

• Develop students' capacity to use the technical terms of writing. Writers must know the terms that describe what they are trying to learn (Spandel 2001) if they are to be able to discuss their writing and others'. Teachers should not only teach such terms as *tone* and *transition*, *development* and *conventions* but should use them regularly in the classroom to model their meaning and usefulness. Moreover, as Spandel argues, students should be able to assess their use of these writing devices, thereby becoming less dependent on the teacher's assessment of the quality of their writing.

• Anchor your writing instruction in the Six Traits (see Figure 38.1) writing assessment. The traits teach them what to look for, how to read their own writing, and how to use that knowledge to improve their writing through revision.

• Display and constantly provide the traits of effective writing for the type of assignment you are working on. Some teachers create bookmarks, others posters; still others provide checklists or rubrics that help develop the writers' capacity by reminding them at all times what they are trying to do when they write, for example, a narrative essay, a biographical sketch, or a business letter.

• Develop students' vocabulary. Expository writing demands precise verbs. Students need models of how writers use these verbs, not to mention clarification on what they mean.

• Provide examples and models so students see what a successful performance of this assignment looks like. When working with expository prose, for example, I choose from their papers examples that illustrate (or don't) what I am trying to teach. I then put a select few examples on a page that I annotate and return to them while the learning is fresh (e.g., the next day). I put one copy of this sheet on the overhead and give them a copy to guide their next round of writing. I then walk through and verbally annotate the page, explaining what the writer did and why it worked—or did not.

If I am introducing a new form of writing, I will provide more intensive scaffolding to support their initial learning. I might give them a sample of the type of sentence or even a partial prompt that I require them to use at this point.

CLASSROOM CONNECTION: LITERARY ANALYSIS WORKSHOP

I fill in the template in Figure 23.1 when I begin the cycle of feedback and guided writing. I title it "Workshop 1.0" and date it because I will generate a series of these pages over the next few weeks, each one designed to push students up to the next level. I am not marking their papers at this phase of instruction; instead, I am reading to assess their work and to find useful, representative examples to include in these workshop pages. As far as grading, I give them a check or some reasonable completion grade to keep track of who did it and make them feel accountable. Only after the students have shown some initial mastery do I begin to respond individually and assign grades.

RECOMMENDED RESOURCE

Spandel, Vicki. 2001. *Creating Writers: Through 6-Trait Writing Assessment and Instruction.* 3d ed. New York: Longman.

Literary Analysis Workshop 1.0

Verbs that describe what the writer or text does:				Literary analysis papers:

Verbs that describe what the writer or text does:

- emphasizes
- defines
- compares
- expresses
- exemplifies

- implies
- juxtaposes
- observes
- organizes
- provides

- demonstrates
- maintains
- argues
- parallels
- echoes

- alludes to
- claims
- illustrates
- reinforces
- implies

Literary analysis papers:

- Embed quotes from the text to illustrate
- Discuss themes, motives, author's purpose
- Use the present tense when writing about a text
- Use appropriate literary terms
- Make connections within and between texts

Discusses author's purpose

Uses quotations to support and illustrate

Explains meaning of quotations and purpose of author's choices

Identifies author's main idea in the text

1. The point that the author was trying to get across was his opinion of human nature and how their minds work. In the beginning of this poem (Billy Collins's "The History Teacher"), the scene was **depicted** in a classroom, ". . . He told them of the Ice Age . . ." I think that the first four stanzas **refer** to the teacher teaching the students in a classroom. While teaching the students, the teacher wants the students to realize that history can be fun and interesting. By making these comparisons "The War of the Roses took place in a garden . . ." and "The Ice Age was really just the Chilly Age, . . . where everyone had to wear sweaters," he's trying to make the children happy and not bored when it comes to learning history. The point that the author was trying to get across was his opinion of human nature and how their minds work. Part of his point was to **illustrate** human behavior in a very specific way. He wants to have the children take the knowledge of history and **compare** it to their lives; and if they're ever in a situation the morals of history that they learned will be their advisory to guide them. (Katy Wallace)

Establishes clear focus on major themes

Identifies changes in the tone or meaning

Embeds quotations to support her claim

2. This poem talks a lot about innocence and censorship. The history teacher in the poem tries to teach his kids important things in history, but ends up changing the truth into something else to protect his kids' innocence. He censors the story, but all the while the children are "tormenting the weak and smart." **I think that the author is trying to say that** no matter what you say to these children they will still learn to be mean, abusive and violent. Protecting them from the truth won't stop them from picking on the weak or different. It is almost a child's nature to do these things. They see it in the media or they see older kids doing it. (Nicole Germanov)

Examines author's intent

"Verb-stanza"—looks for important moments, that is, changes in the text

Draws conclusion based on observations in the text

3. When I first read this poem, I had no immediate response, other than "What an annoying teacher." But then, after I read through once again, **I seemed to have found the verb-stanza of the poem, the point where something happened:** "the children would leave his classroom for the playground to torment the weak and the smart . . ." It was this part which seemed to hold the point of the poem. That their lack of knowledge and empathy for weaker parties or people caused them to be relentless to their weaker, less powerful peers. In all wars there is one strong force (country, bully) picking on a weaker one. And because they had not learned of the horror of that they showed no mercy to the younger ones. (Charlotte Silver)

Extends his ideas

Connects to his own experiences and the world

Attempts "below-the-surface" reading

Makes assertions about meaning; could support with quotations

Lots of great rough-draft thinking

4. This poem is about a history teacher who is trying to protect his students from the truth of the world. I saw that as a metaphor for America. The history represents the government and the press, just like how the history teacher said, "The Ice Age was really just the Chilly Age." The press and government don't always give the American people the whole story. Maybe they will soften the facts to keep the American people thinking they are right. We often aren't told what is happening in any other part of the world. Before Sept. 11 the bulk of the American population probably didn't know where Afghanistan was. It is because of this ignorance that we bully other countries like the students did, "To torment the weak and smart." President Bush just told the world that any country not with America is against America. This is exactly what Billy Collins was talking about. The history teacher is doing a large disservice by not telling the students the truth about the past. If we don't learn from mistakes of the past they will be remade. (Jon Chiu)

FIGURE 23.1 Sample writing workshop page with student examples

Make Yourself Available to Student Writers

24

RATIONALE

Improvement in any domain—singing, skiing, writing—requires guidance and support as the individual masters the skills and, over time, the craft they are learning. Of course, most of the time we are running around preparing to teach or teaching, neither of which leaves big gaps of time to confer with kids. Whereas the college writing instructor has three small classes and office hours during which to confer, we can have five large classes and just barely enough time to get to the bathroom or steal a quick drink of water.

These different demands aside, our students need our guidance when it comes to writing. Making yourself available is different than commenting on papers; being available means making time to sit down with one or more students to talk about their writing. Different students need you at different times. Prior to competency or state writing exams, struggling students might need you to help them prepare. AP students might need additional guidance as they near the AP test or write essays to colleges they hope to attend. Struggling students need writing mentors and informed guidance for projects in other classes; they have never written a controversial essay before, for example, and thus may need additional help that only the teacher can provide.

Writing is a personal endeavor, a conversation into which we enter with ourselves but also with ideas and other people. Dante needed Virgil to show him the way through Hell; while I don't compare school or writing to Hell, students sometimes do, and thus rely on us to teach them how to complete the journey that each writing assignment represents. By making ourselves available to students to help them with writing, we are also able to help them with living; the two are not so dissimilar, as in these early stages, the kids are themselves rough drafts that want much revision. The conversations we can have with them not only about but through discussion of their writing have the power to achieve much more than just stronger verbs or more concrete details.

The book belongs to the author. An editor at most releases energy. He creates nothing.

MAXWELL PERKINS

WHAT TO DO

• Provide students with your e-mail address. While some, even many, will resist this, there are several advantages worth considering. First of all, you can add a proviso stating that access to you via e-mail in no way implies you will be able to help them at this time. They should consult you ahead of time to secure your permission to seek guidance through e-mail. E-mail allows you to check out their writing when you are ready; moreover, since most teachers type well, you can respond more quickly and specifically to an electronic text. Finally, the teachers I know who make themselves available say only a few students take advantage of it.

• Schedule regular conference times and adhere to them. Tell students you will be available every day for thirty minutes after school, but they need to sign up to meet with you; explain that if no one signs up, you will not stay. You can also hold working lunches with students who are committed to improving their writing. While meeting during your precious lunch is generally not good for you—you need time to be with adults and to rest—such meetings can give you a good energy boost if they are with the right kids. Also, some schools encourage teachers to help out with study centers on certain nights or after school. You might consider going to the homework center one day a week and telling kids who need help that they can find you there. *Some* schools will even pay for your time.

• You can also make yourself available to students within class:

  ▶ Meet with ESL or special needs students during certain times (e.g., while others are working in groups) to discuss specific issues you know they face on a writing assignment. Taking five ESL students to the side to develop their topic or discuss their ideas for a paper improves their writing and makes them feel supported.

  ▶ While kids work in groups, move around the room. Sit down at a desk with a group and listen to what they say. If you see an appropriate place to contribute, do it.

  ▶ While kids are writing on their own, circulate. See who is struggling or who is off-topic. If you see someone having a hard time, sit down next to them and talk them through the assignment. If they are stuck, assess the source of their confusion and provide a useful solution. Sometimes providing them with a graphic organizer, questions, or brainstorming strategy can get them back in business.

• When you meet with students, ask them what they would like you to do. If they don't know what you mean, ask them, "Would you like me to listen, to ask questions, to make suggestions, to give you ideas about your topic? What do you need most from me?"

RECOMMENDED RESOURCE

Strong, William. 2001. *Coaching Writing: The Power of Guided Practice.* Portsmouth, NH: Heinemann.

25

Integrate the Teaching of Language and Conventions

RATIONALE

The integrated study of grammar offers these benefits:

• Creates a common, precise vocabulary with which to discuss writing, language, and various texts the students read

• Helps writers and readers troubleshoot complicated or flawed sentences by giving them the tools to identify both the source and the solution of any confusion

• Develops students' respect for language, for its complexity and power to inform, confuse, entertain, and persuade

• Increases writers' choices through the expanded awareness of those choices

• Establishes and reinforces the standard of correctness and commits students to the value of using language effectively and correctly

• Allows students to be better generative thinkers by developing their linguistic and cognitive capacities for thought

The discussion of conventions would not be complete without discussing testing. It is nice to say that kids should get the ideas down and then clean them up; such a process emphasizes the importance of generating ideas from which the student can build better writing through revision. This model only makes sense, though, if kids do revise and if they have a conscience about or commitment to the correctness of their writing. For it is this knowledge of correctness that ends up being assessed on the state and local writing tests. And given that these tests often offer decontextualized sentences in need of repair, it is appropriate—within reason—to instruct your students in how to fix up such sentences, though it is not fair to call such instruction writing instruction, as it will not likely improve their writing performance or their capacity to correct their own work.

WHAT TO DO

I arrived at the following list of things I must constantly remind myself to do or teach my students to do:

- Use grammar to generate ideas, prepare to write, clarify their thinking

- Develop students' grammatical intelligence (through revision, manipulation, direct modeling and instruction, etc.), especially in the following areas:
    - Parallelism
    - Coordination
    - Correlation
    - Subordination
    - Apposition
    - Modification
    - Predication/logic
    - Tense
    - Agreement

- Use strong, precise, active verbs

- Use concrete, specific nouns

- Use different sentence patterns

- Organize paragraphs for clarity, emphasis, and coherence

- Integrate the study of grammar throughout the curriculum (through minilessons, conversations, activities)

- Know the parts of speech

- Understand how the following free modifiers work in a sentence:
    - Absolute phrases
    - Adjective clauses
    - Verbal phrases
    - Appositives

- Establish and reinforce what is correct

- Punctuate for clarity and emphasis

- Use standard American English

- Omit unnecessary words

- Know and use different transitional and organizational structures and devices

CLASSROOM CONNECTION

Were I to list the verbs that best describe what I do when it comes to working with grammar, they would be these: *construction, manipulation,* and *generation.* Prior to writing, we often use the board or their notes to list, for example, the verbs that they could use to describe a character, event, or scene. We might even take a word and generate additional possibilities, or manipulate the current sentence structure into other grammatical structures to test out the difference in effect between, say, an appositive phrase and an adjective clause.

Here, then, are some other strategies or techniques I use in my classes:

Read and take notes on a section in Writer's Inc. (Sebranek, Kemper, and Meyer 2001) about topics such as passive voice, which they then summarize according to the conventions of a well-organized paragraph. They then revise their own current or previous writing samples, focusing on the overall trait of conventions or the specific aspect of passive voice. We follow such discussions up by working through representative examples or unique problems they encountered, then discussing how they solved the problem as well as other viable solutions.

When we focus on the trait of word choice, on the other hand, we *go through the current or a recent draft of a paper* to assess their use of verbs or nouns, as well as modifiers.

On other occasions we will go through a paper they are working on, especially when we are focusing on language study, and *identify the subject and the predicate.* We do this so as to evaluate the clarity of their grammar and guide subsequent revisions.

Annotate directions on tests and assignments to better understand what they tell students to do. I will say, "Find the verbs," such as *describe,* and then tell them to figure out *what* they are supposed to describe by finding the noun (or noun phrase).

Revise the weak or inappropriate verbs (especially *to have, to be, to get*), replacing them with more precise, powerful verbs. This inevitably leads to a serious discussion—usually in conferences at their desks—about the sentence structure and how it must change. We have conversations about the real subject of the sentence, versus the fake subject they originally had. For example:

- *Original sentence:* Telemachus is the character whom we can relate to in the *Odyssey.*
- *Revised sentence:* We identify with Telemachus more than his father, Odysseus, when we read Homer's *Odyssey.*
- *Alternative version:* Telemachus appeals to the modern reader more than Odysseus, the hero of Homer's *Odyssey.*

Identify patterns of usage or error in their writing. Students who underline all the instances of the verb *to be* in their writing suddenly realize they have a problem. The student who uses the verb *is* seventeen times in one paragraph cannot help but realize this is not strong writing; moreover, students then understand there is a pattern they can look for and try to avoid in the future.

Identify all nouns and revise for precision. Students often write *car* when they could write *Ford Mustang*, or *woman* when they mean *bride* or *Penelope, Odysseus' wife*. Sometimes I will have them go through and, after identifying all nouns, write one or two alternatives to the noun over the original word. The alternatives must be more precise, more detailed than the original.

Conduct grammar brainstorms. Draw on the board or have students divide a page into three columns titled Nouns, Verbs, and Adjectives. I have them generate all sorts of active verbs, nouns, and adjectives that they might use to write about a given subject. Then I will have them use as many of the words as they can in a descriptive writing activity.

Facilitate grammatical synthesis. To help students learn how to write about and discuss what they read, I will ask them to generate a list of adjectives that could be used to describe a character. This activity allows us not only to reinforce what an adjective is and how it works but to synthesize a wide range of information about a character. It also expands their vocabulary, especially if you revise the list as you go.

Give them sentence practice. I write on the board the following sentence (or another like it):

> *Setting out on his raft,* Odysseus began his long journey home to Ithaca.

I talk to them about the pattern of the sentence, explaining how the introductory phrase works. Then I have them generate their own, using mine as a model. I try to anchor the examples in the book we are reading (e.g., *The Odyssey*) and limit them to the type of sentence I provided (e.g., gerund phrase). We then put students' sentences up on the overhead and discuss them, stopping to address issues, such as mismodification, as they arise.

Practice sentence combining. To improve their knowledge of how sentences are made and how they work, I will sometimes use sentence combining. If possible, I draw the examples from their reading. For instance:

1. The judge asked Atticus Finch to defend Tom Robinson.
2. Atticus Finch is a lawyer.

3. Atticus Finch is respected.

4. Tom Robinson was a black man.

5. Tom Robinson was accused of raping Mayella Ewell.

One possible combination: The judge asked Atticus Finch, a respected lawyer, to defend Tom Robinson, a black man accused of raping Mayella Ewell.

We then discuss other possibilities and examine how they change the meaning or style of the sentence.

Give them a paragraph logic exercise. I take a paragraph and scramble up the sentences. Students must then rebuild it, depending on such grammatical clues as transitions to help them solve the problem.

RECOMMENDED RESOURCES

Strumpf, Michael. 1999. *The Grammar Bible: Everything You Always Wanted to Know About Grammar But Didn't Know Whom to Ask!* Los Angeles: Knowledgeopolis.

Noden, Harry R. 1999. *Image Grammar: Using Grammatical Structures to Teach Writing.* Portsmouth, NH: Heinemann.

www.grammarlady.com

Prepare Students to Write

26

RATIONALE

Painters do not just start slapping on paint; they prepare the surface, plan ahead, anticipate obstacles, and check to see that the result meets the needs of the person who owns the house. Not only do gymnasts prepare for their performance by warming up and stretching out; they make sure they know the criteria by which their performance will be judged so they know what to include in their routine. So it is with writing: the effective writing teacher not only prepares students but teaches them how to prepare themselves for a range of writing tasks.

How the student prepares depends on the task or context. If they are writing an essay for a state test or an exam like the Advanced Placement exam, they must begin by reading the directions. If they are writing a specific type of expository essay—for example, comparison, persuasive, or descriptive—they must learn and be sure to include the different elements of such a genre. If they are writing an informational report, they must prepare by gathering all the essential information through research. At every step of the process, the teacher should try to provide models that will prepare the students; these models show students what they are trying to accomplish.

The type of preparation also depends on the students' needs. More advanced students might need only a few examples to guide them; other students will need graphic organizers, models, the opportunity to talk about their topic, and guidance in generating ideas. Still other students might need help in simply understanding the prompt itself. One other aspect of preparation merits attention: purpose. Students, regardless of their ability, must set a clear purpose as part of their preparation; those who resist or cannot come up with one should learn how to adapt a prompt to turn it into something about which they do want to write.

Images always come first.

C. S. LEWIS

WHAT TO DO

Before students write:

• Provide them with the rubric or other criteria by which their writing will be evaluated.

• Give students models of the type of text you are asking them to write whenever possible; if you do not have any, try to model the task yourself. Even better, provide examples of different quality and have students create their own checklist for an effective paper based on their analysis of the sample papers.

• Read the directions or prompt aloud; then have them annotate it or turn it into a checklist that describes what they must do when they write. Remind them also to reread the directions while and after they write, as most errors are the result of misreading the prompt.

• Have students discuss their ideas (if possible) so they can generate new associations and gather new ideas from others in the process.

• Gather information and ideas related to their topic so they have a rich pool of details or examples on which to draw when they write.

• Teach them a variety of strategies that will prepare them to write:

> Outlining
> Brainstorming
> Questioning
> Note taking
> Filling out graphic organizers
> Listing possible titles
> Using online search engines to generate ideas
> Identifying natural categories into which information can be organized or from which ideas could be generated

• Show them how to determine what is important so they will know what to emphasize and include in their writing.

• Clarify what you (or whomever) are asking them to write. Inexperienced writers, which include those still learning English, may not have ever heard the word *essay* or might come from cultures where it is entirely inappropriate to persuade others using your own ideas. Thus, one way you can prepare your students is to get to know them well so you know what they know and need to learn.

After they have written their draft, and before they revise, consider these additional ideas for preparing them:

- Have them reread the prompt, directions, and rubric to be sure they are on the right track

- Have them ask themselves, What question is this writing trying to answer?

- Encourage them to have someone else read their paper to give them ideas for revision

CLASSROOM CONNECTION

Generating ideas is difficult for many students. Even advanced students struggle: though they can come up with ideas, they are often unable to distinguish between a decent idea and a compelling one that would inspire better writing (and more interesting reading). The following techniques prepare students to write well yet require little explanation.

Cloze technique. Adapted from the reading strategy, this method helps students generate academic language while it also prepares them to write. The first step is to provide a viable though incomplete claim:

Childhood is a _____ in our life.

I write this on the board. Then we generate different possible words or phrases to complete the assertion. As they suggest these, students discuss why one is or is not a good suggestion. They then choose their own, which they are now prepared to write about.

SSR topic practice. To prepare students to generate their own topics while reading, I use the following sequence:

1. Students read their silent reading book.
2. While they read, they jot down words or ideas that come to mind. These should be words about which they could (and would want to) write. When first using this technique, I read aloud from my own SSR book, telling them what words I would write down and why.
3. When they finish with their silent reading, they should have a list of words. They must choose one to be their topic.
4. They must then generate questions that will prepare them to write well about this topic.
5. They write for the allotted time about this topic.

Figure 26.1 shows Sutton Howard's work from a typical day in my ACCESS class after following this sequence.

Develop Reading   Sutton Howard

Nightmares

Dreams   Why did I pick blood?

Children   What happened that blood came into the Picture?

Nazis   How Much Blood?

Jews

~~Horror~~   I ~~rember~~ remember when I was about eight

Screaming   years old and I was riding my new

Death   bike up and down my street, until my older

Evil   brother wanted me to race down the hill. We

Voices   started to race and I took off, I was going
                                                    no one could
Germans   so unbelievable fast that ~~~~~~~ ~~~~ catch

Soldiers   me. Then I realized that my shoelace

Crying   was untied. The shoelace got caught in the

blood   spokes and I flew over the handle bars

Shocked   and hit a tree head on, smacked my

betrayed   face, and also cut my face open over-

Whispers   flowing with blood. I also remember

brothers   the thick blood all over me, my face, and

Sisters   my clothes. In the hospital the doctors

                     were trying to fix my face and more

                     and more blood came out. I finally got

                     sick of all the blood everywhere.

FIGURE 26.1   Sutton's sample reading response

Quotations Clarified. We often ask students to write about what they read, but often students, especially those with difficulties, do not know how to begin. By using the Quotations Clarified handout (see Figure 26.2), students are able to write with greater confidence about sophisticated quotations.

RECOMMENDED RESOURCE

Atwell, Nancie. 2002. *Lessons That Change Writers*. Portsmouth, NH: Heinemann *first*hand.

Quotations Clarified

English/Burke

Writing about quotes from a text requires practice. When doing the following assignment, keep in mind the need to support your thinking with examples from the text. Please use the back when you run out of room on the front of this page. Find ONE quote from each chapter and explain that quote using the following examples.

Quotations Clarified	Qualities of a Good Quote
• A quote is any word, sentence, or passage taken from a written text. • The words can be but are not necessarily spoken. • Whatever appears between quotation marks should be *exactly* what the text/person wrote or said.	• It is meaningful: to you, the author, or the characters. • It is about something important: an event, person, idea. • You know you can write about it. • It invites/helps you make connections between the book and yourself.

Phase One

Quote	Questions	Response
Write down the quote here.	List 3–5 questions that will help you write well about the quote.	Use the questions to help you write about the quote here.
"I can change that. Can change it big. Better to put my time into that than moaning about the other all day. That little grammar-school girl showed me that." (page 16, "Wendell" from *Seedfolks*)	• What can't he change—and why can't he change it? • Should he change it? If yes, what might happen? • What does he "moan" about? • How did Kim, the "grammar-school girl," show him this?	This is an important moment for Gonzalo: he begins to look at the glass as half-full instead of half-empty. By this I mean he begins to focus on what he CAN do instead of what he can't do. I can't change the attitude or mistakes others will make. Already we see what happens if you change things: Kim's seeds started a chain reaction that is beginning to change the neighborhood and the people in it. She showed people—without meaning to or even realizing it—that anything is possible if you have courage.

Phase Two

What It Says	What It Means	Explanation
"I know what I don't want to become." (page 5)	Jasmine/Jyoti does not want to grow old and live only for what other people decide is best for her. She is a woman who knows what she wants, or at least has decided that she will be the one who decides what she wants. When the astrologer says "Fate is Fate," she rejects it, saying in essence that she is the one who will determine her fate.	She has watched women grow old and live small lives in her village. She has watched them married to men they did not love. She has seen their lives played out at the river bend. There seems to be no room for surprise in her life, so she will make room. This line also means Jasmine is a strong woman, and Mukherjee probably writes this up front to establish Jasmine's character as independent, strong, intelligent.

FIGURE 26.2   Quotations Clarified handout

27 Support Struggling Writers

Begin somewhere; you cannot build a reputation on what you *intend* to do.

HENRY FORD

RATIONALE

Everyone struggles with writing at one time or another, or with one aspect or another. Some students have more difficulty than others, however, and we need to use strategies to help them overcome these difficulties. We must do this without making them dependent on the aids or tricks that we alone can provide though; otherwise they never become independent writers with ideas and strategies of their own (see Reminder 28).

Struggle is a natural part of the writing process, one we must help students to understand so they can master it. Some students might struggle with an assigned topic on a district writing test because they have no experience in that area and thus do not know what to write. This happened to a girl in my class once. The state test asked students to write about an experience with a neighbor. This girl's problem: she lived outside of town on a couple hundred acres. So she sat there wrestling with what to say until she gave up, telling me, "I don't have any neighbors, so I couldn't say anything." Others struggle because they are not prepared; thus we need to teach students how to prepare for a variety of types of writing assignments.

WHAT TO DO

You must seek to understand why the student is struggling. You must, at the same time, develop their ability to self-diagnose the cause of their problem(s) so they can do this on their own eventually. Begin by asking:

- Is it the task (e.g., they do not know what a persuasive essay is, nor do they know how to write one)?
- Is it the topic?
- Did they understand the text they must now write about?
- Are they overwhelmed by the requirements or the time constraints (e.g., on a state writing test that is timed)?
- Do they understand what the directions ask them to do?
- Are they having a tough time just getting started?

- Are they prepared to write (i.e., do they need to do more research or thinking)?
- Are they trying to write about a topic that contradicts or otherwise challenges what they know or believe?

Students often struggle with a writing assignment for other reasons, depending on the subject and the requirements. Ask whether their difficulty is:

- Developmental
- Cultural
- Personal
- Intellectual
- Emotional
- Technological
- Conceptual
- Experiential (e.g., do they have any experience with the subject they are trying to write about?)
- Linguistic (e.g., do they have the language to understand the prompt and to write about the topic?)

A range of solutions or strategies exists; you must learn to use or recommend the one(s) you think will meet the student's needs at the time:

- Confer with the individual—or a small group if they face a common problem, such as not understanding the topic because they are new to the country—to discuss their difficulties. Ask them what they have tried so far and why it did or did not work.
- Use graphic tools to help them generate and organize ideas during different stages of their process (see Reminder 16). These can also be helpful when conferencing with students as you work through the difficulties of the topic and show them how to organize their ideas or information.
- Provide examples of past performances. Whether you are preparing AP students for the timed AP essay or struggling writers for the upcoming state exit exam, models of successful performances help them see what they are trying to accomplish. Either run these off or copy them to transparencies so you can discuss what makes them effective. As an alternative, give students one or a group of papers of varying levels and then ask them to assess them (e.g., using the Northwest Regional Educational Laboratory's 6+1 Traits guide or the scoring guide for that particular assignment) and identify the traits of a successful piece of writing. Then focus on how to incorporate those traits into their paper.

- Model for them how to approach the assignment. You could think aloud to explain how you do this; you could also use an overhead, computer monitor, or whiteboard so they *see* how you solve the problem the assignment presents. Be sure to explain why you do what you do.

- Prepare them to write. Using discussions—paired, small-group, or whole-class—selected readings, images, or video, help students fill up the idea tank so they are prepared to write. Mark Twain said the tank was empty when he couldn't write; to remedy this, he would go do research or talk with others.

- Talk about writing. I have mentioned this in passing already, but Nystrand et al. (1998) and Langer and Close (2001) concluded that talk is one of best ways to help writers work through their struggles, especially inexperienced and low-performing writers. Talk helps them generate, extend, and refine their ideas throughout the composing process.

- Show them how to write their way into the topic. If students are to improve as writers, they must accept that it is a craft, one that demands revision and ongoing conversation with the self and the topic (and, if they are writing about literature, the author and characters). If they are stuck—can't get started, don't know what's next, aren't sure how to end—they should concentrate on getting a "down draft," as Donald Murray (2002) calls it. This means just getting *something* down so they can begin to work with it. Sometimes students must accept that a bunch of writing will not actually be in their paper but is necessary or at least useful to help them figure out what they do think or know about a subject.

- Put up posters on the walls of the class with different strategies for writing; these posters might include samples or appropriate vocabulary to use for different types of writing (e.g., verbs for summarizing).

Structured techniques such as Jane Schaffer's "Teaching the Multiparagraph Essay" offer struggling writers sequential support. You can learn more about her materials and techniques through her Web site *<www.janeschaffer.com>*. Special education teachers often tell me how helpful these materials are; Schaffer developed the materials in response to the low performance and serious needs of her inner-city students in San Diego. Such materials are useful, even perfect for some students, but they must learn to internalize those structures so they become a set of intellectual habits and strategies they can use for independent performance.

CLASSROOM CONNECTION

The three examples that follow each show something different. Dominic's graphic organizer helped him read Gary Soto's short story "Being Mean" but also prepared him to write about the story or his own life (Figure 27.1). Figure 27.2 shows what Nazreen wrote after we generated possible topics and the language to describe those topics as a class. We

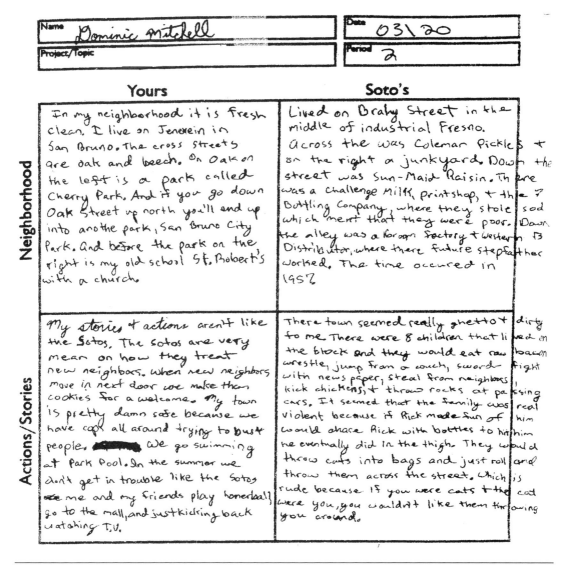

FIGURE 27.1   Sample matrix used to help students generate then organize ideas prior to writing

Introductory Paragraph (Rough DRAFT)

What has a big influence on people. Well, many different things influence us in many different ways.
(- Getting started was hard because I)
(didn't really know what to write in the)
(1st sentence)
One thing that influences us are people. People can influence us in two ways; good and bad. A friend could be very loyal to you then at the last moment betray you, a teacher could tell you something that could make you think differently or change your life forever. Another thing is Experiances, denpending on what you did in the past it can teach you between right & and wrong, or give you a new perspective. Places also influence you, the place you are from or where you ex travel to can change you and the way you think about people

FIGURE 27.2   Student sample

generated several different possible statements, then students chose the one they wanted to develop. In the example below, freshman Nelson Tejada reflects on his year's progress. Though you lack a contrasting example, believe me when I tell you that this letter's clear writing shows substantial progress, as does his attitude. In this letter, Nelson gives us some insights into one student's process of becoming a writer:

Dear Mr. Burke,

I can't believe how much my writing has developed since the beginning of the year. I thought at first that I was misplaced and wanted to get out of your class in a hurry. I remember thinking about how dumb was it for me being in an honors class. I remember all the times I kept giving myself excuses for being lazy saying that I couldn't do the work because it was to hard. Now it's made me wonder if I was wrong all along and I could survive in a class of high expectations. So I thank you, for believing that I could do the work when other people didn't. All the times that you made me focus on my work when I didn't want to. If it wasn't for all your help I probably wouldn't be as good of a writer as I am now.

I think the work that meant the most to me was The Weekly Reader. At first I received such low scores that it discouraged me from doing any more weekly readers. It wasn't until I found out that I had an F in English when I knew it was time to clean up. The way I started was to force myself into doing a weekly reader and checking it over for mistakes. I saw so much improvement in my writing that I myself probably wouldn't believe it in the beginning of the year. And then I finally received my first 20/20 on my essay to prove how much better I have gotten.

I know that one of the reasons my writing has changed is because of the variety of books that I have been reading. I read good books before but this year you have introduced me into different ways of thinking. *Culture Jam* is probably one of the most incredible books I have read before. I think the reason why I liked it so much was because it attacked the way I lived. The author didn't want America to become a brand name. The author knew that everything was now based on material things like money. But the most interesting aspect was that I found some parts true.

If you fail to try again, I now go by that saying. The first time I got a weekly reader I got a low score. Instead of trying again I gave up and let myself slip away. Now I don't get discourage if I don't receive a good score on my work. Now that I got my self set on how to do my work its only up from here. I know my writing is good but not good enough. I must work on my grammar and work ethic. I found out the hard way that last minute work does not pay off and put me in bad positions. And I know the only way to do this is by doing all my work the right way. But as far as freshman year goes, you have given me a great base to work on for the next three years Mr. Burke, and for that I thank you for it.

Your grateful student,
Nelson Tejada

RECOMMENDED RESOURCE

Shaughnessy, Mina P. 1977. *Errors and Expectations: A Guide for the Teacher of Basic Writing*. New York: Oxford University Press.

28 Support Students with Special Needs

RATIONALE

When need is greatest, help is nearest.

GERMAN PROVERB

The following techniques help any students with special needs, though in truth all students benefit from such responsive instruction. What I can accomplish here is limited by space; I have listed two books at the end of this reminder to give further guidance for the different needs I discuss in this section. The term *special needs*, is, of course, a very loaded one; I use it here in its literal sense: students who have needs that are not common to all. I do not mean in any way to imply that English learners have learning differences; having taught special education and learned other languages, however, I realize that many of these techniques benefit both groups. Where the techniques are unique to one group—English learners, for example—I indicate this.

WHAT TO DO

This section focuses on instructional approaches that will benefit all students but particularly those with a range of special needs.

• Be multimodal, use multimedia: It helps all of your students, but the special needs students in particular. Whenever possible, let them hear it, talk about it, see it, and touch it.

• Sequence your activities and assignments logically.

• Provide a weekly assignment sheet to help them check off work they have done or need to do.

• Check frequently for understanding. Do this in a variety of ways (e.g., looking across the room to check in with a student, circling by to look at their work, asking them at the period's end if they understand).

• Discuss learning strategies you think will help the students with specific areas or assignments.

• Allow them more time to answer or react to questions you ask.

• Whenever possible, break up assignments into small units; present them slowly and sequentially; and review frequently.

• Be patient.

• Provide immediate feedback whenever possible to help the students measure their progress.

• Ask the students what helps them the most and what is most difficult for them.

• Provide time to practice or rehearse: whether it is an upcoming writing test or a speech they must give, be sure to give them time to prepare.

• Use small groups: such groups, if made up of fluent speakers and considerate students, provide the developing writer with an opportunity to listen more carefully and speak more often without the usual anxiety of raising their hand and speaking when the whole class is listening. One other tip: do not let them huddle together into single-language groups all the time, as this will not help them become fluent speakers, but do let them help each other by using their primary language to explain things to each other.

• Provide handouts whenever possible. These make it easy for students to follow along; also, they help students by giving them directions to refer to when they get home and begin to do their work.

• Use the board. The board provides visual information that the struggling and diligent alike can write down and clarify later. If they don't understand the words, they can still get the information written down.

• Do not depend on (but feel free to use) verbal directions.

• Do not talk too fast.

• Provide clear, concise directions.

• Allow students to use Cliffs Notes. Though perhaps controversial in the minds of some, such study aids provide much-needed support for the student whose language ability makes it hard enough to understand most English readings, not to mention dialects and slang used by writers like Mark Twain and J. D. Salinger.

• Make yourself available outside of class. Many English learners are reluctant to demand attention until they gain some confidence with their new language; you must then go to them and remind them that you are willing to meet with them if they need the extra help.

To benefit students with learning differences:

• Alter the format of written handouts to reduce the amount of material in the student's visual field, or use graphic displays and diagrams to convey information.

• Let them have a partner who understands their needs and is supportive and willing to work with them.

• Enlist the help of a scribe to share note-taking responsibilities; if one is not provided through the student's Individualized Education Plan (IEP), look for a student in class who would be willing to help in this area.

• Use graphic or other organizers to help with reading. Even if you are not requiring such tools be used on a particular reading, try to make available some helpful means of organizing the information they will be reading (e.g., quickly review how to make an outline).

• Understand the constraints each student's challenges impose on them and do your best to address their needs by clarifying intended outcomes (e.g., students with ADD typically get very tired by the day's end after trying to overcome distraction and confusion all day).

• Provide clear and logical transitions between ideas and units of instruction.

• Provide lots of concrete examples to illustrate any ideas you are discussing, relating them to the student's background, experience, or personal interests (which are usually available in their IEP or student file).

• Seat them away from those people or conditions that would distract them or otherwise undermine their performance; usually up front and close to the speaker and away from noise is best.

• Assess their learning style and inform them how they can best learn different types of info, and allow them to respond in alternative manners (tape recorder rather than written notes, scribe for tests, computer for writing).

• Establish and maintain high but reasonable expectations.

To benefit English learners:

• Assign the ESL student a language partner who is specifically responsible for helping that student understand assignments and words they do not understand.

• Have available a dictionary in their native language. Also there are some dictionaries that are specifically designed for English language learners (see the *Longman Dictionary for American English: A Dictionary for Learners of English* 1977); try to have at least one of these in your class.

- Use gestures to emphasize and illustrate whenever possible.

- Create a questionnaire that asks them specific questions that will develop a profile of them as a student and a learner.

- Allow them, as part of your outside reading program, to read at least one book in their native language.

- Allow them to write first drafts in their primary language as a means of getting their ideas together, then work on the translation and writing in English later.

RECOMMENDED RESOURCES

Levine, Mel. 2002. *A Mind at a Time: America's Top Learning Expert Shows How Every Child Can Succeed*. New York: Simon and Schuster.

Echevarria, Jana, and Anne Graves. 2003. *Sheltered Content Instruction: Teaching English-Language Learners with Diverse Abilities*. 2d. ed. Boston: Allyn and Bacon.

29 Teach Students How to Write Under Different Circumstances

RATIONALE

Successful adults are able to think and function effectively in a variety of situations. Not all of these situations play to our strengths, but we can develop strategies and prepare ourselves to succeed or, in this case, write according to the demands of the situation.

During lectures, students must know how to take effective notes; these notes must be useful when they sit down to write a paper that will synthesize their different ideas. On other occasions, writing might be a means of responding to or reflecting on what they have read, observed, or experienced. Yet another situation is when asked to speak, whether formally or informally; we typically find it helpful to write out what we want to say so that we know what we think and feel better prepared to speak it. Perhaps the most consequential type of writing students encounter is writing on exams for classes or other purposes such as entrance to college. Some of these written exams are timed and formal; others are more informal, asking them to use writing to describe or explain a simple procedure. Students need to be able to write with confidence and competence in all of these situations.

WHAT TO DO

I will focus mostly on the last example—written exams and timed writing tasks—since this causes students the most trouble. While getting started is difficult for many students, it is often more so on an exam. The anxiety of the situation, possibly coupled with the feeling that they don't know what to write, can cripple an insecure or, in some cases, even a seasoned writer. Thus, they must learn how to get started. You can help students master such situations by having them rehearse for a testing situation. AP teachers do this constantly since they know the types of questions the test asks; rehearsals of this sort reduce anxiety by demystifying the task and giving the students strategies to use on such tests. Teachers can also teach students how to anticipate and prepare for exams they might give themselves; they might say, for example, "We have been studying the changing culture of America in the second half of the twentieth century. What would be a good topic for a related in-class essay, one that I might be likely to create?" Such a discussion could, for the attentive student, give them the guidance they need to create their own practice topics so they can write several rehearsal essays prior to the actual exam.

Whatever the situation, students must be able to do the following with ease and confidence:

• Generate ideas, examples, connections, or, in some cases, a topic

• Organize ideas in the most effective way to support their main idea

• Understand the topic or task

• Draw on their content knowledge to be sure they are demonstrating what the test or task is assessing

Teachers can teach students—by modeling, even practicing in class—how to find within the topic itself information about what to write and how to approach the topic. One way to do this is to focus on the directions, specifically the verbs that identify what they must do in the assignment. If the directions say *describe,* that is different than *explain* or *compare.*

When it comes to written exams (see Reminder 52), Scruggs and Mastropieri (1992, 89) identify four steps for writing an effective essay, which they sum up with the acronym SNOW:

• Study the question

• Note important points

• Organize information before writing

• Write directly to the question

Here are a few things students can do to prepare for writing tests:

• Know the task: do they understand what they are begin asked to do?

• If they should learn to respond in one of several ways:

  ▶ Skim through the test to see if other information helps them clarify the task.

  ▶ Ask the teacher for guidance.

  ▶ Generate questions and make connections to what seems related.

• Gather and have with them the necessary and available resources such as notes and books

• Ask if they can bring notes and even make an outline for the test

You can help them in the following ways:

• Tell them ahead of time as much information as you think appropriate so they can prepare effectively

• Ask yourself if it is essential to have students write on this occasion, or whether it would be fair and appropriate to allow certain students the chance to demonstrate their knowledge by talking with you about what they learned.

• Break the writing assignment or exam into smaller units so they don't get overwhelmed; or, teach them to do this on their own so they can be more strategic test takers.

Whatever the situation, whatever the writing problem, it is always ideal to allow students time to debrief. During this time, whether it be after an in-class exam or the AP test, students should talk about the choices they made, the strategies they used, and why these did or did not work. Such conversations yield some of the most valuable learning, as it helps them see there are multiple ways to approach a task or respond to a topic.

RECOMMENDED RESOURCE

Langer, Judith. 2002. *Effective Literacy Instruction*. Urbana, IL: National Council of Teachers of English.

Provide Timely and Useful Feedback to Student Writers

30

RATIONALE

Feedback is essential to improvement. Of course, providing it in a timely and useful form is a tremendous challenge to almost any teacher, since it takes time and you have so many students. My principal once spoke with great admiration and pride about the English teacher at his former school who had a great reputation as a teacher, no family, and hands so ruined from her laborious comments that she sometimes wept with pain as she worked over student papers. Another colleague told me of the woman at her old school who kept a cot in the closet of her classroom so that she could, when necessary, spend the night in her classroom, so committed was she to the notion that students should get their papers back the next day with abundant comments. These women and their example do not inspire me; they scare me, they sadden me.

Still, students cannot improve without feedback, and it must come quickly enough to help and, more importantly, to teach and to improve their writing skills. They need it regularly and it must be specific to their own needs as writers. It must also be meaningful, not comments they never read or, worse, never use to improve their paper or better their skills. Nor should the feedback always be about their grammar or other aspects of correction. Feedback on every aspect of the process is crucial to the writer's growth, for learning how to develop a topic and generate effective examples is just as important as writing correctly. Here, for example, is a brief e-mail exchange between me and a student who was responsible for shaping his own final exam question:

> Mr. Burke,
>
> I have a few questions about my "Final Question" and was wondering if you could give me some feedback on what I have. I haven't come up with a complete question yet, but I want it to have something to do with how your goals affect the journeys in your life.
>
> -----
>
> *A great topic.*

See everything. Overlook a great deal. Correct a little.

POPE JOHN XXIII

143

The text I'm going to use is the *Odyssey.* I am going to use Odysseus's goal of getting home and how it takes him on his journey through many obstacles such as Hades and Calypso's island. And how Telemachus's goal of finding his father led to him finding himself.

You could add further depth to your essay by talking about Jasmine's and Winnie's goal to have the life they want and think they deserve and how that goal sustains them through their trials.

Then I will relate the topic to my life. I will talk about all of the goals that I have set for myself and what journeys they have led to and what effects they have had on my life. I am a little stuck on what to write about for the World aspect of it though.

What you have is good, Nick, but you could see what happens if you think about the consequences of a more competitive world that demands such goals. Thus the goals of the past are not always appropriate to the present. When your grandfather was growing up, it was probably enough of a goal for him to provide a home and meals for his family; now if you (or I!) don't provide love and support to spouse and kids, we are not successful in the eyes of society. All this demands work, a lot of it, and I don't just mean work at the office.

I'm not sure whether to talk about teens' goals in general or what the goals of the world are. I know I am writing to you a little last minute, but if you get a chance I would really appreciate it if you could write back and tell me what you thought of my question and maybe give some ideas for the "World" topic.

It's a great topic, Mr. Buckley. See you tomorrow. Write back if you have questions; I'll be here at my station the rest of the night. It's nice to see you ending the semester so well. Mr. Burke

The point I want to make about feedback—which comes in many forms, from many sources—is that it matters. Mary Pipher, author of *Reviving Ophelia,* has said that one teacher's comments about her poetry in high school kept her from writing any more poetry, something she loved very much at the time, for twenty-five years. Pipher suggests that adolescent girls are especially sensitive to teachers' comments on their papers.

One of my former students, who went on to be a poet, wrote me years later to say: "You really made a difference in my education, and my life. I still carry your words with me, and truly value our relationship and the love of writing that you fostered. You once wrote in a journal of mine next to a poem that 'words like the way you use them, Kassy.' That has stuck with me and made me believe in myself."

Good feedback is:

- Specific

- Limited to a few aspects of the writing

- Focused on patterns or errors or specific traits to which you can direct your instruction

- Timely

- Meaningful

- Respectful

- Connected to current teaching goals and the specific writing assignment

- Culturally sensitive

- Formal or informal

WHAT TO DO

Here is a list of possible solutions and strategies, none of which work for all assignments, all of which are effective in the right measure and on the right assignment:

- *Create forms.* Forms can be generic or specific to the assignment and should allow you to check or circle those aspects that need more work; they should also provide space for additional comments. (see Reminder 18)

- *Create stamps.* Rubber or self-inking stamps are relatively easy to create these days. Northwest Regional Educational Laboratory *<www.nwrel.org>* sells the 6+1 Traits rubric as a stamp and on sticky notes. Investigate theirs or create your own.

- *Use the computer's functions.* While I find autocorrect irritating, Jonathan Mooney and David Cole, authors of *Learning Outside the Lines* (2000) emphasize how useful such immediate feedback can be for the mechanical and grammatical aspects of writing for students with learning differences. These authors both have ADHD and share through this book strategies that helped them enter and succeed in Ivy League universities.

145

- *Provide informal feedback through conferences.* While students work on the assignment, circulate around the room for curbside conferences that allow you to give feedback on the spot about a specific aspect or problem. More personal and effective than written comments on a draft.

- *Confer with students.* While similar to the previous suggestion, this variation is more formal. Schedule conference times with students and have them bring their paper up with the problem they need help with, or read and respond to one predetermined aspect of their paper. If, for example, you are teaching the trait of voice, read for and give the student feedback only about that one aspect of the writing, focusing on what they did and why it did or did not succeed; then discuss what they could do to improve it in their next revision.

- *Have students provide their own feedback.* Too often we think we must collect and respond to the entire paper. Instead, have students read through their own (or another's) paper and look for particular details. One simple example would be to have them go through their paper and find all the weak verbs (e.g., *is, was, were, has, have*). Or they can read just for passive verb formations. In this way you are having them provide the feedback you would otherwise have to spend time giving them. You are training them to find the weaknesses on their own making them more independent writers.

- *Color code.* When we are studying word choice, we spend a lot of time looking at the words kids use in their writing. I will have everyone read their own (or another's) paper and use a yellow crayon or highlighter to identify what they think is strong word choice. I will then read through their paper and, using an orange or blue highlighter, indicate what *I* think are examples of good word choice. This colorful contrast between the two readings inspires useful discussion and effective revisions.

CLASSROOM CONNECTION: THINK-ALOUDS

One of the most useful forms of feedback is thinking aloud about what students are doing. In the early phases of a writing assignment or while introducing some aspect of writing, I do not give individual feedback (usually). Instead, I read through all the papers and find examples that represent what I want and what some are doing. I then put these on the overhead the next day (and give students a photocopy of the same page) and think aloud about what they are doing well and what they need to improve (see Figure 30.1 through 30.3).

RECOMMENDED RESOURCE

Lane, Barry. 1999. *The Reviser's Toolbox.* Shoreham, VT: Discover Writing Press.

Thinking Aloud: How Do I Know What I Think Until I See What I Say?
Burke/English

• I *notice* . . .	• The author is saying that . . .	• A good example of . . . is when . . .
• I *think* . . .	• The characters tend to . . .	• . . . reminded me of . . . because . . .
• I *wonder* . . .	• Certain themes keep appearing . . .	• . . . is important because . . .
• I *suspect* . . .	• As with other books we have read, this one . . .	• One thing that confuses me is . . . because . . .

Annotated Exemplars: Think-Aloud (taken from *Kitchen God's Wife*)

Thinking about the title is always a good idea.

Great idea: always pay attention when a writer embeds a story/folktale within their story. As Cam says, writers always do things for a reason.

1. The story of the kitchen god got me thinking. The title of the book is *The Kitchen God's Wife*. The wife was the perfect wife who was left by her husband, but in the end saves him to no point. The husband (kitchen god) burns himself in shame. I predict this foreshadows a situation that will occur in the book between characters, probably Pearl and Phil. I believe this will happen because I know writers make everything have a point. The story of the kitchen god was put in the story for more reason than to just explain a shrine Pearl's great aunt gave her. (Cameron Duncan)

Note how Cameron speculates about the meaning/implication of the kitchen god story, wondering if it foreshadows what will happen.

Observation: notices a pattern and draws an inference from it. She then elaborates on her observation by including examples from the book and connections to her own life experience.

2. Family seems to be very important to Pearl's family. I observed that each member in Pearl's family has a certain "duty" to their family. I also noticed that, even though most don't want to be there, they still had a family dinner. I wonder if most families feel a certain obligation to their family. I do know, from experience, that most Chinese feel obligated to their family. I suspect this is because Chinese families teach their children such values. I'm not sure if this applies to all families, though. Still I wonder why Pearl feels she *must* go to her cousin Bao Bao's engagement party. She clearly does not want to go. I find this part confusing. (Jessica Gee)

Qualifies her thinking; she is thinking aloud, as she should (e.g., "I'm not sure . . ." and "confusing"). Confusion is the gateway to clarity; Jessica's thinking here will lead to understanding.

Stephen thinks here about the questions he doesn't yet know how to answer. He is on the outside (white, male, young) trying to think his way inside (Chinese, female, adult). Questions like these will get him there.

3. This chapter makes me wonder about things. For example: Is Pearl's father white or Chinese? What race is Pearl? For me the second question is very important and definitely relevant to the story and Pearl's emotions. She really doesn't seem connected at all to her mother or the Chinese culture at times. I also wondered why Pearl is so reluctant to tell her mother about her disease. I understand the surface reasons of fear for her mother's sanity and anger, but I continue to wonder if there is some general thought pattern in the Chinese culture that makes family relationships strained and business-like. Or is it deeper than that? I have noticed that Pearl has a hard time relating to other people in her family, also. (Stephen Hinshaw)

4. Pearl's relationship with her mother is very sad. I think emotional and cultural differences are what separate them the most. (Jen Lescher)

Jen's observation about their relationship introduces an important insight, but she does not elaborate on it.

Note how Jen makes another keen observation here, but then goes on to develop it with examples that she further examines. She shows herself thinking about causes and effects, consequences and implications.

5. The differences between generations in the family are very distinct. The elders are very traditional people and the young generation [their children] is much more modern and American. This makes the family not so close and the kids more free because their parents don't know as much as they do about the society they live in. This then causes competition, the kind of competition that shouldn't happen in a family because that's fake, and if the family showed the love they had for each other they wouldn't have this problem. (Jen Lescher)

FIGURE 30.1 Thinking Aloud 1.0

Thinking Aloud: Exemplars #2
Burke/English

• I *notice* . . .	• The author is saying that . . .	• A good example of . . . is when . . .
• I *think* . . .	• The characters tend to . . .	• . . . reminded me of . . . because . . .
• I *wonder* . . .	• Certain themes keep appearing . . .	• . . . is important because . . .
• I *suspect* . . .	• As with other books we have read, this one . . .	• One thing that confuses me is . . . because . . .

Introduction Use the following exemplars to help you improve your own think-alouds. Remember to refer to the prompts listed above. These all come, once again, from Amy Tan's novel *The Kitchen God's Wife*.

1. **I wonder** why she switched the narrators at the end of the chapter like that. Why not start a whole new chapter with Winnie starting to narrate the story? Or was that not as distinctive as putting a dingbat in the middle of the page? Maybe, maybe not. **I think** she changed narrators and created that section-divider page to get the reader's attention. Make the change sharp and easy to notice. Switching the narrators **I think** makes a dramatic change in the story. First the story was told from a young woman's point of view. Now as her mother is telling the story, **I predict** that the story might show some more wisdom in each sentence. More enticing elaborations in each descriptive quote of hers, telling more about that time period. Knowing and telling more from experience. (Kristin Carranza)

2. **I feel** that Winnie always thinks she is right as well, but when she is wrong, she says it was her luck that turned against her. **I think** that Winnie's luck comes with bad things and visa-versa, so they sort of cancel each other out. **I think** Winnie's luck runs in the family because some of her bad luck was brought upon her by some relative of hers. Old Aunt put the vision of Lin as a lizard in Winnie's mind. The Chinese have a different philosophy than the people in India. In India people believe in fate and mostly marry people they have never seen before. Winnie didn't marry the man she didn't see even though she should have. To an Indian person, she messed up her fate . . . to marry the wrong man. *Jasmine* and *KGW* have another similarity: They both talk about having different lives. (Jacqui deBorja)

3. **Chapter 3 makes me ponder** over many things. For instance: Why didn't Winnie marry Lin? Why, all of a sudden, is she thinking about Lin? Does she have any regrets? **The first question is very relevant to the story because** if she had married Lin, she wouldn't have married Jimmy! Then, the whole story would be turned upside down. **I also wondered** if she was going to tell anybody the real story of Kun. **It seems** a little odd that she would make up a huge lie. Even though everyone knows the "story" of Kun, **I think** Winnie should tell the truth. She is not hurting anyone but herself. **I noticed** that throughout the whole book there has been a theme of hiding. For example, Pearl keeps her disease a secret and Winnie won't tell anyone about Kun. (Jennifer Edl)

FIGURE 30.2 Thinking Aloud 2.0

Observations on the Final Essays

Burke/January

What Worked

- Language: *Most* people used excellent verbs
- Paragraph organization
- Appositives
- Introductions (especially when writers used the models I gave them)
- Organizing essays in a variety of ways to effectively illustrate or support your main ideas, especially with the Heaney essays. *KGW* essays often lacked the same cohesive organization. Distinguished essays were organized to show cause and effect (i.e., how events or experiences shaped Heaney's writing or Winnie's character)

What Did Not Work

Instead of *praising* . . .	try *commenting*
• Seamus Heaney is the greatest poet I've ever read . . .	• Seamus Heaney's reputation as one of the twentieth century's great poets stems from his willingness to confront issues that challenge his readers to question their beliefs.
• Winnie is the most inspiring person I've ever read about.	• Winnie's determination in the face of repeated loss makes her a memorable character, one whom readers can't help but respect as they wonder how they would respond to such crises.
Instead of *summarizing* . . .	**try *making conclusions***
Winnie's mother abandoned her when she was little, so she went to live with her aunts.	Winnie's abandonment at a young age might have scared her more deeply than she shows in the book; it might account for her protective attitude toward Pearl.

What Needs Work

- *Conventions*: Titles!
- *Idea development*: Also, choice, use, and punctuation of quotations.
- *Word choice*: Too much use of (in *many*, not all, essays) *thing, stuff, someone*. Words must be precise: nouns concrete, specific; verbs, as mentioned above, showed greater precision. One person, for example, wrote that "Seamus Heaney *unearthed* . . ." Now *that* is my kind of a verb!
- *Idea development*: Everyone identified important ideas, some more than others; most need to still work hard on learning to elaborate, comment. Once you say something is important, you must explain *why* it is important and provide supporting examples or details.
- *Idea development*: Many still need to work on establishing a controlling or main idea that the essay develops. It's not enough to *have* an idea; the idea must be worthy of your reader's attention and showcase your intelligence.
- *Testing—Pacing*: Written exams, which you will take throughout college, require that you pace your time. Some did a better job of this than others, as evidenced by the final essays, which show some people spent too much time on one essay, leaving them little time to write the other one.

FIGURE 30.3   Sample feedback page on a final essay

31

Provide the Necessary Tools to Teach and Work on Writing

I never write except with a writing board. I've never had a table in my life. And I use all sorts of things. Write on the sole of my shoe.

ROBERT FROST

RATIONALE

You'd never find a repairperson heading off without a toolbox; nor would you be likely to find an athlete going to practice without their gear bag. So it is with writing and the teaching of writing. *Tools* might be expanded to include materials, for writers are picky: not just any notebook will do, nor is any pen or desk acceptable. Some writers spend years in search of the perfect paper or, as writer Annie Lamott has, the perfect chair, for, as she says, you cannot come up with good ideas if you are thinking more about how much your butt hurts.

The tools and materials described here are familiar, though not all of them, nor are they all obvious. Not all will be appropriate for all assignments or students, but they are an accumulation of the tools writers find useful in one situation or another.

WHAT TO DO

Do whatever you can to gather the following materials and tools, then teach your student writers how to use them to improve, or use them yourself to teach even better. Some stores, such as Office Depot, have amazing deals on certain school supplies in August; the resourceful teacher learns to quietly stash the materials they need without causing trouble for their colleagues. Your toolbox might include the following:

- Dictionaries
    - College-level
    - English language learner version
    - Unabridged version
    - Scientific
    - Literary terms
    - Phrase and fable
    - Rhyming

- ◗ Word origins
- ◗ Mythology
- ◗ Visual

- Thesauri

  - ◗ *Synonym Finder*
  - ◗ Antonym/synonym book
  - ◗ Encyclopedia
  - ◗ *Merriam-Webster Encyclopedia of Literature*

- Annotation tools

  - ◗ Post-its
  - ◗ Highlighters (or crayons)
  - ◗ Transparencies
  - ◗ Overhead pens
  - ◗ Overhead projector
  - ◗ Graphic organizers
  - ◗ Butcher paper and markers

- A copy of the text for everyone (unless the activity calls for sharing)

- Bible

- Atlas

- Computers with Internet connection

- Annual almanac

- Extra copies of class texts that everyone is reading

- Cliffs Notes (or their equivalent for special needs students)

- Exemplars of similar assignments for students to consult

CLASSROOM CONNECTION

Some teachers get creative with the tools they make. Teacher Dan Diercks has created a number of bookmarks for his students to use in his class; the samples in Figure 31.1 focus on writing.

RECOMMENDED RESOURCE

Lane, Barry. 1999. *The Reviser's Toolbox.* Shoreham, VT: Discover Writing Press.

Literature Bookmark — Fiction *Continued*

Symbolism - Something in a story stands for itself literally and for something else figuratively.
Example: In Guy de Maupassant's "The Necklace," Mathilde Loisel's borrowed necklace represents her shallow, materialistic values.

Point of View - The perspective from which a story is told.

a. **first person** - told using the pronoun "I" by someone in the story. Perspective is limited to this character's observations.

b. **third person omniscient author** - told by an "all knowing" narrator. Reader sees everything that is happening to everyone in the story.

c. **third person limited** - told by a narrator but from the perspective of only one character in the story limiting the viewpoint to that character.

Allusion - A reference to something, often in history, literature, or even the Bible, that the author assumes the reader is familiar with. A full understanding of the author's point depends on the reader knowing the connection.

Imagery

An author's most powerful tools are those that allow him or her to help the reader create pictures in the mind.

Simile - Comparing two unlike things using the words "like" or "as" to create a new image for the reader.
Example: "Harry stared into Cedric's face, at  his open gray eyes, blank and expressionless as the windows of a deserted house." *From Harry Potter and the Goblet of Fire*

Metaphor - Similar to a simile, a metaphor compares two unlike things, but it doesn't use the connecting words "like" or "as." A metaphor says that something IS something else.
Example: "Morning is a new sheet of paper for you to write on..." *From "Metaphor" by Eve Merriam*

Poetry
The most economical of all literature.

Stanza - Poetry is written in groups of lines, the ends of which are determined by the poet.

Rhyme Scheme - The pattern of rhyming of the ends of lines usually indicated by the use of letters.

Meter - The pattern of stressed and unstressed syllables in poetry.

Free Verse - Poetry that has no regular meter; it may or may not rhyme.

HAGERSTOWN JR.-SR. HIGH SCHOOL
©2001 D. Diercks Hagerstown Jr.-Sr. High School

Literature Bookmark — Fiction

Generally, fiction is literature that is made up–like short stories and novels.

Plot - The sequence of events in the story.

Conflict - A struggle between opposing forces or points of view. There are two categories of conflict:

a. **internal** - man against himself where a character battles with himself.

b. **external** - man against man where one character battles another character; man against nature where a character battles his surroundings.

The **resolution** of the conflict is when it ends, for better or worse.

Characterization - The method by which the author reveals a character's personality. There are two ways of doing this:

a. **direct** - the author comes right out and tells the reader what the character is like. This leaves no chance that the character can be misjudged by the reader.

b. **indirect** - the author reveals the character through his actions and words or from what other characters say about him.

Setting - The time and place of the story. Sometimes this is important to the understanding of the story; sometimes it isn't.

Theme - The general insight or moral an author conveys through his story. Sometimes a theme can be expressed in a single sentence.

Foreshadowing - When an author puts something in a story that hints about something to come.

Irony - The difference between what is said and what is meant. In literature and drama, we have three types of irony:

a. **verbal irony** - a character says one thing but means the opposite.

b. **situational irony** - a situation turns out the opposite of what is expected.

c. **dramatic irony** - the reader (or audience) knows something that one or more characters in a story (or a stage play or film) doesn't know.

Literature Close-up:
Edgar Allan Poe was a master of using setting to create a creepy atmosphere in stories like "The Cask of Amontillado."

My very own grammar Bookmark
Compliments of HHS English Department

▶ Prepositions

Commonly Used Prepositions

aboard	beneath	in	regarding
about	beside	inside	since
above	besides	into	through
across	between	like	throughout
after	beyond	near	to
against	but (except)	of	toward
along	by	off	under
amid	concerning	on	underneath
among	despite	onto	until
around	down	opposite	unto
as	during	out	up
at	except	outside	upon
before	excepting	over	with
behind	for	past	within
below	from	pending	without

Compound Prepositions

according to	because of	instead of
ahead of	by means of	next to
along with	in addition to	on account of
apart from	in front of	on top of
aside from	in spite of	out of
as to		owing to

What can't be inside a prep. phrase?

subject	object complement
verb	predicate nominative
direct object	predicate adjective
indirect object	

How do I recognize a prepositional phrase?
A prep. phrase starts with a preposition and ends with a noun or pronoun.

<u>John left his keys</u> under the *Honda.*
   Independent Clause

▶ Clauses

Clauses are groups of words that contain a subject and verb and act as a part of the sentence.

Independent (Main) Clauses

An independent clause can stand on its own because it is a complete thought like a sentence.

When Jeff left the game, <u>the team began to lose.</u>
   Independent Clause

Dependent (Subordinate) Clauses

A subordinate clause, like a main clause, has a subject and verb but can't stand on its own as a complete thought.

<u>When Jeff left the game,</u> the team began to lose.
   Subordinate Clause

My very own grammar Bookmark
Compliments of HHS English Department

▶ Parts of Speech

Nouns name persons, places, and things.
Pronouns take the place of nouns.
Verbs show action or a state of being.
Adjectives describe nouns and pronouns.
Adverbs describe verbs, adjectives, adverbs.
Prepositions start prepositional phrases.
Conjunctions join words and groups of words together.
Interjections show strong emotion.

▶ Verbs and Complements

Linking Verbs

Linking verbs are being verbs. They don't show action. They link the subject of a sentence to a word that renames the subject (predicate nominative) or describes the subject (predicate adjective). Here are the most commonly used linking verbs:

Forms of the verb 'to be'

am	will be	should be
is	has been	would be
are	have been	can be
was	had been	could be
were	shall have been	should have been
shall be	will have been	would have been
		could have been

Other common linking verbs

appear	grow	seem	stay
become	look	smell	taste
feel	remain	sound	means

Warning: these may also be action verbs!

Action Verbs

Action verbs may show a physical action (like "kick") or they may show mental action (like "understand"). Action verbs can be followed by either direct objects or indirect objects.

Complements

Action verb complements

<u>Direct Object</u> (answers "what?" after verb)
<u>Indirect Object</u> ("to whom?" "for whom?" "to what?" "for what?" after verb)
<u>Object Complement</u> (answers "what?" after the direct object)

Linking verb complements

<u>Predicate Adjective</u> (describes the subject- must be an adjective)
<u>Predicate Nominative</u> (renames the subject- must be a noun or pronoun)

©2001 D. Diercks Hagerstown Jr.-Sr. High School

FIGURE 31.1   Dan Diercks' bookmarks for writers

Use Computers to Improve Writing Instruction

32

RATIONALE

For a long time, writing was arguably the only area of instruction that benefited from the first wave of computers. Even then, however, problems we still face were prevalent: lost time due to equipment failures, slow typing, and lack of ongoing access to the computer lab for the revision process, which made computers useful to writers in the first place. Improved typing skills and the next (or, as some call them, the Net) generation's greater fluency with computers, not to mention teachers' improved ability to use them, make computers much more useful now.

Writing itself has changed and continues to do so with the ongoing integration of technology into our lives. The once-dull typewritten page with one style of font has given way to a dynamic page with multiple formatting capabilities and the expanded dimension of interactivity with the Web, not to mention the integration of everything from sound to images—even video. Thus, today's writer must develop and use their textual intelligence (Burke 2001) to make documents that are effective and efficient. The following contribution to an online discussion about writing and computers sums up the emerging world of writing as it relates to technology (Carbone 2000):

> Date: Tue, 26 Sep 2000 22:35:27 -0600
> From: Nick Carbone
> Reply-To: Writing Program Administration
> Subject: Why Use Computers to Teach Writing?
>
> What writing is depends very much on the technology used to write. We don't teach writing using slate tablets and chalk. We don't teach writing by asking students to etch their words in dirt as we sit outside on a log.
>
> Most of us still teach in brick and mortar classrooms, maybe with some time on the side devoted to talking about word processing or using the Internet for research. I've found that a frustrating way to teach writing. I much prefer being in a networked classroom because increasingly my students are writing on networked computers.

I like writing with a Peacock's Quill; because its Feathers are all Eyes.

THOMAS FULLER

153

Networked computers are the default writing technology; the Internet is the default network. iMacs made a splash in part because you could get online in three steps. Windows makes the browser the operating interface for the desktop. You write in MSWord, and type in a URL, and it becomes a live link. You can save your document in html format, and if you set up your computer to do so, can publish it to a Web site from your word processor.

More and more computers are sold for under a $1,000 and come with an Internet Service Provider.

In more and more workplaces—including ours, including, for example this list—important and necessary communication and community building and collaboration happens with things like e-mail, online chats/MOOs, and shared Web sites, be they online writing centers, class pages, conferences, academic journals, "papers," and other forms of scholarly work.

To say nothing of what happens in the rest of the world. I was watching a zoning board meeting on the local cable access, and residents were discussing a proposed road, where it would go, and how it would affect a neighborhood. Folks were getting up and using PowerPoint slides, overheads, and mixing prepared written remarks with graphics, and other tools to shape their arguments.

So why this technology? Because it's what people write with more and more.

The trick is never teaching the technology for technology's sake, but teaching writing as it can be done with the technology. So even something as simple as cutting and pasting, which involves highlighting and copying, very basic computer skills, should be thought of not as skill, but as a writer's tool. And in a computer networked classroom it's easier to develop an assignment, maybe an in-class peer review assignment, that makes use of cutting and pasting in a way that makes it clear why a writer might want to cut and paste.

I think at some very important fundamental levels you cannot separate writing and the teaching of writing from the technology of writing. I think sometimes we have to, because we don't have enough classrooms to go around where it's possible to really make the connections clear, but I think even then, we need to address technology and writing in a way that gets beyond the usual warnings to save files, make backups, take care with downloading, don't be fooled by spellcheckers or made complacent by grammar checkers and all the other bromides that are now standard fare.

Nick

We must always remember that computers are a tool, a solution, a means of solving a particular problem. They are not an end in themselves. So much instructional time is lost to us through interruptions; computers threaten additional losses if used inefficiently or inappropriately. If the problem is searching for information about a particular topic, the Internet (and thus computers) is often a useful tool. However, if students don't know how to search for and evaluate the quality of resources, or if they don't use the capabilities of computers to revise and improve their documents, then paper and pen might be better.

This last point raises one last issue: students with learning differences often benefit most from using computers and should, whenever possible, be allowed to use them to organize ideas and write their papers.

WHAT TO DO

The following list summarizes a variety of ways teachers, myself included, use computers to teach writing in the classroom or lab.

• Using the monitor in my classroom, which is connected to the Internet, I will type up sentences or whatever we are studying. Depending on the context, I might use the color function of the program to distinguish, for example, all the verbal phrases if we are studying modifiers. If we are studying sentence patterns, on the other hand, I might use boldfaced type or colors to highlight the appositives. Using a presentation program like Microsoft PowerPoint, I might create three slides, each with different variations on a sentence or with different ways of writing about the same subject if we are studying style.

• Other formatting functions make our work more efficient. Using the line numbering feature, for example, when writing up exemplars or models allows for ease of use and quick reference; "Jane, what do you notice in line 17 about the sentence structure?"

• PowerPoint offers both students and teachers a useful means of presenting (as a means of teaching and publishing) to an audience. Students benefit from learning to write in the more telegraphic style and organize their ideas into bullets to convey ideas. In addition, they learn (if taught and required) to organize information by different means: comparatively, sequentially, chronologically. Finally, such multimedia writing further teaches them to incorporate not only words but also images, sounds, and video to convey their ideas in the most effective way.

• Programs like Inspiration *<www.inspiration.com>* and functions such as outlining within word processors allow students to use computers to generate ideas and manipulate information as they create outlines and organize their information. Such capabilities are especially useful for students with learning difficulties.

• Publishing—whether on paper, the monitor, the projector, or a Web site—is a realistic goal for different types of student writing now. Computers allow students to perfect their writing through multiple revisions while also giving them the means to produce impressive publications in different media. Books like *Publishing with Students: A Comprehensive Guide* (Weber 2002) provide teachers with useful guides and abundant resources to help students publish their work.

• One final example merits mention. I have created for my students *The Weekly Reader*, a digital textbook that consists of a wide range of types of texts (see Reminder 7). Students in my English class go online and read different types of texts that they must then use as the basis for a short essay. This assignment integrates reading, writing, and thinking, while providing students choices about not only what they read but how they write about the text they read. The essays themselves must be written on a computer; I use these weekly papers to integrate a range of embedded instruction about features of the computer (e.g., footers and headers) and different aspects of formatting documents.

RECOMMENDED RESOURCES

Weber, Chris. 2002. *Publishing with Students: A Comprehensive Guide.* Portsmouth, NH: Heinemann.

Purdue University Online Writing Lab (OWL): *<http://owl.english. purdue.edu/>.*

Evaluate Your Teaching

and Students' Progress

We must learn not to fear information; rather, we must learn to understand it and make better use of it to improve our instruction and students' performance. No coach or player resists studying the game films from their last outing: they know such data will only improve their performance. Companies and salespeople routinely, even obsessively, examine their performance, using a variety of types of information to track their progress and identify areas of concern, which the data will help them address. Teachers have too often feared data, and for understandable reasons: the information has too often been used in counterproductive ways to judge or otherwise criticize them.

It's time we began seeing errors as invitations and signposts, instead of as judgments and evidence of our failure. Symphony conductor Benjamin Zander (2000) teaches his musicians to call out in a voice of wonder, "How interesting!" when they make a mistake during rehearsals. This is such a more useful, productive response to trouble, for who wants to see in their work more errors than they can possibly learn to fix? Still, writers must learn to monitor their own progress, creating specific goals that will help them improve in those areas of writing they find difficult. Only through periodic reflection and revision can they accomplish this improvement. Such self-examination leads teachers and students to see patterns of error or progress within their own process. Not all students can easily discern these errors, though; some lack the vocabulary to describe what they do wrong, while others simply do not know what it is that effective writers do. Studying the processes of effective and ineffective writers provides students and teachers with a useful window on an individual student's approach.

Such evaluation, of both teacher and student progress, should come from various sources. Teachers and students who maintain portfolios and use them to monitor and reflect on their growth can only improve; this conscious, deliberate attention to the effect of instructional techniques and writing strategies yields insights into what does and does not work. These insights are the ultimate aim of all efforts, for as one becomes more aware of their own strengths and weaknesses, their own processes and practices, they resemble the master whose familiarity and fluency with the tools of the trade give that master a sense of confidence that enables them to confront and succeed in new situations.

The following letter from Snowden Campbell, an English teacher in Colorado, describes far better than I can the ways we can use and discuss writing to help us improve our own teaching while also coming to a better understanding of our own processes as writers.

Our former department chair and current Colorado Writing Project director, Karen Hartman, was looking not only for a way to start our department meetings with a practical application of teaching methods but for a way for our teachers to share through writing. As teachers of reading and writing, says Hartman, we need to recognize the power of reading and writing; we need to practice, we need to build a community of writers, learners, and teachers, helping one another to generate ideas. This practice allows us to communicate in a way only English teachers can—by writing to prompts that we can then choose to incorporate into our curriculum.

Here's how it works: a day or two before each of our meetings, Karen asks one of us to bring to the table a writing idea that may disarm or arm us, to get our creative and teacherly minds flowing before we begin our tasks at hand. This may be something that we have used successfully in the classroom, something we've wanted to try but haven't yet, or just a poem or other piece of writing that's always touched us in some way, that's made us laugh or cry perhaps, and that we'd like to share. After reading the piece, we write for fifteen or twenty minutes and then, those who are willing, share. Sometimes these writings take on issues we have confronted recently in the classroom; others are simply creative expression.

What's important, poignant, and powerful about these too-brief and too-infrequent moments is two-fold. First, they help us "get back to basics," reminding us all why we are here in the first place. We are teachers. Teachers of writing should be writers themselves. And as teachers, it is our responsibility, among so many others, to assume also the role of learner. The very instant a teacher ceases to recognize the need for continuing education, in any form, is, sadly, the same instant that teacher should retire from the profession. Writing reminds us that we always have something new to learn—from our colleagues, as in this case, but also from our students and, of course, from the world at large. By responding in writing to the experiences of others, we discover the value of our own experiences and learn from them.

The second force behind this process is the catharsis it inevitably reveals. Granted, this can take only the form of a five-minute escape from all other thought, but it can also allow for much-needed debriefing. The writings, even if they are not shared aloud, may simply give voice to feelings of frustration, confusion, resentment, etc. but may also go as far as to shed light on possible solutions to recent struggles. These are likely issues related to a profession wrought with hurdles but may also be personal issues that, as is so often the case with teachers, get placed on the back burner to make room for the demands we face daily in our jobs. And of course there are times when writing just gives us the chance to write—something we teach others to do every day but so rarely take the time to do ourselves.

Perhaps the most value in this practice is found in the "putting yourself in another's shoes" category. Without fail, every time I write something—be it a letter, research paper, poem, short story, or even this piece—I worry, rewrite, read, reread, worry, rewrite, worry, worry . . . Writing is arguably the most personal thing one can do, and we ask our students to write every day. So by putting ourselves in their shoes on a regular basis, we are made more sensitive, we are reminded to be aware of the plank we routinely ask them to walk.

33 Establish and Monitor Progress Toward Specific Writing Goals

RATIONALE

Goals give both students and teachers a target to aim at, a context and a purpose. Some goals are waiting at the door the day students first walk in. These goals might include standards created by the state or district that all students must master before they graduate. Other goals might be unique to the teacher, who believes that all students must learn to persuade people or that correctness counts above all else. Thus, we must be aware of the goals imposed on us as teachers and those which we impose, depending on our own biases, on students.

Obviously the goal of any writing course or instruction is effective written communication. To monitor writers' progress in any area, however, teachers must evaluate their current level of understanding and ability. This evaluation may come from the previous year's portfolio or be generated by initial writing assignments designed to show what the student knows and is able to do. In my class, for example, I often use the summer reading as the basis for such a writing assessment, as it shows me not only what they know about writing about literature but also how well they can write in general.

WHAT TO DO

• *Assess their current skills and knowledge.* As mentioned earlier, there are several ways of doing this, but the point is you cannot create or progress toward goals if you do not know what you can and cannot do now.

• *Establish course goals.* This way you'll know what you are trying to accomplish by the end of the course. Such goals should also be aligned with the appropriate standards. Another way of conceiving this is to ask, What do I want them to know and be able to do at the end of this course? Such "backward planning" allows you to figure out the steps that will help you and your students achieve that result.

• *Establish short- and long-term goals.* In his book *Results: The Key to Continuous School Improvement* (1999), Mike Schmoker emphasizes the importance of "rapid results," by which he means short-term goals that can give teachers and students a sense of immediate improvement and create

160

a feeling of momentum, and long-term goals that serve as the foundation of a teacher's or school's program. When instruction, planning, professional development, and curricular resources are aligned with these short- and long-term goals, and implemented in a coherent, competent, and consistent way in a course and throughout the school, improvement is the natural result.

• *Create goals that are appropriate.* Goals must consider the individual student's needs and abilities. While those external goals such as the state exit exam or the SAT matter very much, the students begin where they are. Students arrive in the class at different developmental stages and with a range of needs and abilities. The reason individualized goals are so important is that they can account for students' unique needs; the student with learning differences, for instance, who truly struggles to generate or organize ideas for a writing assignment, can focus on that, making that a priority. The teacher can then teach them strategies and introduce them to software applications and other tools that might help them gain a level of fluency that allows them to write with greater ease and confidence.

• *Align instruction and goals with the standards.* As you plan, begin by asking which standards are most appropriate to this part of your course, and be sure that what your students do builds their capacity to meet such standards.

• *Individualize your goals.* I do not mean that you should create some labyrinth of 143 different sets of goals for each student. Instead, students need to become responsible for their own learning, must develop—with the teacher's guidance through conferences, if necessary—their own goals so that they may internalize these goals. These goals should then be written down, for example, in the students' writing folder or in their binder so they can revisit them easily.

• *Reflect on progress toward their goals.* Both you and the students should evaluate how much progress they are making and the reasons for it. Reflection is key to improved ability; if the writer does not increase their awareness of their craft, of how one choice improves or undermines a piece of writing, they will not develop to their full capacity. Students can engage in such reflection at various times: before they begin, while they are working on an assignment, and after.

• *Refine and revise goals.* As students demonstrate some mastery of a goal, they should make it more specific or move on to new goals that seem the next logical step in their progress as a writer.

• *Focus your feedback.* Instead of giving students feedback about everything they did right and wrong throughout the paper, limit your comments to those goals you are currently focusing on in the class.

• *Measure progress by multiple means using data from multiple sources.* Students and teachers can and should measure improvement by both formal and informal means. An anecdotal comment by a student that it's getting easier for her to write is valid, important evidence of her improvement. Portfolios and writing folders offer more organized means of monitoring progress since teachers and students can thumb through, comparing their recent work with earlier efforts on similar assignments. Teachers can assess the appropriateness of goals and what gains have been made through conferences and curbside chats at the student's desk; for example, the teacher can stop by to see how well a student is beginning the paper, if that is something a particular student has identified as a problem for them. Rubrics also provide targeted feedback about students' performance in a specific domain; ideally the rubric will be aligned with the traits you are teaching. State exit exams, while problematic, are an obstacle students must clear; thus, their score on these tests gives you and the students specific feedback about their performance and those standards that continue to stand in their way.

RECOMMENDED RESOURCE

Zmuda, Allison, and Mary Tomaino. 2001. *The Competent Classroom: Aligning High School Curriculum, Standards, and Assessment.* New York: Teachers College Press.

Consult
the Standards

34

RATIONALE

Standards offer useful guidelines, particularly for new teachers who still lack a complete understanding of all they must teach in any one class. Standards ask and provide answers to the question, What does doing this well look like? They challenge us to demystify for ourselves and others—to make public—what effective writers know and are able to do when writing different types of texts. Standards remind us that our work is not about what we can say we *taught* but what our students can *do*.

WHAT TO DO

• Share, discuss, and post the standards in your classroom and on assignment sheets so students know what they (and you) must accomplish in your subject area.

• Refer to standards without being intrusive, incorporating the language of those standards into your lessons so as to reinforce and remind students of the importance of these skills. Example: "One thing we know good writers do is use questions to generate examples and powerful topics."

• Provide—through a Web site, overhead transparency, or photocopy—examples to help students see what any given standard looks like. This might also include modeling yourself the behavior they are trying to master.

• Identify and explain the criteria by which their performance on any standard will be measured and evaluated. Provide, if possible, examples of the different levels of performance so they can develop a clear understanding of what success looks like.

• Know the different types of standards and how they apply to your subject area:

> *Performance standards.* These articulate the degree or quality of proficiency students must demonstrate to achieve mastery on any standard.

> *Content standards.* These identify and describe what students should know and be able to do in any subject area.

You just shouldn't have standards that inhibit you from writing . . . . I can imagine a person beginning to feel he's not able to write up to that standard he imagines the world has set for him. . . . The only standard I can rationally have is the standard I'm meeting right now.

WILLIAM STAFFORD

163

> *Assessment standards.* These identify and describe the qualities of or means by which standards can be effectively assessed.

> *Delivery standards.* These identify and describe the materials, tools, or other means necessary to help all students achieve each standard.

• Align the standards with your local and state standards and framework to achieve consistency in your interpretation and implementation of the standards.

• Consult the standards when planning and try to use the standards to:

> Identify a topic or essential question

> Design learning and teaching activities (see Reminder 35)

> Decide which products and performances are appropriate to this assignment

> Define the assessment criteria

> Write performance descriptors

> Create appropriate scoring guides

> Collect and display examples

• Remember also to select and emphasize standards appropriate to the assignment, use related local curriculum objectives, and provide multiple means of demonstrating and assessing mastery of each standard in order to accommodate a range of learners.

RECOMMENDED RESOURCES

Jago, Carol. 2001. *Beyond Standards for All.* Portsmouth, NH: Heinemann.

Zmuda, Allison, and Mary Tomaino. 2001. *The Competent Classroom: Aligning High School Curriculum, Standards, and Assessment.* New York: Teachers College Press.

Consult your state's department of education Web site to find your state's standards.

Teach
by Design

35

RATIONALE

Good, effective, powerful teaching is no accident. It is the natural result of conscious, thoughtful planning that juggles the needs of the students, the school, and the state. Intelligent instructional design strikes a balance between skills and meaningful content. It is also an aspect of teaching that many resist. We must, however, accomplish too much to leave instructional design to chance; without thoughtful curricular planning, students with special needs or those needing additional challenges will be neglected; standards won't be addressed; writing and technology will not get integrated. As Edwin Schlossberg writes: "Without a method to properly evaluate excellence, our huge and growing population cannot learn or develop effectively, because learning occurs only when conversations, ideals, and goals have a shared and understandable framework" (1998).

Design is also essential for another reason: it ensures that instruction meets the needs of all students, particularly English learners. Any design, if it is to succeed and be sustainable over time, must accommodate different learners' needs. Such flexibility also helps when the school year's inevitable intrusions begin to chip away at the integrity of the curriculum, threatening to turn it into a bunch of fragments.

The following design tools, all of which will help you align your curriculum with the standards in your state or district, are meant to suggest different ways of teaching by design. All have their merits and are used by different people to help students and teachers do their work better and faster.

> We need a model of curriculum design that begins to account for the complexity of human needs.
>
> NANCIE ATWELL, FROM *SIDE BY SIDE*

WHAT TO DO

(from *The Teacher's Daybook*, Burke 2002b)

BEFORE TEACHING

- Consider students' prior knowledge and experience.
- Establish the criteria by which they will be assessed.
- Provide models to help them understand the task.

- Connect today's lesson with previous learning and other disciplines.

- Give effective directions both orally and in writing.

- Consider students' backgrounds, interests, and developmental cognitive needs.

- Establish and communicate goals.

WHILE TEACHING

- Use a variety of instructional strategies and resources.

- Provide opportunities for students to assess their own learning.

- Treat all students with respect and fairness.

- Encourage all students to participate.

- Enforce expectations for behavior fairly and consistently.

- Employ instructional strategies appropriate to the subject matter.

- Use materials, resources, and technologies to make the subject matter accessible to students.

- Allow students to practice before working independently.

- Follow a logical sequence.

AFTER TEACHING

- Use multiple forms of assessment.

- Consider short- and long-term learning needs.

- Use assessment results to guide further instruction.

RECOMMENDED RESOURCE

Wiggins, Grant, and Jay McTighe. 1998. *Understanding by Design.* Alexandria, VA: Association of Supervision and Curriculum Development.

Review, Reflect, and Revise

36

RATIONALE

A reflective classroom means everyone takes time to think about what's happening, how it's happening, and why. Students reflect on their performance but also their process, their improvement but also their difficulties as they work to better understand what helps them write successfully. Teachers think about and observe students' progress and response, or lack thereof; teachers also reflect on their own goals and responses, noticing which strategies work and which tools and techniques help which students the most. Such reflections occur through direct observation, but also through class discussions, individual conferences, and on the backs of papers, where students can, prior to turning in their assignment, take time to think about what they did and why.

Providing students opportunities to reflect on what they wrote and how they wrote it reinforces both their understanding and the skills they developed or used while writing.

When I'm writing a poem, most of the time I feel like a carpenter.

W. H. AUDEN

WHAT TO DO

These culminating activities can be done using any or all of the following: talking, speaking, writing, drawing.

• Students moving toward independence make choices—about how to approach or write about a given text—while composing, which they must now evaluate as they finish this text. The following questions and activities will help them in this process:

▶ Now that you are finishing or finished, what is the main idea in this paper (see Figure 36.1)?

▶ What strategies did you use to help you write this text? Did they prove effective? Explain how they did or did not help.

▶ Reviewing the habits of effective writers, how would you evaluate your own performance? If possible, provide specific examples to illustrate your remarks about decisions you made or actions you took while writing.

Name: _____

Main Idea Organizer: Reading, Writing, Watching, Listening

Subject:
What are you
writing about?

Subject				

Main Idea:
What are you (or the author)
saying *about* the subject? (I.e., what
is the *point* you or the author
wants to make?)

Main Idea				

Details
- Examples
- Stories
- Quotations
- Explanations

Detail		Detail		Detail	

FIGURE 36.1   Main Idea Organizer

• Have students return to the beginning of the text to see how the end relates to the beginning; do they maintain the same tone and main idea throughout? Rereading their paper with a specific question or purpose in mind—for example, Is my essay organized around this one idea?—gives them added purpose and thus helps you know what to look for while reading.

• Students can go back to their notes to review what they wanted to accomplish with a paper and compare that with what they *did* accomplish. Are there any remaining ideas they forgot to include or fully develop?

• Have students use their learning log for individual reflection or as preparation for subsequent writing or discussions, responding to one of the following prompts:

> ▶ I learned . . .
>
> ▶ I discovered . . .
>
> ▶ I observed . . .
>
> ▶ I was surprised . . .
>
> ▶ I am beginning to wonder . . .
>
> ▶ I now realize . . .
>
> ▶ I would like to find out more about . . .
>
> ▶ I am still confused by . . .

• Ask students what connections they can make to what they read, wrote, and studied before this text.

• Ask students what structures, textual features, devices, or techniques they used in this text that were new to them or particularly difficult. How effectively did they use them, and for what purpose?

• Have students explain what is the best way for the reader to assess and evaluate their reading of this text.

CLASSROOM CONNECTION

These two examples come from students who were asked to reflect on what helped them write about and better understand the texts they had read:

> I believe that getting into pairs and discussing our essays really helped. I got to see another's essay and compare it to mine. It helped me see where I was strong and weak in my essay. It was hard to only view your own words in a class assignment, so seeing how another classmate approached the assignment really

helped me. I also liked how we got to revise it twice in class and make it better. That night it made me think twice about what I wrote and I fixed things that could have been better in my essay.

After we read the poem, *Innocence*, we brainstormed some ideas for our poster. We decided on a boy from the island in *Lord of the Flies* with half a face of innocence and the other half of corruption. The innocent side is clean and sheltered. He is protected with adults that keep him from seeing more than he should. He is clean of violence. The other side portrays a mature experienced young boy. It is the same boy but very changed. He has war paint on his face, burnt skin, ripped clothes, and messed up hair. These are all things a parent can protect their children from. This side of the boy is exposed and very changed. He can now live without a grown-up. He has changed into a corrupted, aggressive, and guilty young boy.

In the poem, Thom Gunn says, "Ran into manhood, ignorant of the past." This quote explains our drawing in a way. This boy had simply run into manhood. It slapped him in the face and made him completely forget the past. In *Lord of the Flies*, Piggy kept on referring to his aunt's instruction while he was on the island. He was still innocent because he still felt guilty when he disobeyed rules that applied to him at home. The other kids immediately disobeyed rules and made up their own. That was a start of corruption. That was the start of the left side of the face.

RECOMMENDED RESOURCE

Hillocks, George Jr. 1995. *Teaching Writing as Reflective Practice*. New York: Teachers College Press.

Look for Patterns of Error and Progress

37

RATIONALE

Patterns are observable. They provide information. They help us see how things—genes, the weather, and, yes, writers—behave. A writer's style reveals patterns of usage and preferences as to how words are arranged. Patterns also give teachers valuable insight into each writer's growth, needs, and understanding of how writing works. For the struggling student, whose writing may resemble a minefield of errors, patterns make improvement possible: we can focus on one type of error the student keeps making or one type of sentence that will help the student begin to communicate more effectively. For the student who is learning English, patterns differ, and often by virtue of the culture or native language; Chinese speakers typically make different decisions or errors than do Spanish-speaking students, for example. Developing teachers' and students' awareness of these patterns enables them to focus on these errors and thereby achieve greater control over what they write and how they write it.

It is easy to associate patterns with errors; however, many patterns indicate growth or the conscious effort to add new skills to the writer's repertoire. Students studying different sentence patterns, for example, will inevitably make mistakes as they fumble toward fluency, learning to control that introductory phrase or properly place the correlative conjunctions. So, too, will students trying to improve in the area of word choice go through an inevitable period of "thesaurus overload" or usage errors as they reach for greater control of and power with language when they write.

> Errors are unintentional and unprofitable intrusions upon the consciousness of the reader.
>
> MINA SHAUGHNESSY

WHAT TO DO

Direct or guided instruction in some aspect of writing (e.g., use of free modifiers or more complicated sentence patterns) often yields patterns of error or misuse that you can anticipate. In *The Teaching Gap* (1999), Stigler and Hiebert describe "lesson study" in Japan, a process whereby teachers create lessons designed to challenge students and extend their fluency in some area. A crucial aspect of this method is to choose problems that will yield predictable errors if students do not understand the concept being taught. The same patterns of error will appear when teaching various aspects of writing, especially grammar and sentence patterns. When teaching some new aspect of writing, or pushing students to become more sophisticated in the use of it, try the following:

• Anticipate the type of errors or difficulties students will have and be prepared to address them through responsive, timely instruction. Consider using sample errors to clarify and illustrate correct and incorrect use.

• Use student examples that represent common patterns of error *and* examples that show effective use or initial fluency. Take these examples and put them on the overhead, a computer monitor, or a handout; then think aloud about what the students are doing. Direct their attention to the appropriate use and the pattern of error so students learn to see them and where to look.

• Discuss, when appropriate, the types of errors you see appearing. These might include:

  ▶ Organizational errors

  ▶ Grammatical errors

  ▶ Syntactic errors

  ▶ Mechanical errors

  ▶ Spelling errors

• Develop your own awareness of the different sources of these errors, in part to remind you that they are not necessarily the consequence of bad or lazy writing. Some possible sources include:

  ▶ Ignorance or misunderstanding of the rule or concept

  ▶ Inexperience (i.e., lack of fluency)

  ▶ Confusion (about what to do, how to do it, or when to do it)

  ▶ Interference (from writer's primary language)

  ▶ Learning differences (e.g., language processing disorder that results in patterns or error)

• Directly teach patterns as an initial step toward greater fluency. You can introduce various sentence or paragraph patterns, for example, through minilessons that respond to emerging needs.

• Make patterns visible. Some teachers, whether using Jane Schaffer's methods or their own, use color to visually reveal or have students correctly identify the patterns. Teachers might ask students, for instance, to use a blue highlighter or crayon to indicate the appositives throughout their paper; or they might have students use a yellow marker to indicate all the verbs in order to study the outbreak of passive verbs the teacher observed on this latest essay.

• When reading papers, use patterns to make your work easier and your conferences more effective. Bill Strong (2001) writes:

> I tried some of the inductive approaches to pattern recognition with the basic writers. Scanning a student text, for example, I might find a transition word or phrase and use this as an exemplar for the concept of signposts. . . . Increasingly, too, when students wanted me to edit their papers, I'd simply put check marks in the margin, each one signaling an error in spelling, punctuation, or usage. I then used the marks as the basis for coaching. (19)

I often use a variation on this technique: When reading a paper that is part of a unit on writing instruction, I write one or two words at the top and put a few check marks in the margins where those patterns appear. So I might write "Transitions" at the top of the paper, and place a check mark where they used, did not use, or ineffectively used a transition; then in a conference, I will hone in on that one aspect of writing, teaching to their individual pattern, which gives them one or two reasonable goals to focus on when revising.

• Some teachers find it useful to have students keep track of their patterns so they know what to look for and have a record of what they've learned. This way of making writing instruction more individualized can be useful in the right setting, though it is difficult to juggle or monitor in larger classes or when the teacher lacks the ability to juggle that extra ball.

• Use the Six Traits rubric (see Figure 38.1) or, when preparing students for the state writing exam, the state scoring guide to teach them those patterns essential to success on the test. Students in California, for example, learn that their tendency to not provide supporting details results in a pattern of vague, uninteresting writing that will earn a score of 2 and thus prevent them from passing the exit exam.

It's important to end with a few positive comments about patterns. Patterns are a blessing to the writing teacher: give me a student who uses the passive verb form throughout his paper any day over the one whose errors are random. A pattern of error is a doorway to targeted, effective, and efficient writing instruction that will result in improvement almost immediately in many cases. Also, error is often, especially in stronger writers, the natural result of reaching for greater power, more control;

173

think of the gymnast who adds a flip to her routine on the balance beam. She will fall many times, each error providing her useful information she can use to adjust her performance, so long as the errors form some sort of predictable pattern. We should also hope to see errors throughout the year, for if students are not making errors, they are not trying new things and thus are not learning or improving. Error is an invitation to both student and teacher to take the next step toward becoming a fluent writer.

RECOMMENDED RESOURCE

Shaughnessy, Mina P. 1977. *Errors and Expectations: A Guide for the Teacher of Basic Writing.* New York: Oxford University Press.

Know the Terms, Principles, and Concepts of Effective Writing

38

RATIONALE

I grew up in Sacramento in the late 1970s, when the greatest swim coach in the world, Sherm Chavor, worked his magic on many kids at my high school. Whenever people spoke of Chavor, they emphasized that he had not been a swimmer himself but somehow knew how to get Olympic performances out of those who did swim. Writing doesn't work that way: you cannot teach what you do not know how to do yourself. When we teach writing, we are attempting to teach much more than how to write a nice sentence; we are instilling habits, developing their ear, improving their capacity, teaching them strategies, and, of course, enhancing their knowledge and skills about what good writing is and how it works.

Teaching students to write the documents essential to a given class (e.g., lab reports for science, research reports or essay exams for social science, essays and speeches for English language arts) requires that the teacher know not just what writing *is* but how writing works and how writers think. They must also understand how to teach it, how one progresses toward mastery of the many different domains and demands of writing. The terms and concepts students need to know depend on the class and its goals. Advanced Placement students, for example, must be trained to use sophisticated literary terms and styles so they can demonstrate a university-level understanding on their written exams. Most students, on the other hand, need to know the basic terms needed to discuss their writing and the ideas of others through their writing on assignments for the class and such state exams as the exit exam.

One reason I like the Six Traits of Effective Writing model is that it is manageable, succinct; no doubt one could come up with the twelve or twenty traits of effective writing, but I can't juggle that many balls. If I can concentrate on knowing these terms, all of which I can use in the classroom and teach to my students (see my one-page synthesis of the six traits in Figure 38.1), my job seems possible, my task more realistic. Moreover, to condense the traits of effective writing into six domains helps to demystify writing and make it seem more accessible to my students, which is the heart of our enterprise, after all.

Writing teachers draw upon three distinct areas of expertise. We must know our students. We must know how to teach. And we must know something about writing itself.

RALPH FLETCHER, FROM *WHAT A WRITER NEEDS*

The Traits of Effective Writing

IDEA DEVELOPMENT: The heart, main idea, or thesis of a text; refers to the details, examples, or images that develop and support the main idea.

5 Text is clear and focused; captures reader's attention.
- ☐ Topic is narrow and manageable.
- ☐ Details are relevant, interesting, vivid, accurate.
- ☐ Point is clear; tells whole story; no trivia.
- ☐ Details support the paper's main idea.
- ☐ Ideas engage, inspire, or intrigue reader.

3 Text's ideas are focused but general, obvious.
- ☐ Topic is fairly broad, but understandable.
- ☐ Details are loosely related, obvious, or dull.
- ☐ Point vague; gives general idea; incomplete.
- ☐ Details provide weak support for main idea.
- ☐ Ideas leave reader guessing; not specific.

1 Text lacks clear ideas, purpose, and details.
- ☐ Topic lacking; no evident focus or purpose.
- ☐ Details are missing, incorrect, or unclear.
- ☐ Makes no point; cannot identify main idea.
- ☐ Details repeat each other; seem random.
- ☐ Ideas confuse and frustrate the reader.

ORGANIZATION: The internal structure of ideas. Effective organization begins with a purposeful lead and moves toward a logical, thoughtful ending.

5 Order compels, enhances, and moves ideas.
- ☐ Introduction intrigues, invites; conclusion resolves.
- ☐ Thoughtful transitions show how ideas connect.
- ☐ Sequencing is logical and effective.
- ☐ Pacing is well controlled and purposeful.
- ☐ Organization flows smoothly; matches purpose.

3 Order moves reader through with confusion.
- ☐ Introduction and conclusion are evident, weak.
- ☐ Transitions often work well; connections are vague.
- ☐ Sequencing shows some logic but lacks control.
- ☐ Pacing is inconsistent but fairly well controlled.
- ☐ Organization offers limited support; inappropriate.

1 Order is missing or random; no identifiable structure.
- ☐ Introduction and conclusion ineffective/missing.
- ☐ Transitions and connections absent or confusing.
- ☐ Sequencing is random; lacks any purpose.
- ☐ Pacing is awkward, frustrating, or missing.
- ☐ Organization makes it hard to identify main idea.

VOICE: You hear the writer's heart and soul, conviction and wit; the text has energy and connects you to both the writing and the writer.

5 Writing is compelling, engaging; aware of audience.
- ☐ Tone is interesting and appropriate for audience and the purpose.
- ☐ Author's presence is evident, powerful.
- ☐ Expository writing is committed, persuasive.
- ☐ Narrative writing is honest, engaging, personal.

3 Writing seems sincere but not engaged; it's plain.
- ☐ Tone is nondescript; shows limited awareness of audience; not very appropriate for purpose.
- ☐ Author sounds earnest and pleasing, but safe.
- ☐ Expository writing shows minimal commitment.
- ☐ Narrative writing is reasonably sincere but plain.

1 Writer is indifferent, distanced from topic/audience.
- ☐ Tone shows no awareness of audience; inappropriate for the audience or purpose.
- ☐ Author sounds monotone, flat, even bored.
- ☐ Expository writing lacks any commitment.
- ☐ Narrative writing shows no attempt at voice.

FIGURE 38.1   Six Traits summary scoring guide. Adapted by Jim Burke from the Six Traits of Effective Writing from Northwest Regional Educational Laboratory. Visit <*www.nurel.org*> for more info.

May be copied for classroom use. Writing Reminders *by Jim Burke (Heinemann, Portsmouth, NH); © 2003.*

WORD CHOICE: The right word, used in the right way, at the right time. The writer chooses words that create the intended effect, impression, or mood.

5 Words are precise, interesting, engaging, powerful.
- □ Words are specific, accurate; meaning is clear.
- □ Words and phrases are striking and memorable.
- □ Language is natural, effective, and appropriate.
- □ Verbs are lively, nouns precise, modifiers effective.
- □ Choices enhance and clarify meaning.

3 Words are common and obvious; they lack energy.
- □ Words are adequate and correct in a general sense.
- □ Words and phrases convey, but aren't memorable.
- □ Language reaches for color; thesaurus overload.
- □ Verbs are passive: nouns common; modifiers dull.
- □ Choices are random: first word that came to mind.

1 Words are simple or vague; limited in scope.
- □ Words are nonspecific, distracting, and vague.
- □ Words and phrases are dull; detract from meaning.
- □ Language is used incorrectly, carelessly.
- □ Verbs, nouns, adjectives show limited vocabulary.
- □ Jargon or clichés distract, mislead; redundant.

SENTENCE FLUENCY: Language that flows with rhythm and grace, logic and music. Sentences are well crafted and want to be read aloud.

5 Writing flows with rhythm and cadence. Elegant.
- □ Sentences are constructed to enhance meaning.
- □ Sentences vary in length and structure.
- □ Sentences use purposeful, varied beginnings.
- □ Connecting words join and build on other words.
- □ Writing has cadence; it moves, has a music to it.

3 Writing moves along but feels businesslike.
- □ Sentences are routine; they lack craft and music.
- □ Sentences are usually constructed correctly.
- □ Sentences are not all alike; there is some variety.
- □ Connecting words absent; reader hunts for clues.
- □ Parts invite reading aloud; choppy, awkward, stiff.

1 Writing lacks flow; it is difficult to read.
- □ Sentences ramble, are incomplete or awkward.
- □ Sentences do not connect to each other at all.
- □ Sentences begin the same way; monotonous.
- □ Endless or no connectives (and, so then, because).
- □ The text does invite reading aloud; no music.

CONVENTIONS: Includes punctuation, spelling, grammar, and usage. It does not include layout, formatting, or handwriting. The final editing phase.

5 Observes and uses standard conventions; few errors.
- □ Spelling is mostly correct, even on difficult words.
- □ Punctuation is accurate, even creative and effective.
- □ Capitalization skills are evident and consistent.
- □ Grammar and usage are correct and enhance the text.
- □ Paragraphing is sound; reinforces organization.
- □ Writer may manipulate conventions for style.

3 Reasonable control of conventions; distracting errors.
- □ Spelling mostly correct; errors on difficult words.
- □ End punctuation mostly correct; internal errors.
- □ Capitalization generally correct; some errors.
- □ Grammar and usage problems are not serious.
- □ Paragraphing lacks cohesion and organization.

1 Errors distract the reader and make reading difficult.
- □ Spelling errors are frequent and distracting.
- □ Punctuation is often missing or incorrect.
- □ Capitalization is random; only easiest are correct.
- □ Grammar and usage errors are obvious and serious.
- □ Paragraphing is missing, irregular, or infrequent.

FIGURE 38.2 *Continued.* Adapted by Jim Burke from the Six Traits of Effective Writing from Northwest Regional Educational Laboratory. Visit <*www.nwrel.org*> for more info.

WHAT TO DO

Learning any language requires constant use and effective feedback if one is to become fluent. The terms and concepts of effective writing are no different. Here are some ways you can learn and teach these principles to your students:

Examine your assignments and state writing tests for academic vocabulary they need to know. See the academic vocabulary list in Figure 38.2 for a sense of what you must know and teach when it comes to writing.

Model the use of writer's language, consciously choosing the words appropriate to the type of writing you are teaching. Thus, if teaching persuasive writing, use those words that apply to argument, such as *fallacies* and *evidence*, words they might know but concepts they may not associate with writing.

Anticipate which terms will be unfamiliar or troublesome for your students and teach them these words immediately. This is especially crucial for English learners who may not be able to succeed on an assignment if they do not know what an *essay* is or are not familiar with the more figurative, academic use of the term *point*, as in "prove your point."

Develop and improve upon your own understanding of writing—its terms, techniques, and concepts—by:

- Reading models of effective writing as well as books and articles about how to teach writing. I find the following books especially helpful:
  - *Write to Learn*, by Donald Murray
  - *Creating Writers*, by Vicki Spandel
  - *What a Writer Needs*, by Ralph Fletcher
  - *Style*, by Joe Williams
  - *Writer's Inc.*, by Patrick Sebranek, Dave Kemper, and Verne Meyer
  - *The Reading/Writing Connection*, by Carol Booth Olson
- Writing with students and on your own (see Reminder 1)
- Reflecting on what you do as both a writer and a teacher that works with different students
- Studying the writing tasks students must master and for which they must prepare (e.g., SAT, exit exams, AP tests) in order to identify the specific skills they must have, terms they must know, and capacities they must develop to be successful

Academic Vocabulary

A thorough survey of various textbooks, assignments, content area standards, and examinations yields the following list of words. You cannot expect to succeed on assignments if you do not understand the directions. The words fall into several categories, which are not identified on this sheet: nouns (e.g., what you read or create); verbs (e.g., what the assignment asks you to do); adjectives (e.g., specific details about what you must do); and adverbs, which provide very important information about how to do the assignment.

1. abbreviate	34. brainstorm	67. confirm	100. describe	133. exaggerate
2. abstract	35. brief	68. consequence	101. detail	134. examine
3. according	36. calculate	69. consider	102. detect	135. example
4. acronym	37. caption	70. consist	103. determine	136. excerpt
5. address	38. category	71. consistent	104. develop	137. exclude
6. affect	39. cause	72. consistently	105. devise	138. exercise
7. alter	40. character	73. constant	106. diction	139. exhibit
8. always	41. characteristic	74. constitutes	107. differentiate	140. explain
9. analogy	42. characterize	75. consult	108. dimension	141. explore
10. analysis	43. chart	76. contend	109. diminish	142. expository
11. analyze	44. chronology	77. context	110. direct	143. extract
12. annotate	45. citation	78. continuum	111. discipline	144. fact
13. anticipate	46. cite	79. contradict	112. discover	145. factor
14. application	47. claim	80. control	113. discriminate	146. feature
15. apply	48. clarify	81. convert	114. discuss	147. figurative
16. approach	49. class	82. convey	115. distinguish	148. figure
17. appropriate	50. clue	83. copy	116. domain	149. focus
18. approximate	51. code	84. correlate	117. draft	150. footer
19. argue	52. coherent	85. correspond	118. draw	151. foreshadow
20. argument	53. common	86. credible	119. edit	152. form
21. arrange	54. compare	87. credit	120. effect	153. format
22. articulate	55. compile	88. criteria	121. elements	154. former
23. aspects	56. complement	89. critique	122. emphasize	155. formulate
24. assemble	57. complete	90. crucial	123. employ	156. fragment
25. assert	58. compose	91. cumulative	124. equal	157. frame
26. assess	59. composition	92. debate	125. equivalent	158. frequently
27. associate	60. conceive	93. deduce	126. essay	159. general
28. assume	61. concise	94. defend	127. essential	160. genre
29. assumption	62. conclude	95. define	128. establish	161. graph
30. audience	63. conclusion	96. demand	129. estimate	162. graphic
31. authentic	64. concrete	97. demonstrate	130. evaluate	163. header
32. background	65. conditions	98. depict	131. event	164. heading
33. body	66. conduct	99. derive	132. evidence	165. highlight

FIGURE 38.2   Academic vocabulary list

May be copied for classroom use. Writing Reminders *by Jim Burke (Heinemann, Portsmouth, NH); © 2003.*

166. hypothesize	205. margin	244. point	283. relevant	322. style
167. identify	206. mean	245. point of view	284. rephrase	323. subject
168. illustrate	207. measure	246. portray	285. report	324. subjective
169. imitate	208. metaphor	247. possible	286. represent	325. subsequent
170. imply	209. method	248. preclude	287. request	326. substitute
171. inclined	210. model	249. predict	288. require	327. succinct
172. include	211. modify	250. prefix	289. requisite	328. suggest
173. incorporate	212. monitor	251. prepare	290. respond	329. sum
174. indicate	213. motivation	252. presume	291. responsible	330. summarize
175. indirect	214. narrative	253. preview	292. restate	331. summary
176. infer	215. narrator	254. previous	293. results	332. support
177. influence	216. never	255. primary	294. reveal	333. survey
178. inform	217. notation	256. prior	295. review	334. symbolize
179. inquire	218. note	257. probable	296. revise	335. synonym
180. instructions	219. notice	258. procedure	297. root	336. synthesize
181. integrate	220. objective	259. process	298. rule	337. table
182. intent	221. observe	260. produce	299. scan	338. technique
183. intention	222. occur	261. profile	300. score	339. term
184. interact	223. omit	262. project	301. sequence	340. test
185. intermittent	224. opinion	263. prompt	302. series	341. theme
186. interpret	225. oppose	264. proofread	303. set	342. thesis
187. introduce	226. optional	265. property	304. setting	343. time line
188. introduction	227. order	266. propose	305. show	344. tone
189. invariably	228. organize	267. prose	306. signal	345. topic
190. investigate	229. origins	268. prove	307. significance	346. trace
191. involve	230. outline	269. purpose	308. simile	347. trait
192. irony	231. pace	270. quotation	309. skim	348. transition
193. irrelevant	232. paraphrase	271. quote	310. solve	349. translate
194. isolate	233. participation	272. rank	311. source	350. typically
195. italics	234. passage	273. rare	312. spatial	351. unique
196. judge	235. pattern	274. rarely	313. specific	352. utilize
197. key	236. perform	275. reaction	314. speculate	353. valid
198. label	237. perspective	276. recall	315. stance	354. variation
199. likely	238. persuade	277. reduce	316. standard	355. vary
200. list	239. place	278. refer	317. state	356. verify
201. literal	240. plagiarism	279. reflect	318. statement	357. viewpoint
202. locate	241. plan	280. regular	319. strategy	358. voice
203. logical	242. plausible	281. relate	320. structure	
204. main	243. plot	282. relationship	321. study	

FIGURE 38.2 *Continued*

May be copied for classroom use. Writing Reminders by Jim Burke (Heinemann, Portsmouth, NH); © 2003.

Teach students the traditional proofreader's marks as a way of developing their awareness of these different terms and aspects of writing. Not only will they learn to use them, but their understanding of the ideas will make them more attentive writers who will, when editing, recognize and repair such errors.

Teach students the terms that govern the conventions not only of writing (e.g., *clauses* and *phrases*) but of layout and design. Using terms like *header* and *footer, italics* and *justified margins* bolsters their knowledge of texts and improves their sensitivity to the different effects these features have on a text and the reader.

When possible, use complementary terms to discuss writing and reading. For example, when talking about a Joan Didion essay or the Declaration of Independence, use such terms as *tone* and *claim*, or *voice* and *transitions*; use these same terms to discuss students' writing.

Have a current, comprehensive, user-friendly writing reference available. I prefer *Writer's Inc.: A Student Handbook for Writing and Learning* (Sebranek, Kemper, and Meyer 2001) because it is so complete and effectively organized. I can learn, for example, about these essential aspects of writing in little over twenty pages:

- *Writing topics:* descriptive, narrative, expository, and persuasive
- *Writing techniques:* allusion, flashback, irony, personification, etc.
- *Writing terms:* argumentation, exposition, inductive reasoning, tone
- *Writing forms:* creative, persuasive, academic, workplace, etc.

RECOMMENDED RESOURCE

Sebranek, Patrick, Dave Kemper, and Verne Meyer. 2001. *Writer's Inc.: A Student Handbook for Writing and Learning.* Wilmington, MA: Great Source.

39

Check for Understanding and Growth

RATIONALE

As writers move along the continuum toward independence, they and the teacher must monitor their progress with a variety of means. Students demonstrate their understanding of new ideas, strategies, and techniques by using each one correctly. Thus, for example, one can check for understanding of the concept of sentence fluency by watching the types of sentences the writer chooses over the course of time, or from one revision to the next. Or they might show their understanding of rhetorical devices or the passive voice by using or not using it accordingly. These concrete aspects of writing, and the improved use of them, offer the most useful, observable signs of progress; for this reason I have always passed when I have been given the chance to have others grade my students' papers. Of course, it would be nice to diminish my paper load, but we cannot let someone else, without any instructional context for or sensitivity to each student's trials and triumphs, do the work that will help us do ours better.

Such information about progress is only useful to the extent that it improves instruction and student performance. Such recursive teaching, in which the teacher and student reflect back on what they were trying to accomplish and then measure their progress against that standard, creates dynamic, responsive class instruction that builds students' capacity to do what we teach and the society expects.

Such a process raises the question of what evidence of understanding and growth we are willing (or, in some cases, able) to accept. The easy answer is that it depends. If, for example, I am teaching students strategies to help them generate ideas, I can observe their proficiency as I move around the room: if they have a web or list of ideas, something is working. Determining how well it is working requires closer scrutiny, which can only happen when I stop to check the quality of what the student is generating, or look at initial drafts as they begin to write. Substantial ideas will yield better writing, though perhaps not fluent writing at first, because of the potential complexity of the ideas; insubstantial ideas will stall, leaving the writer lost, feeling like there is nothing to say about their subject. Another example of evidence might be how they perform on a timed written test, if that is something we have taken time to rehearse or otherwise prepare for. How much they write, how they approach the task and topic—in short, how they behave as writers on such tests—offer insight into their understanding of their own writing process under such conditions.

Several other issues merit brief mention. Having students write in a variety of circumstances (see Reminder 29) gives the teacher the opportunity to see how well the student is able to apply their writing skills; the fluent writer is, like the child who has graduated from training wheels, able to ride the bike in all conditions with confidence. Writing in a variety of circumstances also keeps a check on *who* is doing the writing; sadly, some students have parents or other accomplices who will all but write the paper for them. Thus, having kids write in class on occasion provides important feedback about that student's (versus his parent's or tutor's) current ability and progress. Finally, when assessing understanding of ideas, it is worth remembering that some students come from cultures where it is shameful to admit you do not understand; these students are taught that any failure on their part to understand is an insult to the teacher, implying the teacher is a bad one. By creating a culture of security in the classroom, you can help such students feel more comfortable about admitting confusions.

WHAT TO DO

- Divide your efforts into three phases: before, during, and after:

  - *Before.* Assess their prior understanding of the concept or ability to do what you are asking.

  - *During.* Scaffold instruction using exemplars and guided instruction to support their initial learning as you introduce the concept, skill, or strategy.

  - *After.* Monitor their use and understanding to see if they continue to use and extend what they learned; look specifically for deeper understanding and continued improvement in this or a related area.

- Use portfolios to chart growth over the course of a semester or school year.

- Generate or ask students to provide evidence of their understanding and progress using multiple means and measures.

- Any final assessment information, regardless of the type of task, should be useful and make sense to the student (i.e., help them improve their performance), the teacher, and parents. It is a means, among other things, of explaining the student's performance.

- When designing culminating activities or final assessments, consider using these words in the prompt:

  - Explain
  - Interpret
  - Apply
  - Demonstrate
  - Synthesize

- Design this assessment so it will allow them (and you) to compare their performance on this unit or text with their performance on previous tasks or texts in order to measure their growth.

- When assessing understanding or performance, consider what is adequate in terms of data, time, and task.

- Decide and communicate honestly to your students the purpose of the assessment which might be any of the following:

  - To verify that they read something
  - To measure their understanding
  - To determine mastery of a type of writing or a specific skill
  - To determine what they need to learn or do next
  - To reflect on and thus deepen their understanding before moving on
  - To integrate all the knowledge they've gained in the course of this unit

- Consider what examples of a successful performance (via exemplar or rubric) you can provide them in the process of assessment and make these available early on so they know what success looks like.

- Create assessments that will reveal likely critical misunderstandings or misreadings.

- Allow students to explain or demonstrate their understanding using one of the following means: visual, written, spoken, or performed explanations—or a combination of any of these.

CLASSROOM CONNECTION

Here is the sequence I often use to introduce and improve students' use of new aspects of writing:

1. Give them a handout that explains the assignment and outlines the standards and instructional objectives.

2. Provide little in the way of actual instruction, as I want to see how they approach the assignment (e.g., see Weekly Poem assignment in Figure 45.3), thus establishing a baseline for understanding and ability.

3. Study their first efforts to see what patterns of error or skill appear.

4. Copy representative samples of common problems and successes to a handout and an overhead transparency.

5. In class, I pass back their papers and, using the overheads, think aloud about what the writers did that worked, why it worked, and how they achieved this outcome. I also talk about what they could have done to improve the writing even more.

6. Having further clarified what I expect, what a successful performance looks like, and how they can achieve it, I raise my expectations, sending them home to do it again, but better.

7. When I read the next set of papers, I look for specific progress in that area I focused on, while simultaneously looking for new exemplars I can use to further improve their ability. And so it goes: the best, most representative work at each level informs the others what they need to do to continue improving.

In the following note, a student explains what helped and why. We conferenced about his paper; I felt he was not showing a complete understanding of what he had read and I had taught; nor was he showing the progress I expected by this point in the unit. When the paper was completed and turned in, Nelson wrote:

Mr. Burke,

Thank you for letting me have extra time for my work. I really felt I needed it. I felt out of place since I wasn't here so I tried my best to get caught up. I feel that my writing is getting a little better as I move along because I have been re-reading it and looking for ways to improve it. When you talked to me it helped me think about my writing and how I have not been writing the best I can. I took that into thought and really tried harder. I got help from others and took more time to write. I think that I am improving by the second.

Nelson Tejada

Periodically throughout the year, I ask students to reflect on their growth as writers. The following sequence is one way to do so:

1. I have them jot down their *strengths*, those areas in which they are *improving*, and those areas in which they *need to improve*.

2. Then I ask them to make a continuum with a range of one to ten and identify where along that continuum of performance they are as writers at this stage.

3. Finally, I ask them to explain why they think they are at that point on the continuum (see Figure 39.1).

RECOMMENDED RESOURCE

Wiggins, Grant, and Jay McTighe. 1998. *Understanding by Design.* Alexandria, VA: Association of Supervision and Curriculum Development.

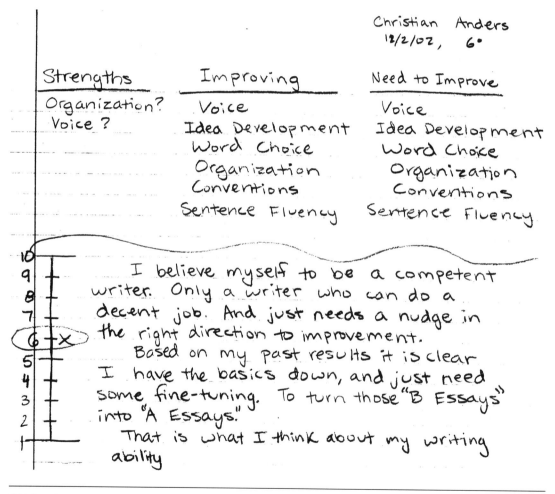

FIGURE 39.1   Self-evaluation done by Christian Anders

Compare Effective and Ineffective Writers

40

RATIONALE

We can only improve if we know the difference between what effective and ineffective writers do. Students working to improve their writing must be students *of* writing, examining what one does, how one works when writing to produce coherent, effective prose or poetry. The following activities offer a range of possibilities that will develop students' awareness of how successful student writers work and think.

Regularly referring to these different habits and techniqes also creates a common vocabulary that allows teachers and students to discuss what they are doing or need to do if they are to become more effective writers. Finally, discussing what writers do demystifies the process of writing, which is sometimes perceived as an activity people either can or cannot do. Donald Murray (2002) makes an effort at demystification by narrating his own process:

> People—many teachers included—make writing a big deal. It is, on many levels, a very complex intellectual issue, the way designing a new downtown hotel, office, and shopping plaza can be for an architect. But I'm just a worker, a carpenter of prose, and my job is obvious and easy. I will start with my first good teacher [for this essay] and work my way to my third and I will start with description, making myself re-see (and eventually my reader see) that first teacher. . . . Where do I start? In the beginning. "When I walked into my sixth grade classroom in September. . . . " (3)

WHAT TO DO

• Generate ideas about what effective and ineffective writers do using a T-chart (two-column organizer). As you generate, discuss, asking when appropriate, "Why do you think they do that (e.g., brainstorm ideas, read their writing aloud, etc.)?"

• Model effective techniques to show them what they look like or how they help.

This is not a novel to be tossed aside lightly. It should be thrown with great force.

DOROTHY PARKER

- Have students swap papers and read, respond to, and discuss what they did and why. This allows them to see other ways they could have approached a writing assignment or solved a problem they encountered when writing. If time allows, have them identify obstacles they encountered and discuss how they solved those problems.

- Discuss and revisit what effective writers do before, during, and after they write (see Figure 40.1). Have students respond to or reflect on their own writing using this approach; thus, they would explain what they did before, during, and after and what difference it made in the final result.

- Study what effective (and ineffective) writers do during different phases or areas of writing:

  ▶ Getting started
  ▶ Developing ideas
  ▶ Editing
  ▶ Revising

- Post the comparison on the classroom wall where everyone can see it. This will allow you to remind them of what they should do while writing in general. Also, add new details to it as time goes on and new insights arise.

- Post the Northwest Regional Educational Laboratory's Six Traits (Plus One) rubric (see Appendix B) on the classroom wall and give a copy to students. This will allow you to review what effective writers do.

- Model the behavior of an effective writer yourself or point out those students in your class who exemplify the different traits. Be sure to use examples from different students whenever possible. If you always showcase the same three students' work, everyone else will think they cannot meet your expectations no matter how hard they try.

- Provide examples of written work from current or past students to help students better understand what certain aspects of writing look like; also, discuss how they achieved the result they did on that particular assignment.

- Use the Six Traits scoring guide (Figure 38.1) in the following contexts to help students focus their attention on how they should write the assigned text:

  ▶ Before they write, review the characteristics of successful writers of such texts, modeling or providing exemplars of work produced on similar assignments to help students see what successful thinking looks like.

  ▶ During their writing, interrupt them and use the scoring guide descriptions as tools to help them reflect on their performance.

Effective Writers	Ineffective Writers

Before You Write

• Determine what you already know and need to learn.	• Begin writing without asking yourself what you know or need to learn.
• Read the directions.	• Ignore or barely look at the directions.
• Establish a purpose or a question you are trying to answer through your writing.	• Do not establish a purpose or, because you did not read the directions, establish an incorrect purpose; write with no question to answer.
• Ask others—classmates or the teacher—if you do not understand what you are supposed to do.	• Do not ask for help.
• Gather any tools, ideas, or materials you might need and determine how best to use them.	• Lack the tools, ideas, or materials that would help you be an effective, informed writer.
• Provide a quiet, studious environment in which to think, read, and write.	• Try to work in an environment filled with distractions.
• Establish appropriate and reasonable goals for the assignment, taking into consideration the demands of the text, your personal writing goals, and the time needed to write this particular text.	• Do not evaluate the demands or difficulties of your writing assignments. You just jump in and start writing without a goal or purpose in mind.
• Identify the type of text or genre so you know how to write it.	• Treat texts equally, writing them without consideration of audience, conventions, or voice.
• Generate ideas using a range of strategies; these ideas involve not only the subject but strategies you will use to write about it.	• Make no effort or do not know how to generate ideas about a topic.

While You Write

• Continually check what you write against the assignment, the text about which you are writing, and the question you are trying to answer through your writing.	• Never or rarely check the topic or the text about which you are writing; you charge on, more concerned with finishing than doing it correctly or well.
• Check for understanding as you write; if you get lost, you use various strategies to help you understand. You are a reflective, recursive writer.	• Pay no attention to whether you understand what you are writing about; if you get lost you do not use strategies to help you get unstuck.
• Make connections between what you are writing and your own experiences and knowledge.	• Do not make any connections; you may not see what you are reading as related to yourself or anything else.
• Ask questions to help you generate examples, details, or connections.	• Do not ask questions, which results in writing that lacks necessary information and useful examples.
• If writing about a text—that is, poem, book, film, or image—you return to it, rereading it to better understand it and find supporting details for the ideas you explore in your paper.	• If writing about a text, you do not reread it.
• Make notes and generate other possible approaches as you write, checking to see if they would improve the paper you are writing.	• Make no notes; do not consider alternative approaches.
• Evaluate and revise as necessary those essential aspects of effective writing: voice, organization, clarity, ideas, conventions, mechanics.	• Make no effort to evaluate or revise; you just get it down so you have something to turn in.

After You Write

• Check for understanding and success, asking such questions as, Do I understand what I wrote? and Did I achieve my stated purpose in this piece of writing? If necessary, you return to the text or consult others who can help you improve what you wrote.	• Do not check for understanding or consult others if you did not understand this assignment.
• Reread the topic or assignment so you can be sure you met the requirements.	• Do not revisit the topic; this may keep you from realizing you went off-topic.
• Edit for clarity.	• Do not edit for clarity.
• Edit for correctness.	• Do not edit for correctness.
• Reflect on what you did and how you did it so you can learn and do better on future writing assignments.	• Do not reflect on what you did. Make no effort to think about what worked or why.

FIGURE 40.1   Traits of effective and ineffective writers

Evaluators commonly use these anchoring sessions to help remind them what a successful performance looks like.

▶ After they've finished, have students use the scoring guide descriptions to evaluate their own performance, identifying those specific behaviors they employed or skills they used to write at that level. They could use the scoring guide in subsequent discussions with their groups, the class, or the teacher, as a tool to help them talk about not only what they wrote but *how*.

▶ Throughout the day or year, revisit the scoring guide to remember what you are helping students learn to master and what you must teach. It is also a good idea to consult the standards periodically (see Reminder 34).

RECOMMENDED RESOURCE

Spandel, Vicki. 2001. *Creating Writers: Through 6-Trait Writing Assessment and Instruction*. 3d ed. New York: Longman.

Use Writing Portfolios

41

RATIONALE

In *Educative Assessment*, Grant Wiggins (1998) offers the following possible uses of portfolios:

• As a showcase for the student's best work, as chosen by the student or the teacher

• As a showcase for the student's interests

• As a showcase for the student's growth

• As evidence of self-assessment and self-adjustment

• As evidence enabling professional assessment of student performance, based on a technically sound sample of work

• As a complete collection of student work for documentation and archiving

• As a constantly changing sample of work chosen by the student, reflecting different job applications and exhibitions over time

Wiggins sees several different implications in these examples. "Portfolios can primarily serve instruction or assessment; they can be focused primarily on documentation or evaluation; their contents can be defined by the student or by the teacher; they can be seen as a résumé, as a representative sample of overall performance (good and bad) or as a constantly changing exhibit" (190).

There are voices that stand out, like the voice at the dinner table whose next sentence you strain to hear.

LOUISE GLÜCK

WHAT TO DO

Many use portfolios to create what Wiggins (1998) calls an anthology. Students keep their work throughout the year, weeding it at the end of each semester and returning to certain pieces at different times for different

191

purposes. In June, I require that they create a final portfolio, which accomplishes several important ends:

• It provides students an opportunity to reflect on what they have done during the year. As Carol Jago writes, "It is important that students reflect on each essay they hand in, as well as their writing over a period of time (2002a, 111)." Such reflection can be especially important for students who forgot that they did some distinguished work during the course of the year. In short, it allows them to see the pieces of their education as forming a more coherent and, I hope, meaningful whole.

• It requires them to evaluate the value of their work and assign to it a final meaning (i.e., important enough to go in my portfolio, meaningless, transitional, etc.).

• It creates an opportunity to involve parents in the process of their child's education. This presentation of work to parents provides an important chance for the student to show them what he accomplished. Such exercises have the secondary benefit of showing the parents what is going on in the schools so when they talk to others, they can say, "Well, you know, the schools aren't all bad. Just last week, her teacher had us read her portfolio and I thought. . . ."

• Others recommend what they call an "active" portfolio (Wilcox 1997). Wilcox describes this type of portfolio as one that has "a diversity of artifacts which are assessed in a variety of ways. Although tests are not mentioned as an outcome of the *active* portfolio, traditional tests can be added to any portfolio. The point is that when different artifacts are evaluated by different evaluators, the chances increase for a more authentic assessment of the final portfolio." (36)

Others argue for a more schoolwide, common approach to the portfolio; such a portfolio might be adopted, for example, by the English department, as often happens. Moreover, such a portfolio might be aligned with state and district standards.

CLASSROOM CONNECTION

Here is one version of the handout I provide students in June as they begin to create their portfolios:

Overview   It's time to create your final portfolio of your junior year. First, sift through it and prepare to write a letter evaluating your work. Your reflective writing should refer to specific pieces of your work as examples of whatever you are saying (e.g., "I learned how to better support and develop my ideas when writing about literature. In my *All Quiet on the Western Front* journal, for example . . ."). Your portfolios provide me with the most insightful evaluation of my teaching and this course; I always look forward to reading through these at the end of each year, as they are (I hope) a validation of your progress and my efforts. They also provide you a final chance to argue your case by presenting evidence of your progress and accomplishments in this class.

Contents　　In your portfolio on the day of the final you should have the following:

☐　Table of contents with the following: date, type, title, strengths, weaknesses

☐　Samples from your journals that show your daily writing

☐　Your outside reading record (i.e., the titles and authors of the books you read)

☐　Evidence of at least one project you've done this year

☐　Your annotated bibliographies

☐　Your portfolio cover letter (placed in front of all your work, so that it serves as an introduction to and commentary on all that follows)

☐　Anything else that you feel completes the picture of your development this year as a reader, thinker, writer, and speaker

☐　Goals for the year

Cover Letter　　Write a letter to a prospective reader of your portfolio in which you provide a careful analysis of your progress since September. This reflective letter should address most of the following questions at some point:

☐　In which area have you progressed the most this year? How would you contrast your work in this area now with your work in September? What helped you improve in this area?

☐　Which piece of work this semester means the most to you? Why?

☐　Which piece of work this semester challenged you the most? Why? In what ways did it challenge you?

☐　How would you characterize your experiences as a reader this year? What did you read and how does that compare with what you read in the past? In what ways have you improved as a reader?

☐ What was your most memorable book this semester? What made it so memorable?

☐ What book did you like least this semester? Why was that?

In your conclusion or introduction, come up with a topic sentence in which you use an adjective or analogy to describe this semester as it relates to your work as a thinker, reader, and writer. Go on to explain what you mean and always use specific examples to support and clarify.

I encourage (and sometimes require) students to show their portfolio to their parents, asking only that the parents sign to show that they did, in fact, see it. Such presentations are one small way I can make public the work we do and help parents better understand their child's progress.

Figure 41.1 shows a sample of a schoolwide high school portfolio cover sheet.

RECOMMENDED RESOURCES

Mahoney, Jim. 2002. *Power and Portfolios: Best Practices for High School Classrooms.* Portsmouth, NH: Heinemann.

Sunstein, Bonnie S., and Jonathan H. Lovell, eds. 2000. *The Portfolio Standard: How Students Can Show Us What They Know and Are Able to Do.* Portsmouth, NH: Heinemann.

Burlingame High School Portfolio

Student Name: _____   ID Number: _____

Graduating Class: _____

	WRITING	9	10	11	12
9	☐ Biographical Essay		▓	▓	▓
9–12	☐ Response to Literature				
11	☐ Research Report	▓	▓		▓
10	☐ Business Letter	▓		▓	▓
10	☐ Technical Document	▓		▓	▓
9–12	☐ Expository: (9) Analytical (10) Persuasive (11) Report (12) Reflective				
12	☐ College Essay/Personal Statement	▓	▓	▓	
11–12	☐ Resume	▓	▓		
9–12	☐ Personal Choice (e.g., poetry, fiction, art, multimedia works)				
9–12	☐ Personal Choice (e.g., poetry, fiction, art, multimedia works)				
	READING				
9–12	☐ Annotated Bibliography				
	SPEAKING				
	☐ Expository/Persuasive Speech				
	☐ Oral Report on Historical Investigation				
	☐ Oral Response to Literature				
	☐ Multimedia Presentation				
	☐ Interview (of someone else)				
	ASSESSING				
	☐ District Writing Assessment (September)				
	☐ District Writing Assessment (June)				
	☐ Gates-McGinitie Reading and Vocabulary		▓	▓	▓
	☐ Golden State Composition Exam	▓	▓		▓
	☐ Golden State Reading and Literature Exam	▓		▓	▓
	☐ California High School Exit Exam	▓			
	☐ SAT 9				▓
	☐ AP Exam	▓			
	PORTFOLIO				
	☐ Goals Essay (Reflective Writing)			▓	
	☐ Portfolio Cover Letter (Reflective Writing)	▓			

FALL TEACHERS		Fall	SPRING TEACHERS	Spring
9				
10				
11				
12				

FIGURE 41.1   Sample department portfolio checklist

42 Revisit the Six Features of Effective English Instruction

RATIONALE

The following six features come from a study conducted over several years by Judith Langer at the Center on English Learning and Achievement. This study, described in *Beating the Odds: Teaching Middle and High School Students to Read and Write Well* (1999), focused on middle and high school English classes, though in truth these same six features would apply equally well to other subject areas. Throughout the report, Langer and her team emphasize that these six features are not independent of each other but are instead interrelated and supportive of one another. Langer provides examples of activities to illustrate how each feature might be addressed in the classroom. The following information is adapted from Langer's report.

WHAT TO DO

Feature One: Students learn skills and knowledge in multiple lesson types.

ACTIVITIES THAT WORK
- Providing overt, targeted instruction and review as models for peer and self-evaluation
- Teaching skills, mechanics, or vocabulary that can be used during *integrated* activities such as literature discussions
- Using all three kinds of instruction to scaffold ways to think and discuss (e.g., summarizing, justifying answers, and making connections)

Feature Two: Teachers integrate test preparations into instruction. Using district and state standards and goals, teachers and administrators work together on the following activities.

ACTIVITIES THAT WORK
- Analyze the demands of a test
- Identify connections to the standards and goals

- Design and align curriculum to meet the demands of the test
- Develop instructional strategies that enable students to build the necessary skills
- Ensure that skills are learned across the year and across grades
- Make overt connections between and among instructional strategies, tests, and current learning
- Develop and implement model lessons that integrate test preparation into the curriculum

Feature Three: Teachers make connections across instruction, curriculum, grades, and life.

ACTIVITIES THAT WORK

- Making overt connections between and across the curriculum, students' lives, literature, and literacy
- Planning lessons that connect with each other, with test demands, and with students' growing knowledge and skills
- Developing goals and strategies that meet students' needs and are intrinsically connected to the larger curriculum
- Weaving even unexpected intrusions into integrated experiences for students
- Selecting professional development activities that are related to the school's standards and curriculum framework

Feature Four: Students learn strategies for doing the work.

ACTIVITIES THAT WORK

- Providing rubrics that students review, use, and even develop
- Designing models and guides that lead students to understand how to approach each task
- Supplying prompts that support thinking

Feature Five: Students are expected to be generative thinkers.

ACTIVITIES THAT WORK

- Exploring texts from many points of view (e.g., social, historical, ethical, political, personal)
- Extending literary understanding beyond initial interpretations
- Researching and discussing issues generated by literary texts and by student concerns
- Extending research questions beyond their original focus

- Developing ideas in writing that go beyond the superficial
- Writing from different points of view
- Designing follow-up lessons that cause students to move beyond their initial thinking

Feature Six: Classrooms foster cognitive collaboration.

ACTIVITIES THAT WORK

- Students work in small and large groups to
  - Share their ideas and responses to literary texts, questions, and so on.
  - Question and challenge each other's ideas and responses
  - Create new responses
- Teachers provide support during discussions and group work by
  - Moving from group to group
  - Modeling questions and comments that will cause deeper discussion and analysis
  - Encouraging questions and challenges that cause students to think more deeply

RECOMMENDED RESOURCE

Langer, Judith. 2002. *Effective Literacy Instruction*. Urbana, IL: National Council of Teachers of English.

www.cela.albany.edu

Consider the Traits of Effective Literacy Instruction

43

RATIONALE

Literacy instruction includes more than reading, of course; writing is at the heart of being literate, as is language. Richard Allington (1999) identifies ten core principles for effective literacy instruction in reading and language arts:

> Much has been learned in the past decade about classroom instruction that effectively develops the reading and writing of all children. The following ten principles provide a brief summary.
>
> 1. *Nothing is better than reading and writing to develop children's reading and writing.* Do kids read for at least one hour each day? Do kids write for at least one-half hour each day?
> 2. *Most reading should be easy reading (high accuracy/good comprehension). An 80/20 ratio (of easy to harder) seems about right.* Do all children have texts of appropriate complexity? Do they choose some of their books?
> 3. *Children do not develop comprehension strategies by answering questions after reading.* Are active comprehension strategies explicitly modeled on a daily basis? In content subjects as well as reading sessions? Do children write daily to demonstrate understanding?
> 4. *Children do not develop composing strategies from red ink corrections (nor from just writing).* Are composing strategies explicitly modeled in front of children on a regular basis?
> 5. *Children do not develop decoding strategies from drills or dittoes (nor from just reading).* Are useful decoding strategies explicitly modeled for children on a regular basis? Is decoding instruction linked to spelling/composing? Are decoding lessons focused on word structure?
> 6. *Children benefit from an integrated, content-oriented reading/language arts curriculum.* Are the interrelationships between the language arts obvious in the curriculum children experience

A student should not be taught more than he can think about.

ALFRED NORTH WHITEHEAD

each day, each week, each year? For instance, is the decoding strand linked to the spelling/composing strand? The composition strand to the comprehension strand? Do each day's instructional activities exhibit linkages? Do children learn from reading?

7. *Some children need access to larger amounts of more intensive instructional support and enhanced opportunities to read and write with instructional support.* Do lower-achieving students (e.g. Title I, learning disabled) participate in instructional support efforts that substantially increase the amount of reading and language arts time they have and is personalized instruction provided? Do they actually read and write more daily?

8. *Thoughtful literacy is the new general goal for reading and language arts instruction. Basic literacy/minimum competence will no longer suffice.* A wealth of school tasks emphasizing summarizing, organizing, synthesizing, comparing, analyzing, creating, and presenting texts is evidence of thoughtful instruction K–12.

9. *Developing independent readers and writers is critical to developing thoughtful, lifelong learners. Easy access to books is critical support for fostering independent reading activity.* Do classrooms have large and enticing supplies of books and magazines nicely displayed and available to read at school and home? Is the school library open weekends and summers?

10. *Access to consistently high quality classroom instruction is more important than which parents children have or which special programs they attend.* Good classroom instruction is absolutely central to student achievement. Do not expect either parents or special programs to solve children's literacy learning problems.

Effective literacy programs balance but include the following needs or traits:

They have cohesion. Allington's guiding principles offer the benefit of his wisdom and research; still others have different ideas we might use to reflect on what makes for effective literacy instruction. Carol Jago, for example, says that lack of effective writing is not always the students' fault. She says, "Our methods of teaching lack cohesion. Within the same English Department, one teacher's writing program may consist entirely of personal journals while down the hall another assigns five-paragraph essays. No wonder students are confused (2002a, 7)."

Goals and directions are clearly and completely articulated. Teachers take time to identify the concepts, skills, and content they are trying to teach.

This means not only instructing students in the conventions that govern the particular type of writing but providing coherent directions for doing the work. When possible and appropriate, such directions will be aligned with the standards students must learn during their time in that course.

Assignments and instructional techniques are culturally sensitive. Writing is a personal act. The topics we create and assignments we design include a range of complex cultural aspects. The simple concept of an argument is dangerous to students from some cultures. Effective writing instruction must anticipate and prepare students from all cultures to develop the academic and intellectual literacies they need to succeed in this one.

Writing workshops, when used, are run by a teacher who:

- Expects that every student will write, read, and find satisfaction in literacy
- Organizes a predictable environment
- Makes regular, sustained time in class for writing and reading
- Allows choices from day one of topic, genre, pacing, and audience
- Works with whole pieces of writing and whole pieces of literature, not paragraphs or excerpts or chapters
- Offers response while individuals are engaged in the acts of writing and reading and moves among the students
- Publishes students' writing and helps writers find real audiences
- Helps readers find real audiences for their reading
- Serves as an editor of final drafts
- Teaches skills, conventions, and strategies to individuals in context
- Keeps records of students' growth and helps students keep their own records
- Evaluates writing and reading for growth over time, in collaboration with students
- Uses minilessons or some other forum as an opportunity to create a frame of reference for students to think together about writing and reading, to create a group "lore" about literacy
- Reads literature for himself or herself and shares it
- Writes literature for himself or herself and shares it
- And acts like a joyful reader and writer to whom students would wish to apprentice themselves (Atwell 1991, 140)

While it is important to consider what effective writing looks like within a classroom, Jago's comments about cohesive writing instruction emphasize the importance of thinking schoolwide when it comes to effective writing instruction, for students write reports in science classes, essays in other classes, and speeches and research papers in still other classes.

RECOMMENDED RESOURCE

Langer, Judith. 2002. *Effective Literacy Instruction*. Urbana, IL: National Council of Teachers of English.

Manage
the Paper Load

44

RATIONALE

Let me begin by reviewing the components of effective responses to student writing. Such responses are:

- Personal but productive

- Specific (e.g., target a pattern of error students can effectively address)

- Immediate (throughout the composing process or directly after writing)

- Focused on no more than three items to work on (e.g., read only for verbs)

- Cumulative (i.e., build on previous responses) so as to maintain continuity and accountability (e.g., "Let's see how you're coming along on that paragraph development this time around, Matt . . . ")

My first response is to balk at the scale of these demands on my time and life. And so we come to the challenge of how to cope with the paper load. Consider the math for a moment, just to put this in perspective: if you have 150 students and each one writes one page that warrants your response, you will spend more than two hours responding to this assignment *if you take only one minute to read each page.* It is easy to see how out of control this can get when you start talking about essays and more formal writing instruction. In *Cohesive Writing,* Carol Jago writes: "Often I am able to find the time to write detailed commentaries on final copies; I just don't beat myself up when it is not possible. Too many good teachers have left the profession over the paper load. Given the imperfect world we live in, I believe it is more valuable if I focus my critical eye on students' drafts than on their final products" (2002a, 109). And yet if there is not another way, many teachers will simply avoid having their students write. Luckily, there are some helpful tricks of the trade, many of which are outlined in *Classroom Practices in Teaching English* (Stanford 1979).

I start my work by asking a question and then try to answer it.

MARY LEE SETTLE

WHAT TO DO

- Ask yourself the following focus questions about your assignment:

  ▶ What am I reading this paper to establish? (Grade? Mastery? Next step in revision process?)

  ▶ What purpose will my response serve? (To improve performance or explain grade?)

- How much time should I spend responding to these papers? (Prioritize your work to achieve the greatest effect on student performance.)

- Have students seek response from various other sources that are able to read a product and say what did or didn't work for them as readers.

- Use checks ($\sqrt{}$, $\sqrt{}+$, $\sqrt{}-$) to indicate that you read and evaluated it for its quality; these marks allow you to satisfy your students' need for evaluative feedback and your need to get out from under the pile of paper.

- Have students read their writing aloud, and enter a mark in your gradebook as they do so.

- Confer with students in class and assess them on the spot through your conversational evaluation.

- Have groups responding to literature or other texts use the overhead projector to display their presentation notes instead of writing them on paper.

- Instead of having thirty-five kids write about the importance of secrecy in *The Kitchen God's Wife*, have them do a quick write, then form groups and use their quick writes to get a conversation started and focused. At end of the period, collect the quick writes and staple them behind a front sheet with the group members' names and notes on it. Give them a grade based on participation in the conversation.

- Use rubric scoring (see Reminder 18). This type of evaluation is based on a general impression and allows for a quick response. You read through a paper and assign a score according to those attributes described in a particular rubric. See, for example, Figure 38.1, my version of the Six Traits rubric, a model that carefully integrates writing and assessment to improve performance.

- Circulate and check off work in class when possible so as to deliver personalized response and, at the same time, direct response to the problems or achievements you encounter in students' writing.

- Have students write a short essay every week but check only that they did it; after they have written four essays, have them pick one to revise, perfect, and hand in.

• Create a rubber stamp based on a local or recognized rubric to use for quick but specific responses to writing. You can buy the 6+1 Traits rubric, for example, on a rubber stamp through the Northwest Regional Educational Lab.

• Respond with "So what?" Based on the assumption that so long as students keep writing and working with the paper, it stays separate from your workload, this method helps students write much deeper into their topic. Ask them to rewrite their entire paper using only this question to drive them deeper into the subject; I've used the response as many as three times for the same paper and found the resultant writing to be remarkable for its depth.

• Check any patterned error such as the tendency to misuse the semicolon or produce sentence fragments; then, upon returning the papers, have students go through and identify the error and make the corrections at that time. Once all corrections have been made, they turn their papers in again for reevaluation.

• Confer with students at your desk in one-on-one meetings in which you use one of the following methods:

▶ Read through their writing quickly and focus on whatever jumps out

▶ Read through for a specific aspect of the writing (e.g., paragraph organization) and provide appropriate feedback—what works and what does not and why—orally, making short notes ("paragraph focus," "verbs") at the top of the paper for quick reference when you meet to discuss subsequent drafts

▶ Have them, prior to the meeting, highlight or underline specific aspects of the paper they want you to attend to

• Ask students to have their parents read their papers and respond to them as they are willing and/or able.

• Photocopy a range of samples (e.g., introductions for the same essay topic) onto one page; then have students, first individually, then collectively, evaluate and rank the samples (see Figure 44.1 for an example I used for our Weekly Poem assignment). Be sure to have them explain (preferably in writing) their reasoning for the ranking; then have them identify the elements of an effective and ineffective introduction. After discussing this further as a class, send them home to revise their own intros with the samples and criteria for effective introductions in hand. Improvement almost guaranteed.

• Skim through a set of papers to identify common areas of concern. Focus on the trait or other aspect of writing you have been teaching them

Weekly Poem Exemplars: Week 2

Burke/Fall

1. I find this poem a true inspiration to build strong relationships with those around me. **This poem describes** the building of a strong relationship (the wall) through the use of scaffolding. **The scaffolding allows the "masons"** to build a sturdy wall from the foundation up. It seems appropriate that a sure wall is needed **because the "old bridges breaking between you and me" or the older links** to each other will not last forever. **Thanks to the temporary structure of the scaffolding, a sturdy wall can be** built. (*Michael Rogers*)

2. **This poem starts out** with a very common idea of how masons would build a building, **but by the end of the poem** it came to me that **it was not just about** such a common idea **but about love**. This **poet showed a relationship** in a form of a building being made stable. **The poem is trying to symbolize the building as a relationship** that is getting built to last forever even when times get rough. (*Jenna Salazar*)

3. *Language:* The tone of the poem is rather **soft and mellow** and the word choice keeps the poem rather **simple**. The style of the poem makes it a very easy read all the way through and makes you want to read it correctly.

   Devices: **The actions of the masons** and the description of what they do really **paints a picture in your mind of the hard but beautiful work**. The most obvious metaphor, the scaffolding, represents love or marriage. The **symbols that they use, to me, represent safety in the beginning**. Everyone wants to be sure they are safe. **Then in the end** the falling of the scaffolding is a symbol of letting things go and being confident that you already did your job.

   Purpose: **The poet is trying to explain and define** the concepts of marriage. **He does this by using** the scaffolding as a metaphor and comparing everlasting love to a brick wall. That when their safety lines go down (scaffolding) it is okay because they were done building the wall of their trust and love. I think the reason he wrote this poem was to put marriage in simpler words and in perspective for people. (*Mimi Franco*)

4. Building a home is like building a relationship. **You need good "masons"** and good support **"scaffolding"** to build the building or relationship to be solid and secure. He uses **the word "scaffolding" which gives the feeling of surrounding oneself. It's a secure word.** In the second stanza **he uses "secure"** to explain. In the third stanza a scaffolding comes down, but leaves behind a solid wall/foundation, so the author could express the scaffolding as first love that helps build the secure foundations later. The fourth stanza **repeats the theme** of the third stanza, **but changes it from the metaphor of a building to people and relationships**. (*Jennifer Hazelwood*)

FIGURE 44.1   Weekly Poem exemplars

lately. Instead of responding to them all individually, copy a few exemplars to transparencies and put these up on the overhead, giving everyone a completion score (e.g., five points or a check, for now). Using these exemplars to guide your instruction, discuss what makes them effective (or not). Then have students identify the key strategies for improving them. Have them, in their journals, practice revising or otherwise rewriting the samples, then discuss what they wrote. Send them home to revise their own papers again. The point, remember, is not to collect them, making the process terminal, but rather to use the writing to improve their skills and sustain the conversation about not only writing but the topic about which they wrote.

RECOMMENDED RESOURCE

Stanford, Gene, ed. 1979. *Classroom Practices in Teaching English 1979–1980: How to Handle the Paper Load.* Urbana, IL: National Council of Teachers of English.

Write in
Many Genres

Cut a good story
anywhere and it will
bleed.

—ANTON CHEKHOV

It's true: state standards documents require that students learn to read and write a variety of types of texts. They all say this in one way or another; so they should, for successful students need to know how to write everything from a resume to a research paper, an essay to a letter, and so on if they are to move through high school and, ultimately, college successfully. Standards are nice, but the world matters more: graduates need to know how to write a range of texts out there. My mother, working as an administrative assistant at a health center, writes all sorts of documents, publishing them on paper, via Web sites, as PDFs (portable document format files), and through e-mail.

Students need to know how to write not only for different purposes but on different devices. The man sitting next to me on the plane to Denver this afternoon composed e-mails on his wireless pager, wrote memos and created PowerPoint presentations on his laptop, and jotted notes on his Palm Pilot. The note on the pager read almost like a digital haiku because of the constraints of its screen.

At the heart of these different types of texts, however, is the thinking they require. Each demands some measure of textual intelligence (Burke 2001), which the student writer uses when making choices about which text, which organizational pattern, which voice, and which medium best suits the purpose and point of the writing. When teaching students to write, we must ask how students need to think during the work and which tools and techniques will best support that work.

This section examines the different types of texts students should be able to write and how to write them. It also describes what each type of text, such as a persuasive essay, must include. Realize that no one should teach all these different types of writing in any given year, though many will be part of your writing curriculum in any given year. You might not directly teach persuasive writing, for instance, but your students will almost certainly need to examine and respond to arguments in writing.

Resumes are not necessarily appropriate for freshmen, but the variations on a resume (see Reminder 65) are most appropriate for freshmen.

It is essential to reinforce the reading-writing connection whenever possible. Reading poetry? Good, then have students use writing to analyze it, but also use journals to respond to and reflect on the poems and their ideas; then have them write their own poems, using the poems they are reading as models. This interaction between making sense (while reading) and making texts honors the original meaning of the word *text* itself. The word *text* relates to weaving (e.g., textiles) or the making of something from many parts; so it is when we read and write: writing the types of text you read helps you understand what you read even as it improves your own writing. One cannot be an effective writer if they are not an active, thoughtful reader.

Write a Response to Literature

45

DESCRIPTION

Writing about literature, the student seeks to answer such questions as, What does it mean? or What does this text say about the human experience? Depending on the genre of the response, writers might also reflect more personally on what the text means *to them*, or they might consider what the text says about *their* experience. At the more advanced or upper-grade levels, response might examine the text's relationship to the larger literary tradition or its insights into history or culture. Writing a response to literature differs from most of the other forms of writing in that it involves reading, understanding, and writing about another text; for these reasons, and the likelihood that such a prompt will appear on any exam students take, this is a crucial form of writing to master.

One always tends to overpraise a long book because one has got through it.

E. M. FORSTER

Of course, there is no one form, but several: essays, journals, letters, and short critical responses. Some genres, such as the essay, come complete with specific conventions that dictate content, voice, and organization. Others—journals, letters, dramatic monologues—have no such constraints and thus allow for more flexibility and imagination. Whatever the genre, writing about literature demands sophisticated thinking. Given time, and proper support, students at all levels can write well. Anderson, Morrill, and Adler (2002) describe how one teacher scaffolded her instruction to achieve successful performances from her diverse urban students:

> Initially, Melissa accepted all written work [in response to *Money Hungry*, by Sharon G. Flake], but as the conversations became more critical, more mature, she demanded more in-depth, longer responses, while continuously praising the work received. Interestingly, when presented with this new challenge, students met and sometimes exceeded Melissa's expectations. . . . Students completed response sheets focusing not only on the facts of the story, but also on predicting, making connections to their lives, and developing literary appreciation by finding lines from the literature that moved them or seemed important in some way. (1)

RESPONSE TO LITERATURE AT A GLANCE

☐ Identify the subject of your response (e.g., a theme, a claim, a character)

☐ Know what you want to say about this subject; formulate it into a statement or controlling idea in whatever form you ultimately choose to write.

☐ Choose an emphasis. Emphasis depends on assigned or chosen purpose, but possibilities include:

  ☐ Evaluating the author's purpose
  ☐ Analyzing the author's style
  ☐ Examining the themes within the text

☐ Engage in critical reading of the literary text, taking notes or annotating the text according to your purpose.

☐ Organize your response according to the conventions of the genre. An essay, for example, might be arranged thus:

  ☐ *Opening.* Makes a compelling point in response to the text, one that engages the reader and establishes a connection to the text. The writer clearly identifies the subject and makes a statement about that subject that the rest of the essay will develop.

  ☐ *Body.* Develops the claim made in the opening, drawing supporting details and examples directly from the text to back up your thinking.

  ☐ *Conclusion.* Sums up what the writer says and extends the ideas, making inferences and drawing conclusions about the author, the text, or the characters that support the main idea established in the opening.

☐ Support assertions, connections, and interpretations with specific examples and quotations from the text; clearly identify and properly format these quotations.

☐ Make insightful inferences and draw thoughtful conclusions that are supported with quotations and examples from the text.

☐ Use and embed within the essay relevant quotations from important characters that shed light on significant events or themes within the text.

☐ Connect ideas within the text, between different texts, and, if appropriate, to yourself, as well as the world beyond.

☐ Examine appropriate and significant aspects of the author's style; this analysis might include the author's use of language, rhetorical devices, imagery, allusions, or ambiguity. Discuss how these aspects of the author's style relate to the point you are trying to make in the essay.

☐ Discuss the importance or meaning of all examples and quotations, connecting these to the main idea introduced at the beginning of the essay.

☐ In most forms of literary response, you should:

  ☐ Use the active voice.

  ☐ Refer to "the narrator," "the author," "the character," or "the speaker," instead of using pronouns (e.g., *he, she, I*).

  ☐ Identify the author by the last name (e.g., Orwell) after first using his full name (e.g., George Orwell).

  ☐ Avoid beginning sentences with "I think," "I believe," or "I feel." Such verbs undermine the effect of your argument; after all, we know already this is what you think, how you feel—otherwise, you wouldn't be writing it.

  ☐ Avoid speculation about scenarios or motivations; anchor your analysis in what the text says, what really happens, or what you know.

  ☐ Discuss literature using the present-tense verbs (e.g., "Cisneros uses Spanish words throughout her novel to add voice and style to her writing.").

  ☐ Focus on the text you are trying to understand and preparing to discuss; do not write about the author's life unless asked to do so.

  ☐ Avoid praise and the other forms of compliment. Tell your reader what the text means and why certain details are important, not how great you think the author is. Consider the difference between these two brief examples:

   • Seamus Heaney is a wonderful author who uses language in so many great ways to describe his family.

   • Heaney uses precise terms familiar to any farmer to describe his father's expertise in the fields.

   • Use appropriate verbs when writing a critical analysis of an author or a work of literature. Examples of these terms include:

Emphasizes	Observes	Develops
Elucidates	Identifies	Provides
Compares	Organizes	Connotes
Suggests	Reinforces	Focuses
Creates	Defines	Balances
Illustrates	Clarifies	Relates
Exemplifies	Contrasts	Expresses
Parallels	Argues	Insinuates
Juxtaposes	Mirrors	Demonstrates
Implies	Shows	
Alludes to	Echoes	

PROMPTS FOR PRACTICE

Here are some sample topics you might consider using or discussing with your students:

- Explain how a character changes over the course of the story.

- Compare characters from two different stories or within the same story.

- Write a letter to a character in which you respond to their ideas or actions.

- Identify and discuss an important theme in a literary text

- Discuss what the main character learns over the course of the story; then compare this with a lesson you learned from a similar experience.

CLASSROOM CONNECTION

These sample prompts as well as other ideas appear in various forms in the following assignments. I have tried to include a continuum of assignments of varying difficulty to demonstrate the range of ways students can respond to literature. Some assignments are preparatory, for struggling readers asked to respond to literature often do not know how to identify what is most important. The double-entry journal is one way to reinforce and extend critical reading and writing skills. Reading Response Notes (Figure 45.1) is an alternative means of developing and reinforcing these skills. This assignment and Tommy Chong's *Rumblefish* response (Figure 45.2) mark an important transition in the process: the words listed up top or on the side are possible topics the students generated themselves while doing silent reading. This progress toward greater independence is essential if students are to meet the standards and be prepared for the challenges that await them.

To improve students' ability to respond to literature, I use student examples so we can stay anchored in the texts we are learning to write about and focus on the level of current performance. Following, for example, Katie Wolfe and Justine Macauley offer their classmates useful, powerful examples of how to write about the Weekly Poem assignment in Figure 45.3 which, in this case, included Seamus Heaney's poem "Clearances."

The title of the poem already reveals that Seamus Heaney will be describing someone who has passed on. There is one major symbol Seamus Heaney uses throughout the poem, this is the potatoes. The potatoes symbolize a oneness between him and the person he is describing (her). "They broke the silence, let fall one

Reading Response Notes

Date 10/3	Period 2°

Name MR. BURKE	Title BREAKING THROUGH

Responding to the Text

IDEA DEVELOPMENT: The heart, main idea, or thesis of a text; refers to the details, examples, or images that develop and support the main idea.

5 *Text is clear and focused; captures reader's attention.*
- ✓ Topic is narrow and manageable.
- ✓ Details are relevant, interesting, vivid, accurate.
- ✓ Point is clear; tells whole story; no trivia.
- ✓ Details support the paper's main idea.
- ✓ Ideas engage, inspire, or intrigue reader.

3 *Text's ideas are focused but general, obvious.*
- ✓ Topic is fairly broad; understandable, though.
- ☐ Details are loosely related, obvious, or dull.
- ☐ Point vague; gives general idea; incomplete.
- ☐ Details provide weak support for main idea.
- ☐ Ideas leave reader guessing; not specific.

1 *Text lacks clear idea, purpose, and details.*
- ☐ Topic lacking; no evident focus or purpose.
- ☐ Details are missing, incorrect, or unclear.
- ☐ Makes no point; cannot identify main idea.
- ☐ Details repeat each other; seem random.
- ☐ Ideas confuse and frustrate the reader.

Developing Your Ideas

- ☐ I think _____ because..
- ☐ A good example of ___ is...
- ☐ This reminded me of _____ because...
- ☐ _____ was important because...
- ☐ One thing that surprised me was ___ because I always thought...
- ☐ The author says that...
- ☐ For example....
- ☐ The author/character wants...
- ☐ The author describes...
- ☐ The author's purpose is...

Performance Standards: Responding to Reading

- Identify main ideas in the text
- Generate useful questions to help you read and write about the text
- Organize your written response in a paragraph that includes:
  - Main idea (answers the question: What's your *point?*)
  - Details, quotations, or examples that support your main idea
- Make connections to your life, the world, major themes, or other books.

- faith
- work/job — hard work
- ambition
- respect — to look back at
- discipline ("like a bird caught in a storm.")
- success is scary — public — responses to
- humility
- desire
- disappointment

We all need someone we do not want to disappoint. This person might be a teacher, a relative, a coach, or a parent. Many parents have made great sacrifices for us, whether by working an extra job or going with-out some pleasure they would enjoy. In Breaking Through, Francisco worked hard to make his parents proud — but also those teachers who have worked hard to help him succeed. So when he gets sick with mono, his first concern is that he will fail school and let his parents down. It is such people that motivate him, make him want to work. His success = their success.

FIGURE 45.1 Sample Reading Response Notes I did to model for the students how to do it

Tommy Chong.
1-30

Rumble fish.

	Good friends.
girlfriend	
work	How can you tell if you have a good
little bro	friend? A friend that will stick by you no matter
Mad	what? You don't. You can't say that someone
fight	is a true friend if you have never done any
good friends	thing to see that.
Making up	
serten girls	I, on ther other hand, do have a true
Promising	and loyol friend, and he has passed meany
getting Pumped up.	test with me. His name is Jeremy. We have
fat.	known euch other ever seance the first day
Little Leaguers	of kindergarden. On that day we sat next to
Vacant lot.	euch other and became the best of friends. To
Fiver.	this day we still hang out almost every
	day.
How do you	
tell you have a	How do I know he is a good friend?
true friend?	I know becuase even though I got in trouble
	numers times he stood next to me and we took
	the blame together, as a team. In the 3rd
	grade we made up a secret hand shake,
	and we still use it today. So because we
	are still good friends now, that shows me
	he is a true, true friend.

FIGURE 45.2   Sample journal from Tommy Chong for the book *Rumblefish*

Weekly Poem

Mr. Burke/English   **Your Name:** _____

Date: _____   **Period:** _____

Overview

1. Read the poem straight through for pleasure—preferably aloud.

2. Then read it again (and again), looking for any of the following literary devices or features:

   ☐ *Language:* Tone, style, diction (word choice)

   ☐ *Conventions:* Punctuation, grammar, poetic forms

   ☐ *Devices:* Imagery, metaphor, symbols, repetition, and more

   ☐ *Design:* Structure, organization of content (e.g., stanzas, past to present)

   ☐ *Themes:* Ideas that run throughout the poem

   ☐ *Connections:* Relate it to the other works we've read, conversations we have had or are having

   ☐ *Purpose:* What is the poet trying to accomplish?

3. Annotate the poem—that is, underline words and phrases; pose questions and make comments *as you read.*

4. Write the analytical paragraph—a single paragraph with a clearly stated main idea—on the back.

5. Consult the *Reader's Handbook* (see page 389) about how to read poems.

6. Read *Writer's Inc.* (page 214) for help on writing about literature.

FIGURE 45.3   Sample Weekly Poem assignment

by one . . . " this line indicates that there might have been awkward silence between the two, or perhaps a welcomed note of peace. Either way, the peeled potatoes were cold comforts between them, things to share. Seamus Heaney sees the potatoes as gleaming in a bucket of water. The potatoes were not only something that both of them shared, but they were also seen as beautiful to him. The beginning of the second stanza changes the direction of the poem. Here Seamus tells about the day of her death. The whole first stanza is merely a flash back to the time when they were, "never closer the whole rest of our lives." (Katie Wolfe)

This poem travels deep into the subject of true love. In the beginning, it uses soft, simple words like "things to share," "I was all hers," "pleasant splashes," and "bring us to our senses" to show that this time for the two people is very special and anticipated. This verse compares the breaking of the silence by potatoes dropping into a bucket of water to solder "weeping off"—that is, being applied—the soldering iron. The next verse is probably a further time from the first and implies that she is dying. Again, it uses simple, soft language to touch upon the subject of death. The last three lines are in the past tense. For example, it says "I remembered," so they could be referring back to the first verse when they were alone and everyone else was at church. (Justine Macauley)

Carrin Tanaka's response to her outside reading (Figure 45.4) is an equally good example of how to respond to a novel she read outside of class; I copied it for the class and posted it to our class Web site so people could study it when writing their own. Furthermore, I put it up on an overhead to narrate what made it so effective.

The Weekly Poem culminates in the final exam, which includes, as part of its requirements, the following Author Study assignment, yet another type of literature response:

Author Study: Seamus Heaney

FINAL EXAM PREPARATION
ENGLISH/FALL

Introduction

There is great value to reading a wide range of authors or poets. However, the close, sustained study of one author offers great insight into that person's writing and character as it evolves over time. This assignment, which you will receive each Friday and turn in every Monday, is meant to challenge you but not overwhelm you, given the other demands of the course. For this reason I will always choose short poems and poems that will reward close reading without taking you all day. I have chosen Seamus Heaney as the poet we will study this semester; by unit's end, we will have read about twenty of his poems in all. The Author Study culminates in the semester final exam, which will require you to write a final paper on Seamus Heaney and his poems, using your notes from the semester to demonstrate your understanding in a well-written essay.

Instructional Objectives

This assignment will develop your ability to:

• Read a literary text closely for style, theme, tone, imagery, and symbolism

• Read the language of a literary text at both the literal and the figurative level

• Annotate and take notes on what you read to improve comprehension, make connections, and prepare to write

Proper header
(see p. 277
Writer's Inc.)

→ Carrin Tanaka
Mr. Burke
English 2H
22 January

Proper Citation Format MLA
(see p. 265
Writer's Inc.)

→ Filipovic, Zlata. *Zlata's Diary: A Child's Life in Sarajevo*. New York: Penguin, 1995.

50-word synopsis
(see p. 277
Writer's Inc.)

→ In this 197-page book, Zlata Filipovic describes her city of Sarajevo as it is torn apart by war. She began keeping her diary just before her eleventh birthday. In her journal Zlata writes about her days, from school to piano lessons, skiing to watching her favorite TV shows, all American. She decided to keep a diary of her experience just as Ann Frank did, finding in her diary a comfort she could not find elsewhere.

Loss

500-word essay on a theme in the book

→ Everyone experiences loss at some point. We lose people, objects, and even games. People lose things every day. If one loses something unwanted, such as an unwanted sickness, then a loss can certainly be positive. But one can also lose something important to them, a friend for instance. Such a loss is negative. The *American Heritage Dictionary* defines loss as: "the condition of being deprived of something or someone."

Zlata experiences a tremendous amount of loss in her life. There is a key cause for her loss, and that's the war that is being fought on the streets right outside of her house. This war prevents Zlata from continuing with her daily activities. She can no longer go to school, play outside, or even enjoy music, because it is unsafe. Coping with the loss of her regular everyday life is very hard for Zlata, but she manages well under the circumstances. She finds new ways to occupy her time. The many restrictions imposed on everyone by the war make finding new activities difficult for her. You can say that her whole city, Sarajevo, lost its freedom.

Surviving for Zlata becomes a challenge. Water, electricity, and food all become scarce. This is just one more loss which Zlata learns to accept. Fresh fruits and vegetables are rare and hardly get into the hungry town of Sarajevo. Even going into the kitchen to use the appliances is dangerous, for Zlata's kitchen faces the street, making it easy to see. Therefore she must keep a low profile at all times. Even if it were safe to enter the kitchen, the electricity would probably be unavailable. Zlata's family finds new ways of cooking to keep from starving. This is almost impossible because Zlata spends much of her life during the war in the cellar, which is the safest place because it is hard to find and out of sight of any invaders. Because of the war, Zlata has even lost her own home.

Zlata lost many things during the war, the most tragic of which were her friends and family. She can no longer see them or even talk to them. Those people most important to Zlata fled to safety in other parts of the world, while others died in the war. Such losses affect Zlata the most and are the hardest to overcome because of the anger and depression they cause her. The war stole Zlata's childhood, leaving her only the terrible memory of complete loss which she records in her diary.

Recommendation
(see p. 222
Writer's Inc.)

→ I recommend this book **enthusiastically**. Zlata is a remarkable girl. High school students would find this story inspiring and exciting. She never loses hope, even as her city is destroyed. If you liked *The Diary of Anne Frank* you will love this book.

FIGURE 45.4 Model paper for outside reading

- Write an essay in which you analyze the content and evolution of one author's style over the course of time

- Learn to use and apply your knowledge of appropriate literary terms when discussing and writing about the author's work

Performance Standards

To demonstrate your mastery of the relevant standards, you must:

- Annotate each week's poem with comments, connections, and insights into this poem in the context of the other poems you have read by this poet

- Write a response to each poem on the back that shows insight and uses quotations and details to support what you are saying about the poem

- Discuss the author's use of language, imagery, symbols, and tone

- Use appropriate literary terms when discussing and writing about the poems in your weekly responses *and* in your final paper

- Write a three- to five-page analytical essay in which you make a claim about Seamus Heaney or his poems, providing supporting details from at least eight different poems you read over the semester

- Write a paper that earns at least a score of 4 in each of the Six Traits domains

Related Resources

Here are a few useful resources for your study of Seamus Heaney:

> *<www.poets.org/poets/poets.cfm?prmID=215>*
> *<www.nobel.se/literature/laureates/1995/index.html>*

Final Exam

On the day of the final exam, you will use the Weekly Poem guidelines to write an essay *in class* on some aspect of Heaney's poetry. Your essay must:

- Be one to two pages long

- Establish, maintain, and develop a central claim about Heaney as a poet or his poetry

- Include direct quotations from and a discussion of *at least* four Heaney poems we have studied this semester

- Organize itself into paragraphs, each with its own main idea that relates to the paper's main idea

On other occasions we might work with poetry in a different way, as the following assignment shows:

Reading Literature: A Poetic Cycle

Overview

This unit asks you to study a collection of poems, focusing on one poem in depth as you teach it to us. The unit concentrates on the close study of literary texts in general and of poems in particular, culminating in a short (one typed page) paper in which you demonstrate your ability to write about themes, embed quotations from multiple texts, and organize your ideas into a coherent paper.

Standards Connection

This assignment asks you to learn about and demonstrate your ability to:

• Read poetic texts closely, annotating and responding to such elements as the poet's use of language, imagery, tone, and other devices

• Identify and compare common themes in multiple texts

• Identify and understand the elements of the specific type of poem (e.g., sonnet) you are studying

• Make a statement about your theme and support this claim with examples and quotations from the texts

• Identify and embed into your paper appropriate direct quotations

• Present and/or discuss the texts, using details to support your ideas

• Use various note-taking strategies to organize your ideas and quotations and prepare to write a literary essay

• Generate useful questions to help you read, write, and speak

• Write a literary essay

Guidelines

Follow these steps to complete this assignment:

1. Read through all and choose *one* of the poems in the packet.
2. Sign up for that poem; no groups may teach the same poem.

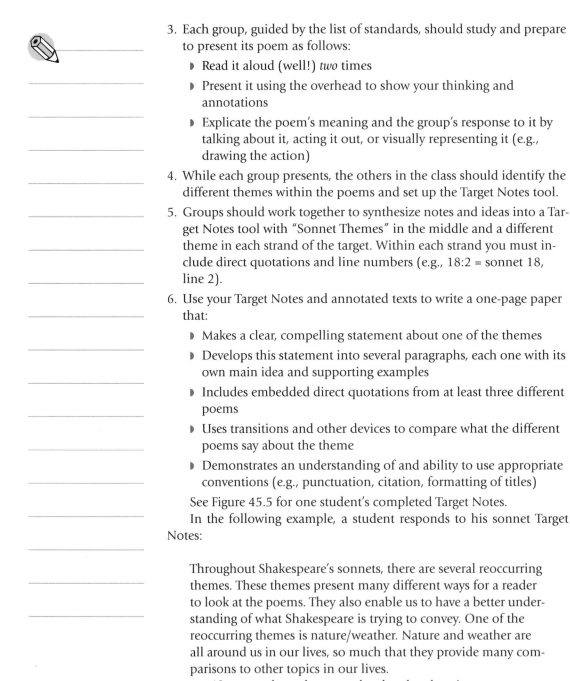

3. Each group, guided by the list of standards, should study and prepare to present its poem as follows:

   ▶ Read it aloud (well!) *two* times

   ▶ Present it using the overhead to show your thinking and annotations

   ▶ Explicate the poem's meaning and the group's response to it by talking about it, acting it out, or visually representing it (e.g., drawing the action)

4. While each group presents, the others in the class should identify the different themes within the poems and set up the Target Notes tool.

5. Groups should work together to synthesize notes and ideas into a Target Notes tool with "Sonnet Themes" in the middle and a different theme in each strand of the target. Within each strand you must include direct quotations and line numbers (e.g., 18:2 = sonnet 18, line 2).

6. Use your Target Notes and annotated texts to write a one-page paper that:

   ▶ Makes a clear, compelling statement about one of the themes

   ▶ Develops this statement into several paragraphs, each one with its own main idea and supporting examples

   ▶ Includes embedded direct quotations from at least three different poems

   ▶ Uses transitions and other devices to compare what the different poems say about the theme

   ▶ Demonstrates an understanding of and ability to use appropriate conventions (e.g., punctuation, citation, formatting of titles)

   See Figure 45.5 for one student's completed Target Notes.

   In the following example, a student responds to his sonnet Target Notes:

   Throughout Shakespeare's sonnets, there are several reoccurring themes. These themes present many different ways for a reader to look at the poems. They also enable us to have a better understanding of what Shakespeare is trying to convey. One of the reoccurring themes is nature/weather. Nature and weather are all around us in our lives, so much that they provide many comparisons to other topics in our lives.

   Nature and weather, two closely related topics, are common themes in many poems, not just Shakespeare's. So what is

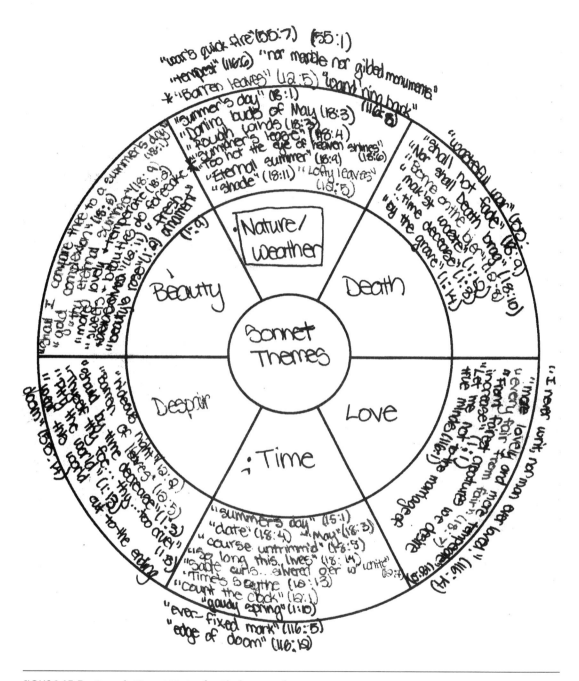

FIGURE 45.5 Sample Target Notes for Shakespeare's sonnets

different about how they are used in his sonnets? He uses them to express deeper meanings of beauty and death. For example, "summer's leases hath all too short a date" (18:4) seems to mean that summer is too short. However, when this line is looked at in comparison with the rest of the poem, it means that the time during which a person is beautiful is too short. Because of the many beautiful things in nature, it was chosen to represent beauty. Also, beauty, both in people and nature, does not last.

Nature and weather are not always beautiful things, though. A tree "barren of leaves" (12:5) surely is not. Trees have no leaves in the winter, the season that is thought to be least happy and beautiful. This use of nature gives us a picture of dead things, and has been used to express death and oldness. In weather, "tempests" (16:6) bring about destruction and confusion, not especially good things either. Nature and weather are not always pleasant.

Nature and weather can be used to convey ideas that are good or bad. It all depends on how they are used. With so many examples of both all around us, it is hard not to see both sides of the picture they depict.

Figures 45.6 and 45.7 show examples of two ways of working closely with student writing about the sonnets. I cut and paste (it's quicker!) representative student work onto a page and then have students evaluate the writing for its effectiveness. Here is Stephanie Ellingson's critique, which grows out of her group's discussion of the examples in Figure 45.7:

1. You should use quotations when writing a literary analysis to support your ideas. By using part of the actual writing, you can more convincingly persuade your audience. Using quotes is most effective when they are integrated with the rest of your writing.

2. The last paragraph uses quotations most effectively. It blends the quotes with the rest of the sentence so effectively that you can't tell where the quotes start and end.

3. The last paragraph is the most effective. It blends the quotes very well and supports each quote.

4. The third paragraph is the second most effective. It clearly supports the quote, but the quote itself is not blended very effectively. The second paragraph is the third most effective because it only supports and uses quotes competently. This first paragraph is the worst because it doesn't have grammar or use quotes well.

① Explain what an effective intro achieves. Support your explanation and give examples — both effective & ineffective — from these opening ¶s.

② ~~Pick the~~ Rank these from most to least effective. Explain your choices.

③ Discuss

④ Write a new opening for your paper using these as examples to guide you.

⑤ Due tomorrow.

---

① As we all know Shakespeare was and still is the best poet ever. My ~~Lancender~~ Elyse evidence is that 400 years after he has written his poems, sonnets, or plays we still are learning and reading them. After learning about all the different sonnets he wrote, I concluded that the theme "Love" was in almost all of his writings He stressed different meanings of love and what it meant to him. He felt that his definition of love was the only correct definition.

② When people think about Shakespeare, they immediately think of *Romeo and Juliet* and the love they shared for each other. However, in my opinion Shakespeare tends to write about death more than love. If you think about it, what happens in the end of *Romeo and Juliet*? They both die! They did die because of their outrageous love for another, but nonetheless they did die.

③ When a man or woman is truly in love with another, the only thing their eyes see is perfection. It doesn't matter what the other person looks like or how they act; Love can make any and every flaw disappear. This is what Shakespeare expresses in his Sonnets 18, 29, and 116. Each of these pieces talks about love in different ways, but all of them somehow relate to the ~~theme~~ idea that, love covers all flaws.

④ Time is only one of the many themes William Shakespeare portrays in many of his sonnets. Time must always go on, it does not relay on any one person or thing to keep it's existance. However, time is the origin of life, and also it's end. Time is what makes the world keep spinning, without it, there is no

⑤ In many of Shakespeare's sonnets love is mentioned and plays a strong subject to his writing. Sometimes love is directly mentioned and other times it is indirectly mentioned. For instance in 18:1, "Shall I compare thee to a summer's day?" Shakespeare indirectly mentions love by asking a question that refers to someone's love for another. 1:1, "From fairest creatures we desire increase..." love plays a major role in this sonnet. Throughout the sonnet Shakespeare writes about how someone loves another so much that they hope that love will never die out, and how they make the other person want to live and how the other person has the ability to make everything perfect and just. It ends saying that the person wants to be with the other one until they die.

⑥ Throughout Shakespeare's sonnets, there are several reoccurring themes. These themes present many different ways that a reader can look at the poems. They also enable us to have a better understanding of what Shakespeare is trying to get across. One of the reoccurring themes is nature/weather.

FIGURE 45.6   I took these from students' draft introductions, choosing samples that would help us identify the traits of an effective introduction.

① Explain why you would use quotations when writing a literary analysis. Provide examples from these →

② Which one uses quotations most effectively? Defend your answer, using examples to support.

③ Rank them in order of effectiveness. Provide examples to support your thinking

④ Discuss.

⑤ Revise your paper.

⑥ Due Monday.

① Sonnet 18 is Shakespeare writing a poem to his own love one. Any girl that read this, Shakespeare could probably steal her heart. He uses the word love, to compare it to other things like a summer's day or heaven. He says," Shall I compare thee to a summer's day? Thou art more lovely and more temperate." This lines mean to me that spending time with her is even better then being outside on a perfect summer's day. She is more pleasant to be around with then the weather.

Sonnet 29 tells the story of a man who feels inferior to the other men around him and is depressed when he thinks about all the fascinating looks and features that they have and he doesn't, ("...look upon myself and curse my fate...Desiring this man's art and that man's scope..." (29:4 & 7). But as soon as he thinks of the one he loves, he forgets about his personal flaws and finds happiness, "Yet in these thoughts myself almost despising, Haply I think on thee, and then my state, Like to the lark at break of day arising From sullen earth sings hymns at heaven's gate..." (29:9-12). Just thinking of the woman he loves changes his whole attitude and makes him happy. His love for her is so great that it not only covers any flaws she might have, but it also hides his own.

Nature and weather, two closely related topics, are common themes in many poems, not just Shakespeare's. So what is different about how they are used in his sonnets? Nature and weather are often used to express deeper meanings of beauty and death. For example, "summer's leases hath all too short a date" (18:4) seems to mean that summer is too short. However, when this line is looked at in comparison to the rest of the poem, it means that the time during which a person is beautiful is too short. Because of the many beautiful things in nature, it was chosen to represent beauty.

Time is what makes the world keep spinning, without it, there is no existance. When you are first born, you are only a, "bud" (1.2), a caring bud or May" (18.3), however, as you grow older you become a "rose" (1:11). You are constantly, "changing course" (18:8) and aging as time goes on. In "brief hours and weeks" (116:11) you may have a totally new view on life and your times passed. Whether it is only a moment or a life time, you are becoming older with time.

FIGURE 45.7 This page shows the second day's collection of exemplars I quickly gathered and prepared to use in class.

5. An effective introduction establishes a main idea and gives support to that idea. It also includes commentary and some opinions. An ineffective introduction does not establish a main point and rambles on. An effective introduction holds the reader's attention and keeps it.

6. The fifth paragraph is the least effective. It does not establish a main point and jumps straight into an explanation. The first paragraph is the second most effective. It establishes a point, but gives too much opinion. The sixth paragraph is the third most effective. It doesn't hold the reader's attention much. The second paragraph is the fourth most effective. It has a main idea and holds the reader's attention. The third paragraph is the fifth most effective. It states a main idea and expands on it. The fourth paragraph is the most effective. It states an idea, expands on it, and holds the reader's attention.

RECOMMENDED RESOURCE

Newkirk, Thomas. 1997. *The Performance of Self in Student Writing*. Portsmouth, NH: Boynton/Cook.

46

Write
a Narrative

DESCRIPTION

A narrative not only describes *what* happened but often discusses *how* and *why* something happened. It is, obviously, a story; such stories can serve a range of purposes depending on the writer's audience or goal. Narrative writing commonly appears on state and district tests, which tend to demand a biographical narrative. This emphasis on writing about others' lives is most likely an effort to keep the focus away from the personal or inner lives of students. While such a shift makes the test less intrusive or personal, it also makes such writing more difficult for some students who, unable to relate the biographical subject to their own lives, struggle to write effectively.

The narrative remains at the core of the writing experience, for what is any writer doing if not telling the story of people, a place, an object, an experience, or an idea? Narrative thinking is deep thinking, inviting us to reflect on not only what people want but why they want it and how one action leads to another to shape our own story as well as others'. It reminds us, if we take it a step further, that our own lives necessarily have a plot, different settings, a cast of characters, themes, and inevitable conflicts that make our lives richer if we can keep them in perspective. Reflecting on the lives of others, on their stories, helps us better understand and realize that we must make our own life worth the telling if we are to say it was a good, interesting life. Benjamin Franklin (2001), in what many consider to be the first autobiography, wrote: "The next best thing most like living one's life over again seems to be a recollection of that life, and to make that recollection as durable as possible by putting it down in writing." (9)

PROMPTS FOR PRACTICE

Here are a few sample narrative topics to consider or adapt for your own class:

• Narrate a series of events that lead up to a specific historical event (e.g., the Civil War, America's entrance into World War II).

• Trace the course of a specific historical movement (e.g., Civil Rights) in the United States.

THE NARRATIVE AT A GLANCE

☐ Emphasizes one important moment in an individual's life

☐ Establishes a main idea; there is a point to the story. What is the question the essay is trying to answer about this person's life? In other words, what purpose does telling this story serve?

☐ Includes specific, compelling details about the person, setting, and other characters involved

☐ Uses telling examples to support your ideas and help the reader better understand what is happening and the importance or meaning of such events

☐ Organizes events in the most appropriate order to reveal how one event leads to or causes another. A narrative typically includes:

    ☐ *Beginning.* Introduces the people, place, and incident around which the essay will be organized.

    ☐ *Middle.* Discusses the event: who said what, where, when, how, and why; includes dialogue. Also focuses on the main event and its importance.

    ☐ *Ending.* Reveals the final outcome and the writer's attitude toward it. Connects to the main idea established in the beginning.

☐ Includes dialogue and sensory details to help the reader see the story as it unfolds

☐ Speculates about the main subject's motives

☐ Considers (if appropriate) the subject or character from multiple perspectives

☐ Draws conclusions about the characters based on their actions and the events that occur

☐ Uses an appropriate tone and mood to describe the character and the events

☐ Chooses a style—voice, language, sentence patterns—appropriate to the subject and themes

The narrative offers the writer many rewarding challenges; the following list offers a sampling of the different approaches you could take to the narrative:

☐ Short story

☐ Personal narrative

☐ Biographical narrative about fictional character

☐ Life study

☐ Case study

☐ Memorable person

☐ Character sketch

☐ Character study

☐ Biographical poem

☐ Internal or dramatic monologue

• Describe the contributions of scientists to the development of major discoveries (e.g., Genome Project, atomic bomb).

• Examine the life of a person who has made a significant contribution to society (see, for example, *Time* magazine's Web site for its lists of the one hundred most important people in different fields in the twentieth century); describe the events in that person's life that motivated them to make this contribution. A similar assignment could be to examine the most important events in the life of an artist, athlete, or a person from your own life who has been influential.

• Write a fictional narrative based on one writer's comment that there are only two stories: (1) a stranger came to town and (2) a person went on a journey.

CLASSROOM CONNECTION

The following assignment allows my students to think about the story of people's lives as well as the fictional narratives they are reading. It allows us to work on specific aspects of writing, such as voice and perspective; we also focus on such aspects of academic literacy as note taking and investigating throughout the course of the unit. While most assignments I create have a more focused structure, the open-ended approach you see here allows us greater flexibility as we work. Instead of a specific assignment, it is more of a description of how we will work, what we will learn and do over the course of a couple weeks. I usually revise the assignment as we go so that I can respond to new directions or instructional needs as they arise. Thus, "2.1" reflects that this is a slightly altered version of a second major revision of the assignment. When I give them 2.1, we take out 2.0 and ceremonially tear it up to avoid confusion between the two. Note also the way students on this assignment are asked to write and think in a variety of ways over the course of the unit, using different types of texts and multiple media types as they go. All early steps develop their understanding of what a good biographical narrative has and does, so that when they write their own in Step 11, they will be ready to write well.

Biographical Narrative 2.1

Overview   What makes one person stand out over another in our memory? We might have twenty-seven uncles and aunts, but there's one who somehow remains in our mind long after the others go to bed. We sit in the classrooms of dozens of teachers in a lifetime, but one or two we never forget. This assignment asks you to think and write about a person who remains very memorable to you. They may still be alive, or they may have died years ago. You might know them, or they might be someone whose life fascinated you so much you learned everything you could about them to better understand them.

Note: Please keep all work from the following steps as you move through the process.

Performance Standards: To achieve the standards on this assignment, you must:

1. Read as a writer to generate questions, connections, and ideas about a memorable person:

    ▶ The *Reader's Handbook* (pages 155–67). Take notes that will prepare you to write

    ▶ Miscellaneous readings (to be provided)

2. Generate the criteria and attributes of a "memorable" person.

3. List *at least* ten people you could write about, all of whom qualify as memorable according to your criteria. (You do not have to know them personally but must know enough to be able to write about them.)

4. Find, print, read, and annotate *two* articles from *<www.time.com/time/time100/>*.

5. Write *one* paragraph in which you compare these two people and why they are memorable. See *Writer's Inc.* (pages 103, 361) for more information about how to write a comparison.

6. Watch Time *Century* video, and take notes on each person; using these notes and examples from the video, write a set of instructions in which you describe what one must do to be remembered. Give it an interesting or at least appropriate title; use the proper voice when writing this document.

7. Visit *<www.nytimes.com/pages/national/portraits/index.html>* and read two "Portraits of Grief." Write a short personal reflection/response about what made these people memorable to those who knew and loved them. These portraits tell the stories of those who died in the World Trade Center.

8. Generate questions for interviewing others about their most memorable person (see *Writer's Inc.*, page 330). Think about the questions reporters asked when interviewing people for "Portraits of Grief."

9. Interview (take notes!) two people about their most memorable person. At least one of the two people must be over thirty; the older the better! These should not be quick-quick talks, but conversations in which the people you interview tell stories and discuss why these people are memorable. Be sure to keep all notes and questions as evidence of completing this assignment.

231

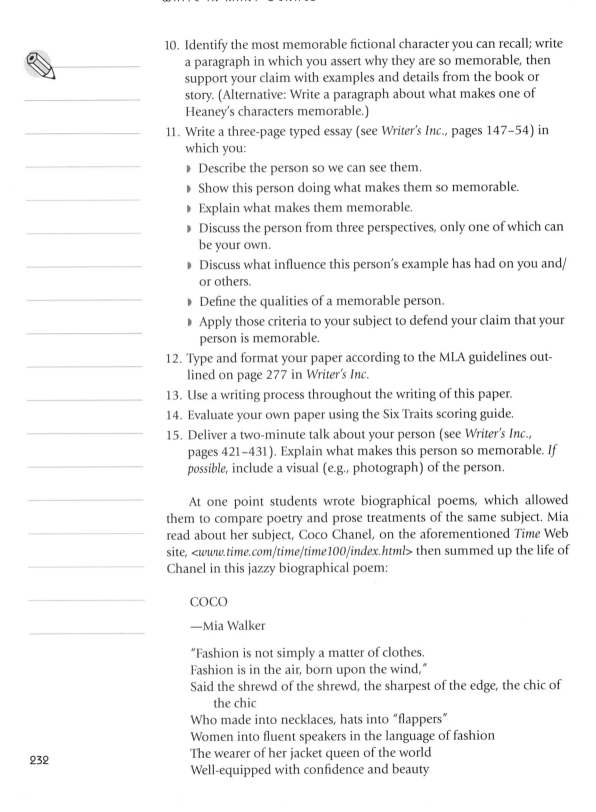

10. Identify the most memorable fictional character you can recall; write a paragraph in which you assert why they are so memorable, then support your claim with examples and details from the book or story. (Alternative: Write a paragraph about what makes one of Heaney's characters memorable.)

11. Write a three-page typed essay (see *Writer's Inc.*, pages 147–54) in which you:

   ▶ Describe the person so we can see them.

   ▶ Show this person doing what makes them so memorable.

   ▶ Explain what makes them memorable.

   ▶ Discuss the person from three perspectives, only one of which can be your own.

   ▶ Discuss what influence this person's example has had on you and/ or others.

   ▶ Define the qualities of a memorable person.

   ▶ Apply those criteria to your subject to defend your claim that your person is memorable.

12. Type and format your paper according to the MLA guidelines outlined on page 277 in *Writer's Inc.*

13. Use a writing process throughout the writing of this paper.

14. Evaluate your own paper using the Six Traits scoring guide.

15. Deliver a two-minute talk about your person (see *Writer's Inc.*, pages 421–431). Explain what makes this person so memorable. *If possible*, include a visual (e.g., photograph) of the person.

At one point students wrote biographical poems, which allowed them to compare poetry and prose treatments of the same subject. Mia read about her subject, Coco Chanel, on the aforementioned *Time* Web site, <*www.time.com/time/time100/index.html*> then summed up the life of Chanel in this jazzy biographical poem:

COCO

—Mia Walker

"Fashion is not simply a matter of clothes.
Fashion is in the air, born upon the wind,"
Said the shrewd of the shrewd, the sharpest of the edge, the chic of
   the chic
Who made into necklaces, hats into "flappers"
Women into fluent speakers in the language of fashion
The wearer of her jacket queen of the world
Well-equipped with confidence and beauty

A revolutionary stylist she was
Receiving gasps and ooh la las as she swept through the
    street
Cigarette dangling from her darkly defined lips
Hat slanted on her forehead, covering one skeptical eye
A genius, bringing then and now and tomorrow into an outfit
Work by a freshman self-assured fan
They all raised their chins and toyed their pearls
That day Ms. Chanel graced the coco trees

Katie Wolfe's poem was inspired by her reading about a man who was lost in the World Trade Center.

EVERYONE'S BEST FRIEND
PORTRAITS OF GRIEF (JOE ZUCCALA)

Time, of all things, is never remembered
Time doesn't reveal why or how, only when.
The size and shape of a person
Is never remembered for long.
The size and shape of the void that they leave
Can never be forgotten.

He didn't know how
He didn't want to
He knew better
To make someone smile
He would dance in front of hundreds of people
Any day.
He didn't hide behind any crowds and
He didn't hesitate to eat his fill of life
Until his appetite was satisfied.
He died on September 11 doing his job.
He was everyone's best friend.

Being six foot five, he stood out enough,
But what is life
If all you are remembered for
Is a number?
Stories will be told as this one has
For hundreds of years, and maybe more.
Each story different,
Because each distinct impression that he made
Will be remembered differently.
However, one idea will remain constant:
Joe Zuccala was everyone's best friend.

For a different assignment, sophomore Neal Cameron wrote a sketch of his great-grandmother. What the paper can't convey is the hard work Neal put into it. His commitment to the subject, one he obviously cared about, inspired him to transcend his usual work habits and learning differences to deliver a remarkable piece of writing:

"SKETCH" OF A FAMILY MEMBER

—*Neal Cameron*

Nona Des, my great grandmother, a woman who to my young eyes seemed never to age, was in a state of permanent antiquity. Older than my grandmother, Nonnie seemed as if she was born old to me, never aging despite the many birthday parties she had at The Leaning Tower Restaurant. I remember them well, the banquet room was decorated in red with carpeting, drapes and that fuzzy wallpaper on the high walls, my cousins and I ran on the sloped aisle in the center of the room, in uncomfortable clothes, I also remember drinking Shirley Temples and Roy Rodgers. She never aged, only got shorter and slowed down a bit, but not getting any older. In the kitchen of Nona Des's house memories are preserved, kept vivid by the refrigerator, stove and table furnishing the room. The white antique refrigerator, short and rounded like Nona herself, housed half-sized cans of Seven-Up, below the one-foot square freezer inside it. The iron stove, also white with its porcelain enamel, boiled water in a teapot atop. The table, covered in a gray granite-like vinyl table cloth, sat four generations, Nona, Grammy (my grandmother), my mom and me who drank heavily sweetened tea the stove had just heated the water for in the pot.

Now, with a great deal of imagination I am able to vaguely picture long ago when Nona's long hair, kept in a tight bun consisting of a single braid wrapped spiraling around itself, reminiscent of Princess Leia, was black not the gray I knew. A time when my grandmother was a child along with her two brothers. My imagination dwindles when imagining the activity taking place inside the house. Perhaps Nona was chasing my great uncles out of the kitchen so she could get some work done, vacating the distractions with threats of the dreaded wooden spoon. An implement larger than most wooden spoons, over a foot in length, sat idly on the ledge of the elaborate molding my great grandfather trimmed the house he built with. Much too nice for such mischief my grandmother would be reading a book, or doing something else quiet and polite, so she would now tell me.

Back to work in the kitchen, Nona would be making the raviolis I remember, before the pre-made frozen varieties, which lay joined like Siamese twins on frosty sheets of white waxed card board, took their place at family dinners. Nona would mince the several types of meat that compose the raviolis, beef, veal, pork and of course the brain of a cow, these ingredients which the butcher had put through his meat grinder were again ground after being browned in a pan. Later atop the stove a huge pot of water would be boiled dominating the burners. In here the raviolis were cooked. Preceded by a meticulous and methodical process involving mincing as mentioned along with rolling thin sheets of dough, in which the mixture of meat was individually packaged the blanket of dough pinched around each one by Nona's careful fingers, which were short and fat with time. This waffle-like sheet was later sliced apart into the individual ravioli. Finally cheese would be grated over a tin grater as old as Nona herself it was mounted in a maple box which had a handle and a drawer with a porcelain knob, the cheese was contained after having a saw-dust-like consistency. More importantly every mishap, cut finger or forgotten step would be accompanied by its own soliloquy, "God . . . this," and "Jesus Christ . . . that," or the equivalent in Italian, in a peculiar gospel of swearing. This trait of Nona Des is one I have been told much about yet remember hearing none of it. All this and the mouth watering smells omitted from the foods prepared is how I imagine Nona Des, my great grandmother long ago.

The following assignment asks students to write the biography of a fictional character, gathering information, making inferences, and drawing conclusions as they read the novel.

Fictional Character Biography

Overview   A biography is the study of another's life. Biographies have different emphases. Some focus on what a person accomplished; these biographies might emphasize Benjamin Franklin's different inventions and contributions to our country's principles. Other biographies concentrate on what influenced the subject most profoundly; such a biography about Eleanor Roosevelt might look closely at the people she met, books she read, and experiences she had, and how all these shaped her thinking. This assignment asks you to write a short biographical essay about a character from a novel you are reading.

Objectives While our primary objectives are to read the book and have great discussions, I also want you to:

• Make inferences about the main character based on what they do or say

• Identify, collect, and use appropriate quotations from the book to support your statements about the character

• Choose and use details and examples to illustrate and further support what you say about the character

• Organize your essay and paragraphs around main ideas (see *RHB*, 60)

• Develop a compelling thesis about the character, which your essay supports

• Use embedded quotations from the text (see *Writer's Inc.*, 258)

• Use transitions to make your ideas flow (see *Writer's Inc.*, 104)

• Take organized Cornell Notes, which you can use when writing your essay

Directions When you are finished reading this novel, you will write an essay (see format guidelines) about the protagonist (or, if there is adequate information about them, some other character in the story). Complete the following steps in order:

1. Identify the character you will study.
2. Take notes (*indicate the page number for easy reference*)—using the Cornell Notes format—about the following aspects of the character:
    ‣ Physical features (i.e., what they look like)
    ‣ Personality traits (i.e., how they act, think, respond)
    ‣ Values and their sources (i.e., what they think is important)
        • Concentrate on cause-effect relationships (see *RHB*, 739; 202)
    ‣ Crucial decisions (i.e., what the character decided—and *why*)
        • Discuss *why* the character made each decision
        • Discuss the consequences and/or implications of each decision
    ‣ Others' perspectives (i.e., what others think of this person)
        • Discuss *why* these other characters think or feel this way
        • Explain why these other characters' opinions matter
    ‣ Your perspective (i.e., what *you* think about this person)
    ‣ Themes in this person's life

3. Use your notes to write a biographical essay about this character. The essay should be:

- Three pages long
- Double-spaced
- Typed
- Written in twelve-point font (either Times Roman or some other serif font)
- Properly formatted (see *Writer's Inc.*, 20, 276–77)

RECOMMENDED RESOURCE

Langer, Judith. 1995. *Envisioning Literature: Literary Understanding and Literature Instruction.* New York: Teachers College Press/International Reading Association.

47 Write an Expository Essay

OVERVIEW

Expository writing is as much about thinking as it is about writing. Its purpose is to explain, to inform; in the process of explaining a process, for example, we must analyze what is most important and choose the most appropriate way to convey this information in writing. Hall and Birkerts describe exposition as follows:

> Exposition is explanation—exposing a subject for an audience, making it clear. The word itself comes from the Latin verb meaning "to set out," and it becomes an English noun meaning "something displayed for public inspection." Expository writing is far and away the most common mode of expression. We write exposition not only in college; most writing required in professional life is expository—in business, in teaching, in technology and science, in law and medicine. When social workers deliver papers, when geologists make reports, when hospital officials release information on new diagnostic equipment, when marketing managers report on activities of their competition, they write expository prose. Newspapers, brochures, and guidebooks are all exposition. We might, therefore, think of exposition as the foundation on which most essays, including those of the argumentative or persuasive sort, are built. (1994, 228)

Perhaps you can understand it best by seeing how exposition differs from narration. The first example is a narrative, while the second is exposition:

> The girl slumped in her chair, her left hand playing an invisible piano on her desk. She stared out the window, as if looking for some answer to a question her mind kept asking. As she watched the sky pass by the dirty windows of the classroom, Allison began to hear words gather in her like a small storm; suddenly she realized these were the words to the song she had been up late—too late—trying to write. She bolted up in her chair and, pushing aside the class assignment, hastily began scribbling the words in the little notepad she always kept with her.

Many students today feel lost or so they appear. Sitting in a typical high school classroom, you notice kids staring off into space, their eyes glazed over with apparent indifference. Appearance can be deceiving, however; we know from recent interviews that most kids have active imaginations, which they use to solve the problems they encounter in their daily lives. A boy might be puzzling through why he lost the tennis match the day before; next to him, a seemingly distracted girl might be working through a song she spent much of the previous night trying to write. Teenagers are, to adapt an old saying, a country all their own; they do things differently there. But the point is they *do* things, interesting things, often when the lights seem most out and no one could possibly be home.

State exit exams and other such tests typically require abundant expository reading and as many as two different expository essays. Teachers must develop students' textual intelligence (Burke 2001) about how these informational texts work so students can both read and write them with equal fluency. Thus, students must learn strategies they can use to generate, organize, and analyze the subject they must explain. The tools for thought (Burke 2002c) and writing strategies teachers and students use will ultimately depend on the writer's purpose.

While students might write a paper to describe something—a person, a place, a process—they rarely use only one mode of thinking. In describing a place, for example, the writer finds it useful to compare this place with others to help readers understand what it is (and is not) like. Similarly, when describing a place, one might also be quietly asserting this place's supremacy over others; such might be the case in an informational brochure or article about the beauties of Ireland over, say, Scotland or England. Finally, writers may incorporate into their exposition other devices—images, graphics, figures—that can help them more fully convey their ideas. One would hope, for instance, to see photographs of those aspects of Ireland that the writer is celebrating, and perhaps a map to visually illustrate the proximity of other wonders in the area.

PROMPTS FOR PRACTICE

• Explain how a process or object (e.g., computer) works.

• Explain how to do something.

• Write a report that investigates and answers a serious research question.

- Write an observation report about what happened in a specific situation.

- Write a news article about an event.

- Describe a place (e.g., your room).

- Write a letter to incoming students telling them what the school (or a program) is like and how to get the most from it.

- Write a research paper about a historical event or the evolution of an idea over time.

- Evaluate and discuss the traits of a good (for example) soccer player, band, or coach.

- Describe the culture of your school and compare it to that of your previous school.

- Explain how one event or person affected other people or a historical period.

- Compare several different literary works (e.g., poems, stories, novels) by the same author or several different authors' comments about the same subject.

CLASSROOM CONNECTION

Not all expository writing comes in the form of an essay, of course. A steady diet of expository reading and writing develops students' awareness of and ability to use different organizational patterns and rhetorical modes. The example assignment on page 242 comes from my ACCESS class and illustrates an effective sequence of actions that helped students read and write effectively. The assignment corresponded with our reading of the *Reader's Handbook* (Burke 2002a), which we were using to

---

THE EXPOSITORY ESSAY AT A GLANCE

Expository writing includes more attributes of informational texts as time goes on and the nature of texts changes (Burke 2001). Such writing will only become more multitextual over time, incorporating hotlinks, images, diagrams, graphics, and eventually audio and video clips, until expository writing may well look more like today's multimedia encyclopedias than an essay. See Figure 47.1 for a list of the many forms of expository writing often required of students.

California Assessment Program Categories

AUTOBIOGRAPHICAL
- Focus on a single incident—a moment, a few hours, no more than a day; also give reader a sense of what this meant to you personally
- Re-create the experience by using vivid sensory details, scene description, dialogue, action, internal thoughts, personal commentary, explanations
- Use essay format—beginning, middle, end

OBSERVATION
- Focus on the topic (e.g., a specific place to describe)
- Imagine that you are a reporter and a cameraperson all in one
- Re-create the scene by using vivid sensory details, names of people and places, action, dialogue, personal observations
- Give the reader a sense of movement and perspective—in and out of the scene, move around, giving a sense of the writer's attitude toward the observation as expressed through the choice of language and detail
- Have an organization—beginning, middle, end

INTERPRETATION
- Take a stand (i.e., have a clear thesis) and support it
- Give good reasons, examples, "for instance," factual information, experiences that support
- Organize into clear paragraphs; topic sentences
- Provide logical supports—don't stray from the topic
- Conclude with both summary and an extension of your ideas

EVALUATION
- Take a clear stand—for or against the issue—to evaluate
- Establish criteria for evaluating—these are the points by which you judge something to be good or bad, right or wrong, pleasant or unpleasant. They may be stated directly at the beginning and then used throughout, or they may be scattered throughout the essay as you argue your points
- Use specific examples and details to support your arguments. These may be taken from your own or others' experiences or from what you have read or seen or heard
- Begin essay with your position—thesis—statement in the introduction. Organize all subsequent paragraphs logically into main points to develop your thesis
- Conclude with summary and a good recommendation that fits your thesis

REFLECTION
- See the instructions for the Autobiographical Essay. This essay is similar, but more sophisticated
- Use the technique of re-creating an incident, but raise your commentary and observation to a philosophical, universal level. How does this incident reflect a truth about life in general or about something universal to human experience? As you develop your paragraphs, you will want to include commentary that is more reflective about the meaning of events

CONTROVERSIAL ISSUE
- Take a side on the issue given. Argue either for or against
- Write an introduction that does what you have been taught—hook the reader, give background material, present a clear, arguable thesis
- Organize your main arguments into logical paragraphs with clear topic sentences
- Support your arguments with specific examples and details drawn from your own friends' or family's experiences. Don't worry about having to use precise statistics, but do use logical, well-known "facts"
- Use counterarguments; these are points that someone on the other side would use and that you demolish with your own arguments
- Write a conclusion that pulls together your main ideas and provides perspective and a recommendation

Traditional College Rhetorical Modes

NARRATIVE
- Answers the question, What happened and when?
- Emphasis on chronological order of events; use of traditional words helps such events flow smoothly from one to the next
- Point of view is important as it shapes the voice, tone, and purpose of the story
- Mood is of fundamental importance as it directs the reader's response: is this a fond memory of a loved one or an angry account of an event that left a lasting scar?

DEFINITION
- Answers the question, What is it?
- Attempts to explain any important word or concept to the reader
- Uses negation to also clarify what the word does *not* mean
- Might focus on the origins of the word as a means of establishing its meaning

DIVISION/CLASSIFICATION
- Answers the question, What kind is it? or What are its parts?
- Arranges information into categories in order to establish and articulate the relationships between items in each category
- Categories should be distinct to avoid confusion
- Exemplary essay "Friends, Good Friends—and Such Good Friends," by Judith Viorst

PROCESS ANALYSIS
- Answers the question, How did it happen?
- Two choices: how *to do* something or how something *was done*
- Establishes who your audience is so you know what must be carefully explained
- Uses modes such as narration to explain the process

CAUSE AND EFFECT
- Answers the question, Why did it happen?
- Carefully examines what happened and why
- Clear, logical writing is crucial in order to be effective
- Descriptive writing helps illustrate the relationship between the cause and the effect

ARGUMENTATION/PERSUASION
- Answers the question, Why should I want to do or think that?
- The thesis is especially important as this is what your essay will convince the reader to think or do
- Logic is crucial so as to make argument effective
- You must anticipate the counterarguments and address them in your essay
- *Argument* focuses on the logical appeal
- *Persuasion* focuses on the emotional appeal

COMPARISON/CONTRAST
- Answers the question, What is it (not) like?
- In the *comparison*, the similarities are carefully established and developed
- In *contrast*, the differences between the two elements or sides are emphasized
- You must clearly establish early on the basis of the comparison so as to provide a context for all that follows it

EXAMPLE/ILLUSTRATION
- Answers the question, For example?
- Clarity depends on concrete, vivid examples that reveal the concept being discussed or the position advocated
- Active verbs will help the reader by showing him/her exactly what this subject does
- Exemplary essay: Nikki Giovanni's "My Own Style," in which she illustrates her way of living by describing specific objects and explaining how they exemplify her lifestyle

Source: South California Department of Education (California Assessment Program)

FIGURE 47.1   Various types of academic writing students are often asked to do

learn more about how information in textbooks is organized so students could read, in this case, their history books more successfully.

1. *Set a purpose.* Tell them why they are reading and what they are trying to find (examples and details).
2. *Preview the text.* Skim through it with them to get a sense of the text's content and organization so they know what to expect.
3. *Make a plan.* Use the Main Idea Organizer (see Figure 47.2) to help them take notes toward the point they will make about the subject (in this case, Muhammad).
4. *Read with a purpose.* As they read, have students evaluate the information for possible ideas and details to support the point they want to make about the subject.
5. *Pause and reflect.* After finishing the reading, during which your class has discussed how the information was organized within the chapter and paragraphs, ask them to make sure their details support the point they want to make about the subject. Have them discuss in small groups or pairs to see that everyone is in agreement about what the text says.
6. *Write.* Have students use their notes, now organized into a Main Idea Organizer, to help them write a well-organized paragraph about the subject.

Julia Heredia's example, written about Muhammad, follows. A quick glance reveals how helpful such tools as the Main Idea Organizer (Figure 47.2) are for the students learning to write expository writing.

Muhammad was a strong religious leader that spread Islam religion all over the world. Muhammad came from a very powerful family and had met his wife, Kaadijah, when he worked as a businessman and trade manager. Even before his inspiration from what he thought was Allah (God), he was a very religious man. He would always pray and meditate a long time. When the angel Gabriel appear to him he thought it was Allah and the angel told him that there was only one God. From there on he started to preach and some people converted into Islam, which means submission to the will of Allah. In the year 622 AD they resettled in Yathria because back in Mecca they were treated bad because of Islam religion. This migration was called Hijrah. In 630 AD Muhammad and 10,000 men marched in Mecca and won. With that great victory he destroyed all idols in the Ka'aba to show that there was only one God.

Main Idea Organizer: Reading, Writing, Watching, Listening   Name: Julia Benedict

Subject — What are you writing about? **MUHAMMAD**

Details • Examples • Stories • Quotations Explanations	Detail — Business	Detail — Religious	Detail — Military/Political
	• POWERFUL FAMILY • trader + business manager for Khadijah ← wife	• time alone in prayer + meditation • while praying in cave outside Mecca — angel Gabriel spoke to him — he thought it was Allah • Allah = 1 + only God • "Muslim = one who has submitted" • Islam → "submission to the will of Allah" • 613 he preach publicly in Mecca • 622 he settle in Yathrib (Medina) 200 miles from Mecca — migration known as Hijrah • Umma or Muslim religious community	• Fashioned agreement w/ Arab + Jews • leader in hostilities b/w Mecca + Medina (Yathrib) • 630 Prophet + 10,000 follower marched to Mecca • Prophet won • write to Kaaba + destroy all idols — 1 God only

Main Idea — What are you saying *about* the subject (i.e., what is the *point* you are trying to make)?

Muhammad was a strong religious leader that spread Islam religion all over the world.

FIGURE 47.2   Sample Main Idea Organizer that Julia used to prepare herself to write about Muhammed

The following additional assignments show a range of types of expository writing typical of my class. Other reminders get more detailed about particular forms, such as persuasive and reflective writing, both of which are types of expository prose. The first assignment, Write of Way: Entering the Public Dialogue, grew out of new legislation restricting teen drivers; I know a rich and useful opportunity when I see one. My sophomores, all of whom were living for their licenses, were passionate about this subject, so the assignment was a successful one.

Write of Way: Entering into the Public Dialogue

Overview Last week several laws were passed that specifically affect you. One, AB99 (Runner, R-Lancaster), makes it illegal for anyone to perform body piercing upon a person under eighteen unless the piercing is performed with the consent of a parent or guardian; ear piercing is exempted. The second law, SB1329 (Leslie, R-Roseville), puts more restrictions on teenage drivers concerning driving at night and driving with passengers under twenty years of age.

Objective The objective of this project is to accomplish the following:

- Teach you to access information via the Internet

- Improve your ability to comprehend difficult texts and summarize their main ideas

- Improve your ability to use facts to support an argument

- Improve your writing through writing to real audiences (e.g., newspaper and radio and state representative)

- Improve your ability to communicate your ideas orally by giving a brief speech to the class on your topic

- Improve your ability to use computers by typing up your letters and essays

- Improve your ability to generate ideas during the prewriting stage

- Involve you in the actual political process

Requirements Each of you will do the following:

- Read and summarize the main points of the laws as outlined in the *San Francisco Chronicle* article and the text of the law itself.

- Using the graphic organizer provided, list three reasons for the law and three reasons against it. You should include notes in your cluster to support your reasoning for and against.

- After reading the sample letters to the editor, write your own letter to the editor and type it up. You are limited to 150 words. The top three will be submitted to the *Chronicle* for consideration.

- After reading the sample "Perspective," write a radio commentary that you will subsequently read before the class; the top three will be submitted to KQED for consideration.

- After using the Internet to find out who your state representative is and what their address is, write them a letter using the proper letter format. In this letter you should outline your position on the driving laws, taking time to support your argument with specific examples. This letter must be typed and perfect.

- Explain the following relationships in your journal:

  ▶ How is the relationship between the British and the American colonialists similar to that of a parent and their adolescent son or daughter? Explain with examples.

  ▶ How is the recent law regarding teen driving similar to laws passed by the British prior to 1776? Explain using historical examples to illustrate.

- Complete the following activities in your journal:

  ▶ Write a bill of rights for American teenagers and explain your reasoning behind your proposed bill of rights.

  ▶ When you are forty-five, will you still support your bill of rights for teens? Please explain your thinking.

Evaluation Rubric

Distinguished

- Each required piece is typed (except for journal)

- Each price is perfectly proofread

- Each piece is well written

- You use examples to support your reasoning

- Your language is appropriate and effective in supporting your arguments

- You use proper formatting for your letters to editor and legislator

• Your speech is delivered in a clear, articulate voice we can all hear and enjoy

Good

• Your work is typed

• Your work is generally well proofed but has minor errors

• You develop your main argument but do so without effectively supporting it with examples or explaining how the examples relate to your main idea

• Your argument is weakened by inappropriate language that is not able to persuade the reader (e.g., they hear a teenager whining about the law)

• You do not follow the proper letter format in your letters

• You speak but need to work on articulating your words, projecting your voice, showing us your eyes while you speak

Inadequate

• Your overall work lacks sincere effort to do the work or the thinking necessary to be taken seriously

• Your argument is not developed and lacks specific examples

• Your work suffers from unacceptable errors that could have been caught during proofreading

• Your letter does not follow the proper format

• Your speech was unsuccessful because you mumbled, you were not prepared, or you did not give it

The French Revolution Digital Storybook, which history teacher Steve Mills assigns in his freshman modern world history class, provides a useful example of expository writing that incorporates much more than just words:

French Revolution Digital Storybook

Directions for creating a digital storybook of the French Revolution.

1. You and your partner will create a digital storybook that chronicles major events of the French Revolution and describes how the revolution contributed to the rise of democracy. It should be written in simple, clear language so that a ten-year-old could read and enjoy it.

2. Your digital storybook will contain the following features (TEN TOTAL SLIDES):

   ▶ A visually appealing cover slide with an appropriate title

   ▶ A brief introduction slide that describes the conditions in France in the late 1780s

   ▶ A separate slide for each of the following events: the meeting of the Estates General, the Tennis Court Oath, the storming of the Bastille, the march on Versailles, the Reign of Terror, and the rise of Napoleon. Each of these six slides must contain the following:

     • A graphic or illustration of the event

     • Thought or voice bubbles coming from the characters in the graphic or illustration with dialogue specific to that event

     • A summary of the event and how it was related to the French Revolution

     • A brief explanation of whether the event represented a step toward democracy

     • All the vocabulary in the word banks that appear on Student Handout 1.4B (diagrams of the six events)

   ▶ A conclusion slide that briefly explains how the events of the French Revolution contributed to the growth of democracy

   ▶ A resources slide that documents where you gathered your information from

   ▶ Additional touches to make the storybook artistic and visually appealing—use of color, sound, video, additional graphics or visuals, page numbers, and so on.

3. Your digital storybook of the French Revolution is due on _____. Web sites for research: go to *<http://home.pacbell.net/smills/history resources.html>* and scroll down to the Age of Revolutions section to find links to help you with this project.

Short expository papers provide students the opportunity to work with papers in different ways over the semester while at the same time giving them the chance to practice writing essays. The Weekly Paper (see more about the *Weekly Reader* digital textbook in Reminder 6) invites students to read and write about a variety of types of text. In the following essay, a student writes about a work of art titled *Trash People*:

We throw things away every day, a gum wrapper, a magazine, an apple core, dirty binder paper, what does it matter? It is trash to us and has no meaning in our busy life. The things we don't need take up too much time, causing us to disregard some

247

things as if nothing is important to the human soul, only your money and career. We treat our inner most thoughts, feelings, and dreams as trash because they take up too much time and we think they are unpractical, resulting in us treating our most precious thoughts and wants like the trash we throw away daily.

Garbage Men, by H. A. Schull is an interesting piece of art. It is life-size human sculptures that stand along the Great Wall of China. When I first saw the photograph of the sculpture I had my own idea of how the artist was connecting trash to humans. What I saw and observed about life, including my own, is how we throw so much away without a thought. We often don't take ourselves seriously and don't listen to our instincts that scream at us. We throw away our views, emotions, dreams, until we lose our shine. We no longer reach out to others, say unexpected things, and do beautiful or unusual things. We give into society and turn into the manufactured human. The sort of human that can no longer tell trash from goods, and our lives become plastered with trash that we can't even find ourselves.

Just because you see most people walking around without a twinkle in their eye, without a spring in their voice, without a flicker to their movement, doesn't mean you don't have a polish. People forget that there are dreams out there to achieve, and that they can listen to their blaring dreams and instincts without throwing them away like trash. People become plastic just like their trash, and they start to blend in even when their thoughts are different. We walk around like robots without souls because we have learned to play in a world where nothing matters, but it matters. We need to start saving ourselves and throwing away the real trash.

While related to the fictional character biography, the following sketch of a character is more of an expository exercise. The assignment asked students to work on writing but also made them more attentive readers, as they had a purpose for their reading.

WEN FU CHARACTER SKETCH

—*Chana-Rivka Foster*

Wen Fu has a very complex character, more complex than most people's, because he is not one but two people. Inside of Wen Fu are two connected, yet very different identities. One of these identities is the sweet, charming boy Winnie met on the streets with Peanut. The other man is a monster, a vicious, demanding person who alters the minds of people and twists them to get what he wants. Of course, these different characters are not even identities: they are simple roles Wen Fu shuffles between, like a spoiled child, to get the best of the situation. For example, in order to marry Peanut, and to be part of a rich family, Wen Fu is faithful, kind, honest, and loving, in order to win Peanut's love, and ultimately to become rich. At the same time, Wen Fu is still able to receive what he wants from Winnie: obedience, loyalty, respect, and the like, just by being mean, rude, and disrespectful towards her. Through these two fake roles that he plays, Wen Fu is somehow able to win the respect and friendship of others, even though an artificial character is being displayed, not his own. His different roles make it easier to trick people, so Wen Fu has become different people.

Generating topics presents challenges for many students, particularly those for whom writing is difficult. Many students have "output" difficulties; for this reason, I try to model my own process of getting ideas out, showing them that I get it down, saying yes to anything for the moment. As I stand at the overhead jotting my ideas down, I think out loud, telling them how one idea leads to another.

After I have finished showing them how I generate ideas, they get going on their own.

RECOMMENDED RESOURCE

Hall, Donald, and Sven Birkerts. 1994. *Writing Well*. New York: Harper-Collins.

48 Write a Description

DESCRIPTION

Descriptive writing answers the question, What is it like? Description underlies all effective writing and is, inevitably, embedded in most other types of writing. Through description the writer helps the reader see and thus better understand the object, process, place, or event about which they are writing. Some descriptions are objective, offering no commentary, no larger context created by the author's mood or the text's tone. Other descriptions are subjective, dealing as much if not more with the author's attitude toward the subject as with the description of the subject itself. When a writer like Joan Didion, for example, describes something—a governor's mansion, Alcatraz Island, a city—she has a point she wants to make and an attitude to convey through the words and images she chooses to use.

We describe many things when we write: people, places, processes, events, even abstract subjects such as ideas and feelings. A few years back, the state writing test asked California students to describe an interesting building, something many found difficult. They struggled with not only how to write such an essay but what to write about; many arrived at the same topic: a building in downtown San Francisco with wild colors and pieces of furniture (e.g., desks, chairs, couches) affixed to its exterior walls. Despite the curious aspects of the building, however, most did not know what to say about it; their descriptions had details but no point. Had students been invited to describe a subject about which they cared, the state might have received powerful word paintings of cars, places, computers, sports equipment, and so on.

PROMPTS FOR PRACTICE

Here are some sample topics you might consider discussing with your students. Consider discussing with them how they would begin; what they would say; how they might organize their information; what examples they can come up with and why they are so effective. They might describe:

- A person
- A process

THE DESCRIPTION AT A GLANCE

☐ Focuses on a clearly defined, manageable subject.

☐ Makes a point about this subject. If, for example, a student is describing their car, they might say, "While not the most stylish car on the road, my 1981 Ford Maverick offers something not even the most expensive car has: great memories."

☐ Organizes information within the composition in the way most appropriate to the subject:

    ☐ *Space.* If you are describing a room, building, or other space, the description might begin at one point (e.g., the doorway or the top) and move in a logical, linear way through the rest of that space until you reach the end (e.g., the last room, the bottom).

    ☐ *Aspect.* One alternative to organizing your paper spatially is to focus on one aspect, such as color, then move on to another characteristic, like texture. In an essay about baseballs, for example, Roger Angell moves from seams, to cover, to core, describing each aspect in fine detail and in relationship to the others.

    ☐ *Perspective.* Writers can also describe the same subject—whether object, process, or event—from multiple perspectives to paint a more complete picture of that subject. When describing different wars, writers such as Stephen Ambrose and Bruce Catton typically include the perspective of the men in the field as well as that of the men in the White House; the older, more experienced soldiers and the fresh new recruits; the enemy and the allies. Such comparative descriptions offer a range of insights into the subject being described that the writer's own perspective cannot achieve.

☐ Establishes and maintains throughout a sense of purpose, which answers the questions, What is it? and Why am I describing it?

☐ Selects details that will create a strong visual sense or impression of the subject described. Of all the details available, the writer chooses only those that will most effectively contribute to this impression.

☐ Takes a stance or adopts a perspective toward your subject. Possibly include in your description how other people feel about or would describe this subject.

☐ Includes such practical details as what people do with it, what it is made of, its surroundings, its distinctive features or markings, as well as any other precise details that would help people see and understand what you are describing and what you are saying about the subject.

☐ Surprises the reader in some way by allowing them to see whatever you are describing in a new way or from a different perspective.

☐ Includes details that draw on as many of the five senses as possible so as to help the reader see what they are reading.

☐ Includes, depending on the writer's underlying purpose, other rhetorical modes. In addition to describing a basketball player, for example, the writer may be trying to persuade you that this player is the best. The writer describing Patton and Eisenhower not only describes the two leaders but defines the traits of effective military leaders, drawing examples from these two men to support the point he wants to make.

☐ Matches word choice and sentence style to the subject and purpose; thus, if the object is one toward which the writer feels reverence, the words and style should reinforce that mood if the writer is to succeed.

☐ Uses devices—for example, metaphors and similes—to make abstract concepts or unfamiliar subjects more concrete, more visual to the reader.

- An object

- A place

- An event

- A procedure

- A feeling or emotion

Here is a sample sequence teachers can adapt for any of the subjects just listed. Note the connection between reading and writing and how one complements the other.

1. Students read a passage from a book, article, or poem or watch video, look at an image, or observe a process.

2. As they read, they look for and take notes about the precise details of a place, person, or object. The details must be of use in rendering a precise *drawing* of the subject. Thus, if students are reading *Lord of the Flies*, for example, they might take notes on the layout and appearance of the island as described by Golding. This is a good opportunity for close discussion of nouns (*palm* trees, not just trees), verbs (*slashed*, not cut), and adjectives (*violet*, not purple).

3. Using their notes to guide them, they make the best, most precise, accurate drawing they can of the subject.

4. Using the drawing as a variation on prewriting, have students describe what is happening in the drawing, what the viewer sees.

5. Have them compare with other students to see how they responded to the same or different subjects.

CLASSROOM CONNECTION

The following assignment comes from the Life Study Project my students do each spring. This project takes most of a semester and embeds all different kinds of writing. Here is one assignment from the much larger unit:

Overview   Whether you are writing about Muhammad Ali or Mother Teresa, your grandfather or a cherished aunt, your subject is most alive, is their truest self in a particular situation. This is when you see what they are all about, what makes them unique or simply reveals their excellence. If it's an artist, it is at some point during the creative process; for mathematicians or scientists, it might be at the chalkboard, or simply while thinking through an idea. Einstein, for example, used to write all over the tablecloths while illustrating his ideas, moving plates and glasses to the side to make room. (Waiters would then fight over who got to keep the great scientist's tablecloth.) Whatever the subject of your life study does, there is an element, a situation in which they are most at home. Your job is to figure out what that situation is and show them in it.

You are *not* writing a report or a summary; you are, instead, writing a word portrait, one that shows your subject *doing* what it is they do best. To write this portrait successfully, you must think carefully about the verbs and nouns needed to evoke an image of your subject. How do you describe the wrist movements or hand gestures of a painter, sculptor, or composer so we can see them when we read? What words will capture the intensity of their eyes or the sound of their voice as they play out the drama of their life? Finally, what is that setting—and how can you help your reader see it—in which you must describe them at work if you are to be true to your subject?

Exemplars   Consider this excerpt written by Paul Krupnov, a freshman writing about the mathematician John Nash. I have italicized Paul's verbs to draw attention to them as they are the key to his successful writing:

. . . He [John Nash] *scrambles* through [his papers], *searching* for a specific one, the one where he made a rather important discovery. He *picks up* his pen, as if to start writing again, but instead *scratches* his relatively large ears, still *staring* at the many sheets of paper lying on the table. Finally, he finds it, and moving his eyes back and forth along the many lines, he finds his error. He quietly *murmurs* something to himself, *reaches* into the left pocket of his dark-colored jacket and takes out a tiny piece of chalk. He once again *murmurs* something to himself, something

253

which obviously displeases him. Then, he stands up and turns around to face an open window, one that is almost entirely covered in white writing. He quickly *erases* the x^2 from a previous equation, and in its place writes x^3. Seemingly pleased, he *nods* his head in contentment, and sits back down.

Guidelines

Your portrait should:

- Use active, precise verbs that help the reader see your subject

- Use concrete, precise nouns so the reader can, again, see what you are describing

- Include little or no exposition or background; save that for the full report or your presentation

- Include dialogue so we can hear your subject speaking, unless part of their character is their silence, in which case you should find a way to represent that

- Focus on a specific moment, in some cases only a minute long. Film them with words. Make sure that your portrait represents them, their character, the work and ideas that made you want to study them in the first place

- Be at least one page long, typed, double-spaced, in a 12-point, serif font.

A different kind of assignment, one common to English classes at all grade levels, is describing a character from a work of fiction. Figures 48.1 through 48.3 show a sequence of activities we used to write about characters from Homer's *Odyssey*. First you will see the Main Idea Organizer (Figure 48.1), which students used to make a claim about the subject, then generate and organize details around that subject that they could use in the subsequent paragraph. Figure 48.2 shows a related step: creating a Conversational Roundtable for Telemachus. Both of these activities, combined with in-class discussions of their notes, prepared students to then write well-organized paragraphs such as the one in Figure 48.3.

RECOMMENDED RESOURCE

Atwell, Nancie. 2002. *Lessons That Change Writers*. Portsmouth, NH: Heinemann *first*hand.

Main Idea Organizer: Reading, Writing, Watching, Listening

Overview This tool helps you identify the main ideas while reading a text, watching a video, or listening to a lecture; it also prepares you to write by helping you organize your ideas and determining **what you want to say about those ideas.**

Subject: What are you writing about?

Details
- Examples
- Stories
- Quotations
- Explanations

Main Idea: What are you saying *about* the subject (i.e., what is the *point* you are trying to make?)?

Handwritten grade: 20/20 Very good. Thinking + writing win. Rose

Subject: Penelope

Detail	Detail	Detail
Courses	Suitors	Telemachus
Her husband went to war and has been lost for 20 years so Penelope is left to raise her son	- Invaded her home	- First, he has little confidence and shows little potential to be king
Telemachus on her own	- Disrespect her son	- He leaves her without telling her
	- Refuse to leave	- is in danger of suitors
	- Use up resources	
	- food drink lounge around all day	
	- Threaten to kill Telemachus	

Main Idea

Penelope is very unhappy for different reasons.

Hot Tip: Turn your "Main Idea" into your thesis statement or topic sentence; how-

FIGURE 48.1   Main Idea Organizer for Penelope

255

What he says/Does	What Others Think about Character
- Orders his mother to her room	- Suitors don't have much respect for Telemachus, when he asks them to leave, they do not
- Called assembly with suitors, asked them to leave	- mother is surprised + proud He is taking authority
- Acts properly around leaders better + better throughout voyage	

Telemachus

How character looks and feels	How I feel about Character
- Looks like his father	- Feel bad because father is gone
- Tall and handsome	- Feel bad b/c suitors wont listen
- God like	
- Felt powerless in beginning with suitors	- Lucky b/c Athena is helping him
- After athena's help - begins to feel like king's son	- Hopeful - hope he finds his father

FIGURE 48.2   Conversational Roundtable for Telemachus

Telemachus

When the story begins Telemachus is young and insecure. He has never had a father to help him become a man. It's not until Athena comes to help him that he begins to grow confidence. He shows his new strength when he orders his mother to her room. When this happens, his mother is very surprised, but proud that her son is finally taking authority. The suitors, however, have a different reaction when Telemachus tells them to leave. Obviosly, they have little respect for him, and refuse. During his journies, Telemachus shows more and more confidence, and gets respect from the leaders he meets. Most of the leaders he meets describe him as tall, handsome, and godlike and immediately identify him as Odysseus's son. It is sad that Telemachus has never had a father and that the suitors have taken over his home, but he is very fortunate to have a god, Athena, there helping him.

FIGURE 48.3 Initial writing on Telemachus, in which the student draws on her preparation with the Main Idea Organizer and the Conversational Roundtable

49 Write a Persuasive Essay

Beauty itself doth of itself persuade
The eyes of men without an orator.

SHAKESPEARE, FROM *THE RAPE OF LUCRECE*

OVERVIEW

Our country exists in large part because of a group of men's ability to persuade people to think and see differently. In *Founding Brothers: The Revolutionary Generation*, historian Joseph Ellis writes about James Madison:

> John Marshall [observed] that [Patrick] Henry might be the all-time oratorical champion in his capacity to persuade; but Madison was his superior in his capacity to convince. . . . Appearances, in Madison's case, were not just massively deceptive; they actually helped to produce his prowess. Amid the flamboyant orators of the Virginia dynasty, he was practically invisible and wholly unthreatening, but therefore the acknowledged master of the inoffensive argument that just happened, time after time, to prove decisive. (2002, 53)

About one of the other "founding brothers," Thomas Jefferson, Ellis writes:

> Madison, who knew [Jefferson] better than any man alive, fully realized that there was an invisible line somewhere in Jefferson's mind above which lay his most cherished personal and political ideals. Cross that line and you set off explosions and torrents of unbridled anger of the sort that got spewed at George III in the Declaration of Independence. (Jefferson did not regard such occasions as arguments, but rather as holy wars to the death.) (68)

Of course many of the arguments we encounter today—whether written, spoken, or visual—are attempts to sell us not a new republic but better shoes, faster computers, or whiter teeth. When attempting to persuade us, these arguments tap in to a set of basic human needs for comfort, safety, control, tradition, friendship, nurturance, recognition, success, independence, variety, curiosity, and enjoyment (Osborn and Osborn 1997). Effective arguments also recognize and make use of a set of universal values: power, achievement, tradition, enjoyment, self-direction, security, unity, benevolence, conformity, and stimulation (Osborn and Osborn 1997).

While arguments come in different forms—spoken (oral), visual (e.g., advertisements), and written—I will focus on written, recognizing that most of what applies to one type applies as well to the others. Persuasion is perhaps the most common form of thinking we use, whether with ourselves or others. We write letters and proposals; kids write essays to colleges; others write reports or other papers meant to persuade people to support, change, or *not* change certain beliefs, policies, or decisions. Of course, I do not include the endless—and failed—efforts to persuade my three children to eat their dinner, stop attacking each other, and clean up their rooms.

PROMPTS FOR PRACTICE

Have students do any of the following:

• Write their local legislators to argue for or against some pending legislation that is before the government. An alternative would be to have students write a letter calling for some new law or an alteration to an existing law that affects teens.

• Write letters to the editor or op-ed columns about some pressing issue of compelling interest to them.

• Convince someone that something—a movie, a method, some kind of food—is the best.

• Write a letter to someone explaining why it is important for them to do something (e.g., do well in school, improve their diet, go to college).

• Write a letter to their teacher arguing for the grade they feel is most appropriate.

• Answer the question, Who is the most important person of this century?

• Answer the question, What is the most important event or discovery of the last century or millennium?

• Argue for or against a school rule (e.g., the dress code) in an essay, speech, or letter to the administration.

• Write a letter of complaint—about a product, service, or experience—in which they argue for some resolution, change, or compensation.

• When finishing a novel, write a persuasive response in lieu of a literary analysis. For example, students finishing *All Quiet on the Western Front*

THE PERSUASIVE ESSAY AT A GLANCE

☐ Choose a subject that is both interesting and controversial.

☐ Make a statement about this subject; this will be the thesis of your essay (or whatever form your argument uses).

☐ Gather information from multiple, reliable sources to support your claim.

☐ Organize your ideas, identifying the most significant details; consider whether it is more effective to place these powerful details up front or at the end, as a dynamic closing.

☐ Anticipate objections, biases, and assumptions your readers may have; structure or adapt your argument to address those challenges.

☐ Consider what the audience does and needs to know about this subject.

☐ Know and observe the distinction between fact and opinion when supporting your claim. Effective ways to support your argument include using facts, examples, stories, quotations from experts, and images that graphically depict the point you are trying to make.

☐ Know which kind of opinion statement you are making:

    ☐ Statement of fact (i.e., whether something is true or not)

    ☐ Statement of value (i.e., the value or worth of something)

    ☐ Statement of policy (i.e., whether something should be done)

☐ Acknowledge the other side's perspective; by conceding the opposing side has some merit, you undermine the effect of its argument.

☐ Be consistent: take a stand and hold it throughout your essay; any wavering or second-guessing compromises its effectiveness.

☐ Avoid the use of logical fallacies:

    ☐ *Appeal to authority.* This technique involves citing "authorities" who in fact are not experts in the field the writer is discussing in the essay.

    ☐ *Appeal to fear.* Such efforts to persuade play on people's fears and employ threats.

    ☐ *Appeal to pity.* This common technique plays on people's emotions as opposed to their reason. The writer tries to make the reader feel sorry for their or another's situation.

    ☐ *Begging the question.* This approach lacks support for the stated conclusion; the argument is often circular, saying, in effect, that something is enjoyable because it is . . . enjoyable.

    ☐ *Equivocation.* This involves the intentional manipulation of ambiguous language to support a position or achieve an outcome. Those with greater capacity with language will often employ this technique in an effort to confuse the reader.

    ☐ *False-analogy.* The writer compares two things, or some aspect of these two entities, that are not, in fact, similar.

□ *False cause.* Some writers will falsely attribute a result to some series of events that did not, in fact, lead to that outcome. Some call this fallacy oversimplification, as it offers a handy explanation for a complicated result.

□ *Either/or thinking.* The writer implies there are *only* two ways to think about this issue: good/bad, right/wrong, for/against. Their argument permits neither alternative possibilities nor a gray area between the two.

□ *Hasty generalization.* The writer's argument is based on insufficient data; for example, they have a small sample of people who may also be unrepresentative of the larger population.

□ *Personal attack.* In such arguments, the writer attempts to undermine the opposition's argument by attacking the person making that argument, typically in an abusive way that makes it a personal affront as opposed to a reasoned discussion.

□ *The domino theory.* The writer asserts that to take one step will inevitably lead to others, all of which are either fatal or otherwise undesirable. Sometimes also called the slippery slope.

□ *Special pleading.* This defense asserts that this is an exception to the rule, or that what the writer is arguing is truly different than what someone else is arguing for.

might write a persuasive essay against war; students who read Toni Morrison's *Beloved* could argue against slavery.

• Write both sides of an argument to see how the same information could be used to support one side as well as the other using different tactics.

• Write an advertisement in 120 words or less. For fun, they can deliver them orally in class.

• Deliver any of the above persuasive writings as a speech to the class.

CLASSROOM CONNECTION

The following sequence demonstrates one way to approach persuasive thinking in the classroom. It demands that students read a variety of types of text, all of which attempt to persuade, and then communicate their ideas in writing and a visual representation.

The Art of Persuasion

Overview   The purpose of this mini-unit is to improve our understanding of how ideas and images are used to persuade people to believe, feel, or act in certain ways. We face such propaganda every minute of the day in the form of advertisements. During wars and other periods of crisis, such tools of persuasion become especially important, as the accompanying poster art shows.

Analysis of Originals   Before you begin to create your own project, do the following, using the attached page of sample World War Two propaganda posters from Germany and America. Pay attention to how the artist uses the following to persuade people: color, typestyle, images, fonts, language.

- "Read" through the different posters to familiarize yourself with them.

- Make a list of the elements used in these posters (i.e., answer the question, What are these posters (and their arguments) made of?).

- Explain how the posters work to persuade people, drawing examples from at least two posters to support your assertion.

- Choose two posters—one German, one American—and analyze them in depth, explaining *what* they are trying to accomplish, *how* they are trying to accomplish it, and the extent to which you think they would be successful.

- Choose two posters—they can be the same two from the previous step—and write a paragraph in which you compare and contrast them, specifically referring to the ways in which they are similar and different and which one is more effective (and why). Support all thinking with examples from the posters.

Possible Products   You are free to produce any of the following as a means of persuading people of your point:

- Poster
- Postcard
- Web site
- Song
- Commercial

Requirements   A completed project will have the following parts:

- Your analysis, as outlined above under "Analysis of Originals"
- Your product (poster, song, etc.)
- Slogan (should be included in your product)

- Written explanation that includes the following:
  - ▶ The objective (i.e., what you are trying to accomplish through your product)
  - ▶ Basis of the argument (e.g., we are trying to link national pride with fighting in the war)
  - ▶ Analysis of overall effectiveness of your effort that evaluates:
    - Words
    - Images
    - Ideas
  - ▶ Presentation of your product to the class next Friday

Guidelines   While we are studying *All Quiet on the Western Front*, a novel about war, I would like you to use this assignment to think about how to persuade people to think a certain way about an idea or issue that is important to you. Thus, you may do your project on something unrelated to war if you prefer. Use the attached examples or visit *<www.adcouncil.org>* to get ideas.

Here is one student's analysis of the originals (of various propaganda texts from World War Two):

Analysis of Originals

1. These posters are made of many elements. On the side of the Germans the posters are cheap posters with a few German words, and the American posters are well completed painted pictures with slogans. The pictures don't make the American posters better than the German posters, the pictures just make the poster stand out and make you think about enlisting to help our country win. The American posters tell the country that they must save any usable resources so that they won't run out during battle, and the German posters say that the country is now in the hands of the people, and if they don't fight then their future will not be what they expect.

2. The American posters persuade people in little ways by telling and showing: that everyone needs to save valuable items, fight together as a team for your country, and for the people back at home to keep the country running smoothly so that when they win the men can come home without any problems to deal with. The German posters have simple sayings that say if you join the fight against the Americans, your country will be proud of you. They tell you that you must be

very strong and love your country enough to help defend it and win a battle. A poster with Hitler's quote "No one can get past the German soldier," is used as an inspiration to make the German soldiers feel like they are superior to the Americans and to fight harder to show that they're unstoppable.

3. The American poster that I think would be the most successful is the poster on the top right that says, "United We Win." This poster, just through the words tells that if everyone does a little part in this war to help out, then the Americans will win because of them. United means to bring together, so if the country comes together, we will be unstoppable and beat the Germans. The picture has many words also. There are two men who look like they are welding together some steel or making ships for the Americans. In the background there's an American flag stretched across the poster. The picture symbolizes American pride with the flag. The two men working symbolize that even if you aren't a soldier, they need any and every man with skills to help out. If you are good at metal work, start making ships; if you are good at making guns then start making guns for our soldiers to fight with. Along with winning in every war means that you lose less men and if you work together to win, there will be many more men that return home to America unharmed and fortunate. The German poster that I think would be the most successful is the poster in the middle on the left. This poster has words in German from their leader Adolf Hitler that say, "No one can get past the German soldier." There is no artwork but it is a good poster that would encourage Germans to join the army, if they weren't forced in. The quote is said by the German leader, which would tell the Germans that he will help them out if they need but tells them that they are unbeatable. By saying no one can get past, it doesn't just mean win the war it means they can't even penetrate the German territory. It tells the Germans that they are tougher and smarter, therefore, they should be able to win the war.

4. There are many similarities and differences between these two different poster-making styles. In both posters, there are words which are little encouraging words to their countries. Both sides say that we will win if we stick together as a team, instead of individuals. "The time is yours. What happens with it depends on you." This is the general saying for both Germans and Americans. From both sides, people were dragged into the army whether they wanted to fight or not.

So they must have thought that as long as we are here fighting, let's win it for our side and go home unharmed. Both posters also have many differences. The German posters are just quotes with encouraging words from their leaders written on them. The Americans spent a lot of time to put together colorful well drawn posters and wrote little captions on the poster that point out a specific thing: work together and we will win, we can do it back here in the U.S., without the men's help we will run this country, man the guns and help win the war. The American posters were more effective for one reason: They were colorful and caught the eye of the everyday person. Hanging in local stores and other public places may have made many men look at it and think to themselves that they can be a war hero. The other poster for the women would inspire all the housewives to get out of the house and take over the vacated jobs left by the men. This was a big opportunity for women to show that they are more useful than just making meals and cleaning the house.

The following step is not so much about persuasive writing; rather, it shows one way to get kids to reflect on and evaluate their own efforts to, in this case, persuade others.

Analysis of Persuasion Project

Overview   Now that you have made your project, it is time to evaluate your product and the process through which you created it. Working on your own or with the members of your group, please respond to the following questions and comments. The goal of this assignment is to help you better understand what you did and learned by allowing you to evaluate your work and the thinking that informed the work.

(*Note:* Please answer all questions on a separate sheet of paper and turn in with your Art of Persuasion project.)

• What did you try to persuade people to do (e.g., believe, feel, etc.)?

• Who was your primary audience?

• What special considerations did you have to make when trying to persuade this particular group of people? Please explain in detail, providing examples if appropriate.

• What medium—poster, song, video—did you use to persuade people?

• Why did you choose that particular medium? What did it allow you to do that the other media did not?

- What special features—images, fonts, colors, music—did you incorporate into your project? Be sure to provide examples and explain how they contributed to the overall effectiveness of your argument.

- If, as we discussed last week, some of the war posters used guilt to persuade people to act or think a certain way, what tactic does your argument use? Explain why you feel this was the best approach.

- What is Erich Maria Remarque trying to persuade us to think, feel, or do through his novel *All Quiet on the Western Front*? How and why is he trying to do that? (If you are not sure, speculate and offer whatever support you can.)

- To what extent does/would your project succeed in persuading people? Why do you think that?

- Final evaluation of your work with comments about the following:

  ▸ Quality of the final product

  ▸ Quality of the process—individual or group?

  ▸ Evidence of work: notes, samples, drafts, etc.

  ▸ Extent to which you demonstrate your understanding of persuasion as evidenced by your process and final product

  ▸ Grade you deserve on this assignment and why (If you feel a different grade is appropriate for certain members of your group, please explain and provide examples to support your argument.)

RECOMMENDED RESOURCE

Cooper, Sheila, and Rosemary Patton. 1997. 2d ed. *Writing Logically, Thinking Critically.* New York: Longman.

Write a
Comparative Essay

50

DESCRIPTION

We constantly compare one thing, one person, one place with another. It is more than a way of thinking; for humans it is a habit, a tradition. Students need to be able to make observations in science based on intelligent comparisons of data, behavior, or conditions; in social studies classes they must compare eras, cultures, historical figures. Students in my honors English classes must, as a culminating project for the semester, compare different aspects of the Indian and Chinese cultures as part of a collaborative project with their social studies teacher.

Comparing is a more complicated activity than it first appears; students need to learn to determine the criteria most appropriate to use when comparing different entities. Comparing also lends itself to either-or thinking; such dichotomous thinking results in saying one country or group is better than another. Tools such as Think in Threes (Burke 2002c) force students to think in three directions or on three different levels (see Figure 17.3). Thus, instead of comparing two items, students examine an idea or subject from three perspectives, which yields much more insight.

Everywhere I go I'm asked if I think the university stifles writers. My opinion is that they don't stifle enough of them. There's many a bestseller that could have been prevented by a good teacher.

FLANNERY O'CONNOR

PROMPTS FOR PRACTICE

• Write a review in which you compare different recordings or books by the same person.

• Write a review in which you compare different musical bands, films, or books by different people about the same subject.

• Analyze and compare different works of art by the same artist or by different artists about the same subject.

• Write a stylistic analysis about different speeches in which you compare the use of various techniques.

• Investigate a historical era (e.g., the Civil War) and compare it with another (e.g., World War Two).

THE COMPARATIVE ESSAY AT A GLANCE

☐ Identify what you are comparing. Examples include:

   ☐ Performances
   ☐ People
   ☐ Places
   ☐ Objects
   ☐ Products

☐ Determine the criteria for identifying and choosing details to compare and support what you want to say when comparing.

☐ Make a compelling statement about the subjects you are comparing. Be sure to say more than the predictable, "There are many similarities and differences between India and China when it comes to religions."

☐ Know and convey your purpose (to persuade, to evaluate, to illustrate).

☐ Organize your comparison according to the qualities of your subject and purpose: spatially, chronologically, order of importance, classification (i.e., different traits that can be classified).

☐ Use transitions to maintain order and flow as you move between the subjects you are comparing.

   When comparing, students will find several tools especially useful:

☐ Graphic organizers such as those found in my book *Tools for Thought* (2002c):

   ☐ Venn diagram
   ☐ T Notes
   ☐ Think in Threes
   ☐ Target Notes
   ☐ Comparison Notes (see Figure 50.2)

☐ Questions

   ☐ How did the characters change between the beginning and the end of the novel?
   ☐ How are the patterns of these two stories similar?
   ☐ How do women and men during Homer's era compare with women and men of our modern society?
   ☐ Compared with *what*?
   ☐ Is this a comparison of two or more meaningful (i.e., significant) aspects of this subject?

• Write a comparative study of two (or more) people who represent strong contrasts within their field. Examples might include two (or more) musicians with different styles (Bing Crosby and Elvis Presley), military or political leaders (Lee and Grant), athletes, or artists.

CLASSROOM CONNECTION

I often have students compare characters between different stories we read. A variation on this is to have them compare the characters in a book with parallel characters in a film version of the same story. This has the benefit of forcing them to look more carefully at the decisions the writer and director made when creating their respective productions. In Figure 50.1, you see Cameron comparing characters and events from Bharati Mukherjee's novel *Jasmine* with Homer's epic *The Odyssey*.

Comparison Notes, a tool I created to help students on papers and presentations, gives students a way to generate, organize, and evaluate details and domains for comparison. To show them how to use the tool, I filled one in myself (in part, to be sure it worked) so I would have an example (see Figure 50.2).

I don't mean to privilege essays in this reminder; throughout the year, especially while studying paragraphing and comparisons, we write many paragraphs so we can focus on how to organize the details. On other occasions, we simply do the thinking—with Venn diagrams or other tools—and use that to talk about the subjects we are comparing.

RECOMMENDED RESOURCE

Sebranek, Patrick, Dave Kemper, and Verne Meyer. 2001. *Writer's Inc.: A Student Handbook for Writing and Learning*. Wilmington, MA: Great Source.

Comparative Reading

Directions In comparing the two texts, find parallel examples (i.e., matching) from each. The following examples illustrate the types of comparisons you could make:

- Similar events for different reasons (e.g., both went on journeys, one to escape, the other to discover)
- Different events for similar reasons (e.g., one went on a journey, one opened business—both to find wealth)
- Similar devices or organization of information (e.g., flashbacks from present to the past, related episodes)
- Crucial moments in the life of related characters (e.g., Jem from *Mockingbird* and Telemachus in *Odyssey*) that have similar outcomes (e.g., force them to grow up or change them in some similar way)
- Important relationships (e.g., between two characters, between a human and a place, a person and god or an animal)

Please offer a brief explanation of how the two ideas/events/examples are related. If you think of other types of comparisons (e.g., themes, use of language, etc.), please include those and provide examples that illustrate the comparison.

EXAMPLE	**EXAMPLE**
The Odyssey	**Jasmine**
Similar Event: Odysseus kills Cyclops	*Similar Event:* Jasmine kills Half-Face
Cyclops: Odysseus kills the monster in order to save himself and his men; alters his story because he now ends up with Calypso.	*Half-Face:* She kills him, overcoming her biggest obstacle on her journey. This event changes her and her story.
<ul><li>Odysseus believes in his gods.</li><li>Odysseus flashes back to how he got to Phaecia.</li><li>Prophets tell Odysseus his future and it comes true.</li><li>Odysseus leaves his home for a task, but ultimately goes on a journey to reach his previous home and life again.</li><li>Odysseus lands on Phaecia, which is the beginning of the improvement of his life.</li><li>Nausicaa is like Lillian Gordon; she gets Odysseus back on his feet again.</li><li>Telemachus is like Darrell: he has to someday fill his father's shoes.</li></ul>	<ul><li>Jasmine believes in god (Brahman).</li><li>Jasmine flashes back on her life and how she got to America.</li><li>The village astrologer foresees Jasmine's future and it comes true.</li><li>Jasmine goes on a journey, leaving her childhood home in order to find her final place away from India.</li><li>Jasmine lands in Tampa, which marks the point in her life when things begin to go well for her.</li><li>Lillian Gordon is like Nausicaa: she helps Jasmine get on her feet.</li><li>Darrell is like Telemachus because he must take over his father's estate.</li></ul>

FIGURE 50.1   Sample comparative reading notes

Comparison Notes

| Name | Mr. Burke | Date | |
| Topic | 3 Contrasts: Winnie / Jasmine | Period | |

1. Winnie   Jasmine

Winnie	EDUCATION	Jasmine
• little formal schooling beyond the basics • minimal academic sensibilities • experience is her main teacher		• Masterji said she had extra talents • great faith in edu. • Prakash taught her to read tech. manuals • scholarly experience with professors in the US / NY.

Main Idea/Summary Both are very smart women; it's what enabled them to survive their trials. While both are "street smart," Jasmine has academic talents that Winnie never developed.

2. Winnie   Jasmine

Winnie	FAMILY	Jasmine
• dysfunctional + inhospitable • abandoned by mother • unhappy experience • important to Winnie (wants what she did not have).		• supportive family • poor: unable to provide savvy • appreciated her intelligence and courage, independent • complete family – traditional

Main Idea/Summary They both appreciate family, but for different reasons. Winnie wants what she never really had. Jasmine's family loved and supported her — which is why she treasures it.

3. Winnie   Jasmine

Winnie	VALUES	Jasmine
• traditional in many respects • combination (later in life) of East + West • Independence • Family		• Origins of her values come as much from thinker as life experiences. • Darwin — values survival and happiness over all else.

Main Idea/Summary What they value is shaped by what they lost. Winnie, for example, lost both her dignity and her independence; Jasmine lost her love — and with it her reason to live

FIGURE 50.2 Sample Comparison Notes I completed to show students how to use this tool to compare characters in two novels

51

Write a Reflective Essay

It's never too late to be
what you might have
been.

GEORGE ELIOT

DESCRIPTION

To write is to think—or so we hope. Students need time and incentive to pause and reflect. The very act of writing invites reflection by both students and teachers (Hillocks 1995). This reflection can take place in journals, letters, poems, speeches, formal essays, or more informal, personal essays. Whatever the form they use, students this age should see writing as a means of thinking through the changes and dilemmas that they and others face. The word *reflect* itself means to look back. However, the larger question is, Why do it, what can they gain from it? Obvious answers include they gain insight into themselves and others; appreciation of how much they have changed or improved; understanding of the larger implications of certain events or actions. Reflection is, in short, a "habit of mind" (Costa and Kallick 2000), which writing cultivates most effectively in students.

Some moments demand reflection—as opposed to observation, description, or narration—more than most. Beginning high school, for example, or the wake of a powerful experience whose meaning and importance students may not fully appreciate yet. Juniors might find themselves considering the meaning of America and how that meaning applies to not only themselves but others. Seniors bound for college have the ultimate invitation to reflect: their college essay (see Reminder 63), the most public and consequential of reflections.

PROMPTS FOR PRACTICE

Here are some sample topics.

- Give students a proverb or, better yet, a page of them organized around a central theme; have them choose one or several to support their reflection on that theme.

- Some people say we receive three names: the one our parents give us when we are born, the one our friends give us, and the one we must make for ourselves. Ask students to write about this topic as it relates to themselves.

THE REFLECTIVE ESSAY AT A GLANCE

☐ Considers or responds to a significant event or idea and what that idea means to the writer and the larger world.

☐ Answers the questions, Why? and So what?

☐ May be either serious or humorous in tone, though it tends to be serious.

☐ Is often anchored in small, even familiar details or occasions that the writer makes more meaningful.

☐ Incorporates a variety of forms, including narration and description.

☐ Makes it clear not only what the event means to the writer but what it might mean to the reader.

• Have students in a senior class write their own graduation speeches; at the end of the year, create an occasion in the class during the last week (or, dare I say it, on the day of the final!) for them to each deliver their graduation speech as part of a more private ceremony.

• Colleges often ask students to write a personal statement. Such a statement is meant to give students an opportunity to represent themselves and their ideas to the world. Have students write their own personal statements or credos, then explain them through short papers.

• Have students draw a continuum with September at one end and June (or January) at the other. Have them list those words that best describe what they thought, felt, were like in the beginning. They should add words to the continuum at whatever point things changed, then list the event that caused the change. This continuum should then serve as the basis for reflective writing about the year and the changes they went through.

CLASSROOM CONNECTION

Teachers who ask students to reflect, and who take time to think alongside their students when possible, create thoughtful communities within the classroom. They create a place where students have permission—from themselves and those around them—to think, to ponder, to reflect on who they are, what they are, and what it all means in light of where they are going. The following response to *Iron and Silk* illustrates the value of such opportunities to reflect.

OUTSIDE READING REFLECTION: *IRON AND SILK*
THOUGHTS FROM *IRON AND SILK*

It's interesting to know how different people think about your country. That's how I felt when I chose to read the book *Iron and Silk* by Mark Salzman, which is a book about his journey in China. When I found this book, I was half-excited and half-afraid. Since I moved to California from China, I have heard plenty of all kinds of talking about China. Some of them are nice; some of them are not. At the beginning, I didn't know how to respond. I was mad because of some ridiculous talking, and I was happy about some nice talking, and things that I couldn't even decide if that was right or wrong struck me. I wondered how this book would be like. Surprisingly, I had such a good time reading it. That became one of my favorite books. Salzman did a such good job on telling the true lifestyle of Chinese people that when I was reading it, I felt like that were some snap shots of my daily life back in China. At one moment while I was reading, I suddenly understood that there are always two sides in every countries, one is ugly, and another is decent. We don't need to turn one down because of its ugly side, and we don't need to set one as perfect model for others because of its decent side.

I guess this has been always a critical topic for me to talk about China with my friends, since we all from different places, like Taiwan, or Hong Kong. And we basically have our own point of views. I struggle to find a position that would fit me well. I have to admit that I love my country very much, even though I am one of the people who do not satisfy the condition China is in at this point. I am disappointed by how Chinese government functions and manage its country, however, I can't stand when people look down on China or make fun of it. One thing that I can't stand most is that when I see people from China make fun of its own country to get others attention. Unfortunately, that happens occasionally. People do that in various ways, by languages or their behaviors. I feel sorry for them because they are blind to see all the good aspects of their own country, and also the improvements that China is making. I feel mad for them because they act without using their conscience. After all the things happened in the past two years, I am proud of where I am from. In spite of everything, that's where I grew up, that's where I learned to be person I am right now. My dearest family lives there, so do my friends, my teachers, and all the people I've known since I was little. I believe deeply and honestly that China will be prosperous, but it will take some time to correct all the shortcomings it has.

I think it's a sort of funny that once a friend of mine from Taiwan told me that I am the most patriotic person he has seen from China. I laughed. I don't think anyone would allow people to hurt the ones that they love and care about in any ways. I am just doing the same thing. Love one's country doesn't mean we can't see the ugly parts of it. We should look at the good sides rather than the bad ones, while we should improve the bad ones as much, and as quickly as possible.

It takes me a while to realize I should be proud of where I am from just as I should be proud of who I am instead of some-one else. To think so, I have to act so. To be proud of my country does not mean I will just say so, instead, I will work hard to show people that I am not weak as how they think I might be, and I am just little part of the strong force where I come from. An ant can't do anything, but one million unified ants can move the rock.

Ashley Arabian's poignant reflective response to the photograph of two soldiers shown in Figure 51.1 reminds us what a powerful invitation to writing (and reflecting) pictures can provide. She wrote her essay in re-sponse to the Weekly Paper assignment (see Reminder 7).

WHAT WE LIKE TO THINK

—Ashley Arabian

My heart stopped when I saw this picture. You never see a man being comforted by another man like this. I suppose that is what the war does to you. You need comfort from anyone. I sometimes think how it must have been for the men in war. Were they afraid? Were they excited? Nervous? Grim? I can only think that I would be horrified at the sight of others being killed in front of me, let alone having to kill others. What they had to go through was entirely inadequate. None of them had to go to war and kill like that. The world could have gotten along in the first place, but instead we had to put our citizens through this.

Why do we fight? Why did we fight? There are the historical explanations for why we fought the war, but people still wonder why we argued. I speak for almost everyone when I say world peace is extremely important to citizens. What if there was a World War Three involving your country? What if you had to go

FIGURE 51.1   Photograph from National Archives, which we used with the *Weekly Reader*

and fight? Leave your family to kill people. Does that seem right to you? It never seemed right in the first place. Yet we have a Vietnam Memorial wall. There are graveyards filled with soldiers. So many questions come to the mind when we learn about war. Sometimes there are not any answers. When there are no answers to the questions we ask about war, doesn't the fact of someone dying for an unanswered question seem illicit? It is really something to think about.

I have thought about this kind of stuff a lot and peace always is the answer to my questions. If we can keep peace in the world, do you think we will abide? I believe we can survive as a planet, not as humans, if we agree with each other on worldly issues. Is it so hard to believe that one day, even if it is for one day, every country will have peace with each other? I have hope for that day. I have hope that I will live to see that day. I have hope that we all have hope for world peace. Hope is a human need. Can peace be a world need? If we have been surviving without it, maybe not, but many like to think so.

Throughout our study of *All Quiet on the Western Front*, we examined what boys/men lost and how that related to what they *need*. Indy Johal's work in Figure 51.3 prepared him to write this opening for the human needs assignment in Figure 51.2:

Losses are something that everyone has to go through sometime in their life. I have suffered many losses in my life, and I'm not yet sixteen years old. I can't even imagine how many I might go through until I'm gone. Paul Baumer is another individual who had suffered many losses in the novel *All Quiet on the Western Front*. Paul had losses that will stay in his life forever. There are some losses that when you suffer them you can forget about them easily. Permanent losses are with you every day, from the moment you wake up in the morning until you go to sleep at night. Macbeth's losses are very hard on him as well as others who are affected by his actions. What Macbeth had was a permanent loss which is with him every day until the day he has died.

Near the end of the grading period, I try always to have students reflect on their own standing and progress. Here is one such assignment:

Reflective Writing: Personal Progress Report

Overview   As the grading period draws to an end, it is time for both of us to reflect on your progress so far. While I won't just give you the grade you suggest, I will listen to your argument and take it into consideration when reflecting on what grade you have earned in this course.

Guidelines   When writing this short essay, be sure to:

• Make a clear statement about the grade you feel you deserve

• Include specific details and examples that support your assertion

• Organize your essay and its ideas to support your main idea

• Anticipate my responses and biases, and address these in your essay

• Use transition words (e.g., *although, however, of course*, etc.) to make the writing flow and improve your argument

 ▶ Example: *Although* I have read only one book so far, it is a long book and one I have learned to read faster and better, as my reading record shows.

What We Need: A Study of Fictional Characters and Ourselves

Overview   Stories often chart the development of a character over the course of time and in response to different events. How characters respond can often be understood by examining what they need at different points throughout the story. Needs themselves, however, fall into different categories, as these two quotes from Mark Twain show:

- Adam was but human—this explains it all. He did not want the apple for the apple's sake, he wanted it only because it was forbidden.
- It's much easier to tell the truth on a full stomach.

Steps   This assignment has several stages to it:

1. List three to five questions you should ask to identify, categorize, and rank the different human needs.
2. Brainstorm a list of as many human needs as possible. These needs should be appropriate and applicable to all people in one form or another, at one time or another. This should be a big messy list full of ideas, some of which you will omit later.
3. Using your list of needs, come up with five to ten categories into which all your list items could be organized.
4. Represent/organize your ideas: list the five to ten most important needs common to all humans and rank or arrange them according to one of the following models:
   - Continuum
   - Pyramid
   - Ranked list
   - Other (e.g., flower or other metaphorical diagram)
5. Compare your model to the following other models (which I will provide) and then revise yours based on any new information or insights you gain from these models:
   - Maslow's Hierarchy of Human Needs
   - Mr. Firpo's Twenty Human Needs
6. Using the graphic organizer provided, identify five important needs and compare a character (or characters) in *All Quiet on the Western Front*, one (or more) character in a book you read outside of class this semester, and yourself. Be sure your comparison reflects how their/your needs change over time or through different periods of their/your life.

Example: The Need for Success		
Paul (from *All Quiet on the Western Front*)	Cedric Jennings (from *A Hope in the Unseen*)	Myself
Examples/Details/Explain	Examples/Details/Explain	Examples/Details/Explain

Remember as you begin to think about your prospective essay that you might write, for example, about how a character was *unable* to meet a certain need, even though it is a crucial and very human need. You might then discuss why the character did not satisfy that need and what the consequence of that failure was.

Final Exam   Now that you have completed the preparatory stage of this process, you are ready to use all these notes and examples to take the final exam.

FIGURE 51.2   What We Need assignment handout

Brainstorm

Myself - losses
- my great grandma
- my grandfather
- my love for soccer
- my childish behavior
- some friends
- concentration
- girlfriends

Questions
1) Why do we lose things in life?
2) What are the most important losses I have came up with?
3) How could have Paul avoided the losses he's suffered?

All Quiet on the Western Front (Paul) - losses
- being a student
- friends
- staying with family
- soldiers that were his friends
- he's lost himself, who he really is.

Macbeth
- the loss of the king
- Macbeth has lost faith in himself
- others have lost faith in Macbeth
- his family and other major families don't think of him the same way, the use to.

Fight Club
- Tyler Durden, going losses to main character
- Sleep
- different organizations
- Marla, Tyler
- the Fight Club, project Mayhem

FIGURE 51.3   Indy Johal's brainstorm about losses in his own life and the texts we read

- Discuss your progress in all areas of the course:
  - ▶ Reading
  - ▶ Writing
  - ▶ Thinking
  - ▶ Speaking
  - ▶ Working
  - ▶ Participating
- Limit your essay to *no longer than one page*

Assessment   I will use the Six Traits scoring guide to assess your essay.

On other occasions, I ask students to reflect on such subjects as those people and experiences that have influenced them:

Overview   We are the result of many influences. People shape our beliefs, our values, and our attitudes; but so do experiences and the eras in which we live. Where we come from, the culture we are born into, our gender and race—these, too, affect us. This assignment asks you to think about these different influences in general and about those that have made the biggest impact on you.

1. Generate ideas: brainstorm all the different influences that come to mind. Use the Target Notes tool to identify key categories (e.g., People, Experiences) and generate examples and details (e.g., who/what influenced you and *how* they did).

2. Respond to your initial ideas by doing a fifteen-minute quick write in which you think about how all these factors have influenced you. Whether you write, list, or cluster, *do not stop writing* until the fifteen minutes are up.

3. Discuss your quick write with one other person; tell stories, explain what you mean. When one of you has a question about something, ask it! Give each person equal time.

4. Write more: With your notes and discussion fresh in your mind, go back to the paper and write down any additional stories, details, or examples that come to mind.

5. Prepare to write your introductory paragraph. Use the Main Idea Organizer to generate and organize the ideas you will use in your introductory paragraph.

6. Share and compare your Main Idea Organizer with two other people; note what they include and add new ideas to your own if you find some.

7. Draft your introductory paragraph, using your Main Idea Organizer to guide you.

   ▸ Read pages 55 and 97 from *Writer's Inc.* about opening paragraphs.

8. Respond to and revise your opening paragraphs using response groups.

9. Type up your introductory paragraph on the computer; incorporate revisions.

10. Generate details about your most important influence using a Conversational Roundtable.

11. Draft body paragraphs using details from the Conversational Roundtable.

12. Respond to and revise your body paragraphs while typing them on the computer.

13. Draft your conclusion.

14. Read and respond to essays in writing groups.

15. Revise and print your essay.

16. Adapt essay into a speech using the Speech Outline tool.

17. Rehearse.

18. Deliver Influential Person speech to introduce yourself at the Toastmasters International Youth leadership Program.

RECOMMENDED RESOURCE

Hillocks, George. 1995. *Teaching Writing as Reflective Practice.* New York: Teachers College Press.

52 Write an Essay Exam

DESCRIPTION

Essay exams represent a particular domain of writing, one that is associated with stress, consequences, and ability. Kids encounter such exams in our own classes at a unit's end or on the final exam at semester's end; they find them on state and district tests; and they encounter sometimes daunting essay exams on such tests as the Advanced Placement exam and the SAT. Many are timed tests, a factor that adds that much more pressure to the testing situation; others are not timed or are so short that the term *essay* seems hardly to apply. Unlike the other types of writing described herein, this type of writing is a performance, one for which the student must prepare intellectually, physically, and emotionally.

CLASSROOM CONNECTION

Donald Graves (2002) offers an interesting idea, one I've begun to experiment with in my own classes, for essay exams. Don suggests that kids create a list of ten topics they want to learn about within the context of your class; as the semester unfolds, they take notes and reflect on these ten topics, thinking about what they would say about them in an essay. They are responsible for creating, refining, and preparing to write about the different topics. On the day of the exam, students bring in their topics and all their notes for each one. The teacher then walks around and circles one of each student's ten topics—all of which they are theoretically interested in and able to write about—and tells each student to write an essay about that topic by the end of the period.

Of course, that's not the way the world works all the time. Students in AP classes must learn to write timed essays about significant literary works. Students in most states have timed writing exams called competency or exit exams. These come with their own unique challenges and demands, some of which are more difficult for some students than others. (In my own classes, I tend to make my culminating final exam an essay. See the example from my ACCESS class shown on pp. 17–20.).

THE ESSAY EXAM AT A GLANCE

Any essay exam begins and ends with the writing prompt; this includes the elements evaluators will expect to find in the student's essay. Thus, students must:

☐ Read the essay topic and all directions closely, marking it up if possible. Some key words offer specific instructions about what to do (e.g., *describe, examine, compare*); they must find these words and be sure to include in their essay whatever the directions say to do.

☐ Understand what they can and cannot do, bring, or use on the essay exam. If, for example, it is permissible to use the dictionary, then announce it; if it is not, announce it, providing a clear, reasonable rationale for not allowing the use of this resource.

☐ State a thesis.

☐ Know the criteria that judges or teachers will use to score the exam. If for instance, they are taking the AP exam, they can find the scoring guides and annotated sample papers on the Educational Testing Service (ETS) Web site. Most states also post scoring guidelines and sample essays for exit exams and other state writing exams on their department of education Web site.

☐ Be able to transform the prompt into a list of things to do or to include that they can check periodically.

☐ Read the essay topic several times, each time for a different purpose. Some suggest that students rewrite the topic in their own words to better understand it, to make it their own.

☐ Develop and refine the thesis.

☐ Generate ideas or questions that will help them write about this subject and read about it effectively also.

☐ Read the documents or text on which their essay is based. They should jot down notes and examples they think will support or illustrate what they are trying to say in their thesis statement.

☐ Return periodically to the directions to be sure they are doing or including what the test requires.

☐ Come prepared. This means they have completed all the prior reading or other tasks in preparation for this task. This also means that they have come rested, well fed, and mentally prepared to do their best.

☐ Find and organize details and examples from the text that effectively support what they are saying about this issue.

☐ Ask for extended time on tests if they require special education accommodations; it's not a given, and they must learn to see this as an important aspect of their success.

Sandy Briggs (2002), ESL coordinator for my school district, and one of my mentors, outlined what effective teachers do to weave essay test instruction (crucial for English learners' success) into the curriculum. Here are her guidelines:

I.   How I weave this into our writing program:
  ☐ Students write from the first day they come into ESL.
  ☐ About one month before the exam will be given, we talk about the competency exam, giving the students an explanation of the overall competency program.
  ☐ We present it as a challenge.
  ☐ We emphasize the ninth-grade writing types: autobiographical and observational.
  ☐ We emphasize autobiographical writing. We have student samples for them.
  ☐ They work on first drafts.
  ☐ We emphasize strategies they can use to do their best.

II. The importance of a simulation:
  ☐ We all know that you get better at something if you practice.
  ☐ A few days before the real exam, setting up a simulation that gives them a chance to write one of these essays in the conditions under which they will write the real essay is very powerful for the students.
  ☐ I give them the scores I think they would receive on these practice exams. Students share their essays in groups and we talk about how to do our best.

III. The real exam:
  ☐ They take it in my classroom with me.
  ☐ I read the essays before I send them in. They get effort points from me. I also give the essay a preliminary grade and tell them what I think.
  ☐ It takes about six weeks to get the results back. We celebrate the successes and we look to the future for the rest of the students. The real emphasis is on participating in the process, and we know that there will be other chances.

IV. Discussion

While Sandy's course of study prepares students to meet the needs of school and state exams, I include it here to show you that you must make some systematic plan for preparing English learners to succeed on these tests, which too often prevent them from demonstrating their full knowledge and potential. The above guidelines are for teachers, obviously. On the next page is the handout Sandy gives to students; notice how it seeks to demystify the essay exam for students, telling them what they need to do and showing them (through a packet of examples that she includes and which they study and critique over time) what that looks like.

ESL 3-4: Writing Competency Exams: Autobiographical Incident

When you write an autobiographical incident, you write about something that happened to you in no more than twenty-four hours. You can mention events that happened before or after that day, but the focus needs to be on telling a story about something that happened in one day. Your writing needs to have:

1. *A beginning, a middle, and a conclusion.* It needs to have shape like the stories that we have read; it shouldn't just be a list of things that you did. For example, if you are writing about going to a new school, tell how afraid you were before you went into class and then how welcoming the first class was, what the people were like in that room and what the people said to make you feel welcome. End by telling that you knew it would be a good place to go to school.

2. *Sensory words and images.* Help your readers see, hear, touch, taste, and smell what you are talking about. For example, if you are talking about a family dinner, talk about the noise of getting the table set and the food prepared. Tell about the smells of hot soup and steamy rice. Tell how slippery that lime Jell-O feels on your tongue.

3. *As many details as possible.* Details make the readers feel as if they are there. For example: I sat down next to a tall kid with a sweatshirt that said BHS Panthers on it. I didn't know what Panthers were. The teacher was short and she had a big smile. I remember that she was wearing a pink skirt and a white blouse, but I don't remember what she said to me. I only knew that this place would be my new home.

4. *Showing rather than telling.* This also makes the readers feel a part of your story. For example, you may be writing about how afraid you were. Instead of saying, "I was afraid," say, "My heart was pounding and sweat was running down my back."

5. *Direct quotations.* Giving the words that people really said makes your story more exciting, and the people who evaluate these essays love quotes. For example:

The teacher smiled and said, "Rudy, we are glad that you came to this school."
"Hey, where are you from?" the short kid with brown hair asked me.

You should write about a page and a half. If you don't write enough, the evaluators will think you can't write more. If you write too much, you may make too many mistakes. Your story counts much more than your spelling and your verb tenses, but you need to use complete sentences with good verbs and spell pretty well. Not everything that you tell has to be the real truth; you can invent details and such. However, be careful not to tell things that will upset the evaluators. They don't know you and they might be worried if you write about a really terrible experience that you had.

Having given them this orientation to the test they will take, Sandy then provides them with a series of sample prompts, focusing on how to read the directions and the prompt. She has them compare and discuss a range of samples written by past students for the practice exam topics. At times, her students practice just beginnings; on other occasions, if they must first read and take notes on a text in response to a specific topic, they rehearse that with a series of similar articles.

Advanced Placement students have their own unique needs when it comes to essay exams. Effective AP teachers train their students to incorporate into their essays "what AP readers long to see" (1994). Teachers and students can find useful information and resources, including sample questions and essay prompts, on the College Board Web site: *<www.collegeboard.com/ap/students/english/index.html>*. The following list describes what AP exam readers want to see students doing in their essays:

1. *Read the prompt.* It hurts to give a low score to someone who misread the prompt but wrote a good essay. While the reader will try to reward you for what you do well, you must answer the prompt.

2. *Do everything the prompt suggests.* If the prompt suggests that the student "may wish to discuss" the character's effect on action, theme, or other characters' development, be sure you discuss all three areas.

3. *Think before you write.* Plan your response. You need not outline extensively, but a little organization will help you avoid extensive editing or crossing out of lines or paragraphs. It's no fun for the reader to pick over the remains and try to decipher sentences crammed into the margins.

4. *Make a strong first impression.* Build your opening response artistically. Don't parrot the prompt word for word.

5. *Begin your response immediately.* Don't beat around the bush with generalizations such as "There are many great novels. . . . " Try for a creative opening that immediately sets up a specific central idea or thesis of your own, based on the prompt.

6. *Use clear transitions.* Help the reader follow the flow of your essay. Keep your paragraphs organized. Don't digress.

7. *Avoid plot summary.* Your essay can follow selected plot sequences in the order in which they appear in the work, but your central idea or thesis—not the plot—should dictate your overall organization. You are proving an assertion, not telling a story.

8. *Don't use canned quotes or critics' comments if they do not fit.* Use only evidence and support material that fit your thesis.

9. *Write to express, not to impress.* Keep vocabulary and syntax within your zone of competence. Students who inflate their writing often inadvertently entertain, but seldom explain.

10. *Demonstrate that you understand style.* Show the reader how the author has massaged the selection to create a desired effect. This indicates that you are aware of the creative process.

11. *Maintain a sense of simplicity.* The best student writers say much, but say it very succinctly.

12. *Let your writing dance with ideas and insights.* You can score moderately well with a lock-step approach, but the best essays expand to a wider perspective.

13. *Write legibly.* If a reader can't read half the words, you won't get a fair reading.

14. *Let your work stand on its own merits.* Avoid penning "pity me" notes ("I was up all night," "I have a cold," etc.) to the reader.

15. *Always address the meaning or theme of the work early in your answer.* The prompt may not seem to ask for this in an obvious way, but all prompts really do. Work the meaning or theme into your introduction or thesis statement. Everything you are asked to discuss will ultimately be based on the author's meaning in the work—style, imagery, point-of-view, and so on will always connect to meaning or theme.

16. *Use strong, specific supporting evidence.* Select telling details and appropriate quotations from the work to substantiate every generalization you make.

RECOMMENDED RESOURCE

Scruggs, Thomas E., and Margo A. Mastropieri. 1992. *Teaching Test-Taking Skills: Helping Students Show What They Know.* Cambridge, MA: Brookline Books.

53 Write a Research Report

DESCRIPTION

Few aspects of the curriculum have changed and faced such challenges as the research report. Teachers in all subjects, but in history and English for sure, complain about the lack of time in light of the material they need to cover. Will Fitzhugh, editor of the *Concord Review*, a journal devoted to publishing student research papers, found a dramatic drop over the last ten years in the number of history teachers who require students to write research papers (Manzo 2002, 1). But, as Carol Jago writes in her book *Beyond Standards* (2001), "Technology has made research sexy. Students who would never in their lives delve into tomes of the *Reader's Guide to Periodical Literature* now find manipulating a search engine a cool thing to do, not a bit nerdy. No longer is the preparation of a footnoted manuscript a laborious task, because most students are reasonably able on a keyboard" (56).

Between the way students work and the tools available, the experience has been overhauled. Ethical issues such as plagiarism and reliability of sources (Burke 2001) raise serious issues. Citation issues (e.g., format) and the allowable number of Web site sources remain, for some, serious issues. These other issues are secondary, however, to the larger changes that continue to confront the research project: the actual form and content of the project in a multimedia, multitextual world. As the sample assignments in this reminder illustrate, students may be thinking like researchers, but they are producing reports like documentary filmmakers, journalists, and Webmasters more and more. This blending of genres and media will only continue as the technology and students' fluency with it evolve.

CLASSROOM CONNECTION

English teacher Diane McClain, who teaches in the room next to mine, has her students do an American Cultural Studies Project their junior year. Aside from informal and quick check-ins, she has them send her a "postcard" from wherever they are in their project. She does this about halfway through, when the kids have begun to get their hands dirty and have something to report or are in deep enough trouble that they need

THE RESEARCH REPORT AT A GLANCE

☐ Before you begin, you must answer the following questions:

    ☐ What is the goal of this research project?

    ☐ What standards will it help my students meet?

    ☐ What evidence of their understanding am I willing to accept? This question can lead to various answers, but the most important one at this point is the form of the research project. Possibilities include:

        • "I search" paper

        • Multigenre paper

        • Senior project

        • Expert project (multiple sources; search Web for "expert project" to find samples, guidelines, and suggestions)

        • Formal research paper (visit the *Concord Review* Web site at *<www.tcr.org>* for sample guidelines and research papers)

    ☐ What configuration is appropriate for this project? For example:

        • Individuals

        • Pairs

        • Small groups

        • Whole class (i.e., each person investigates some aspect and contributes that section to the research project)

    ☐ How much time can I afford to spend on the whole project and, over that period of time, how much in-class time can I devote to it?

    ☐ What skills (e.g., conducting an Internet search, taking notes) do I need to teach students? When and how can I best teach these skills?

    ☐ What resources will I need to make available for students to successfully complete this project?

☐ Write up the research project assignment in a format similar to those included here as examples (e.g., with check boxes, sequencing) to help students stay organized.

☐ Generate possible topics appropriate for this subject or assignment.

☐ Have students select the one they feel most interested in investigating.

☐ Have students write a proposal to you explaining why they want to do this topic, what they think they will find out, and why they think that.

☐ Next, students develop and refine their thesis. Related to this crucial aspect of the project is what some standards documents describe as the ability to generate possible research questions. Some state tests, such as California's, include different research questions and ask students to identify which of them would be best for a research project. Hidden within this standard is an important skill: recognizing and creating viable research questions or topics.

☐ Provide opportunities for them to talk about their ideas, findings, or processes so they can learn from and help each other.

☐ Ask them to gather information for their project from a variety of sources:

    ☐ Books

    ☐ Web sites

    ☐ Surveys

    ☐ Interviews

    ☐ Observations

☐ Teach minilessons on such topics as evaluating the quality of sources, creating surveys, formulating a thesis, and using and citing direct quotations.

☐ Follow the Big6 steps in the research process (see Figure 53.1).

Such projects require students to embark on a journey of sorts. They need both a road map (e.g., a project plan that outlines what they need to do, by when, and who can help them accomplish this) and a means of "phoning home" if they get lost along the way. Sometimes topics that first seemed compelling turn cold, with the trail leading off into the woods. They'll need your help to get back on track.

intervention. Here is one example (which originally came in what looked like a postcard, complete with stamp and address) from two juniors who decided to study homelessness:

Dear Mrs. McClain,

HI! How's it going? Gena and I are doing great here in San Francisco. We have been able to visit and talk to so many people about our topic, volunteering and the effect it has on the homeless. Last weekend, we went to Saint Anthony's Dining Hall in the Tenderloin of San Francisco. It was a life-altering experience that we will both never forget. We interviewed the volunteer coordinators, and even got to talk to some of the homeless people while we were serving them food. It was such a drastic change coming from Burlingame. As we watched hundreds of families, children, disabled, veterans, immigrants, and mentally and physically ill people come into the soup kitchen due to starvation, we recognized how secure they felt to have a place where they could eat without being prosecuted or asked any questions. We have also visited many homeless shelters, the Salvation Army Programs, and Red Cross Organizations. In addition, as Gena and I spend our time here in San Francisco, we have

Big6 Overview for Research Projects

People go through these Big6 stages—consciously or not—when they seek or apply information to solve a problem or make a decision. It's not necessary to complete these stages in a linear order, and a given stage doesn't have to take a lot of time. We have found that in almost all successful problem-solving situations, all stages are addressed.

In addition to considering the Big6 as a process, another useful way to view the Big6 is as a set of basic, essential life skills. These skills can be applied across situations—to school, personal, and work settings. The Big6 Skills are applicable to all subject areas across the full range of grade levels. Students use the Big6 Skills whenever they need information to solve a problem, make a decision, or complete a task.

A Big6™ Skills Overview
(by Mike Eisenberg)

The Big6
The Big6 is a process model of how people of all ages solve an information problem. From practice and study, we found that successful information problem solving encompasses six stages with two substages under each:

1. Task Definition
1.1 Define the information problem
1.2 Identify information needed in order to complete the task (to solve the information problem)

2. Information-Seeking Strategies
2.1 Determine the range of possible sources (brainstorm)
2.2 Evaluate the different possible sources to determine priorities (select the best sources)

3. Location and Access
3.1 Locate sources (intellectually and physically)
3.2 Find information within sources

4. Use of Information
4.1 Engage (e.g., read, hear, view, touch) the information in a source
4.2 Extract relevant information from a source

5. Synthesis
5.1 Organize information from multiple sources
5.2 Present the information

6. Evaluation
6.1 Judge the product (effectiveness)
6.2 Judge the information problem-solving process (efficiency)

Big6 Process: What You've Done Checklist
In this column, write down what you have done that corresponds with each task on the left. When, for example, you have defined your task, write down 1.1 and spell out the information problem you have created or identified for this project. Be sure to begin each subpoint with a verb that describes what you should do.

1. _____

_____

_____

_____

_____

_____

_____

_____

_____

_____

_____

_____

_____

_____

_____

_____

_____

_____

_____

_____

_____

_____

_____

_____

_____

_____

_____

FIGURE 53.1   Overview of Big6 steps for research projects

May be copied for classroom use. Writing Reminders *by Jim Burke (Heinemann, Portsmouth, NH); © 2003.*

had the fortunate chance to walk the streets of San Francisco. We have learned about the astonishing and depressing reasons that led them to become homeless people. One of the most important things we were reminded of was by Mike Green, a volunteer coordinator at St. Anthony's, and that was that the homeless are people that have feelings too. We have all walked down the streets of San Francisco and noticed poor and homeless people's conditions and hardships they have to face, but we mostly just try to ignore them. We have been through so many more amazing experiences, and we are looking forward to sharing them with you. See you soon!

Sincerely,
Eleni Alevizos and Gena Svedise

The following sample projects are pretty self-explanatory. I do at least one project a year that requires my students to investigate a serious topic. Writing is not always the only option when they are ready to communicate what they learned; it is, however, a core element in any project, as the assignments show. I see such projects as intellectual rites of passage, experiences that leave most students changed, that give them a feeling of achievement that other assignments cannot muster. The girls in the preceding letter will never feel that way about an exam; they are entering into a serious conversation with themselves and their world about an issue that troubles or intrigues them.

The Personal Project

Overview   The Personal Project develops new skills and improves upon existing ones by having you study something of personal importance. You might study the life of someone important, whose example or ideas inspire you. Or you might investigate an invention or product that intrigues or excites you; topics include everything from guitars to cars, careers to cultures, ideas to identity, fashion to Picasso, and everything else. This project gives you the freedom to work more effectively in class—on your project if you prefer, or on work for a class if you need to. Everyone must, however, complete this assignment: it is your final exam.

Criteria   Any subject is fine so long as it is:

- Meaningful (to you)
- Substantial

- Researchable (by multiple means: interviews, visitations, reading, observing)

- Narrow and manageable

- Appropriate

Guidelines   *Target Notes.* Generate possible topics

Topic selection. Choose the most interesting one that meets the previous criteria

Main Idea Organizer. Complete the Main Idea Organizer about your topic

Proposal. Use the Main Idea Organizer to write a one-page typed proposal explaining:

- Why you want to investigate this subject

- What you already know about it

- What you want to find out about it

Research. Investigate your subject by doing as many of the following as possible:

- Read about your subject from multiple sources (newspapers, books, etc.)

- Interview others who know about this subject

- Observe or shadow people or places associated with your subject

- Conduct a Web search

Progress report. On Fridays, people will write about and discuss what they did, found, and learned that week with me, a small group, or the class

Time card. Keep track of the time you spend on this project using the attached time sheet

Outline. Make an outline for your topic; this will become the basis for your final speech

Infotext. You must use your outline to create a one-page, two-sided brochure on a computer

Presentation. You must teach us about your subject in a ten-minute presentation

Notes/evaluations. Listeners must take notes on all speeches: evaluate, respond, reflect

Letter. Using your notes and your own experience with the project, write a letter in which you reflect on what you accomplished, what you learned, and what you would like to learn about next (i.e., possible topics)

Bibliography. You must include a properly formatted bibliography for your project. It must be typed on the computer. It must include at least three of the following:

- Newspaper article
- Book
- Web site
- Magazine article
- Other (CD, interview, etc.)

Options   You may, if you prefer:

- Work in *pairs*, but not larger groups

- Propose an alternative form or format for your Personal Project (Web site, multimedia production, performance, etc.) so long as it meets the guideline requirements outlined

The America Project

Introduction   Throughout *Jasmine,* Bharati Mukherjee examines the different Americas in which people live. Some of these Americas are cultural, others are regional, some are generational; still other differences result from race, wealth, and gender. Other distinctions are evident throughout the story as people move between identities, roles, values, and problems. This project's primary objective is to examine some aspect of our culture from multiple perspectives and, by studying it, arrive at some new insight into such questions as:

- Who is American?
- What does it mean to be American?
- What does America mean or represent?

In the course of your investigation, you will also be working on the following skills:

- Developing useful, insightful questions about complicated subjects

- Searching for, organizing, and interpreting different types of information that represent a range of perspectives

- Making connections between ideas and expressing your ideas through words and images using the most effective media and formats

- Presenting your findings through images and words (written and spoken)

Finally, you must look at your subject from three perspectives. Here are some examples:

- *Music.* Rock, rap, blues; past, present, future; three musical artists' views of America (e.g., Bruce Springsteen, Tupac, Bob Dylan)

- *Film.* Three directors' work on the same theme (e.g., John Waters' series of teen films); films about war from three different directors, eras, or perspectives; three very important films and what they say about American culture (e.g., *Citizen Kane, Saving Private Ryan, Gone with the Wind*)

- *America.* What it means to someone from India, someone born in Burlingame, and a homeless person; what it means to a ninety-year-old, a forty-five-year-old, and a fifteen-year-old

- *Art.* Three different artists' perceptions of America (e.g., Andy Worhol, Walker Evans, and Wayne Thiebeau)

- *Poetry.* Using the book *Americans' Favorite Poems* (I have three copies of it) and its companion Web site *<www.favoritepoem.org>*, read a sequence of poems that provides three different views about America (*Note:* reading three poems would not be adequate.)

Useful Sources

- Music: see Rock and Roll Hall of Fame site *<www.rockhall.com>*

- Poetry: *<www.favoritepoems.org>*; *<www.poetry.org>*; *<www.poems.org>*

- Values: What does America believe in?

- Images: _#_ ways of looking at America

- Film

- Religion

- Art: *<www.time.com/time/time100/artists/index.html>*

- Ideas: *<www.time.com/time/time100/scientist/index.html>*

- Leaders: *<www.time.com/time/time100/leaders/index.html>*

- *DoubleTake Magazine: <www.doubletakemagazine.org/teachersguide/ activities/index.html>*

- Culture: The following Web sites all contain excellent content:
    - Lost & Found Stories: *<www.npr.org/programs/lnfsound/stories/index.html>*
    - American Memory: *<http://memory.loc.gov/ammem/amhome.html>*
    - National Archives Exhibits: *<www.nara.gov/exhall/exhibits.html>*
- Wars: see Stephen Ambrose's book *Americans at War*

Requirements

READING

- Bibliography of what you read, watch, and listen to (including Web sites, articles, books, films, and so on) during the course of your project. Must be properly formatted (see *Writer's Inc.* for guidance in this area).

WRITING

- Three-page typed reflection on what you found out about your subject, the answers to your question(s).

- Examples from and discussion of all three domains in your paper.

- *Alternative.* A series of poems written about your subject with a one-page analysis of what your poems say about the subject, complete with quotes from your own poems to support your ideas.

- *Alternative.* A video or other multimedia production that includes a one-page analysis of what your production says about the subject (i.e., discusses what you were trying to accomplish through your video, what it says about America).

- *Alternative.* A musical performance of either original or carefully selected American music that includes a one-page analysis of your selections and how they relate to your subject.

- *Alternative.* An original work of art (or multimedia presentation of art collected online and organized into a show focused around an idea) with a one-page typed analysis of or introduction to the show.

THINKING

- Think in Threes graphic organizer.

- Evidence of planning, thinking, working.

- A list of the questions you asked to help you and those questions you were trying to answer through your research.

SPEAKING

- Be prepared to present on _____ .

Assessment   Your work will be evaluated according to the:

- Quality of your:

  - Production
  - Presentation
  - Thinking
  - Writing
  - Work (all projects are to be done individually, though PAIRS may lobby me for special consideration)

- Degree of creativity, originality, and intellectual risk you demonstrate

RECOMMENDED RESOURCE

Ballenger, Bruce. 2001. *The Curious Researcher: A Guide to Writing Research Papers*. 3d ed. Boston: Allyn and Bacon.

54 Write Creative Fiction

DESCRIPTION

All writing is creative; when we speak, however, of creative writing or creative fiction, we speak specifically of the imagination. This type of writing, unless taught and studied in creative writing classes, gets increasingly short shrift, as teachers feel they must teach what's tested. The constraints of this book preclude going into much detail about this type of writing, but let me say that it matters and can, in fact, develop students' textual intelligence (Burke 2001) by improving their understanding of narrative design and the elements of fiction. More important than the practical, however, is the personal: Maxine Greene (2000) contends that English is the last bastion of the imagination, the last class whose curriculum routinely invites students to occupy others' perspectives, an experience central to a complete education in the humanities.

What students write depends on why they are writing it. If they are studying style or author's craft, they might mimic the authors they are reading to see how they shape their voice, their style. If you want to use creative fiction to help them understand the characters or the text as a whole, have them write into the story, adding scenes or chapters in the author's voice.

Creative fiction also invites fun into the classroom. In recent years, contests for short-short stories (e.g., of 50 words, 99 words, 250 words) have appeared, some of them sponsored by America Online or National Public Radio. Such short stories provide students the opportunity to play with and even publish and perform their stories through classroom anthologies or readings. Such writing allows students to examine the elements of voice and the differences between fiction and nonfiction. Writing fiction also invites classes to discuss the patterns of stories—to note, for example, that the journey, the return (e.g., of the prodigal), the rite of passage, or the dilemma typically lies at the heart of any story.

PROMPTS FOR PRACTICE

• Have students write a straight-ahead, traditional work of creative fiction inspired by their own life, a book the class is reading, or some other, more original source.

CREATIVE FICTION AT A GLANCE

☐ Story must have characters—some major, some minor

☐ Characters must face some situation

☐ Story must be set in place and time

☐ Story must have some central, guiding ideas

☐ Story must have some tension(s) that draw it forward and that the story attempts to resolve

☐ Story's central problem(s) must eventually be resolved as the story moves toward its conclusion

☐ A narrator must tell the story from a specific point of view (first, second, third)

☐ The writer must decide what genre—poem, play, novel, short story, dramatic monologue—is most appropriate to the subject matter and story

---

• *Recast the text.* Have students take one text—a poem, play, novel, biography—and recast it as a work of creative fiction. If it is already a work of fiction, they can recast the story in a different era, from a different perspective, in the voice or from the perspective of another character in the story.

• *Write into.* Find a section of a work of fiction you are already reading where an opening appears. Then have students add a whole new scene, such as a dramatic monologue, that fits in style and content with that chapter. Examples include the scene when Holden Caufield waits in the diner for the phone to ring and the scene when Huck whiles away the afternoon on the raft by the river.

• *Add a chapter.* In books such as Mark Twain's *Huck Finn* and Bharati Mukherjee's *Jasmine,* the novel ends with the character walking into the future, with no clear ending in sight. This is typical of most novels unless a character dies, such as in *Hamlet.* Have students write an additional chapter or epilogue that is consistent with the tone, style, and perspective of the novel; in this addition, they should portray the character and what they think happens to that person in the future.

• Have a short-short story contest, bringing in examples of stories from books like Jerome Stern's *Microfiction* and Paul Auster's *I Thought My Father Was God* and *Sudden Fiction.* Study models from these books and have students publish and/or perform their own texts.

• Have students write dramatic monologues for imaginary characters (Jago 2002a), historical figures, or characters from stories you are already reading.

CLASSROOM CONNECTION

Here is a sample assignment that illustrates the previous idea.

Overview   Now you need to take on the persona (become someone else, a character in a story) of a teenager who is talking about the world and life from their point of view. Think of Esperanza from *Mango Street* or Holden from *Catcher*. Focus on their VOICE in the stories and how it evoked their character.

Assignment   Write a monologue in the voice of a teenager who is fed up with all the troubles of this world, who is confused by it all, who does not understand why things can't just be nice and simple. Or you might prefer to write a similar monologue in the voice of a character with a very strong attitude about something else; they might, for instance, hate cynical people.

Due   This draft is due tomorrow. Focus on developing the VOICE and the CHARACTER of your narrator in the story. It should be at least one page long.

RECOMMENDED RESOURCES

King, Stephen. 2000. *On Writing: A Memoir of the Craft*. New York: Scribner.

Le Guin, Ursula K. 1998. *Steering the Craft: Exercises and Discussions on Story Writing for the Lone Navigator or the Mutinous Crew*. Portland, OR: Eighth Mountain Press.

Write
a Speech

DESCRIPTION

We speak more than we will ever write; ironically, public speaking routinely ranks as the number one fear for people in the United States. What once was a straightforward task that demanded one stand and deliver has since become a more complicated challenge as speakers feel compelled to incorporate other media into their presentation and use powerful applications like Microsoft PowerPoint to communicate their ideas.

Thus, when we speak about speeches, we must realize we are also talking about presentations that range from simple to complex, owing to their multimedia components. Speeches such as these ask us to think differently. Instead of minutes, we think of screens as we create a Web site presentation or PowerPoint presentation. Such thinking requires ideas to be effectively bulleted and explained in short sentences. Other speeches are less ambitious, as the example of classroom minutes on page 307 shows.

In my own classes, students present in a variety of situations (see Figure 55.1). We try to begin each day with the minutes from the previous day's class; I appoint a different person each day to take the minutes. In addition to minutes, this student reads a poem from Billy Collins' *Poetry 180* Web site *<www.loc.gov/poetry/180/p180-list.html>* or some other short daily piece from one of the Web sites I've listed for them. Through my collaboration with the social studies teacher, the kids participate in several simulations during the year, the most ambitious of them involving presentations and performances. In my ACCESS classes, sophomores participate in the Toastmasters International Youth Leadership Program; this program develops their confidence by having students accomplish what they did not think they could (give two speeches). The program has shown me the difference speaking can make and convinced me that I must make a permanent place for speeches in my curriculum.

Most people would rather be in the coffin than giving the eulogy.

UNKNOWN

Components of an Effective Presentation or Speech

OVERVIEW

The following ideas are designed to help you speak to either one person (e.g., a coach, a teacher, a prospective employer in an interview) or a large group in a formal setting. Speaking in front of people is considered, by most Americans, the most stressful experience imaginable; these strategies can help ease some of that stress by getting you prepared.

PREPARATION

First, clarify your topic. Try the business card test: you have only one side of a business card to state your main idea. Aside from this, the following points are essential, even if they do seem obvious:

- **Preparation:** Know your material cold so you can worry not about *what* to say but about *how* to say it.
- **Rehearsal:** This might mean walking around your bedroom all afternoon repeating your lines over and over; it might also mean practicing in front of friends, parents, mirrors, even video cameras or tape recorders.
- **Audience:** How you speak, what you include, how you act will be determined by the answers to a few simple questions: To whom am I speaking? Why am I speaking to them? What do they know—and what must I explain? How much time do I have?
- **Tools and aids:** What, if any, visual or other aids (props, handouts, transparencies, posterboard, computer presentation, video) should I use to convey this information to my audience most effectively?

VISUAL AIDS

When your purpose is to convey complex or abundant information to your audience, use visual aids to help them keep track of your main ideas. These aids also let the audience know what to expect; for instance, in the example provided below, the audience can relax, knowing the speaker will take questions when they finish their presentation.

Consider using one of the following:

- Posterboard
- Overhead transparencies (with colored pens or photocopied)
- Presentation software such as PowerPoint, HyperStudio, ClarisWorks, or similar
- Handout with the same information as displayed on your visual aids so they don't have to take notes but can pay closer attention or supplement your notes with their own

CHARACTERISTICS OF EFFECTIVE PRESENTATIONS/SPEECHES

- Visual aids:
  - Are clearly visible and readable to all members of the audience
  - Use large, basic fonts such as Helvetica for clarity and neatness
  - Include minimal text for emphasis and readability

> - Overview of presentation
>   - Background
>   - Current status
>   - Proposed changes
>   - Implications
>   - Summary and questions

- Use concrete, precise words that will not confuse the audience
- *Do not* include graphics or images that compete with the information
- Effective, engaging speakers:
  - Pace their speech so that each word gets the proper enunciation and emphasis
  - Look at their audience as much as possible
  - Project and inflect their voice in order to engage the audience and emphasize those ideas they feel are important
  - Use humor or other such devices to engage and maintain their audience's attention
- Effective presentations:
  - Provide an overview of the presentation at the beginning
  - Provide a summary of the presentation's main points at the end
  - Provide strong supporting examples to clarify the ideas
  - Follow a logical, coherent progression from idea to idea
  - Avoid any theatrics that will undermine the speaker's ability to effectively convey the information to their audience
  - Anticipate the audience's questions and are ready to answer them
  - Restate questions from the audience to clarify (and provide time to compose a thoughtful response to the question)
  - Use transitions to clearly mark where one idea ends and the next begins; these transitions also make for a more fluid, coherent speech
- Presentation strategies:
  - **Note cards:** These can contain either cue words or main ideas across the top of the card, followed by ideas or scripts as needed.
  - **Outline:** Helpful, abbreviated script that supports but allows you to speak instead of read. Also helpful as checklist of what you've discussed.
  - **Memorize:** If you have time, memorize what you will say, especially if you are presenting your information dramatically. Actors reading off 3 × 5 cards just doesn't work too well.
  - **Write your outline or script in large type and triple-space** it so you don't have to search through the document to find your place.
  - **Have style:** Whether this is the handouts, your way of speaking, your humor, or the guiding metaphors and analogies you use to help them understand, make sure your speech engages their attention and their heart if at all possible. Give them something to remember.
  - **Avoid words you can easily trip over** during the course of your speech. This is particularly important for speeches that cause stress.
  - **Monitor your audience:** If you see that you are losing them, adjust your speech, improvise, project yourself more forcefully.
  - **Cue words:** On note cards or outlines, such words, if the speaker is well prepared, allow the speaker to recall all they want to say about a topic once they see the word. Example: *Implications* signals the memory to recall the list of five different implications for the expanded use of technology in every aspect of our lives.

FIGURE 55.1   Components of an effective speech

May be copied for classroom use. Writing Reminders *by Jim Burke (Heinemann, Portsmouth, NH); © 2003.*

PROMPTS FOR PRACTICE

What your students speak about depends on what they are studying in your class. Speeches serve a range of purposes, each with its own conventions and nuances. The following list represents some of these possibilities:

• Have speakers persuade the class about the importance or value of an idea or event, or the quality of an item (art review), experience (restaurant review), or performance (movie or performing arts review).

• Have students address the class as a historical character about an event such as the American Revolution, World War Two, Japanese internment, or Dustbowl migration. Students can research the event and that person's likely perspective on it in preparation for the speech. An appropriate follow-up to the activity might be to explain (from their perspective, that of the character, and, ideally, someone else from that era who might see things differently) why they acted as they did.

• Students can address the class as a character from a book the class is reading. You could have Atticus Finch talk about a certain issue or invite Macbeth to speak about ambition, leadership, or power.

• Have students write and produce their own commercial about a product they invent. Students can do this as either a serious or a satirical project.

• Seniors could write graduation speeches and deliver them as part of a culminating activity for your class. Hold your own private graduation ceremony in class the week before graduation. Let students invite family members and bring food. Memorable occasion guaranteed. Invite the principal to come and say a few words, too.

• Have students find (or provide them with) a proverb or compelling quotation on a subject (e.g., evil) related to what the class is studying (e.g., *Lord of the Flies* or *Macbeth*). Each student explains and discusses the proverb or quotation in a one-minute speech. Options include having students give the speech from the perspective of a character or the author (e.g., have Roger from *Lord of the Flies*, or William Golding, the book's author, discuss what he thinks about the proverb from his perspective). One other alternative is to have students deliver speeches already given by historical figures, then explain and discuss *as that person* what they meant, what they were trying to accomplish, or analyze what *they* think the person was trying to say in this speech and support why they think that.

Other examples appear in the assignments that follow.

CLASSROOM CONNECTION

Natalie Miles' speech (which the class voted best speech of the day) is about the need to change so you can improve, a theme central to the AC-CESS program. It's hard to get a sense of what an achievement this speech was, but her delivery, her admissions, her success that day are what make speeches such memorable occasions.

WHY DO PEOPLE CHANGE—AND HOW DO THEY?

—Natalie Miles

Everyone has a life of their own, that they can live by however they want, and most people make the choices that please them. Some choices however, are not ones that please them, and they can't help but choose them sometimes. And so some of those people may not be happy at all in what they are doing. No one's perfect, so no one makes perfect decisions, where they can lead the happiest life ever. However, I know that everyone wants to change something, whether big, small, physical or mental, things they do, people they see, to help themselves lead a happier life.

People want to change usually because they're not happy in themselves or what they're doing. Something new or better is always good for someone. In order to do some of those things, it's not easy, and a person must take some steps. Some people don't want to change though, most likely cause they're afraid of something different, or something they might have to put effort in and work at. Like say . . . you want to do something big to change, like stop drinking or smoking. There are many steps that go into stopping. Like you might have to leave friends behind, or family, or just overall things that might influence you to do those things, maybe even the environment you live in. Or say you want to change something small, like your looks. Well, first you have to decide how and what you want to look like, then you have to make efforts, like buying those new clothes, or trying that new make-up. I guess what I am trying to say, is that no change, big or small comes like that (snap). It takes all your heart and soul and determination to make that change happen.

There are many things I want to change about myself: my study habits, my horrible procrastination. But what I really want to change is my low, low self-esteem. Believe it or not, I do have low self-esteem; it's just hidden under my "happiness." Not only is it bringing me down in just my life, but in school, work, and my social life. I want it to go away so badly. But it's one of the hardest things that I've ever tried to do. And I am constantly trying to change the way I think, but I need to make really honest efforts, and do things to change it. It's not that I am afraid of changing, it's I am afraid of the things and efforts I have to do to change. But it's something that I have to do, just like any other change, and it all takes work, and determination.

Figure 55.2 shows the notes from our conference about her speech. They show how such tools for thought (Burke 2002c) help students generate and organize their ideas prior to writing.

When working with kids on speeches, I use several tools for thought (see Figure 16.1). Speech Outline is, however, the most common tool for obvious reasons (see Figure 55.3).

The guidelines for the daily minutes assignment appear on page 308; see Figure 55.4 for Danielle Hobart's sample daily minutes.

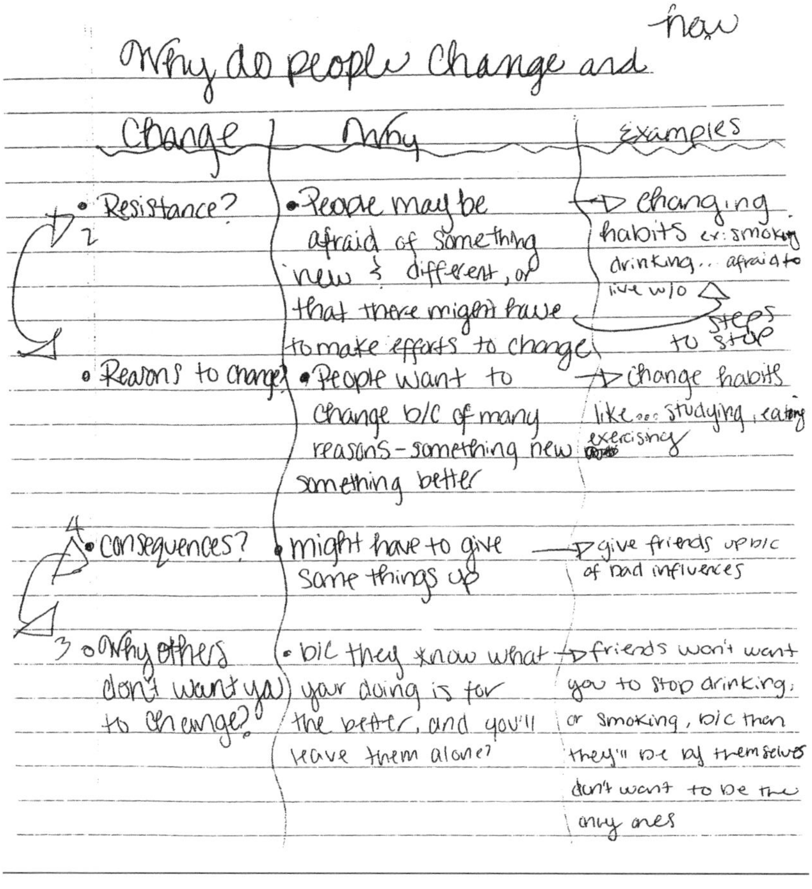
Why do people Change and new

Change	Why	Examples
• Resistance? 2	• People may be afraid of something new & different, or that there might have to make efforts to change	→ changing habits ex: smoking drinking... afraid to live w/o → steps to stop
• Reasons to change?	• People want to change b/c of many reasons - something new something better	→ change habits like... studying, eating exercising
4 • Consequences?	• might have to give some things up	→ give friends up b/c of bad influences
3 • Why others don't want ya to change?	• b/c they know what your doing is for the better, and you'll leave them alone?	→ friends won't want you to stop drinking, or smoking, b/c then they'll be by themselves don't want to be the only ones

FIGURE 55.2 Notes from conference session with Natalie Miles

Speech Outline Notes

Name: _____ **Date:** _____

Topic: _____ **Period:** _____

Main Idea/Subject _____
(What is the question your speech is trying to answer?)

Introduction _____

Details/Examples A. _____

Consider:
- Asking a thought-provoking question
- Beginning with a good/funny story
- Opening with a demonstration
- Making a strong statement
- Using a prop or visual

B. _____

C. _____

D. _____

E. _____

Body of My Speech _____

Details/Examples A. _____

Remember to:
- Organize your speech in order of importance, chronological order, comparison/contrast, cause/effect, order of location, or problem
- Use interesting details, examples, or stories
- Consider your audience's needs and question
- Make a strong statement

- _____

B. _____

- _____

C. _____

- _____

D. _____

- _____

E. _____

- _____

Conclusion _____

Details/Examples A. _____

Remember to:
- Tell one last interesting fact or story
- Explain why the topic is important
- Sum up the most important ideas in your speech
- Make a strong statement

B. _____

C. _____

D. _____

E. _____

FIGURE 55.3   Sample Speech Outline Notes page, which students can use or adapt to help them prepare for their speech

May be copied for classroom use. Writing Reminders *by Jim Burke (Heinemann, Portsmouth, NH); © 2003.*

Minutes For December 3, 2002   Danielle Hobart

Presented on December 5, 2002   °6 12/5

Done by: Danielle Hobart   Mr Burke

Period 6. Q. When?   A. December 3, 2002

Q: Where were we?   A. In the Imac Lab

Q: Who was there?   A. Mr. Smith, Mr. Burke, students.

Q: What did we do?   A. We participated in the freshmen career
                            inventory. Every english class did this to
                            open our minds to job opportunities and
                            select a field of study that we might
                            excell in. We filled out two forms. One
                            was a sheet with spots for our first and
                            second semester scedules. We added
                            the possible changes to them. After we did the
                            online test, we did further reasearch about
                            our first choice of job. The other form
                            asked us what we thought about the
                            job, what level of education was needed,
                            and how you could reach the level of
                            position. We handed everything back to
                            the counslers and were dismissed.

Q: Homework?   A. The homework was to read pgs 1-64 in
                            Kitchen God's Wife. Then you had to make a
                            list of major and minor characters.

Reading from Poetry 180: "The Death
                          of Santa Claus"
                          by Charles Webb.

FIGURE 55.4   Danielle Hobart's sample daily minutes

The Daily Minutes and a Poem or a Word

Introduction   Successful adults are able to listen well, take useful notes, read critically, and speak clearly to a group of people. They use these skills as employees, consumers, and community members. This daily assignment provides an interesting way to develop these skills while having some fun. Each day a different student will do the following:

• Take notes (using Cornell Notes) on what we discuss, do, or turn in

• Go online (visit <*www.englishcompanion.com/room82*> for links) and find *either* a poem to read (see Poetry 180) *or* a word whose story you'll tell

• Begin the next day's class by reading the poem or telling the word story, then reporting (from your notes) on what we did the previous day

Instructional Objectives   This assignment challenges students to become better:

• Listeners by requiring them to take notes on important ideas in class

• Note takers by having them to use the Cornell Notes format

• Speakers by reading to and discussing ideas with their classmates

• Researchers through online investigations into words and poems

• Readers through close reading of literary (poetic) texts

• Users of language by learning new words

Standards   To meet the standards on this assignment, you must:

• Identify and include in your Cornell Notes the most important ideas, events, and information (e.g., assignments, due dates) from class that day

• Use the Cornell Notes format as intended

• Find, print, and turn in your daily poem or word

• Read your notes and poem (or daily word) to us with eye contact, clear voice, and appropriate pacing (not too slow, not too fast)

• Show some style when you speak so we will enjoy and *remember* what you say

The rubric in Figure 55.5 illustrates one way to evaluate speeches.

RECOMMENDED RESOURCE

Franklin, Sharon, and Deborah J. Clark. 2001. *Essentials of Speech Communication*. Boston: Nextext.

Presentation Evaluation

Student Names: _____

Period: _____

Topic of Presentation: _____

OVERALL QUALITY					NEEDS IMPROVEMENT · · · · · · · GOOD · · · · · · · EXCELLENT
1.	1	2	3	4	5	**Ideas and content:** Your presentation addresses meaningful and interesting subjects that challenge you and your audience to think about what you say.
2.	1	2	3	4	5	**Process:** You prepared your materials and speech for this presentation; it does not look like you made it up as you spoke.
3.	1	2	3	4	5	**Delivery:** You make eye contact, project your voice, and speak clearly. **OR:** You facilitate a discussion. You get the conversation started and keep it going; engage class or group in meaningful discussion; you challenge their thinking by asking thoughtful questions and asking them to support their arguments and ideas.
4.	1	2	3	4	5	**Creativity:** You solve the problems the assignment presents; your work is original; you try different approaches to solve problems; you take intellectual and emotional risks.
5.	1	2	3	4	5	**Knowledge/expertise:** You demonstrate a complete and fluent understanding of the topic. You answer people's questions. You use examples to support and illustrate your thinking. You answer the question, What is important to know about this subject?
6.	1	2	3	4	5	**Visuals/aids:** You use (if appropriate) a visual or multimedia aid to present your information or ideas. The information is organized and chosen to achieve a specific outcome: for example, compare, persuade, define, illustrate. Everyone can read the words. The aids complement your speech and are integrated into the talk for maximum effectiveness.
7.	1	2	3	4	5	**Participation (*if appropriate*):** All members of your group participated in and contributed to the project or presentation *before and during* the actual presentation. Refers both to quantity *and* quality of each member's work before and during the presentation.
GRADE						**COMMENTS**

FIGURE 55.5   Speech or presentation evaluation sheet

56 Write a Letter

DESCRIPTION

Most of our students will not write poems or stories, essays or speeches in their adult lives, but they will almost all write letters. Partly because of e-mail, the letter is enjoying a renaissance; in fact, it is being overhauled, turned into a multimedia communication that will, over time, include more video, images, and sound. Different occasions and situations require different types of letters, each written in a different voice, according to various conventions. Letters of complaint, condolence, and gratitude are each important when appropriate. In fact, these are some of the most important letters we write. My power as a writer allowed me to scare Apple Computers so badly in one letter of complaint that they shipped me a replacement overnight. My deep commitment to letters no doubt grows out of my experience in the Peace Corps, for it was through two years of letters that I won over my wife, letters that taught me to see, gave me an audience to please, and provided a purpose that made every writing task personal and meaningful.

In the course of a school year we write many different types of letters: e-mails to colleagues, memos to administrators, letters to organizations. I write others, including cover letters to applications for programs, proposals, and inquiries. In my work as a writer, I send off a miscellany of other letters, such as book proposals, business letters about contracts, and letters thanking the many people who have sent me letters about my books.

The letter remains one of the most common, useful forms of writing—so common that some don't even think it needs to be taught or don't see how to fit it in the curriculum. Something is amiss, however, when no one in a senior English class knows how to address an envelope or format a letter to a college they hope to attend. One letter I wrote turned into one of the more powerful classroom encounters of my career: I dashed off a letter to the editor of the *San Francisco Chronicle* lamenting my students' attitudes toward reading; the response—more than one thousand pages of letters—became my second book, *I Hear America Reading* (1999b).

THE LETTER AT A GLANCE

☐ Determine your audience

☐ Consider the appropriate tone

☐ Be clear and informative, but succinct

☐ Format the letter according to the conventions of the genre

☐ Establish your purpose both to yourself and your reader

☐ Choose the medium—paper or e-mail—appropriate to your audience and purpose

☐ Choose the means—handwritten or typed—according to the occasion and audience

☐ Organize the letter according to your stated purpose. If, for example, the letter's purpose is to inform, make that clear up front

☐ Be cautious about salutations, as they can cause offense

☐ Consider the effect you wish to create when choosing paper, ink, and envelope

☐ Close the letter appropriately (e.g., not with "Luv," "C-YA!" or some other such parting words)

☐ Format the page and envelope according to standard guidelines

CLASSROOM CONNECTION

Students in my class write a variety of letters, both formal and informal. Some are for real audiences, others, such as the *Huck Finn* Rationale letter, are persuasive writing assignments based on actual letters people do write in the world. Still others, such as the *Jasmine* letter, provide a way for students to enter into a character's mind and think and speak as the character would in a certain situation. A letter such as Jessica Perez's (see page 460), on the other hand, offers an important opportunity for the writer to reflect on an experience such as their year in my class. I will typically give them guidelines for such letters so they can be sure to give me the information I need to improve my class the next year.

In addition to the assignments just mentioned, consider having students write letters to:

• The editor about a local issue of particular concern to students

• The administration (or other school authority), advocating or responding to a change in school policy

• Someone (a character in the book; a similar character in a different book; a friend of theirs) about an issue related to a book they are reading in class

311

- Classmates about a book they are reading; think of it as an unplugged, offline chatroom

- Characters about issues related to the book

- Dear Abby letters to characters in novels, historical figures, or students themselves about important issues

- Incoming students (e.g., to freshmen from those who will be sophomores), offering them advice about how to succeed and survive

Letters allow students to write and think in more reflective ways than essays. I typically have students write letters at the semester's end—sometimes to themselves, other times to me—to reflect on where they are after a semester's or year's work. Here is Jessica Perez's letter, which she wrote at the end of her freshman year. I include the whole letter here, as it provides a useful overview of many aspects of a full year's course of study:

Dear Mr. Burke:

Throughout my freshman year, you have taught me a great deal of information, which I thank you for. When I first entered into Burlingame High School, I was nervous and didn't know what to expect of my teachers, just like most average teenagers. I didn't enter your class until the next week because I was placed in CP English class. I remember my first day in your class; you welcomed me with kindness. I thought I wasn't going to be able to make it through the Honors system for long. I was thinking of getting out because I thought it was going to be extremely hard and it was only for the smart kids. Well, with you as a teacher, I got through it and it wasn't as bad as I thought it would be. I'm not trying to suck up or anything that's just how I feel.

You taught me how to annotate a poem. I liked learning that, you began the process of my thinking. You helped me take a few sentences and write a review on it and how to relate it to books I've read or things that have happened in my life. I didn't know how to do it at first, but then you helped me to understand the poem. You taught the class that it's okay to guess as a reader. I couldn't get that concept for the longest time. In the beginning of my reading I would always try to avoid the questions. But in the end I ended up always asking questions.

My essays are much better now. Before I used to do the usual format of an essay: (1) Intro. (2) Body (3) Conclusion. You taught me to break away from that concept and write how I wanted to while still making sense. Organizing my paragraphs to lead to one another. I tried and tried to write an essay while connecting main ideas. I finally got it when you brought in the "I am Picky . . ." assignment. Then I understood how to lead from one idea to another. I had a struggle with the Weekly Reader essays. At first I didn't think there was any point to writing an essay about a picture with a small caption to go by. It was a new project for everyone to get used to. I didn't like writing them for the longest time. But then after a while I got to understand what I thought it was helping me achieve. I feel that, that assignment was to help us take one idea and write about something that pops off the top of our head when we look at the picture or read that poem. I always tried to ask my family what to write about. But they had no clue on what to write. They really didn't help much with my problem. Everyone kept asking me what to do and I would tell them "Just try to write about the first thing that comes to mind . . . " It turns out the Kristen Carranza got an A when she got her paper back. I looked at mine and I got a C. I asked her what she did, and she said, "I followed what you said to do." I was mind boggled! So I had to learn how to find out when my best writing occurred. It turns out it is late at night when I am about to doze off and I can barely read what I am typing. It worked! Then the next essay I got it turned out to be a B. I was so happy I began writing all my essays and projects at night. Now I talk to my sister and she asks me what to write about in a picture, and I can name at least five different areas of information that she can put in. She wonders how I did it. I do too sometimes.

This is very odd writing a letter to you. I am so used to writing a formal essay of something. My favorite group project that we had was the Lit Circles. I liked being in control of the game. It was like being you, a teacher for a day. It was great. The only thing I didn't like about that assignment was the time frame. We really didn't have a lot of time to read our book so we couldn't go into much depth or question many things. We kind of had to just skip some ideas and head for the next because of the deadline. Besides that, it was great. My group and I thought we had reached our goal. We worked excellent with each other. I am really happy that we got to pick our own groups. For future reference, you should try to let the students pick their groups because we feel more comfortable and not so pushed down to do an assignment. We can have more fun with it, it doesn't seem like such a sophisticated project.

I would have to say that the middle of the school year I saw the most progress. I now look back on some of the work I have done and I think "Wow! I wrote that?!" It's funny sometimes but others it's like, "Wow! I wrote that?!" in a negative way. I think the most important project we have done would be the Lit Circles. It helped

313

me become in control and it was fun. I felt that the *Kaffir Boy* was the most important book that we've read during the school year. It helped us connect ideas with today, history class, and the book. We were able to take on roles in which we would relate to the character in the novel. I didn't like *Kitchen God's Wife*. I really didn't do well with that book. I couldn't connect my thoughts to the book.

This year, I feel that my reading level of books has been raised. Before I used to have a tough time getting into a story and taking down notes. I also wasn't able to read aloud with others. With the book *Othello*, I was able to read with my group and if I messed up, I didn't feel embarrassed. That was a hard book to read, but it was a great challenge for me to overcome. I enjoyed that book a lot. I am now able to read more quickly and understand words. I also have a larger vocabulary now from the weekly vocab.

Next year I hope to enroll and still be able to go to Honors English. I feel that in this system I am challenged to new experiences and learning. This year has been like a tossed salad. At the beginning (lettuce) we were all put into a classroom (mixing bowl). Then we had assignments such as Weekly Readers, Annotated Poems, Vocabulary, Reading, etc. (tomatoes, carrots, croutons, bacon bits, etc.). At the end of the year we had expanded our minds to new horizons and now we are ready for new challenges (salad dressing and now it is being served). This year was a lot of fun. I enjoyed being in your class. You taught me a lot of useful information.

Your Student,
Jessica Perez

Writing letters to officials or other genuine audiences offers students an opportunity to participate in public discourse. Here is one way to simulate such an otherwise authentic type of letter:

HUCK FINN RATIONALE
JUNIOR ENGLISH

Overview   This week, a group of parents formally demanded that Mark Twain's book *The Adventures of Huckleberry Finn* be barred from the classroom at Burlingame High School. This group, composed of parents and community members of different races—including both whites and blacks—based its argument on several assertions:

• The book perpetuates outdated and unjust stereotypes of African Americans through its depiction of Jim and the use of the word *nigger* more than two hundred times.

- There are other books that can be read and studied to understand the nature of that period of our history that are written from a more balanced cultural-historical perspective.

- The last portion of the book, considered by such respected, award-winning authors as Jane Smiley to be flawed writing, undermines the quality of the whole work's literary merit.

The book, because of many of the reasons listed above and the fact that some classes at Burlingame High have no African American students to lend their voice to the discussion, harms those who read it because of its "racial bias," which thereby harms the society as a whole.

Assignment   You are asked to write a one-page defense of *Huck Finn* in which you explain why it should be read and kept as part of the curriculum. It is appropriate to include in your argument why the book and our discussion of it was personally meaningful to you. You do *not* have to limit your argument to discussing the book but may, for example, base part of your argument—especially if you did not like the book—on the discussions the book allowed us to have (e.g., about racism, becoming an adult, etc.). You should, in the end, explain what you got out of our reading and discussions in class over the last six weeks. It is entirely appropriate to include in your discussion such other readings as the Emerson essay on nonconformity, the *Time* article on teens and race, and Nathan McCall's book *Makes Me Want to Holler*.

Prewriting   Thursday we will spend the period doing the following in order to prepare for this writing assignment, which will be done in class on Friday:

- Reading through and discussing what, exactly, this assignment asks you to do

- Preparing notes or even outlines for the writing assignment

- Asking me questions as needed to help you prepare

- Rebecca Chappell's letter, which follows, shows a student writing the type of letter she may well need to be able to write as an adult. Written just after reading *Huck Finn*, her letter makes clear the purpose from the beginning:

Dear Board of Directors:

One of the most amazing things happened to me while reading the book *Huckleberry Finn* in my junior English class. I learned about myself, about my own nature, and even more importantly, about my

315

world. A thousand textbooks could never provide me with the portrait that this book drew of my country's history. Like the light switch flipping at 6:00 a.m., I awoke to a new idea, a new understanding about society and the people within our society. Mark Twain accomplishes so much in this book, providing the reader with a newfound love for the past, and for learning. Not only should *Huck Finn* be included in the junior reading list, but it should be embraced as the ultimate commentary on humans and the world we create.

When I read *Huck Finn* it was in conjunction with a history chapter of the same period. For the first time in my six plus years of history, the topic came alive. The issues in the book, the facts in my history, and my emotions wrapped me in a complete understanding of the topic. No other educational tool would have been nearly as effective as the story by Twain. He is historically correct, but also manages to force the reader into the atmosphere of the time period. From farming to river boats, trickery to slavery, the reader becomes part of the southern society that Twain brings to life. At one point in the story Huck is faced with the dilemma that chased him through his whole journey: slavery. Huck had just discovered that Jim had also run away to the same island. Huck has to make the first of many decisions about whether or not to turn Jim back in. Eventually he said, "People would call me a low down abolitionist and despise me for keeping mum—but that don't make no difference." From that one line the reader is shown how much pressure there is from society, what society deemed appropriate, and even more so, how the people feel about society. The problem that Huck dealt with when assisting Jim was one that plagued many people of the time. No source could have more accurately shown the inner turmoil caused by the plight to follow one's heart, and in doing so, going against the grain of society. *Huckleberry Finn's* historical accuracy allows the reader to be part of the history that society today is based upon, and provides the reader with the ability to understand their own past.

Perhaps the most in depth discovery within the book is that of the human. Twain examines human nature and presents his observations to the reader, the most dominant of which is the lack of strength within the human soul. Man created societies that confine them to the mass beliefs that strip people of their individuality. Sherben's speech is virtually words spoken directly from Twain's own lips. He tells the townspeople that they only borrow strength from each other and when not united they are cowards. This is also shown when the Duke and Dauphin are pretending to be the brothers of a dead man. The town's doctor reveals their identities as frauds but the people isolate him as the only believer of that and go on with the charade as a collective group. Other human tendencies, like believing what is easiest to believe, the unwillingness to go against the majority, and the employment of religion only when convenient, are also depicted in the story. Twain makes profound conclusions about humans in this story that should be read, or else we will be doomed to perpetuate these errors.

Some opposition may be directed toward this book from unsatisfied readers. One complaint is the foul language used. Unfortunately, however, those words were used and frequently by people in that historical period. Twain finds no use for masking the truth, and definitely no reason to pretend things were any different than how they really were. Others may say that topics in the story are negative and serve only as reminders of a dark past. That, however, is the point of this book: to remember the past. There is that saying, history will repeat itself if it is not learned from. The people who oppose this book simply do not want to think about the horrible parts of our nation's history. That form of censorship, though, would only achieve a second coming of what they so much want to avoid. The past cannot be escaped. This book shows readers why it is so important to ensure that we must not revert back to that past.

Huckleberry Finn serves the readers with morals and education in our own nature and history. Taking this book out of the curriculum would hurt the people of our country, especially the students, more than anything within the book.

Sincerely,
Rebecca Chappell

Sometimes it helps students enter into the mind of characters if they write letters to or from those characters. In the following letter, one student writes as if she were Jasmine, the main character in Bharati Mukherjee's novel of the same name. Jasmine writes here to her common law husband, Bud, telling him why she left him.

Dear Bud,

Hi, I just wrote this letter to explain to you why I recently left and to see how things are going. First, I would like to apologize to you for leaving so abruptly. I will update you on how the baby is doing every chance I get.

The reason why I left you was because I wasn't truly happy there. My happiest times were when I was with Taylor, and ever since I left New York I longed for those times and wouldn't be a full person until I was with him. In any event, I really love Taylor but am grateful to you for the relationship we had. I hope you can find a way to understand my decision.

Love,

Jane

RECOMMENDED RESOURCES

Andrew Carroll has published several amazing collections of letters.

See also <*www.americasstory.com/cgi-bin/page.cgi*>. The American Memory section of the Library of Congress includes many famous and remarkable letters linked to major historical events.

Write a Précis or Summary

DESCRIPTION

The ability to summarize is essential. It is an intellectual skill we use both as readers and as writers, one that depends on our ability to determine what information matters most. Without the ability to summarize, students could not take notes effectively, nor could they perform successfully on state or content area exams, where they often face questions such as this one from a modern world history class:

> What aspect of Napleon's character or personality do you think was the most responsible for the collapse of his empire? In your response, summarize Napoleon's three costly mistakes.

We often ask students to write a summary, but our reflexive use of this word ignores the other variations: the paraphrase, the abstract, and the précis. A summary includes the *major* points in your own words and cannot be longer than the article it summarizes. A paraphrase, on the other hand, is like a translation of a passage into more familiar words. A paraphrase might update antiquated language or use different examples, whatever is necessary to make the meaning more clear. Abstracts typically appear at the front of scholarly articles and offer an overview of the main ideas and findings in the article that follows. Finally, a précis uses the voice and perspective of the original text, but is brief, using paraphrases instead of direct quotations.

Other questions arise when teachers consider when, how, or why to have students write a summary. Sometimes it is useful to have students summarize all they know about a subject before they investigate further; this type of summary serves as a form of assessment, giving them a sense of what they already know and thus need to find out when they begin their research. At other times it can be useful to write a summary of all they have learned so far, sort of an interim report to themselves and a way of checking on their progress toward the final destination. Most often, however, students summarize what they read after they finish reading. Such summaries are more structured, formal pieces of writing, as the Summary Notes page and accompanying sample show (see Figure 57.1). While summaries allow the student to assess how well they understand a

> The beautiful part of writing is that you don't have to get it right the first time, unlike, say, a brain surgeon.
>
> ROBERT CORMIER

319

Summary Notes

Name _____   Date _____

Topic _____   Period _____

BEFORE

1. Determine your purpose.
2. Preview the document.
3. Prepare to take notes.

DURING

4. Take notes to help you answer these questions:
   - Who is involved?
   - What events, ideas, or people does the author emphasize?
   - What are the causes?
   - What are the consequences or implications?
5. Establish criteria to determine what is important enough to include in the summary.
6. Evaluate information as you read to determine if it meets your criteria for importance.

AFTER

7. Write your summary, which should:
   - Identify the title, author, and topic in the first sentence
   - State the main idea in the second sentence
   - Be shorter than the original article
   - Begin with a sentence that states the topic (see sample)
   - Include a second sentence that states the author's main idea
   - Include three to five sentences in which you explain—*in your own words*—the author's point of view
   - Include one or two interesting quotations or details
   - Not alter the author's meaning
   - Organize the ideas in the order in which they appear in the article
   - Use transitions such as "According to (author's name)" to show that you are summarizing someone else's ideas
   - Include enough information so that someone who has not read the article will understand the ideas

   Sample verbs: The author:

• argues	• focuses on
• asserts	• implies
• concludes	• mentions
• considers	• notes
• discusses	• points out
• emphasizes	• says
• examines	• states
• explores	• suggests

Sample summary written by Jackie Ardon

In "Surviving a Year of Sleepless Nights," Jenny Hung **discusses** *success and how it may not be so good*. Hung **points out** *that having fun is better than having success and glory*. Jenny Hung survived a painful year because of having too many honors classes, getting straight A's, and having a GPA of 4.43. Why would any of this be bad? It's because she wasn't happy. She describes working so hard for something she didn't really want. **At one point she says,** "There was even a month in winter when I was so self-conscious of my raccoon eyes that I wore sunglasses to school." She says she often stayed up late doing work and studying for tests for her classes. After what she had been through, she decided that it was not her life, and chose her classes carefully once sophomore year came around.

_____

_____

_____

_____

_____

_____

_____

_____

_____

_____

_____

_____

_____

_____

_____

_____

_____

_____

_____

_____

_____

_____

_____

_____

_____

_____

_____

FIGURE 57.1   Sample Summary Notes template from *Tools for Thought* (Burke 2002c)

May be copied for classroom use. Writing Reminders by Jim Burke (Heinemann, Portsmouth, NH); © 2003.

subject, they do the same for the teacher, giving the teacher a clear sense of the depth and clarity of the student's understanding so far. For example, students can respond to the following two questions at the end of class, then turn in their response:

1. What is the main idea that you learned in class today?
2. What is still not clear to you about this subject at the end of class today?

In his book *Making the Most of College* (2001), Richard Light found both teachers *and* students derived profound benefit from this quick exercise: teachers used the feedback to adjust their instruction and students were able to better monitor their understanding of material as they studied it.

Teaching students to write summaries—or any of the variations described earlier—gives the teacher a perfect opportunity to show students how to take useful notes, how to determine the criteria for what is important enough to include (in notes or subsequent summaries), and how to annotate what they read. Determining what is important is crucial: students cannot write effective summaries (or much else) if they do not know what information, what details, what examples are essential to the subject; taking time to teach students to evaluate the value of details and information matters and pays off.

The word *summary* (and *summarize*) raises the issue of academic vocabulary. When students take state and other consequential exams, they encounter (as they do on assignments and in textbooks) words that have specific meanings; thus, when students must "write a summary," or are told to "please summarize," they must know what that word means and how to do it if they are to succeed.

PROMPTS FOR PRACTICE

The following short list offers some examples of when it might be appropriate to have students write a summary:

- Before, during, or after they read an article
- After reading one or more Web sites to find out about a subject
- During and after a lecture or instructional video they are watching

• At the end of each page, chapter, or section in a challenging book they are reading

• For a sample sequence and summary, see the "Classroom Connection" section on page 240.

RECOMMENDED RESOURCE

Sebranek, Patrick, Dave Kemper, and Verne Meyer. 2001. *Writer's Inc.: A Student Handbook for Writing and Learning.* Wilmington, MA: Great Source.

Write
a Bibliography

DESCRIPTION

It would be absurd to go into detail here about preparing a bibliography; after all, this is not a reference book. For that, you can consult *Writer's Inc.* (Sebraneck, Kemper, and Meyer 2001) or *The New St. Martin's Handbook* (Lunsford 1999). I like to take what is familiar and ask what more we can accomplish with it (see Reminder 65). In the case of the bibliography, the answer is that we can accomplish much more. What is a bibliography anyway but a list of experiences (in the form of books, articles, etc.) that you had while reading? A good bibliography reads like an itinerary of places you visited along the way.

Most state tests check students' knowledge of the different parts of a bibliographic entry. California's state exam includes questions like this: "Which part of the sample bibliographic entry provided tells you where the book was published?"

When we are collecting books, we are collecting happiness.

VINCENT STARRETT

CLASSROOM CONNECTION

I have students write different types of bibliographies for different purposes. At semester's end, for example, I have kids write up an annotated bibliography of what they read that semester, such as the one that follows. This not only teaches the form and its conventions but also provides them with an impressive record of what they accomplished as readers.

ANNOTATED BIBLIOGRAPHY

O'Brien, Tim. *The Things They Carried*. Penguin Books: New York, 1990. 273 pgs.
These stories, compiled into a novel, represent Vietnam, the men who fought there, the stories they have, and how it impacted their lives. The stories O'Brien writes are stories of love, stories of war, stories of courage, stories of depression, stories of superstition. All of them have their own impact on the reader. O'Brien reveals much of the horror of fighting in Vietnam, the horror of being alone in a foreign country with your life on the line. His style of writing is almost blunt, but it catches

323

you in a way that makes you see things differently. The stories he writes tell of how things went in Vietnam, what guys did to cope, what nineteen-year-old boys just out of high school did. It is fascinating and horrifying at the same time. Vietnam greatly affected our country, the people in it and how we go about doing things. O'Brien writes, sometimes with pain, about trials and triumphs and things that went on in the Vietnam war.

My colleague Diane McClain had a conversation with her class one year about their annotated bibliographies. "Reading isn't the only thing we do that matters, you know," they challenged. This led to an interesting discussion and the birth of Diane's Cultural Collage assignment, which she had her juniors do. They discussed what else should be included in this collage besides reading; what, they asked, amounted to a meaningful encounter with our culture? These are the categories they developed and that students could include material for in their Cultural Collages, all of which came with brief explanations about what the students did and what the event or experience meant to them:

• Readings (by genre), which included the original short fiction her students wrote and read to the class

• Movies they watched

• Television shows

• Plays they attended

• Concerts

• Museums

• Sporting events

• Magazines

• Newspapers

• Religious services or other traditions

• Experiences

• Internet sites they visited

Here is an excerpt from Lindsay Rosenthal's Cultural Collage:

PLAYS

• *The Lady in the Van*

• *The Complete Works of William Shakespeare in 90 Minutes*

• *Spend, Spend, Spend*

All of the plays, or at least the ones I can remember at this time, I saw in London over winter break. So, for this assignment, they don't help a lot with the American culture aspect. However, *The Complete Works of William Shakespeare in 90 Minutes* was performed by a group stationed in London at the moment, but originally from UC Santa Cruz. It was hilarious and often over-the-top with comical devices, but still very entertaining. More importantly, I could tell that most of the people in the audience were tourists from the US. Thus, it seems that the American tourists were interested in getting a quick fix, rather than a more intellectual interpretation of Shakespeare while in London.

MOVIES

- *Kadosh*

- *American Beauty*

- *The Red Violin*

- *Erin Brokovich*

- *Return to Me*

- *The Cider House Rules*

- *Sleepy Hollow*

- *Anywhere But Here*

Overall, I think, more than average years, the movies this year have been very well done. The movie industry has to become more and more creative it seems in producing movies that people will enjoy, but are not based on a formula plot that has been done before. Most of the movies I saw are pretty well-known. Out of the other movies on my list, I would have to say that "American Beauty" relates most to the American character and dream. In a way I think this film dug beneath the proposed American character and revealed the dysfunctional mishaps that take place in our nation, whether we like or not.

MUSEUMS

- San Francisco Museum of Modern Art

- British Library

- British Museum

- Tate Gallery

- The Globe Theater

- The Roman Baths of Bath
- Israeli Air Force Museum
- Yad Vashem
- Herod's Quarters
- The Tower of London
- Churchill's War Rooms
- Others: see Sojourn to the Past section

I am beginning to like visiting art museums more and more after my visits this year. It took me awhile, but I can now appreciate a lot of different kinds of art, even modern art. I particularly like SF MOMA, sometimes purely for the architecture within the building of the museum itself. As one can tell from the rest of the list, I have also become an avid visitor of archaeological and historical museums. Being in Jerusalem last summer was amazing because I got to visit so many holy sites, but also because I began to comprehend the incredible age of many of the relics and sites. For example, the Kotel, or Western Wall, was built over four thousand years ago and is still standing today.

CONCERTS

- Sheva

Though I have tickets for the Dave Matthews Band in August, the Sheva concert is the only one I made it to this year. Sheva is a group most Americans probably have never heard of, but this summer I fell in love with their music. "Sheva," in Hebrew means, seven; the group is made up of a mix of seven Palestinians and Jews from Israel, singing mostly songs about peace. The group is funded by a grant called the Abraham fund, which hopes to bring Arabs and Jews closer. Their most famous song is "Salam," which is Arabic for Shalom (Hebrew) meaning peace, hello, and good-bye. It is a really simple, beautiful song that we used to sing on a lot of our hikes. The day before I left Israel, I went to four music stores in Jerusalem trying to find the album with "Salam." I couldn't find it, but an Israeli friend promised to find it for me and mail it to me. A few months after I returned I got a postcard in the mail from the Bureau of Jewish Education that Sheva would be performing soon at the Great American Music Hall. I screamed!

I ended up going with a small group of close friends. We went nuts when they played "Salam!" I will never forget that night.

SPORTING EVENTS

• Burlingame High's Girls tennis team regular season matches, play-offs, and CCS individuals and team

• Little Big Game

• One or two Forty-Niner games

To me, even in high school sports, the true American competitive spirit always seems to surface. This year Burlingame's Girls tennis team was very successful—we won the league and made it to the third round in CCS, but were defeated by past state-champions, Menlo School. Rebecca Chappell and myself also competed and finished first in PAL individuals as a doubles team, and then went on to CCS individuals. This year I went to a limited number of Burlingame football games, because in the past they've been an enjoyable social event, and this year only a few of my friends went. I enjoy seeing my friends compete, but the team wasn't anything spectacular this year. In the fall, I'm often bitter that so much attention is focused on football and hardly any on tennis. While sports events overall are competitive and often rowdy, they can also be fun social events to share with family or friends.

TV PROGRAMS

• *Dawson's Creek*

• *Friends*

• *ER*

Though it may seem, I'll admit it . . . that these three shows are often corny, over-dramatic, and typical "teenager dramas," they have served me well this year as a wonderful release at the end of the week. I say the end of the week, as most of the time, I find myself forced to tape these shows since I run out of time during the week with homework. I look forward to relaxing on my couch Friday afternoons after a long week in order to plug into my three shows and detach from reality for two and half hours (minus the commercials, of course). The one show that I actually make a point of watching and not taping is ER. It has become a tradition in my family to stop pretty much everything and get together on the couch for ER every Thursday night at ten. While my dad consistently insists that we make him watch it, in truth I think we all not only enjoy the show, but the familiarity of the tradition and spending time together. In my opinion, unfortunate as it is, I think a lot of American families see watching TV together as quality family time.

RECOMMENDED RESOURCE

www.thewritesource.com

Write
a Poem

DESCRIPTION

What does poetry offer the writer—even, or especially, the one most re-sistant to the invitation to write poems—that prose cannot? Poetry is an easy and frequent target of contemporary educational critics; they em-phasize that kids can write poems but not address envelopes, can write sonnets but not essays, write rhymes but not resumes. Ours is, after all, a practical culture, one that always wants to know the point or value of any activity. I will say only that poetry serves different purposes and draws on, even as it develops, different faculties within us if we spend time reading and writing it. Poetry asks the writer to pay attention to the smaller aspects of the world, while helping us see in those smaller details the larger world of which they are a part. Poetry asks us to pay atten-tion—to the world inside of us as well as the world outside ourselves. Bringing poetry into the class—the writing and the reading of it—en-sures that the imagination has a role in students' education.

It is not every day that the world arranges itself into a poem.

WALLACE STEVENS

CLASSROOM CONNECTION

A recent conferencing session with John, a gregarious sophomore in my ACCESS class, reminded me how much poetry offers us if we keep it in perspective and don't force it down kids' throats. John's English teacher asked his students to write an ode about anything that interested them. John barged into my class the next period saying, "Uh oh, Mr. Burke, I have a *real* problem. I do *not* write poems, and Mr. Dowd just told us to write an ode. I have *no* idea what to do! I don't even get what an *ode* is!" Having established his policy on this issue, John and I sat down and be-gan a conversation about what odes are and what they do—and why people write them. Our discussion focused on things he could write about. Within minutes we went from nothing to cars to *red Ferraris,* about which he said he knew everything. Working at the board—while other kids in class were working on independent assignments—John and I brainstormed the details that would bring his ode to life. We had a fantastic conversation about what makes the *red* Ferrari so great; and as we talked, played with words, and interacted, John could feel the poem coming together. Here is what he had written by the time we finished filling the board with notes:

Sleek, flawless, beautiful
The Ferrari shimmers
as it moves
toward the horizon,
the sun reflected in the paint
that glows not red
but Ferrari red
as you pass through the world
that is slower than the speed
you are traveling
everyone
looking not, at you
but at the Ferrari
as it passes like fire
moving across places
known only by the Ferrari
the appearance of the color
the Ferrari red
gleaming under that sun.
When you strap into
Those Italian leather seats
all your worries
will go away
when you think Italian
you think of Ferrari and
the color, Ferrari red.

On a different occasion I wanted students to examine the difference between poetry and prose, to see how they treated the same subject differently. This assignment, called the Memorable Person Paper, asked students to write about a person they found memorable. When they had a good draft of their essay, I asked them to write a poem about that person using details from their paper. I added one other requirement, which they all appreciated: they had to read their poems aloud that Friday. Mimi Franco's poem is exceptional, but others wrote good poems, too, since their essays had helped them gather all the details about the person. Here's Mimi's poem:

BILL BROWN

Walk down the swaying street
Twitching energy

Pack of Brazilian humidity
Silence, in a random house
Swish blanket down
Sliding samba sound.

Spin, snap, swish, swack, swirling in the
Silky samba sound
Vibrant dark light he glows
People come
Clap, clap he smacks
Party starts
Heat jumps, I feel the beat, look up out to the street
He's gone
Myth in my mind, Bill Brown.

One final thought about poetry (though I have many many more than space here permits): When students suffer traumas, such as the death several years ago of one of my students, poetry is the only thing that makes sense to them. I didn't know this until Mikey, the student of mine, died. Kidsp—some of them big, tough, football boys—who went to school with Mikey since kindergarten didn't know where to go with their feelings. They began asking if they could write poems, and these poems helped.

EXAMPLE ASSIGNMENTS:

List poem. See "I Hear America Singing," by Walt Whitman. An accessible form that allows for a variety of uses in the class.

Found poem. See Annie Dillard's *Mornings Like This* or Julius Lester, whose found poem "Parents," is about a young girl who shoots herself when her parents try to force her to shoot her dog, both devastates and inspires my students. You can have students create powerful found poems from the text of stories and novels they read.

Thirteen Ways of Seeing. Taken from Wallace Stevens' poem "Thirteen Ways of Looking at a Blackbird"; you could also use James Wright's poem "Three Sentences for a Dead Swan" as a similar model. Examples of poems students have written: "Thirteen Ways of Seeing Hamlet" and "Thirteen Ways of Looking at Winnie" (in response to *The Kitchen God's Wife*).

"Autobiography in Five Short Chapters." Written by Portia Nelson, this poem's structure offers students an effective and powerful way into writing about their own life or that of some character in a story (e.g., what would Huck Finn write in such a poem when thinking back on the different stages of his life?).

Ode. Kids love Pablo Neruda's *Elemental Odes.* They can adapt this form to their own lives ("Ode to My Telephone") or a character or object from a story.

The Irish Curse poem. A poem in which the writer or narrator rains down a long and delicious curse of all they hope will happen to some offending party in brutal, powerful language. (For more on this poem, see Sandra MacPherson's poems or her appearance on Bill Moyers' PBS series *The Language of Life.*)

Journal poem. Inspired by Stanley Kunitz's poem "Journal for My Daughter," in which he writes nine entries in elegant verse, each entry made up of a different event or period in his daughter's life. The same idea could easily be adapted to a student's own life or the lives of different characters in a story.

Ancient Chinese and Japanese poems. These beautiful poems, many of them translated by Kenneth Rexroth, offer models that can help students find their way into a good poem about their world or the story they are reading. (See Czeslaw Milosz's excellent anthology *A Book of Luminous Things,* 1996). I wrote the following example as a model based on Winnie from *The Kitchen God's Wife:*

I have been alone for many years now.
Out back leaves fall from my plum
tree like children leaving home.
They will not return. They think
they are different, that life will be
different—even better.
My daughter visits according to the
rituals of birth and death and holidays.
At night, when she visits,
I offer her my slippers worn thin
by all the years of walking these halls
looking for her.
Outside the plum tree sleeps
while in the cold, wet earth the leaves
dream of the arms that once held them.

Spoon River Anthology poem. Based on Edgar Lee Masters' anthology of voices and characters, this poem consists of voices in poetic form all talking about some central theme or set of characters. See also Dylan Thomas' play for voices, *Under Milk Wood,* which follows a similar format and offers other ideas for students.

Dialogue poem. I got this idea from Louise Glück's brilliant book *Meadowlands,* which uses Homer's *Odyssey* as a metaphor for a failing marriage. Poems use alternating stanzas to indicate different voices discussing a topic often suggested by the title. Examples to consider: Hamlet and Ophelia, Holden and Phoebe, Huck and Jim, Winnie and Pearl, Lenny and George.

Letter poem. I use Ezra Pound's translation of Rihaku's "Exile's Letter" as an example of this form. The poem's structure is simple: I sit here thinking about you and these different memories while we are apart and send this poem or letter off, thinking of you. Examples to consider: Holden to Phoebe, Huck to Tom, Jim to his wife or kids, Celie in *Color Purple* to her sister or God (you could even take this last example and turn her letters from the book into found poems).

Question poem. A very fun poem that allows for playful use of language and imagery as well as intelligent speculation. The best example that comes to mind is Pablo Neruda's poem "Enigma," in which he begins by asking what the lobster is spinning in his nets down in the ocean. Such poems often begin with a question that the rest of the poem tries to answer: for example, What is the meaning of all this wandering?

Journey poem. The journey poem asks the student to choose a metaphor that best describes the journey they or some character is on and explore it through the poem. Some students choose bridges (e.g., that help you cross from adolescence to adulthood), others pick roads; the most common choice, however, is a mountain, something that seems to embody all their different obstacles. I offer students an example of a poem I wrote to help them get the idea. It's somewhat difficult, but the exercise creates a context for their thinking in more metaphorical terms; this helps them to be able to understand the assignment better.

RECOMMENDED RESOURCE

Wormser, Baron, and David Cappella. 2000. *Teaching the Art of Poetry: The Moves.* Mahwah, NJ: Lawrence Erlbaum Associates.

60 Keep a Journal

DESCRIPTION

Journals are to writing what the weight-lifting room is to football players or the rehearsal hall is to the performer. They offer all writers, professional and novice alike, the space to learn and permission to play so that they might learn and think in private what they must eventually be willing to write or say in public. They offer readers a place to converse—with themselves, the author, or some characters—throughout the reading process. Like the artist's sketchbook, they give the writer a place to practice but also produce different possible openings for the essay they are trying to write. Like Leonardo da Vinci in his amazing notebooks, they give the student a drawing board on which to sketch out all sorts of new and emerging ideas, a place to which they may return for further thinking or ideas.

Journals can serve other purposes for student writers. They can designate pages to keep words they love or need to learn as they encounter them. Other pages can list favorite lines from texts they read throughout the year. More practical concerns might include a page that lists their common writing errors or words they typically misspell; they can, as part of their writing process, turn to this page and check it as they enter into the editing and proofreading phases. Yet another page might contain a running list of books they've read and want to read, perhaps with little notations to remind them what each book is about or why they thought they would like to read it.

Journals are the safe houses of the student writer's world. They must be free to take risks with their thinking, trying on one idea or style after another to see which one is right for the job. The absence of judgment and opportunity to write offered by a journal are especially helpful for struggling writers and English language learners, who need to develop their fluency without fear.

Several traits distinguish effective journals in the English class:

• They promote fluency of thinking and writing and thus are *never* graded based on conventions.

• Students use them for a variety of purposes but most commonly as a place to think about a subject they will discuss, a text they will study, or aspects of their life.

- They promote, indeed require, experimentation as a means of learning to write or think in new ways without the fear of judgment.

- They belong to the student, who is able to personalize the book through word and visual art, photographs and color.

High school kids often lack room and opportunity to think about all that their lives are asking them to consider. Such considerations as who they are, where they are going, and what they think about the world around them demand time and space.

One final note about journals: With all the talk about risk and privacy, they can be fertile ground for dangerous thinking. I tell students that if they write about hurting themselves or others, or if they write about doing things that are against the law, I am required to report this and I will assume they are asking me for help by including it. In ten years I have had incidents that required attention, and I wonder what would have happened if these students had lacked the opportunity to communicate that sensitive information. Students themselves seem grateful for the journal.

THE JOURNAL AT A GLANCE

☐ Invite students to use a journal that makes them want to write, that feels right to them. My only proviso about this is that the journal be at least a certain size (standard composition book size).

☐ Encourage them to personalize it using art, colors, images, whatever.

☐ Determine the purposes for which you want to use it and communicate these to the students clearly.

☐ Tell them how you want the entries formatted on the page. For example, do you want the date and subject in the margin? Do you want the entire journal formatted in Cornell Notes style?

☐ Use the journal regularly and for a variety of purposes, including daily warm-ups, quick responses to some text they are reading, one-minute essays at the end of the period synthesizing what they learned, and notes during a lecture.

☐ Provide students with clear assessment guidelines so they know how you will grade their journals; if possible, include exemplars.

☐ Check their journals regularly; many teachers accomplish this by circulating through the room while the students read or take exams.

☐ Use the journal to cut down on your own paper load, but also be consistent about which assignments students should do in their journals and which they should do separately and turn in.

PROMPTS FOR PRACTICE

Sometimes students have a tough time getting started when writing in a journal. Here is a handy list of prompts to get them going. Some (myself included) take these or other such prompts and put them on bookmarks the kids can keep in their books for easy reference when writing about what they read.

- I wonder . . .
- I began to think of . . .
- I suppose . . .
- I don't see/I see . . .
- I like the idea . . .
- I know the feeling . . .
- I noticed . . .
- I love the way . . .
- I was surprised . . .
- I can't really . . .
- What if . . .
- I thought . . .
- I can't believe . . .
- If I had been . . .
- I was reminded of . . .
- Why did . . .
- Maybe . . .
- I wish . . .
- I don't like . . .
- It really bothered me when . . .
- My first thought was . . .
- One thing that grabbed my attention was . . .

CLASSROOM CONNECTION

A quick list of what to do in the journal might include the following:

- Make lists (of words, ideas, characters)
- Draw (images, scenes, clusters)
- Include quotes (from the radio, books, friends)
- Write poems
- Write early drafts
- Write sketches (from life, art, books)
- Incorporate lyrics (their own or others)
- Ask questions (of themselves, the teacher, characters)
- Make observations (about life, people, books)

Assessing journals is easier if you define your expectations and establish the criteria up front through a scoring rubric. Figure 60.1 shows an example of one such rubric.

On some occasions, I will have students use their journals to help them be more interactive, critical readers. Figure 60.2 shows one example of such an assignment. While it is for the *Odyssey*, a teacher could easily replace that title with any other. Note, however, the inclusion of an example to establish what I expect in terms of format and quality of content.

A variation on the *Odyssey* journal is to have students keep a journal from the perspective of one of the characters in a book. The following example is based on *Lord of the Flies*, but again, it could be adapted for any other book in a snap.

Lord of the Flies Character Journal

Directions   You will become one of the characters in the novel. The catch is that you must choose a character in the novel and keep your journal as though you were that character. In other words, if I chose to be Ralph, I might begin my journal something like this:

> First day on the island: very hard day. First I thought I was the only one who survived the crash. I was so overwhelmed by the beauty of the sea, though, that I forgot about all of that and went for a swim. It was right after that that I met this kid named Piggy. He is rather an odd duck . . .

Yes: you will be keeping this journal throughout the whole book, but whereas the past logs and journals have asked you to write chapter by chapter, this assignment allows for, indeed, demands much more

Class Journal Rubric

Name _____

Period _____

EFFORT

- ❏ **Complete:** Includes all assigned work.
- ❏ **Readable:** Is legible, presentable, coherent.
- ❏ **Used:** Is used to think, learn, practice, understand.
- ❏ **Improved:** Shows overall improvement since last time.

WRITING

- ❏ **Fluent:** Writes with ease about a range of subjects.
- ❏ **Developed:** Includes examples, details, quotes when appropriate.

UNDERSTANDING

- ❏ **Thorough:** You write for the full time; your entries show you trying to fully understand or communicate an idea in writing.
- ❏ **Insightful:** Shows deep understanding of ideas; goes beyond the obvious.

REQUIREMENTS

- ❏ **Format:** All entries clearly list *in the margin:*
  - ❏ Date of entry
  - ❏ Title of entry (e.g., "*Odyssey* notes")
- ❏ **Organization:** Entries appear in chronological sequence or as otherwise assigned.

- ❏ **Notes:**

FIGURE 60.1   Sample journal rubric

May be copied for classroom use. Writing Reminders *by Jim Burke (Heinemann, Portsmouth, NH); © 2003.*

Odyssey Journal Overview

DIRECTIONS   For each book of the *Odyssey*, you must identify what you think is the primary event (i.e., the most important event) that happens in that chapter. In your analysis, you must explain WHY it is important to the story, the character, or to you. I have provided a specific example from later on in the book.

You should have such an entry for each book in the *Odyssey* and keep these entries together in a separate place (e.g., separate sheets of paper that can be turned in at the end as your *Odyssey* Journal. You will write in this and add to it as directed.

I would strongly recommend that you think ahead to the essay you will write (see handout on in-class essay) and keep notes on those themes you might choose to write about in that essay.

Sample Reader Response Log: *The Odyssey*

BOOK	EVENT (that is of fundamental importance)	ANALYSIS (meaning; importance of event to character, book, story, reader, studies in history class)
10	Odysseus' men, after leaving Aeolus' island and being told NOT to open the bag, proceed to open the bag, thinking it contains treasure that Odysseus is keeping from them.	This [opening the bag of wind] was not heroic but an act of stupidity and greed that cost them dearly. Their lack of trust for Odysseus cost them the respect of Aeolus and his people and the progress they had made towards home. It also cost the crew what little morale or strength they had left since this put them back to square one just when they thought they were about to get home. Such actions, however, further reinforce the idea that Odysseus' reckless actions cost him credibility in the eyes of his crew who no longer trusted him as they should and as they need to if they were to survive. (FYI: This analysis was written by a freshman, *not* by your teacher. This is important since it shows you what we expect you to be able to do, given that other freshmen before you have been able to do it.)

FIGURE 60.2   *Odyssey* journal assignment

creativity, for it will be assessed not only on its thoroughness but more importantly on the degree to which it sounds like your character, I would also encourage people to make it look like a journal that survived such an island experience so that it has that authentic air about it. In other words, do not do it in our regular journal. Be fun and original about it. And pick someone you can really enjoy becoming.

Evaluation   Journals will be evaluated based on the following criteria:

- How successfully you evoke the character (through attitudes, tone, insights)

- *Voice.* The extent to which the writing here sounds like your character

- *Consistency.* The extent to which your journal sustains the voice and style throughout the work

- *Insight.* If you just summarize what happened in the character's voice, you will receive a C as you show no insight into the character or the story or the other characters

- *Thoroughness.* The extent to which you delve into the character and follow him through the entire story. If you do Simon, you must find a way to follow him throughout the entire story—same goes for the one lost to the fire

During class discussion, issues or ideas may arise that merit more private, individual response. One day we returned from a schoolwide assembly on tolerance. It had been a powerful assembly, mostly dealing with racism. At that time, my freshman class was studying South Africa in their modern world history class, and we were reading South African novels like *Kaffir Boy*. To help them digest and prepare for a follow-up discussion, I had them write in their journals from the perspective of the role they were playing in a South African simulation that week. Here is one student's response from the perspective of a black South African student:

I am a black South African student visiting America for the first time. It is amazing to me to see how most everyone accepts at least some people that are different from themselves. Most tend not to extend that to its fullest. While some may not have a problem with a black girl like me, they might be very intolerant and rude to someone who is, for example, gay. We should learn to accept everyone. We interact with so many people different from ourselves in America and you would think that by now we could be able to accept *all* good people no matter what race, color, or belief. I know I like, in fact love, to be accepted and when judged or made fun of can be very hurt and feel uncomfortable with my own self. The best gift you can always give someone is compassion and you should not shut yourself out to anyone because they are not like you.

These are all important uses and useful examples; journals remain, however, a personal space, a place to do the thinking we need to do but cannot always discuss in public. When reading aloud, I typically have students jot down possible topics to write about and then respond to one of them in their journal. In my ACCESS class, I was reading from *Tuesdays with Morrie*, a book that gave everyone plenty to discuss and think about. Here is an excerpt from Nicole Cinti's journal. She was so moved by this portion of the book that she lost herself in her writing that day and wrote seven pages. Here's just the first:

I have thought about things like this before. Well, only because a year ago my grandpa passed on. I guess that was the hardest time I have ever really had. I didn't know what to think! I mean it was such a big change in everyone's life. I didn't realize how important someone really was until that person is gone. Now my grandpa meant the whole world to me. He was always thinking about how he could make the day enjoyable. He would light up a room with his smile and his stories! I never really got over the fact that he is gone. I have kept it all bottled up inside. It is very odd that I am even talking about this now. I mean if you ask anyone in my family you will never even hear me say his name. I guess that is really bad for me to do. When I was at his funeral, I took a look at him. Just laying there brought tears to my eyes, knowing that he is never coming back. As many people sat behind me, I just stood there for so long. And of course inside of me, I talked to him. I know that seems sad, but I did. We had this relationship that could never be replaced. As time went by I thought it would get so much easier, but it hasn't. I became very depressed. Not wanting to do anything. I guess I realized that I needed to go on. I mean words just can't express how much I miss him, loved him, and care about him. We moved in with my grandma because it was really hard being in that big house all by herself, coming home to nothing, no one. But I know this was something we had to do. . . .

RECOMMENDED RESOURCE

Fletcher, Ralph. 1996. *Breathing In, Breathing Out: Keeping a Writer's Notebook.* Portsmouth, NH: Heinemann.

61

Write an Infotext

DESCRIPTION

Informational writing attempts to inform the reader using a mix of formats and media. Such writing often involves design as much as writing; these are texts people *use*, after all, so they want their info clear, quick, and concise. Web sites often incorporate infotexts as they give you the rundown on some product you are evaluating. Labels on food containers, manuals for computer programs, directions for cell phones—infotexts abound these days. They serve obvious, explicitly stated purposes and use a different voice than expository prose. Infotexts are neutral, objective, removed from the realm of persuasion. The only standard one might apply to any infotext is clarity: does it say what it says in clear English and in a format that helps the reader?

PROMPTS FOR PRACTICE

A cautionary note about including this kind of writing in your class: timing and context are important. It can lead to the worst kind of decontextualized, contrived writing imaginable. You don't interrupt your reading of *Catcher in the Rye* to have students write sample menus for the restaurant at which Holden breakfasts with the nuns. You might, however, have students write some infotexts if they are reading a novel like *1984* or *Brave New World* because that is appropriate to the text. It's also worth pointing out that such writing is more appropriate to classes other than the English class: health classes can write recipes, product labels, directions; industrial arts classes can write policies, directions, and product descriptions; technology classes can write directions, manuals, and policies for use of the machines.

• *Minutes.* Have a different student each day keep minutes for the class; the following day, begin class with that student reading the minutes back. (See Reminder 55 for an example of minutes)

• *Pamphlets/brochures.* Students can create these for a variety of purposes, but they should be, if at all possible, for real audiences. One example might be a pamphlet describing the school or (in the case of my school

---

THE INFOTEXT AT A GLANCE

☐ Short, telegraphic sentences

☐ Immediately establishes the subject and purpose

☐ Uses language appropriate to the audience and subject

☐ Minimal or no use of analogies

☐ Concrete nouns

☐ Limited or no use of jargon

☐ Bulleted lists and other such devices (e.g., numbered steps) help the reader move quickly through the text

☐ Headers and subheaders help the reader navigate the text more efficiently

☐ Specific focus on a process, object, or aspect of the subject; not an analysis of the subject

☐ Diagrams, images, or other graphics such as graphs can help convey information

☐ Clear purpose to the information: to help you choose, understand, produce

☐ Includes only essential information: who or how to contact, what to include, which steps to follow, what it is made from, and so on

☐ Effective page layout designed for quick use and maximum clarity

---

as I write this) telling people how to find everything during the reconstruction process. This type of assignment offers some of the most useful, appropriate opportunities for integrating instruction in technology and formatting.

• *Web sites.* Keep in mind that Web sites need not be actually done on the computer or in html; rather, they can be done on paper as a way of designing what would go on the computer. Nearly all Web designers work on paper first; I do all my Web designing for my site, *<www.english-companion.com>*, on paper first.

• *Directions.* This can be a fun assignment and can be coupled with either a how-to speech or diagrams illustrating how to do something. Some teachers have fun with a common assignment such as having students write directions for how to create a peanut butter and jelly sandwich. Those wishing to have great fun with this can go online and search for the "Jean-Paul Sartre Cookbook," in which he describes the process for making an omelet. Variations on this assignment include how to do something, how to get somewhere, how something works.

• *Policies.* Have students generate, discuss, evaluate, and write up proposed classroom policies—for example, regarding behavior, class library, computer use, or tardies. The class can then compare and evaluate the policies and adopt those that are most effective and best written and post them. This is a good opportunity to discuss word choice and language in general, for, as Orwell reminds us, policy language is a minefield of trouble.

CLASSROOM CONNECTION

While working on their Memorable Person Paper, students read about different memorable people on the Time 100 Web site <*www.time.com/time/time100/*>. To have them synthesize their reading, I had them write up directions for how to be memorable. Here are Michael Rodgers':

HOW TO BE FAMOUS

So, you want to be famous? Have people remember your name? Make "*Time's* 100 most memorable people list"? Well, you've come to the right place. Below is a set of directions (compiled through hours of exhaustive research) for the people out there who can't deal with being normal, who need that something extra, who want to be famous.

1. Be born into poverty or the lower class. (You don't have to overdo this one; if you weren't born into a social disaster just have an amazing success story, like you won the Olympics with only half a brain, or something sappy like that.)

2. If you are rich use your hoard of cash to help the lower dregs of society. (Another good idea, if you are rich, is to give up all your wealth and live with the dregs of society.)

3. Do something totally radical and shocking. (You know what I mean, something that all the people over 30 are tsk-tsking and everyone else is worshipping.)

4. Develop an idea that changes the world. (This would definitely be for those of you looking for the more difficult path. Also, the more put-down and ridiculed the idea is the better.)

5. Do something extremely evil. (Probably the easiest and most successful thing to do. The more evil and sadistic it is the longer you will be remembered. For that little extra touch you can also have a unique name or title like "Sidius" or ODimitrovff.)

6. Fight for a seemingly "lost cause." (That way, when you win, you'll be a hero.)

7. Be assassinated right after achieving your goal. (Only for people who want to go the extra mile. Since you will be dead, make sure that your will and mausoleum are in order.)

A more ambitious assignment is to create a large project to which everyone can contribute their piece of information. Such projects can make for excellent service learning projects. Students could, for example, create a directory for all the stores in one area, interviewing owners and writing up brief descriptions for a brochure of the shopping area. One year, a group of my seniors created, in conjunction with a community organization called Burlingame Together, the *Burlingame Community Resources Directory*. This fifty-two-page directory required abundant interviews, phone calls, and general research; desktop publishing and general computing skills; and precise, perfect writing. During the course of the project, we realized we needed some software and additional hardware; students wrote grant proposals to the superintendent who was so impressed (and surprised), he couldn't say no. (See Figure 61.1.)

Here is a rubric I created for such assignments:

Rubric: Informational Document/Pamphlet

5   LAYOUT/DESIGN

- ☐ Appearance distinguishes it (neat, finished look)
- ☐ Essential info is clearly and effectively emphasized
- ☐ Fonts and symbols and used to enhance the document
- ☐ Space is used to great effect

3   LAYOUT/DESIGN

- ☐ Appearance neither attracts nor detracts
- ☐ Essential info is not emphasized
- ☐ Fonts and symbols do not enhance document
- ☐ Space is not used to great effect

1   LAYOUT/DESIGN

- ☐ Appearance detracts (messy, rushed, careless)
- ☐ Essential info is either lacking or buried in document
- ☐ Fonts and symbols detract or distract
- ☐ Space is wasted or used with no purpose in mind

Introduction

This Burlingame directory was initially conceived the summer of 1995 while members of Burlingame Together attended a community development workshop in Palm Springs. Sitting in those air conditioned rooms with representatives from Burlingame's community, we found ourselves talking of all there was to do and work within our community. While other communities there wondered where to find the resources to do what they dreamt, we realized that we had only to better know what we had in order to implement the programs we discovered that summer. This directory began as an idea that only took root when a group of seniors at Burlingame High School accepted the challenge the community and their teacher, Jim Burke, put to them: to use their English class to research and create this directory. In the course of the year, they learned not only about their community, but how to use computers, how to solicit support for the development of the computer lab. Most importantly, these students learned that they could do anything they set their minds to. The students would like to dedicate this directory to Mr. Crawford Hill, who worked all year with the students as a mentor, guide, and community resource.

This directory was created by the following students:

Dorian Alpen	Consuelo Martinez
Mike Childers	Vicente Martinez
Maria Ferrera	Stephanie Olson
Rudy Gonzales	Carlos Ortega
George Jensen	Fulton Recio
Edwin Joachin	Victor Torres
Nick LePera	Christina Wieland
Jason Marquez	Daniel Young
Karen Marriscolo	

We hope this directory will help the people in Burlingame know and better use the vast resources available to them in their community.

Table of Contents

FIGURE 61.1   Two inside pages of the *Burlingame Community Resource Directory,* created by my senior English class

5 INFORMATION
- ☐ Information is interesting to the reader
- ☐ Information is accurate/correct
- ☐ Information is thorough/in-depth despite space limits
- ☐ Essential information (e.g., contact info) is included

3 INFORMATION
- ☐ Information is basic but informs the reader
- ☐ Information is outdated or of questionable accuracy
- ☐ Information is superficial or obvious but relevant
- ☐ Essential information (e.g., contact info) is included

1 INFORMATION
- ☐ Information is not interesting to the reader
- ☐ Information is incorrect/dishonest
- ☐ Information is missing or irrelevant
- ☐ Essential information (e.g., contact info) is missing

5 PROCESS/TEAMWORK (IF APPROPRIATE)
- ☐ Uses time efficiently to get work done
- ☐ Uses a variety of tools and resources
- ☐ Accepts responsibility and completes portion of work
- ☐ Contributes to the team's enterprise
- ☐ Organizes time, materials, tasks effectively

3 PROCESS/TEAMWORK (IF APPROPRIATE)
- ☐ Uses time to work—but not efficiently
- ☐ Uses limited resources but with reasonable success
- ☐ Not entirely dependable
- ☐ Does not contribute to team's work
- ☐ Organizes time, materials, tasks—sometimes

1 PROCESS/TEAMWORK (IF APPROPRIATE)
- ☐ Wastes time
- ☐ Uses no resources or one that is inadequate

347

☐ Cannot be depended upon to work, help, or meet

☐ Undermines the group with behavior

☐ Lacks organizational skills

RECOMMENDED RESOURCE

Koechlin, Carol, and Sandi Zwaan. 2001. *Info Tasks for Successful Learning: Building Skills in Reading, Writing, and Research.* Markham, Ontario: Pembroke.

Write
a Review

. . . .

62

DESCRIPTION

Reviews offer students the opportunity to look at and examine subjects of personal importance. Students have something to say about bands, movies, cars, consumer products, and even books. They respond to the "Two thumbs up!" format. Moreover, it is a common type of reading in their world; thus, learning how reviews work, how information can be used to bias readers about products, for example, is important.

One fun addition to the study of reviews is the Internet. Kids can go to Amazon.com, epinion.com, or other such online databases of product and performance reviews. There they will find a range of examples written in different voices with different perspectives. In fact, part of the assignment might include the review of some reviews or reviewers. To push it a step further, they could compare the quality of reviews by an Amazon.com "Top 50 Reviewer" and a random Amazon.com reader, distinguishing between the two by asking what one does that the other does not.

Finally, having students write reviews offers teachers the chance to introduce or revisit such issues as bias and credibility. Some media observers have suggested, for example, that negative reviews often don't get posted on sites like Amazon.com since their business is, after all, to *sell* books, not post reviews that would prevent people from buying them. Such discussions about sources allow for a substantial talk about *authority* and *objectivity*, conversations that would help students understand what these words mean and why they matter when it comes to reviews.

If one person says you're a donkey, don't mind. If two say so, be worried. If three say so, go buy yourself a saddle.

YIDDISH PROVERB

PROMPTS FOR PRACTICE

In general, students can review anything that qualifies as a performance, product, service, or process. Specific subjects they might review include:

- Movies

- Restaurants

- Cars

349

THE REVIEW AT A GLANCE

☐ Focuses on a particular performance, person, or product

☐ Compares key aspects of the subject with others (previous performances, earlier editions, others in the same class)

☐ Establishes the reviewer's authority on this subject

☐ Maintains an objective tone throughout

☐ Identifies and applies the criteria by which the subject is being evaluated

☐ Clarifies the purpose of the review: to inform, to persuade

☐ Limited in scope, includes only essential aspects appropriate to the purpose, subject, and criteria

☐ Includes telling examples that illustrate or support the reviewer's opinion

☐ Offers balanced treatment: for example, examines and concedes flaws in this product or strengths in others of comparable quality

☐ Knows and anticipates the questions and needs of the intended audience

---

- Clothing
- Electronic products
- Television programs
- Music (one CD or band)
- Web sites
- Other consumer products of interest to them
- Books
- Magazines

CLASSROOM CONNECTION

Students must learn which questions to ask when writing a review. Before beginning, brainstorm possible questions that students should ask the designer, user, or maker. Discuss each question, asking why it is a useful question, perhaps even what kind of answer they would expect to get from such a question. If time permits, it is useful to allow students to present their reviews as short speeches. While such speeches can get the class out of hand—I once lost an entire period after asking the simple question, "So what is the best movie of all time?"—they similarly invite passionate discussion, an essential ingredient to any class hoping to earn a good review from our most ruthless critics.

Having students write a review of a movie based on a book you read demands that they look closely and compare the two texts' treatment of specific events. It is also a useful, if subtle, way of making sure kids read the book: they have to be able to discuss choices the director made and the effect of those changes on the film. When, for example, students watching *Lord of the Flies* see that the modern director made the English school boys American military cadets, they must ask if that is an appropriate or effective departure from the original text. Thus, reviews ask students to be critical readers of multiple texts by forcing them to compare and evaluate as they read and watch.

The following example comes from the Weekly Paper assignment. Students could choose to review and recommend a Web site for inclusion on my Weekly Reader Web site for the class. Here is one student's review of the Web site Learn2.com:

LEARN2.COM

—Reviewed by Chana-Rivka Foster

How do you dry flowers without turning the petals brown and moldy? Or how do you turn down those pesky telemarketers who call you every night in hopes of subscribing you to some magazine? The answer is simple: all you have to do is go to Learn2.com. This intriguing website is something completely new and original (to my own experiences at least). It's an easy, interesting way to learn to do something fun, useful, and (gasp!) even educational.

So what is this website anyway, and what's great about it? To most people, a title like Learn2 is pretty scary. Who has time to learn these days except in school (if even there)? We are all so overloaded with jobs, school, family, and kids, that we tend to shy away from the unknown. But once you take a few minutes to try this site, I can almost guarantee you'll be hooked, like I am. Where else can you learn to make homemade paper in step-by-step detail? This site is especially captivating because not only can you type in a keyword to learn about something, but there are also daily features that include titles such as "How to soothe a sore throat" and "How to read music." Each step appears in categories according to what you are making (e.g., paper-making might appear in categories entitled "Preparing your paper" to "Drying"). Each page is adorned with little tidbits of information,

351

such as interesting items to add to your paper, and advice on how to make your paper a certain texture. The steps can either appear one by one, or altogether in a printable version. The best part about it is that while creatively offering information, this site takes away the strict, black and white learning rules, and creates new extremes that make learning fun.

For fun and easy information, Learn2.com is definitely the place to go. Once you get there, you'll have wished you found it ages ago. It's the perfect site for all of your needs: arts and crafts, job-oriented, informational, and everyday. So next time you go on-line, don't forget to check out Learn2.com, the best place to learn.

RECOMMENDED RESOURCE

Sebranek, Patrick, Dave Kemper, and Verne Meyer. 2001. *Writer's Inc.: A Student Handbook for Writing and Learning*. Wilmington, MA: Great Source.

Write a College Application Essay

63

DESCRIPTION

It is late October, lunchtime, and I am sitting in my room, whose windows show the first signs of autumn outside. At the desk next to me sits a young woman from Taiwan who came to the United States specifically to get the best education she could. She is a senior. She wants to go to Columbia. She has asked me, even though I am not nor have been her teacher, to look at her college essay. I immediately notice that my colleague Elaine's comments are on there in her immaculate purple script (compared with my scrawl). I have spent most of my lunches this week meeting with kids to look at their essays. Because the essays are often personal reflections on their journey through the last four years, I find these sessions very informative and often inspiring: the essays show they changed and learned.

This young woman, Helena, wants me to say Elaine's comments are off the mark; she wants me to say, "Oh, Helena, this is just perfect as it is. Really! Here, let me give you a stamp so you can mail it now!" And when I say the same things as Elaine, when I tell her that she should hack out about 75 percent of it and start over using her concluding paragraph, she looks crushed. She wants me to do her work for her, to give her words, images, a heavy ring of keys that will open up not only the essay but the future she is trying to enter. I don't do that. My role in this process is to help them see their real subject and let them write the essay.

One young woman I worked with examined the role her voice coach played in her life. The essay said what the coach *did*, but did not examine the precise ways she had "influenced" the student's "development." Not only this: the student did not have a sense of her topic—to speak of how someone develops your voice is, frankly, not so interesting or important.

What are the colleges and universities *really* asking? Do they really want to hear about how your voice got more tone and strength to it—or are they interested in your intellectual, emotional, moral growth? Face it, a question like this is asking: What kind of person are you, and are you the kind of person we want at our university? What will you have to offer us? Schools get applications from thousands of kids with remarkable talents and grades; they prefer, in the balance, to give the nod to kids they think have character and will help create a great culture at their school.

Training is everything. The peach was once a bitter almond; cauliflower is nothing but cabbage with a college education.

MARK TWAIN

353

Penn State, for example, receives applications from approximately sixteen thousand hopefuls annually, 80 percent of whom are qualified for admission based on their numbers alone. However, only 25 to 30 percent can be admitted. The difference, according to one admissions officer, is *often* their essay because this is a variable "over which they have control." In other words, amidst all the statistics about their performance, the essay provides a chance for the student to really show who they are.

Another admissions officer I interviewed said, "There are three things you don't ever want to watch being made: one is sausage, one is legislation, and the other is college admissions because the process is sometimes so random, given the number of kids that come across our desk. I read a thousand applications, each one of which has to have an essay, and I give each application about ten minutes in the first read-through. Anything that kid can do to connect with me as their reader, to make them stand out in that essay, which in many cases is the most important piece of the puzzle, helps me . . . When we read them, though the scale is one to ten, we mostly calibrate it to a two, five, and eight: two means the essay negatively affects the student's application; five means it does nothing to advance their application; eight means it moves it forward toward acceptance, though other factors are, of course, considered." And this: "Given the assumption that all kids have spell checkers on their word processors, we are now merciless when it comes to spelling errors: we are looking to take 25 percent of all the applications we receive; so even a spelling error can tip the balance against the student in such a competitive environment." Finally, colleges feel insulted and are annoyed by silly essays such as the person who writes an essay about the Little Engine That Could in response to the topic "Write about a fictional character that had an influence on your thinking or beliefs."

Once I accepted the job of reading eighth-grade writing tests for the state exam. About eighty of us came every day for four days to a large, dull-colored room at a suburban high school. It was summer. I knew no one. We could not talk. I could not listen to a Walkman. We could not have drinks on the table with us because, they argued, we might spill them and the tests were legal documents. I read papers for four days, scoring them on a rubric of 0–6. It was hell on earth: each paper was the same as the last one but with different handwriting. And every once in a while, suddenly, I would pick up a paper and it would make me laugh, would make me think, would help me settle into the world a bit more. It was those I remembered at day's end. I can only imagine that college admissions officers feel the same way every fall when they get snowed in by the blizzard of papers students send off at midnight.

THE COLLEGE APPLICATION ESSAY AT A GLANCE

☐ *Originality.* What can you write about that others cannot? Even if you are going to respond to a topic that invites predictable subjects—"Please write about the book that has had the biggest influence on you"—you must find a way to write differently about it. *To Kill a Mockingbird* is a wonderful book; in fact, so many kids think so that any university with such a topic is likely to receive hundreds of essays about Atticus' philosophy of "walking around in another person's shoes for a while." Turn it inside out: write about an unusual character like Dill or the judge. Better still, write about a different book, one that others are unlikely to have read: this will show you are a reader, that you are a thinker, that you don't walk the common path.

☐ *Correctness.* Your essay must be error-free. Errors are moral and intellectual checkmarks against you in this situation. Each one says you are not conscientious and take no pride in your work.

☐ *Details.* They want to know:

   ☐ What your goals are

   ☐ How you prepared yourself for the future while in high school

   ☐ How you interact with other people in an increasingly diverse and crowded society

   ☐ What you will have to offer their school and its community as a person and a scholar

   ☐ That you will succeed and survive at their school (particularly important if you would be coming there from far away, another region and climate: they don't want to choose people who will leave because they're too far from home or because it's too cold when they could give the spot to someone who won't have those troubles)

   ☐ How you will contribute to the school's diversity and enrich its community

   ☐ If you have any links to the college (e.g., relatives who were alumni)

   ☐ Your extracurricular activities: this includes not only clubs or athletics but non-school-related activities like political or church groups, Boy Scouts, and jobs

   ☐ If there is an area in which you are, relative to your age, a "master." This is good to show because it suggests commitment to learning and excelling; shows a passion for something that can be transferred into other areas to ensure success and distinction at their school

   ☐ That you are someone who takes on projects and achieves whatever you set out to do (e.g., the student whose love of photography in high school led him to start his own photography business while still in school, which helped to pay for the college he will attend)

☐ *Pluck* (according to one admissions officer). The gumption to write about something in a way that makes it stand out but not for the sake of standing out. The classic example in recent years is the essay in which a young man lists all the things he has done, exaggerating each one to the extreme—detailing that he has raised a million dollars to help the poor and jumped over tall buildings—but admitting in the end that the one thing he has yet to do is go to college, which he is hoping they will let him do. Such spirit sells you so long as it seems intelligent and a reflection of your character, not just a joke.

☐ *Ownership*. Write the story that is yours to write. Not everyone can write, as one student did in their opening line, "I was born in the Alaskan bush on the kitchen table."

PROMPTS FOR PRACTICE

The best bet is for students to go online and visit the sites for schools they want to attend. Most will have application information and sample prompts. Since these prompts are not timed, students should be sure to do plenty of drafting and brainstorming, getting feedback from a range of knowledgeable sources. Some schools even post the scoring guidelines they use to evaluate essays.

CLASSROOM CONNECTION

When teaching students to write their essays, emphasize the following strategies and tips:

• Read the topic many times to get clear what it is asking.

• Underline any word in the application that seems essential to the topic: verbs such as *reflect, describe, examine;* nouns such as *person who most influenced you, an experience that changed yo*u. If you cannot write on the application, make a copy of it so you can.

• Look for those words in the application that the college is likely to use in their scoring rubric: In a *one-page* essay, please *reflect* on *one person* who has had a *strong influence* on your *development*. Each of the italicized words signals a different aspect of the "story" they are asking you to write.

India Meshack, whose essay follows, was in my sophomore English class. This essay helped get her into Loyola Marymount University (her first choice!).

Write about yourself or a topic of personal concern and how that issue affects you.

THE UNKNOWN EPIDEMIC

"Small opportunities are often the beginning of great enterprises."

—DEMOSTHENES

One of the most dangerous epidemics in the world today is not a disease or virus, it is a state of mind—ignorance. It spreads at unstoppable rates and has only one remedy—knowledge. Ignorance is a condition that begins at birth, and spreads by various sources: sometimes from parent to child and other times from media to public. By definition, ignorance is a lack of information. This deficiency can cause levels of harm varying from subtle to extreme. The scary reality of ignorance is that it is blind. Most ignorant people are unaware that they lack the necessary knowledge. I too was included in this natural phenomenon. A critical area in which I lacked knowledge was in my cultural relationships. My ignorance came from opinions I had formed based on surface observations, stereotypes, and stories I had been told by others. I did not gain understanding by reading a book or watching television; I learned through a first-hand experience, which proved more valuable than any other source of wisdom.

I am accustomed to encountering a variety of cultures on a daily basis and have always had great enthusiasm for learning about different backgrounds; however, I never truly embraced races that differed from my own in my daily life. My relationships were customarily with only a select group. While this tendency was not premeditated, I believe that unconsciously, it was intentional. My classmates were always a racially diverse group, however, I tended to associate predominantly with the African-American students and alienate those of other nationalities; but while the familiarity was comfortable, I came to learn that maintaining the status quo prevented growth and new experiences.

During my sophomore year of high school I was placed into a class setting different from any other that I had encountered. I knew none of my classmates, and most spoke a language different than my own. I was the only person of my race in the entire class. In the beginning I felt much like a stranger in a foreign land. The atmosphere was awkward and uncomfortable, however, as time progressed, a few students gravitated towards me.

One girl, Regina, was from El Salvador, another, Sera, was from Turkey and another, Jackie, was from Mexico. At first it seemed as if we had absolutely nothing in common, however, after further associating with these girls, I learned that we were not altogether so different. While their backgrounds were very different from my own, we shared many commonalties such as mutual values, similar family experiences and a strong religious faith. I was awestruck that four such different people could have so much in common. We became very close friends.

Even though we were from entirely different worlds, when we were together, that fact became trivial. We often shared with each other different aspects of our own cultures; they taught me phrases from their languages and I gave them a better understanding of my own. We had very fond times together. My friendship with them taught me to be more open to forging bonds with those outside of my race. I realized how my own ignorance prevented me from meeting great people my entire life. Getting to know culturally different people was an enriching experience, which taught me that, at our core, human beings are basically the same.

My means for choosing friends are now much more broad-minded. I no longer emphatically gravitate towards the familiar and I approach relationships with people for who they are rather than what they look like. I now even make a conscious effort to approach people unlike myself. Those shared experiences were some of the most crucial and beneficial moments of my life. My own ignorance could have deterred me from ever embracing the differences that made us unique and special. This experience was a great lesson in self-realization and it allowed me to grow into a more evolved person. Making those friends was an opportunity whose impact on my life was profound and unforgettable. I would encourage everyone to break down the barriers that cause ignorance and to seek the knowledge that brings forth understanding.

RECOMMENDED RESOURCES

Curry, Boykin, and Brian Kasbar. 1990. *Essays That Worked: 50 Essays from Successful Applications to the Nation's Top Colleges*. New York: Fawcett Books.

Georges, Christopher J., and Gigi E. Georges. 1991. *100 Successful College Application Essays.* New York: Mentor.

www.petersons.com

The Web site of any school to which students are applying: Most universities and colleges post useful tips and guidelines for application essays on their Web sites.

64

Write
a Proposal

Create the best in any-
thing, and there's usu-
ally a market for it.

RICHARD BRANSON

DESCRIPTION

Teachers often talk of the importance of creating opportunities for authentic learning, by which they mean the chance for students to apply
their work in their English, math, science, or other classes to the "real
world." Indeed, proposals offer some of the most exciting and genuine
opportunities to do just this. When I wanted to convert a small office
into a computer lab, my remedial seniors wrote the letters proposing the
change, soliciting the funds, and requesting the structural changes. Students in shop classes at my school routinely seek funding to expand
their growing entrepreneurial program, approaching tool companies for
donations of hardware, which they then ask local stores to match with
other tools or equivalent investments.

As state standards increasingly focus on the importance of "func-
tional writing," English teachers especially find themselves struggling to
address this standard in a way that makes sense in their curriculum. This
reminder shows you one way to incorporate such writing assignments
into your class. Even if you cannot create a real occasion for your students, you can integrate proposal writing into larger projects, as I will
show you further on.

Such writing is not familiar; students need guidance, they need tools
to help them learn the ropes. Throughout the process, I remind them of
the consequences of their writing, that every detail might make the difference between getting funded and merely getting thanked.

CLASSROOM CONNECTION

Personal Project/Grant Proposal Guidelines

Overview   Your grant proposal should be very well written and look as
professional as possible. You must type it on the computer. The questions
listed under "The Proposal at a Glance" are meant simply to help you.
Each section should be written as a paragraph; consider also that people
who read through such grants often have a large stack to get through and
really like it when writers use formats such as bullets to make them easier
to read. (To make a bullet on a Mac, press the option key and eight.) Each

THE PROPOSAL AT A GLANCE

PURPOSE AND SIGNIFICANCE:

☐ What is the overall purpose of your study or project?

☐ What question are you trying to answer in this study?

☐ What problem do you hope to solve through this study?

☐ What will you create or be able to offer as a result of this study?

☐ Why is this project important to you?

☐ How will this project benefit your community or the world?

PREVIOUS EXPLORATION OF THE TOPIC:

☐ What have you already done to explore this topic?

☐ What have others done in this area—and how is your proposed work different or in what way will it add to what we already know?

☐ What readings or experts in this field have you consulted?

☐ What experience do you have in this area?

METHODS FOR CONDUCTING THIS STUDY OR PROJECT:

☐ What kinds of information will you have to consult to provide a good background for your project?

☐ Explain what you plan to do and how you plan to do it.

☐ Provide a detailed time line that outlines how much time you will need and how you will organize your tasks.

BUDGET:

☐ How will you budget the money?

☐ Give a specific breakdown of your expenditures.

☐ Will you need more than the requested amount to complete your project? If so, why and how do you propose to raise that money?

REMINDERS:

☐ This proposal cannot be longer than one typed page yet must include the information outlined above as it relates to your request.

☐ The way you format your page—font, margins, layout—can make a significant difference in what you are able to communicate and include in your request.

answer should be very specific; remember, you are asking them for money and must convince them you are worthy of investment. In a grant, everything depends on the extent to which you can instill in them a sense of confidence in you and your proposed enterprise.

The next step is to look at a model of an actual proposal. When they come in the next day with their notes or drafts, I pass out the following actual proposal. I explain to them that this proposal is a good example for them to study because it is also asking for books; I also point out that it was funded, that the books we've been using for the past semester were purchased through the grant they are studying. This adds to the assignment's sense of authenticity and helps students to understand how the process works.

> Burlingame High School (BHS) students study American history their junior year. Too often, however, this course neglects the history of the students' own cultures and, more personally, how their families or cultures ended up in California. A recent poll of American high school students claimed students named history their most "boring" subject, a statistic and attitude I found particularly discouraging. The California Project asks all students to study the culture, history, and literature of California and create a range of demanding products that will demonstrate their learning. The project itself will address the following needs:

> - Reading a wide range of demanding texts that include both fiction and nonfiction
> - Writing for a variety of purposes and audiences
> - Employing technology as a tool for research and communication
> - Speaking before audiences for various purposes
> - Learning to work effectively in groups in order to create a final product
> - Engaging students through compelling educational content and experiences

> The project's objectives demand that all students:

> - Learn to use the Internet as a tool for research
> - Write and send formal letters to organizations or individuals
> - Read two books by California authors or about some aspect of the state's culture or history
> - Write a biography about a prominent Californian

- Present their biography to the class in a formal speech or presentation
- Create the following products, working in groups at different stages:
    - An encyclopedia of California culture and history
    - One mural (per class) that represents California's diverse history and culture
- Interview older adults about how and why they came to California
- Create a Web site to house all our information, images, and related Internet links
- Compile an anthology and bibliography of California writers

The requested books will provide the foundation for the course. These two texts—*Many Californias: Stories from the Golden State* and *Where Coyotes Howl and Wind Blows Free*—offer valuable resources for the many projects and core texts for reading that will bring much-needed diversity into the curriculum. The grant would allow us to purchase one class set of *Many Californias* (which is ideal for an in-class text because its selections—including journals, letters, poems, memoirs, and stories—are short) and one copy of *Where Coyotes Howl* for each student so they can read the entire book outside of class.

I also like these two texts because they will allow us, through their shorter works, to focus carefully on reading skills, as this is a crucial deficit for many of our students these days. The department purchased copies of Amy Tan's *Joy Luck Club* to read for this project. Also, the school is applying for a grant to the Anson Burlingame Pacific Rim Studies program; this unit I am developing would tie in very nicely with that course of study if the school wins that grant.

Many Californias: Literature from the Golden State (Western Literature Series)
Gerald W. Haslam
Published by University of Nevada Press
Unit Cost: $13.00
Quantity: 40
Total: 40 @ $13.00 = $520.00 (+ taxes @ 8.25%) = $562.90

Where Coyotes Howl and Wind Blows Free : Growing Up in the West
Alexandra R. Haslam, Gerald W. Haslam (editor)
Published by University of Nevada Press
Unit Cost: $12.95
Quantity: 110
Total: 110 @ $12.95 = $1,424.50 (+ 8.25%) = $1,542.02
Total Grant Request: $2,104.92

Such assignments and the thinking they inspire—not to mention the sense of pride if they are funded!—bring life to the classroom by linking its learning to the world for which the students are preparing themselves. Moreover, such assignments offer rich opportunities for teachers to discuss and even teach aspects of language, document format, style, and voice that are often hard to address successfully in the "regular" curriculum.

One other approach to the proposal is to have students write a proposal for a project they intend to do. This forces kids to think about and explain what they plan to investigate and why; moreover, it asks them to detail how they will proceed and explain the project's importance. This extra step before they launch out on their journey helps them think their topic through and, sometimes, makes them realize how inadequate or uninteresting their initial topic is. A few students always come up and say, "I realized that my topic won't work, can I do it about this instead?" Sure, I say, just write up your new proposal.

RECOMMENDED RESOURCE

Burke, Jim, and Carol Ann Prater. 2000. *I'll Grant You That: A Step-by-Step Guide to Finding Funds, Designing Winning Projects, and Writing Powerful Grant Proposals.* Portsmouth, NH: Boynton/Cook.

Write
a Resume

65

DESCRIPTION

To write a resume is to reflect on what you have learned, done, and accomplished. Resumes simultaneously look back and forward: you consider what you have done and how that prepares you for or relates to what you hope to do next. Anna Quindlen (1999), speaking to graduates at Villanova University, said of resumes:

> People don't talk about the soul very much anymore. It's so much easier to write a resume than to craft a spirit. But a resume is a cold comfort on a winter night, or when you're sad, or broke, or lonely, or when you've gotten back the test results and they're not so good. Here's my resume:
>
> - I'm a good mother to three children.
> - I have tried never to let my profession stand in the way of being a good parent.
> - I show up. I listen. I try to laugh.
> - I no longer consider myself the center of the universe.
> - I am a good friend to my husband. I have tried to make marriage vows mean what they say.
> - I show up. I listen. I try to laugh.
> - I am a good friend to my friends, and they to me. Without them, there would be nothing to say to you today, because I would be a cardboard cutout. But I call them on the phone, and I meet them for lunch.
> - I show up. I listen. I try to laugh.

While I agree with Quindlen's comments about the cold comfort of a resume, I also believe it can accomplish more than we traditionally let it. Of course, kids need to know how to write one by the time they graduate; still, how many of them have done enough to actually fill out a resume? My first resume, at about sixteen, was nearly ten typed pages. I recall that I listed every lawn I ever mowed, every job I ever lost, every child I ever baby-sat. My mother nearly hurt herself laughing when I showed it to her.

If you aspire to the highest place it is no disgrace to top at the second, or even the third.

CICERO

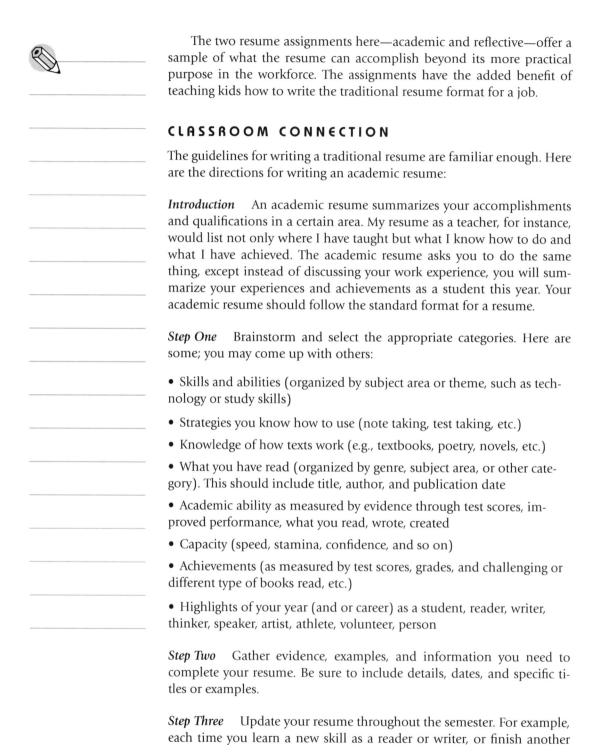

The two resume assignments here—academic and reflective—offer a sample of what the resume can accomplish beyond its more practical purpose in the workforce. The assignments have the added benefit of teaching kids how to write the traditional resume format for a job.

CLASSROOM CONNECTION

The guidelines for writing a traditional resume are familiar enough. Here are the directions for writing an academic resume:

Introduction An academic resume summarizes your accomplishments and qualifications in a certain area. My resume as a teacher, for instance, would list not only where I have taught but what I know how to do and what I have achieved. The academic resume asks you to do the same thing, except instead of discussing your work experience, you will summarize your experiences and achievements as a student this year. Your academic resume should follow the standard format for a resume.

Step One Brainstorm and select the appropriate categories. Here are some; you may come up with others:

• Skills and abilities (organized by subject area or theme, such as technology or study skills)

• Strategies you know how to use (note taking, test taking, etc.)

• Knowledge of how texts work (e.g., textbooks, poetry, novels, etc.)

• What you have read (organized by genre, subject area, or other category). This should include title, author, and publication date

• Academic ability as measured by evidence through test scores, improved performance, what you read, wrote, created

• Capacity (speed, stamina, confidence, and so on)

• Achievements (as measured by test scores, grades, and challenging or different type of books read, etc.)

• Highlights of your year (and or career) as a student, reader, writer, thinker, speaker, artist, athlete, volunteer, person

Step Two Gather evidence, examples, and information you need to complete your resume. Be sure to include details, dates, and specific titles or examples.

Step Three Update your resume throughout the semester. For example, each time you learn a new skill as a reader or writer, or finish another book, add this information to your resume.

Step Four Write your resume using the proper resume format. The completed resume must be:

- Typed

- Presented in a 12-point standard (serif) font

- Properly formatted (check to see if your computer has templates or stationery for preformatted resumes)

- Complete insofar as it includes information about what you can do but also what you have read. Completed resumes must include what you read not only in this class but also in all other classes (including textbooks)

Step Five Proofread and edit for clarity, correctness, and conciseness.

Step Six Turn it in on the day of the final exam.

Here is Molly Choma's academic resume; I give students this or another example to help them see not only what such a resume looks like (i.e., formatting) but what it includes.

ACADEMIC RESUME
Molly Choma

Objective	To attend a four year college after high school graduation and then start a career in graphic design.

Academic Skills and Achievements Freshman English (Burke)

- Wrote essays weekly
  - Autobiographical essays
  - Literary analysis essays
  - Comparison essays
  - Observational essays

- Read six books
  - *The Odyssey,* by Homer
  - *Jasmine,* by Bharati Mukherjee
  - *The Kitchen God's Wife,* by Amy Tan
  - *Lord of the Flies,* by William Golding
  - *Othello,* by Shakespeare
  - *Cry, the Beloved Country,* by Alan Paton

- Learned how to annotate a poem

- Created three PowerPoint presentations

Modern World History (Firpo)

- Read the textbook *Tradition and Change*
- Wrote two research papers
- Participated in five class simulations
- Learned to read in depth
- Learned how to think on my own
- Learned how to relate
- Completed three country studies
  - India
  - China
  - South Africa

Algebra (Stoehr)

- Read the textbook *Algebra 2*
- Completed eight studies
  - Quadratic Formula
  - Exponents
  - Factoring
  - Substitution
  - Linear Combinations
  - Absolute Value
  - Graphing
  - Polynomials

Biology (Kodros)

- Read the textbook *BCS Biology*
- Recorded all data in a lab book
- Completed nine studies
  - Population
  - Protist and Fungi
  - Darwin's Theory and Evolution
  - Plants—Form and Function
  - Animals
  - Genetics
  - Cells
  - Bacteria
  - Taxonomy

Spanish (Woods)	• Read the book *Todo el Mundo*
	• Learned vocabulary
	  ▶ Medical
	  ▶ Anatomy
	  ▶ Travel
	    • Hotels
	    • Trains
	    • Airplanes
	  ▶ Learned how to conjugate verbs
	    • Preterit
	    • Future
	    • Commands

Extra Curricular Achievements	• Student Government
	  ▶ Served as Vice President to my class
	  ▶ Learned how to organize events
	  ▶ Learned how to take charge
	  ▶ Learned the rules and regulations of office
	  ▶ Know how to be a leader
	
	• Volleyball
	  ▶ Learned advanced volleyball skills
	  ▶ Learned how to work on a team
	  ▶ Learned how to respect other players' roles on the court
	  ▶ Learned to communicate on the court
	
	• Basketball
	  ▶ Learned advanced basketball skills
	  ▶ Perfected dribbling
	  ▶ Perfected my free throw
	  ▶ Worked on my three-point shot
	  ▶ Developed an awareness for the ball
	  ▶ Learned to play man-to-man defense
	
	• Badminton
	  ▶ Learned basic badminton skills
	  ▶ Learned how to play singles
	  ▶ Learned how to stay strong in a match
	  ▶ Developed an immunity to frustration

An alternative form for resumes is the reflective resume. Here is the handout I give for the reflective resume, followed by an example from Jen Edl.

Overview

The word *résumé* means a summary of one's professional qualifications, achievements, and experiences. It is a story of what you have done and are trying to do. It is a portrait of your talents and contributions. We are always more than what our resume says; however, when someone is deciding whether to interview or hire you, it is all they have. So you want it to be a flawless, persuasive description of who you are and what you know and are able to do.

Part One: The Reflective Resume for Yourself

Using the attached sample and template reflective resume as a worksheet, create your own. The guiding principle behind the reflective resume is to think about what gifts you have and which ones you need to develop, what you know and what you must learn to be able to do the work you want. Your reflective resume must be:

• Written on a computer

• Properly formatted (see sample)

• Carefully proofread

• Critiqued by an adult over thirty. As a minimum, they should sign the back of your resume to indicate they read it. I would prefer it, however, if they could take the time to respond to it with more personal, specific comments about what you have done and want to do. Be sure to take time to thank them.

Part Two: The Reflective Resume for Someone Else

Using the same reflective resume worksheet you used for yourself, you must interview an adult who is over thirty. You should respect their privacy if they do not wish to include some information, but you should also be sure to choose someone who will be willing to take the time to answer these questions thoughtfully. Try to choose someone who does work or who lives in the world in a way you respect, so that you can, through this discussion, find out how they achieved this life.

Part Three: The Reflective Resume for Your Life Study Subject

Using the same reflective resume worksheet, and adapting it as necessary to meet the needs of your subject's life and times, create a resume for your subject.

Part Four: Write a Business Letter

Using the samples I will provide, write a business letter inquiring about opportunities or thanking someone (e.g., for doing the interview, for a job shadowing experience). This letter must be:

- Written on a computer
- Properly formatted (see sample)
- Carefully proofread
- Properly addressed, in a stamped, unsealed envelope: I will send them when I am finished reading and grading them. If they are not able to be sent because of errors or improper formatting, they will receive no credit and will be returned to you.

Jen's resume is followed by a short note from her mother. Students had to show their reflective resumes to their parents so the parents had a sense of what the students wanted to do with their lives. Such assignments provide potentially meaningful opportunities for students and their parents to have serious conversations.

Jennifer Edl

OBJECTIVE:	To achieve academic excellence in order to attend a top university to fulfill my goal of being a Forensic Scientist.
HIGHLIGHTED QUALIFICATIONS	• Completed third quarter of 9th grade with a grade point average of 3.6 in honors classes. • Future courses include Chemistry, Physics, and one AP science class. • Future math courses include Algebra 3–4, Trigonometry, and Calculus.

EDUCATION (Birth–17)		
	1991–1995	Graduated, Audubon Elementary School
	1995–2000	Graduated, Bowditch Middle School
	2000–2004	High School Diploma (with honors), Burlingame High School

EDUCATION (17–28)		
	2004-2008	BS, Forensic Science, Stanford University
	2008-2012	MS, Medical Science, Stanford University
	2012-2016	PhD, Medical Science, Stanford University

EMPLOYMENT (17–28)		
	Waitress	Friday's, 2004
	• Waited on tables in busiest section.	
	Sales Person	Macy's, 2005
	• Sold shoes in the athletic department.	

EMPLOYMENT *(17–28)*	*Manager*	Macy's, 2005

Manager   Macy's, 2005
- Trained all new employees.
- Responsible for cash receipts on a daily basis.

Receptionist   San Diego Hospital, 2008
- Answered all incoming calls.
- Responsible for keeping doctor's schedules.
- Responsible for organizing patient files.

Forensic Scientist Assistant   Federal Bureau of Investigation, 2009
- Performed DNA experiments to obtain results.
- Assist in pathology experiments.
- Attend autopsies to learn skills.

SKILLS AND
ABILITIES (Now)

Science	Working knowledge of all aspects of Biology.
Math	Good grasp of Algebra and Geometry.

SKILLS AND
ABILITIES
(Future)

Science	MS, BS, and PhD in Forensic Science.
Law	Expert witness for criminal cases.
Computer	Working use of technology to assist in criminal cases.

EXPERIENCES
(Birth–18)

Travel	Foreign Exchange Student, Spain.
Volunteer	Mills/Peninsula Hospital.

EXPERIENCES
(18–Death)

Travel	Extensive European Travel.
Sports	2008, Summer Olympics; 2012 Women's World Cup.
Medical	Awarded highest honors in Forensic Science. Develop new technique for DNA sequencing.

REFERENCES
(Current)

Andrea Sarap

Margaret Benton

Heather Knapp

Joanne Andrew

REFERENCES
(Future)

Professor at Stanford University

Jim Burke, *jburke@englishcompanion.com*

Robert Taylor, Director of FBI

Jennifer's mother, responding to this resume, wrote:

I think Jennifer has accomplished a lot during her young life. She has achieved excellent grades. Her resume shows a lot of thought and focus on her future. She wants to achieve a lot in her future and if she keeps on her path she will achieve her objective and more.

—*Susan Edl*

66

Prepare a Web Site

DESCRIPTION

Soon everyone will write for the Web. They won't even think about it: they will write up a document in a program like Microsoft Word and, instead of (or in addition to) printing it, they will merely save it as a Web page to be uploaded later or sent as an e-mail attachment. I know it will happen because it already is. And it will change our writing, for the conventions of such writing will be shaped by the space we have to fill. That space—on computer monitors, PDAs, cell phones—grows smaller every year; thus, tomorrow's writers will need to be able to convey detailed information in concise language about the length of a haiku.

Web sites are a type of infotext (see Reminder 61) but merit their own chapter. They ask writers to think not of pages but screens, or windows. They are the ultimate infotext when it comes to format: written and formatted to be read—and *used*. No one curls up with a good Web site; they want to read it without reading it. As Jakob Nielsen (1997) writes:

- Users do not read on the Web; instead they scan the pages, trying to pick out a few sentences or even parts of sentences to get the information they want.

- Users do not like long, scrolling pages: they prefer the text to be short and to the point.

- Users detest anything that seems like marketing fluff or overly hyped language ("marketese") and prefer factual information.

CLASSROOM CONNECTION

Web pages serve as thinking tools, for they demand the writer-designer think about the following questions:

- Who is my audience?

- What purpose will the information on this site serve?

374

THE WEB PAGE AT A GLANCE

All of my ideas about how to write for the Web come from Jakob Nielsen *<www.useit.com>* or my own experience as a Web designer *<www.englishcompanion.com>*. Nielsen's studies of the Web are based on how users read or how people use the Web. He found that the three main guidelines for writing on the Web are:

☐ *Be succinct:* write no more than 50 percent of the text you would have used in a hardcopy publication

☐ *Write for scannability:* don't require users to read long, continuous blocks of text

☐ *Use hypertext to split up* long information into multiple pages

Nielsen goes on to say:

SHORT TEXTS

Reading from computer screens is about *25% slower* than reading from paper. Human-factors research usually says that users feel unpleasant when reading online text. As a result, people don't want to read a lot of text from computer screens: you should *write 50% less text* and not just 25% less since it's not only a matter of reading speed but also a matter of feeling good. We also know that users don't like to scroll: one more reason to keep pages short.

The screen readability problem will be solved in the future, since screens with 300 dpi resolution have been invented and have been found to have as good readability as paper. High-resolution screens are currently too expensive (high-end monitors in commercial use have about 110 dpi), but will be available in a few years and common ten years from now.

SCANNABILITY

Because it is so painful to read text on computer screens and because the online experience seems to foster some amount of impatience, users tend not to read streams of text fully. Instead, users scan text and pick out keywords, sentences, and paragraphs of interest while skipping over those parts of the text they care less about.

Skimming instead of reading is a fact of the Web and has been confirmed by countless usability studies. Webwriters have to acknowledge this fact and write for scannability:

• Structure articles with two or even three levels of *headlines* (a general page heading plus subheads—and sub-sub-heads when appropriate). Nested headings also facilitate access for blind users with screenreaders

• Use meaningful rather than "cute" headings (i.e., reading a heading should *tell* the user what the page or section is about)

- Use *highlighting and emphasis* to make important words catch the user's eye. Colored text can also be used for emphasis, and hypertext anchors stand out by virtue of being blue and underlined

HYPERTEXT STRUCTURE

Make text short without sacrificing depth of content by splitting the information up into multiple nodes connected by hypertext links. Each page can be brief and yet the full hyperspace can contain much more information than would be feasible in a printed article. Long and detailed background information can be relegated to secondary pages; similarly, information of interest to a minority of readers can be made available through a link without penalizing those readers who don't want it.

Hypertext should *not* be used to segment a long linear story into multiple pages: having to download several segments slows down reading and makes printing more difficult. Proper hypertext structure is not a single flow *"continued on page 2"*; instead split the information into coherent chunks that each *focus on a certain topic*. The guiding principle should be to allow readers to select those topics they care about and only download those pages. In other words, the hypertext structure should be based on an *audience analysis*.

Each hypertext page should be written according to the "inverse pyramid" principle and start with a short conclusion so that users can get the gist of the page even if they don't read all of it. (Nielsen 1997)

- Why is a reader clicking onto the site (i.e., what are they hoping to find)?

- What are the primary categories into which information on this Web site should be organized?

Not all Web writing must be done on computers or even for actual Web sites. This idea came to me one year when Tommy Chong, a junior at the time, asked if his group could do its project as a Web site instead of whatever I had assigned. I was intrigued, but declined the offer, saying we had no access to the necessary software or computers. "Oh, we don't need a computer; we will just do it on paper, Mr. Burke." Having since designed and built my own Web site, I have a keen appreciation for the amount of thinking involved in setting up a Web site. Such thinking, as well as the related design skills, will become a more integral part of the writer's repertoire in the near future.

In the course of writing, studying how to write, or preparing to write for the Web, students should make good use of models. They can review selected sites of their own choosing or go to specific sites you have determined are appropriate for your assignment. Such critical analysis of Web sites will aid in the creation of or writing for their own while it simultaneously prepares them to read all sites better, thanks to their improved textual intelligence (Burke 2001).

I knew things were changing when, some years ago, before the Internet got big, a freshman turned her final project in on an index card with only a URL written on it in her own handwriting. "What's this?" I asked.

"That's my project. Log on there and you'll find everything."

"Oh," I said. I had no other idea how to respond, so taken was I by the novelty and her own calm assurance that this would be okay. It was the harbinger of all that has come our way and all that awaits us in the future.

RECOMMENDED RESOURCE

www.useit.com

Albom, Mitch. 1997. *Tuesdays with Morrie: An Old Man, a Young Man, and Life's Greatest Lesson*. New York: Doubleday.

Allington, Richard. 1999. "Ten Principles for Looking at Reading/Language Arts Lessons in Your Classroom." Accessed on the National Council of Teachers of English Web site at <*www.ncte.org/ chronicle/allingMay1999.html*> 15 May, 2000.

Anderson, Melissa, Laura Morrill, and Mary Adler. 2002. "Keeping Expectations High While Helping Lower-Achieving Students Meet Them." CELA *English Update* (Fall): 1–3.

Atwell, Nancie. 1998. *In the Middle: New Understandings About Writing, Reading, and Learning*. Portsmouth, NH: Heinemann.

————. 1991. *Side by Side: Essays on Teaching to Learn*. Portsmouth, NH: Heinemann.

————. 2002. *Lessons That Change Writers*. Portsmouth, NH: *firsthand*.

Bell, Madison Smart. 1997. *Narrative Design: A Writer's Guide to Structure*. New York: W. W. Norton.

Briggs, Sandy. 2002. San Mateo Union High School District. Unpublished papers.

Burke, Jim. 1999a. *The English Teacher's Companion: A Complete Guide to Classroom, Curriculum, and the Profession*. Portsmouth, NH: Boynton/Cook.

————. 1999b. *I Hear America Reading: Why We Read • What We Read*. Portsmouth, NH: Heinemann.

————. 2000. *Reading Reminders: Tools, Tips, and Techniques*. Portsmouth, NH: Boynton/Cook.

————. 2001. *Illuminating Texts: How to Teach Students to Read the World*. Portsmouth, NH: Boynton/Cook.

————. 2002a. *Reader's Handbook: A Student Guide for Reading and Learning*. Wilmington, MA: Great Source.

————. 2002b. *The Teacher's Daybook*. Portsmouth, NH: Heinemann.

————. 2002c. *Tools for Thought: Graphic Organizers for Your Classroom*. Portsmouth, NH: Heinemann.

Burke, Jim, and Carol Ann Prater. 2000. *I'll Grant You That: A Step-by-Step Guide to Finding Funds, Designing Winning Projects, and Writing Powerful Grant Proposals*. Portsmouth, NH: Boynton/Cook.

California Department of Education. 1997. *The English-Language Arts Content Standards for California Public Schools (K–12)*. Sacramento: California Department of Education.

————. 1999. *The California Language Arts Content Standards*. Sacramento: California Department of Education.

Carbone, Nick. 2000. <nick_carbone@hotmail.com>Reply-To: Writing Program Administration To: WPA-L@asu.edu Date: Tue, 26 Sep 22:35:27 -0600, Subject: Why Use Computers to Teach Writing?

Costa, Arthur, and Bena Kallick. 2000. *Habits of Mind*. Alexandria, VA: Association for Supervision and Curriculum Development.

Daniels, Harvey, and Steve Zemelman. 1988. *A Community of Writers: Teaching Writing in the Junior and Senior High School*. Portsmouth, NH: Heinemann.

Echevarria, Jana, and Anne Graves. 2002. *Sheltered Content Instruction: Teaching English Language Learners with Diverse Abilities*. Reading, MA: Addison-Wesley.

Ellis, Joseph. 2002. *Founding Brothers: The Revolutionary Generation*. New York: Vintage Books.

Fearn, Leif. 2001. E-mail correspondence. 23 July.

Fletcher, Ralph. 1993. *What a Writer Needs*. Portsmouth, NH: Heinemann.

———. 1996. *Breathing In, Breathing Out: Keeping a Writer's Notebook*. Portsmouth, NH: Heinemann.

Franklin, Benjamin. 2001. *The Autobiography of Benjamin Franklin and Selections from His Other Writings*. New York: Modern Library.

Freedman, Jonathan. 2000. *Wall of Fame: One Teacher, One Class, and the Power to Save Schools and Transform Lives*. San Diego, CA: Avid Academic Press.

Freedom Writers, with Erin Gruwell. 1999. *The Freedom Writers Diary: How a Teacher and 150 Teens Used Writing to Change Themselves and the World Around Them*. New York: Main Street Books.

Gadda, George, and Faye Peitzman. 1994. *With Different Eyes: Insights into Teaching Language Minority Students Across Disciplines*. New York: Addison-Wesley.

Gardner, Howard. 1999. *The Disciplined Mind: What All Students Should Understand*. New York: Simon and Schuster.

Graves, Donald. 1994. *A Fresh Look at Writing*. Portsmouth, NH: Heinemann.

———. 2002. Personal conversation.

Greene, Maxine. 1995. *Releasing the Imagination: Essays on Education, the Arts, and Social Change*. San Francisco, CA: Jossey-Bass.

———. 2000. NCTE convention keynote speech.

Hall, Donald, and Sven Birkerts. 1994. *Writing Well*. New York: HarperCollins.

Handbook for Planning an Effective Writing Program. 1983. Sacramento: California Department of Education.

Heard, Georgia. 2002. *The Revision Toolbox*. Portsmouth, NH: Heinemann.

Hillocks, George Jr. 1995. *Teaching Writing as Reflective Practice*. New York: Teachers College Press.

Jago, Carol. 2001. *Beyond Standards: Excellence in the High School English Class*. Portsmouth, NH: Boynton/Cook.

———. 2002a. *Cohesive Writing: Why Concept Is Not Enough*. Portsmouth, NH: Heinemann.

———. 2002b. *With Rigor for All: Teaching the Classics to Contemporary Readers*. Portsmouth, NH: Heinemann.

Lamott, Anne. 1994. *Bird by Bird: Some Instructions on Writing and Life*. New York: Pantheon Books.

Langer, Judith A. 1999. *Beating the Odds: Teaching Middle and High School Students to Read and Write Well*. Accessed at http://cela.albany.edu/eie2/index.html. November 15, 2002.

———. 2000. "Six Features of Effective English Instruction: How Do They Play Out in Middle and High School Classrooms?" *English Update* (Spring).

———. 2002. *Effective Literacy Instruction*. Urbana, IL: National Council of Teachers of English.

Langer and Close. 2001. *Improving Literary Understanding Through Classroom Conversation*. Albany, NY: Center for English Learning and Achievement.

Light, Richard J. 2001. *Making the Most of College: Students Speak Their Mind*. Cambridge, MA: Harvard University Press.

Longman Dictionary for American English: A Dictionary for Learners of English. 1997. New York: Longman.

Lunsford, Andrea. 1999. *The New St. Martin's Handbook.* Boston: Bedford/St. Martin's.

Manzo, Kathleen Kennedy. 2002. "Relegating Student Research to the Past." *Education Week.* (November 20): 1.

Maxwell, Rhoda. 1995. *Writing Across the Curriculum in Middle and High Schools.* New York: Allyn and Bacon.

Milosz, Czeslaw. 1996. *A Book of Luminous Things.* New York: Harcourt Brace.

Mooney, Jonathan, and David Cole. 2000. *Learning Outside the Lines: Two Ivy League Students with Learning Disabilities and ADHD Give You the Tools for Academic Success and Educational Revolution.* New York: Fireside.

Murray, Donald. 1985. *A Writer Teaches Writing.* Boston: Houghton Mifflin.

———. 2002. *Write to Learn.* Canada: Heinle.

Newkirk, Thomas. 1997. *The Performance of Self in Student Writing.* Portsmouth, NH: Boynton/Cook.

Nielsen, Jakob. 1997. "Be Succinct! Writing for the Web." Accessed online at <*www.useit.com/alertbox/9703b.html*> 16 December 2002.

Nystrand, Martin, with Adam Gamoran, Robert Kachur, and Catherine Prendergast. 1998. *Opening Dialogue: Understanding the Dynamics of Language and Learning in the English Classroom.* New York: Teachers College Press.

Olson, Carol Booth. 2003. *The Reading/Writing Connection: Strategies for Teaching and Learning in the Secondary Classroom.* Boston: Allyn and Bacon.

Osborn, Michael, and Suzanne Osborn. 1997. *Public Speaking.* Boston: Houghton Mifflin.

Peitzman, Faye, and George Gadda. 1994. *With Different Eyes; Insights into Teaching Language Minority Students Across the Disciplines.* Reading, MA: Addison-Wesley.

Quindlen, Anna. 1999. *A Short Guide to a Happy Life.* New York: Random House.

"Relegating Student Research to the Past." 2002. *Education Week* XXII (12): 1.

Remarque, Erich Maria. 1995. *All Quiet on the Western Front.* New York: Fawcett.

Schlossberg, Edwin. 1998. *Interactive Excellence: Defining and Developing New Standards for the Twenty-First Century.* New York: Ballantine Books.

Schmoker, Mike. 1999. *Results: The Key to Continuous School Improvement.* Alexandria, VA: Association for Supervision and Curriculum Development.

Schoenbach, Ruth, et al. 1999. *Reading for Understanding: A Guide to Improving Reading in Middle and High School Classrooms.* San Francisco, CA: Jossey-Bass.

Scruggs, Thomas E., and Margo A. Mastropieri. 1992. *Teaching Test-Taking Skills: Helping Students Show What They Know.* Cambridge, MA: Brookline Books.

Sebranek, Patrick, Dave Kemper, and Verne Meyer. 1999. *Write Source 2000: A Guide to Writing, Thinking, and Learning.* Boston, MA: Great Source.

———. 2001. *Writer's Inc.: A Student Handbook for Writing and Learning.* Wilmington, MA: Great Source.

Spandel, Vicki. 2001. *Creating Writers: Through 6-Trait Writing Assessment and Instruction.* 3d ed. New York: Longman.

Stanford, Gene, ed. 1979. *Classroom Practices in Teaching English, 1979–1980: How to Handle the Paper Load.* Urbana, IL: National Council of Teachers of English.

Stigler, James, and James Hiebert. 1999. *The Teaching Gap: Best Ideas from the World's Teachers for Improving Education in the Classroom.* Boston: Free.

Strong, William. 2001. *Coaching Writing: The Power of Guided Practice.* Portsmouth, NH: Heinemann.

"Teaching Composition: A Position Statement from the Commission on Composition, National Council of Teachers of English." Accessed online at *<www.ncte.org/positions/teaching_composition.shtml>* 25 December 2002.

Tomlinson, Carol Ann. 1999. *The Differentiated Classroom: Responding to the Needs of All Learners.* Alexandria, VA: Association for Supervision and Curriculum Development.

Tsujimoto, Joseph. 2001. *Lighting Fires: How the Passionate Teacher Engages Adolescent Writers.* Portsmouth, NH: Heinemann.

Weber, Chris. 2002. *Publishing with Students: A Comprehensive Guide.* Portsmouth, NH: Heinemann.

"What AP readers long to see." 1994. This information is derived from a list compiled during the 1994 AP English (Literature) Reading at Trinity University, San Antonio, Texas.

Wiggins, Grant. 1998. *Educative Assessment: Designing Assessment to Inform and Improve Student Performance.* San Francisco, CA: Jossey-Bass.

Wiggins, Grant, and Jay McTighe. 1998. *Understanding by Design.* Alexandria, VA: Association of Supervision and Curriculum Development.

Wilcox, Bonita. 1997. "Writing Portfolios: Active vs. Passive." *English Journal* 86 (6): 34–37.

Williams, Joe. *Style: Ten Lessons in Clarity and Grace.* Boston: Longman.

Zander, Rozamund Stone, and Benjamin Zander. 2000. *The Art of Possibility: Transforming Professional and Personal Life.* New York: Penguin.

Zmuda, Allison, and Mary Tomaino. 2001. *The Competent Classroom: Aligning High School Curriculum, Standards, and Assessment.* New York: Teachers College Press.

Ideas and Content (Development)	Organization

5 This paper is clear and focused. It holds the reader's attention. Relevant anecdotes and details enrich the central theme.

   A. The topic is **narrow** and **manageable.**

   B. Relevant, telling, quality details give the reader important information that goes **beyond the obvious** or predictable.

   C. Reasonably **accurate details** are presented to support the main ideas.

   D. The writer seems to be writing from **knowledge** or **experience**; the ideas are **fresh** and **original.**

   E. The reader's questions are **anticipated and answered.**

   F. Insight—an understanding of life and a knack for picking out what is significant—is an indicator of high-level performance, though not required.

3 The writer is beginning to define the topic, even though development is still basic or general.

   A. The **topic is fairly broad**; however, you can see where the writer is headed.

   B. Support is attempted, but doesn't go far enough yet in fleshing out the key issues or story line.

   C. Ideas are **reasonably clear,** though they may not be detailed, personalized, accurate, or expanded enough to show in-depth understanding or a strong sense of purpose.

   D. The writer seems to be drawing on knowledge or experience, but has **difficulty going from general observations to specifics.**

   E. The reader is **left with questions.** More information is needed to "fill in the blanks."

   F. The writer **generally stays on the topic** but does not develop a clear theme. The writer has not yet focused the topic past the obvious.

1 As yet, the paper has no clear sense of purpose or central theme. To extract meaning from the text, the reader must make inferences based on sketchy or missing details. The writing reflects more than one of these problems:

   A. The writer is **still in search of a topic,** brainstorming, or has not yet decided what the main idea of the piece will be.

   B. Information is **limited** or **unclear** or the **length is not adequate** for development.

   C. The idea is a **simple restatement** of the topic or an **answer** to the question with little or no attention to detail.

   D. The writer has **not begun to define the topic** in a meaningful, personal way.

   E. Everything seems as important as everything else; the reader has a hard time sifting out what is important.

   F. The text may be **repetitive,** or may read like a collection of **disconnected, random thoughts** with no discernable point.

---

5 The organization enhances and showcases the central idea or theme. The order, structure, or presentation of information is compelling and moves the reader through the text.

   A. An **inviting introduction** draws the reader in; a **satisfying conclusion** leaves the reader with a sense of closure and resolution.

   B. Thoughtful transitions clearly show how ideas connect.

   C. Details seem to fit where they're placed; **sequencing is logical** and **effective.**

   D. Pacing is well controlled; the writer knows when to slow down and elaborate, and when to pick up the pace and move on.

   E. The title, if desired, is **original** and captures the central theme of the piece.

   F. Organization **flows so smoothly** the reader hardly thinks about it; the choice of structure matches the **purpose** and **audience.**

3 The organizational structure is strong enough to move the reader through the text without too much confusion.

   A. The paper has a **recognizable introduction and conclusion.** The introduction may not create a strong sense of anticipation; the conclusion may not tie up all loose ends.

   B. Transitions often work well; at other times, connections between ideas are fuzzy.

   C. Sequencing shows **some logic,** but not under control enough that it consistently supports the ideas. In fact, sometimes it is so predictable and rehearsed that the **structure takes attention away from the content.**

   D. Pacing is fairly well controlled, though the writer sometimes lunges ahead too quickly or spends too much time on details that do not matter.

   E. A title (if desired) is present, although it may be uninspired or an obvious restatement of the prompt or topic.

   F. The **organization sometimes supports the main point or story line**; at other times, the reader feels an urge to slip in a transition or move things around.

1 The writing lacks a clear sense of direction. Ideas, details, or events seem strung together in a loose or random fashion; there is no identifiable internal structure. The writing reflects more than one of these problems:

   A. There is **no real lead** to set up what follows, **no real conclusion** to wrap things up.

   B. Connections between ideas are confusing or not even present.

   C. Sequencing needs lots and lots of work.

   D. Pacing feels awkward; the writer slows to a crawl when the reader wants to get on with it, and vice versa.

   E. No title is present (if requested), or if present, **does not match** well with the content.

   F. Problems with organization make it **hard for the reader to get a grip** on the main point or story line.

Voice	Word Choice
5 The writer speaks directly to the reader in a way that is individual, compelling, and engaging. The writer crafts the writing with an awareness and respect for the audience and the purpose for writing.	**5** Words convey the intended message in a precise, interesting, and natural way. The words are powerful and engaging.
A. The tone of the writing **adds interest** to the message and is **appropriate for the purpose and audience**.	**A.** Words are **specific** and **accurate**; it is easy to understand just what the writer means.
B. The reader feels a **strong interaction** with the writer, sensing the **person behind the words**.	**B.** The words and phrases **create pictures and linger in your mind**.
C. The writer **takes a risk** by revealing who he or she is consistently throughout the piece.	**C.** The language is **natural and never overdone**; both words and phrases are **individual** and **effective**.
D. **Expository or persuasive** writing reflects a **strong commitment** to the topic by showing **why** the **reader needs to know this** and why he or she should care.	**D.** **Striking words and phrases** often catch the reader's eye—and linger in the reader's mind. (You can recall a handful as you reflect on the paper.)
E. **Narrative** writing is **honest**, **personal**, **engaging** and makes you **think about and react** to the author's ideas and point of view.	**E.** **Lively verbs** energize the writing. **Precise nouns and modifiers** add depth and specificity.
	F. **Precision** is obvious. The writer has taken care to put just the right word or phrase in just the right spot.
3 The writer seems sincere, but not fully engaged or involved. The result is pleasant or even personable, but not compelling.	**3** The language is functional, even if it lacks much energy. It is easy to figure out the writer's meaning on a general level.
A. The writer seems aware of an audience but discards personal insights in favor of **obvious generalities**.	**A.** Words are **adequate and correct in a general sense**; they simply **lack much flair and originality**.
B. The writing communicates in an **earnest**, **pleasing**, **yet safe** manner.	**B.** Familiar **words and phrases communicate**, but rarely capture the reader's imagination. Still, the paper may have **one or two fine moments**.
C. Only **one or two moments here or there** intrigue, delight, or move the reader. These places may **emerge strongly for a line or two, but quickly fade away**.	**C.** **Attempts at colorful language** show a willingness to stretch and grow, but sometimes it goes too far (thesaurus overload!).
D. **Expository or persuasive** writing **lacks consistent engagement** with the topic to build credibility.	**D.** The writing is marked by **passive verbs, everyday nouns and adjectives, and lack of interesting adverbs**.
E. **Narrative** writing is **reasonably sincere**, but doesn't reflect unique or individual perspective on the topic.	**E.** The words are only occasionally refined; it's more often, "**the first thing that popped into my mind**."
	F. The words and phrases are **functional**—with only a moment or two of sparkle.
1 The writer seems indifferent, uninvolved, or distanced from the topic and/or the audience. As a result, the paper reflects more than one of the following problems:	**1** The writer struggles with a limited vocabulary, searching for words to convey meaning. The writing reflects more than one of these problems:
A. The writer is **not concerned with the audience**. The writer's style is a **complete mismatch** for the intended reader, or the writing is **so short** that little is accomplished beyond introducing the topic.	**A.** Language is so **vague** (e.g., *It was a fun time, She was neat, It was nice, We did lots of stuff*) that only a **limited message** comes through.
B. The writer speaks in a kind of **monotone** that flattens all potential highs or lows of the message.	**B.** "**Blah, blah, blah**" is all that the reader reads and hears.
C. The writing is **humdrum and "risk-free."**	**C.** **Words are used incorrectly**, making the message secondary to the misfires with the words.
D. The writing is **lifeless or mechanical**; depending on the topic, it may be overly technical or jargonistic.	**D.** **Limited vocabulary** and/or frequent **misuse of parts of speech** impairs understanding.
E. The development of the topic is **so limited** that **no point of view is present**—zip, zero, zilch, nada.	**E.** **Jargon or clichés** distract or mislead. Persistent **redundancy** distracts the reader.
	F. Problems with language **leave the reader wondering** what the writer is trying to say. The **words just don't work** in this piece.

© Northwest Regional Educational Laboratory

Sentence Fluency	Conventions

5 The writing has an easy flow, rhythm and cadence. Sentences are well built, with strong and varied structure that invites expressive oral reading.

A. Sentences are constructed in a way that underscores and enhances the **meaning**.

B. Sentences **vary in length as well as structure**. Fragments, if used, add style. Dialogue, if present, sounds natural.

C. **Purposeful** and **varied sentence beginnings** add variety and energy.

D. The use of **creative and appropriate connectives** between sentences and thoughts shows how each relates to, and builds upon, the one before it.

E. The writing has **cadence**; the writer has thought about the sound of the words as well as the meaning. The first time you read it aloud is a breeze.

5 The writer demonstrates a good grasp of standard writing conventions (e.g., spelling, punctuation, capitalization, grammar, usage, paragraphing) and uses conventions effectively to enhance readability. Errors tend to be so few that just minor touch-ups would get this piece ready to publish.

A. **Spelling is generally correct**, even on more difficult words.

B. The **punctuation is accurate**, even creative, and guides the reader through the text.

C. A thorough understanding and consistent application of **capitalization** skills are present.

D. **Grammar and usage are correct** and contribute to clarity and style.

E. **Paragraphing tends to be sound** and reinforces the organizational structure.

F. The writer **may manipulate conventions** for stylistic effect—and it works! The piece is very close to being **ready to publish**.

GRADES 7 AND UP ONLY: The writing is sufficiently complex to allow the writer to show skill in using a wide range of conventions. For writers at younger ages, the writing shows control over those conventions that are grade/age-appropriate.

3 The text hums along with a steady beat, but tends to be more pleasant or businesslike than musical, more mechanical than fluid.

A. Although sentences may not seem artfully crafted or musical, **they get the job done in a routine fashion**.

B. Sentences are **usually constructed correctly**; they **hang together**; they are **sound**.

C. **Sentence beginnings** are not ALL alike; **some variety is attempted**.

D. The reader sometimes has to **hunt for clues** (e.g., connecting words and phrases like *however, therefore, naturally, after a while, on the other hand, to be specific, for example, next, first of all, later, but as it turned out, although*, etc.) that show how sentences interrelate.

E. **Parts** of the text **invite expressive oral reading**; others may be stiff, awkward, choppy, or gangly.

3 The writer shows reasonable control over a limited range of standard writing conventions. Conventions are sometimes handled well and enhance readability; at other times, errors are distracting and impair readability.

A. **Spelling** is usually **correct or reasonably phonetic on common words**, but more difficult words are problematic.

B. **End punctuation is usually correct**; internal punctuation (commas, apostrophes, semicolons, dashes, colons, parentheses) is sometimes missing/wrong.

C. **Most words are capitalized correctly**; control over more sophisticated capitalization skills may be spotty.

D. **Paragraphing is attempted** but may run together or begin in the wrong places.

E. **Problems with grammar or usage are not serious** enough to distort meaning but may not be correct or accurately applied all of the time.

F. **Moderate** (a little of this, a little of that) **editing** would be required to polish the text for publication.

1 The reader has to practice quite a bit in order to give this paper a fair interpretive reading. The writing reflects more than one of the following problems:

A. Sentences are **choppy, incomplete, rambling, or awkward**; they need work. **Phrasing does not sound natural**. The patterns may create a sing-song rhythm, or a chop-chop cadence that lulls the reader to sleep.

B. There is little to **no "sentence sense"** present. Even if this piece were flawlessly edited, the sentences would not hang together.

C. Many **sentences begin the same way**—and may follow the same patterns (e.g., *subject-verb-object*) in a monotonous pattern.

D. **Endless connectives** (*and, and so, but then, because, and then*, etc.) or a **complete lack of connectives** creates a massive jumble of language.

E. The text **does not invite expressive oral reading**.

1 Errors in spelling, punctuation, capitalization, usage and grammar, and/or paragraphing repeatedly distract the reader and make the text difficult to read. The writing reflects more than one of these problems:

A. **Spelling errors are frequent**, even on common words.

B. **Punctuation** (including terminal punctuation) is often **missing or incorrect**.

C. **Capitalization** is **random** and only the easiest rules show awareness of correct use.

D. **Errors in grammar or usage are very noticeable**, frequent, and affect meaning.

E. **Paragraphing is missing, irregular, or so frequent** (every sentence) that it has no relationship to the organizational structure of the text.

F. The reader must **read once to decode**, then again for meaning. **Extensive editing** (virtually every line) would be required to polish the text for publication.

Presentation (Optional)

5 The form and presentation of the text enhances the ability for the reader to understand and connect with the message. It is pleasing to the eye.

A. If handwritten (either cursive or printed), the **slant is consistent**, letters are clearly formed, **spacing is uniform** between words, and the text is easy to read.

B. If word-processed, there is **appropriate use of fonts and font sizes**, which invites the reader into the text.

C. The use of **white space** on the page (spacing, margins, etc.) allows the intended audience to easily focus on the text and message without distractions. There is just the right amount of balance of white space and text on the page. The formatting suits the purpose for writing.

D. The use of **title, side heads, page numbering, bullets**, and evidence of correct use of a style sheet (when appropriate) make it easy for the reader to access the desired information and text. These markers allow the hierarchy of information to be clear to the reader.

E. When appropriate to the purpose and audience, there is **effective integration of text and illustrations, charts, graphs, maps, tables, etc**. There is clear alignment between the text and visuals. The visuals support and clarify important information or key points made in the text.

3 The writer's message is understandable in this format.

A. Handwriting is readable, although there may be **discrepancies in letter shape and form, slant, and spacing** that may make some words or passages easier to read than others.

B. **Experimentation with fonts and font sizes** is successful in some places, but begins to get fussy and cluttered in others. The **effect is not consistent** throughout the text.

C. While margins may be present, **some text may crowd the edges**. Consistent spacing is applied, although a different choice may make text more accessible (e.g., single, double, or triple spacing).

D. Although some markers are present (titles, numbering, bullets, side heads, etc.), they are not used to their fullest potential as a guide for the reader to access the greatest meaning from the text.

E. An **attempt is made to integrate visuals** and the text although the connections may be limited.

1 The reader receives a garbled message due to problems relating to the presentation of the text.

A. Because the letters are irregularly slanted, formed inconsistently or incorrectly, and the spacing is unbalanced or not even present, it is **very difficult to read and understand the text.**

B. The writer has gone **wild with multiple fonts and font sizes**. It is a major distraction to the reader.

C. The **spacing is random and confusing** to the reader. There may be little or no white space on the page.

D. Lack of markers (title, page numbering, bullets, side heads, etc.) leaves the reader wondering how one section connects to another and why the text is organized in this manner on the page.

E. The visuals do not support or further illustrate key ideas presented in the text. They may be **misleading, indecipherable, or too complex** to be understood.

6 + 1 Traits™
of Analytic Writing Assessment Scoring Guide
(Rubric)

- Ideas
- Organization
- Voice
- Word Choice
- Sentence Fluency
- Conventions
- Presentations

WOW!
Exceeds expectations

(5) STRONG:
shows control and skill in this trait; many strengths present

(4) COMPETENT:
on balance, the strengths outweigh the weaknesses; a small amount of revision is needed

(3) DEVELOPING:
strengths and need for revision are about equal; about halfway home

(2) EMERGING:
need for revision outweighs strengths; isolated moments hint at what the writer has in mind

(1) NOT YET:
a bare beginning; writer not yet showing any control

© Northwest Regional Educational Laboratory

Guiding Principles for Parents

- You must help your child write the best paper they can at this stage; they are the writer, not you.
- You need their permission to work with them or they will resist and undermine your efforts.
- Resist the immediate and urgent desire to correct their writing; that will not help and they will not want to work with you anymore.
- Allow them to maintain control over their own writing and your role. If you do this, they will value your help and seek it as they need it.

Step One: Clarifying

First, go through the actual writing assignment (e.g., essay topic) and highlight any words that seem essential to the assignment. Look for words like *explain*, *describe*, *analyze*. Look for phrases like ". . . a significant *experience that changed the way you thought* about someone or something," or ". . . *person who had a lasting influence on your personality*." Understand what your must write about before you write at all.

Step Two: Before Writing

Try one of these strategies to help your child get started on the assignment. Help them think about what they need to do or what they have to say once they start writing.

- ☐ *Talk about it:* While your child talks about the topic, make notes, asking them such questions as: Why do you think that? Why is that important? Can you tell me more about that? How does that relate to the writing assignment?
- ☐ *Make a list, cluster, or outline* without worrying too much about rejecting any ideas: just get ideas out of your head for now.
- ☐ *Write a letter, quick write, or quick draft* to get your ideas down before writing an actual draft of the essay.

Step Three: Writing!

Write a draft of the assignment, checking the assignment periodically to be sure that you are addressing what it asks.

Step Four: Revising/Rewriting

- ☐ Use the ending as the new beginning: so often we do not know what we want to say until we reach the conclusion; then we try to bring it together. Take the last paragraph and put it up front in the next draft, then write a new draft of your paper with that paragraph as the introduction.
- ☐ Ask your child what they want you to focus on when you read it; if they don't have specific directions, read it first without saying or correcting anything. Then walk through it *with them*, pointing out those specific problems you can help them resolve by asking them focus questions such as those listed (see "Talk about It").
- ☐ Remember: Your role at this stage is to help them clarify their ideas and address the assigned topic so as to achieve a working draft of the paper which can then be refined for style, mechanics, and tone.

Step Five: Refining the Writing

- ☐ *Voice.* Read through the paper and highlight those sentences where the language wakes you up or seems especially effective. Explain *how* these sentences create this effect and help them find places where they can add still more of these details.
- ☐ *Proofreading.* Read through the paper with *one purpose at a time* to better find errors: for example, read through only to check punctuation. Don't depend on the spell checker: read it through with your own eyes, specifically looking for words like *to* that should be *too* or *not* that should be *note*.
- ☐ *Paragraphing.* Read the paper to look at paragraph focus and organization: What is the main idea and how does each sentence relate to it? What examples do they provide to support and illustrate their ideas?
- ☐ *Style.* Strengthen their verbs and nouns for voice and clarity: go through the paper and identify all nouns and verbs. What can they do to make these nouns more specific, these verbs more active, more precise? Example: Change "The dog ran across the field" to "The dachshund waddled across the just-cut wheat field."

Step Six: Finishing

When your child has made their last revisions and fixed their last misspelling, have them print up a final draft of the paper. Encourage them to include all notes and earlier drafts with the final draft, even if their teacher doesn't ask for them; this will show the teacher how hard they worked. (Such evidence of hard work impresses teachers much more than fancy, colorful cover pages done on the computer!)

10 Things You Can Do to Support Your Child's Writing

1. *Create a dedicated, comfortable space for writing.* Preferably, they have a desk and a decent chair, both of which demonstrate a commitment to them and their studies while sending the message that their work is important. They need quiet; they may also prefer to listen to music that seems impossible to write to; let them listen to it or they will be more distracted.

2. *Buy them books.* Many studies show that reading has profound effects on our writing ability. Reading provides models of style and thinking that help shape our own voices as writers. Such books are great presents that again show interest in their work; they are also—or can be—random gifts that come during a time when your relationship is going through some serious renegotiations. Also, you must read yourself and let them see this; talk to them about what you read and ask them about what they are reading so they know you are interested in them.

3. *Provide them good reference books.* Every student needs a good dictionary (*American Heritage* is excellent; the *Oxford Desk* is good). Also recommended: *The Synonym Finder* or *21st Century Dictionary of Synonyms and Antonyms. Writer's Inc.* and *Write for College* offer the two most succinct and helpful reference resources for high school students.

4. *Buy your child a computer.* Used models with printer and software are available for as little as $150.00. This investment in your child shows that you are interested in them and that their writing is important.

5. *Ask to read their work.* It shows interest in them and their work; it shows you take them seriously. It allows you to monitor their progress. It allows you to say, "I've got some extra time tonight—d'you want to work on this together "a bit?"

6. *Write the assignment yourself.* You can each do the assignment on your own and then compare what you came up with; this creates an opportunity to talk, clarify, or think together, activities that are hard for teens and parents.

7. *Use writing in your house.* The family journal exemplifies this best. Get a nice (but not too nice) journal and keep it near the kitchen table (or wherever your family's central spot is). Write notes, questions, observations to each other to keep talking, to improve communication, to better understand each other, to improve your writing—and theirs! I know people who swear this saved their relationship.

8. *Buy them writer's gifts.* If you are at the office supply store, buy them some colorful Post-its, nice paper, a cool pen—anything that will please them and make working with writing more fun to them. Again: invest!

9. *Celebrate their successes.* Movies, special meals, a bulletin board in kitchen . . .

10. *Play family games that involve language:* Balderdash, Scrabble, Magnetic Poetry . . .

Index